Triadic Game Design

Casper Harteveld

Triadic Game Design

Balancing Reality, Meaning and Play

Springer

Casper Harteveld
Delft University of Technology
Delft
Netherlands

ISBN 978-1-4471-5923-0 ISBN 978-1-84996-157-8 (eBook)
DOI 10.1007/978-1-84996-157-8
Springer London Dordrecht Heidelberg New York

British Library Cataloguing in Publication Data
A catalogue record for this book is available from the British Library

Cover design: deblik

Printed on acid-free paper

Springer is part of Springer Science+Business Media (www.springer.com)

To the "GameBoys" and "GameGirls"
at Deltares

Preface

To know the road ahead, ask those coming back—Chinese proverb

I remember the day that I received my first game console, an Atari 2600, very well. I was about 6 years old and at that time I could be considered among the happy few to get a first hands-on experience with today's classics as *Frogger*, *Pong*, and *Space Invaders*. The world has changed dramatically since that time. Nowadays masses of people are playing games. They are playing anytime and anywhere thanks to technological advances as the Internet and mobile telephony. They are also playing anything, from playing music in *Guitar Hero* to shooting aliens and other mean looking creatures in *Halo*. Most importantly, the people of today are playing anyhow and anyways. Games have unmistakably become an even more so important part of our culture than what Johan Huizinga once described in his masterpiece "Homo Ludens."

While more and more people are playing games, I suddenly started to barely play anymore. This loss in appetite actually surprised myself, because I never thought I would play less. I remember clearly how much I used to "love" games. After my Atari 2600 I bought almost all game consoles available, from the GameBoy to the first Playstation. My life simply evolved around "games" (and my parents can acknowledge this). At that time, I figured that I would never, but never not play again. Even if I would get married, have children, have a busy job, and so on, I would still play games. I was a bit wrong though.

Because just around finishing secondary school and going to the university I lost my desire to play games. It did not have to do with growing up or women. Simply, when I played a game, I constantly had the feeling that I have "been there, done that." Many games offered the same kind of experience in a different setting, or even worse, the same sort of game with some small improvements. I was done with saving princesses, finding keys to unlock doors, and precisely timing my jumps to get from platform to platform. Games did not keep my attention anymore. I never really stopped playing at all, but I became a "softy." I only played occasionally.

Despite my loss in appetite for games, my youth love did sort of influence my eventual career, because another vivid memory is how much I felt attracted on an open house at a university to these dynamic graphical calculators that were used to understand complex problems in today's society, such as traffic congestion and air port capacity management. These were what I now consider "hardcore simulation models." With these tools, we can "simulate" what could happen by calculating different outputs based on varying inputs. To me this meant I could "play around" with variables to see how I could defeat the "evil" problem at hand. It almost felt like playing a game, but then one with a meaningful purpose. I was sold and started studying this "Systems Engineering, Policy Analysis, and Management" (SEPAM).

While I was busy passing my exams, certain scholars at the university realized the limitations of these hardcore simulation models. The human element or the "socio-political complexity" is missing from these tools. Decisions are not made rationally and processes, especially if these involve humans, are difficult to capture with algorithms. What is needed is to involve humans into these simulated models. And if we incorporate humans into a simulated environment, let them make decisions, and give them feedback about these decisions, we get a "game." Largely unaware of these developments at the university, I was missing the human element in my study as well. For this reason, I decided to start studying psychology in addition to SEPAM.

At the time some scholars at my university experimented with the use of gaming within the policy domain, others looked into the application of games in completely other domains, from the military to education, and into the positive effects of games in general. So it happened that more and more people started to recognize the potential of gaming and games were being developed for a huge variety of serious purposes, from recruiting personnel, societal critique to advertising brands and goods.

All of these developments were beyond my awareness as well until by mere coincidence I got into touch with the scholars involved with gaming at my university. This made me fall in love with games again. The puzzle pieces seemed to fall into place: my youth admiration of entertainment games, my attraction to hardcore simulation models and my desire to use these to solve societal problems, and my interest in psychology. Since then I have been involved with using games for serious purposes. This book is a result of my involvement so far.

To be clear, the book is not about culture, gender and health issues, violence, generation differences, business models, programming, and graphics. Rather, it is about the *design* of games that are used for serious purposes. This involves thinking of the concept behind those games: the aspects and mechanics that make such games work. Specifically, it lays out the idea of a "design philosophy" called "Triadic Game Design" that may help in thinking about these concepts and may help in eventually designing "good" games with a serious purpose. As the subtitle suggests, creating a "good" game involves balancing the triad of Reality, Meaning, and Play. Each are "worlds" with their own aspects, criteria, people, and disciplines that designers need to take into account.

I conceptualized this philosophy during and after the design of in particularly *Levee Patroller*. This is a game to train inspectors the knowledge and skills of inspecting levees, the barriers that protect a land from flooding. This "journey" gave me the experience and observations to reflect on. In this respect, my journey is somewhat comparable although by no means of the same scientific significance to Charles Darwin's journey of the Beagle. His journey, which lasted 5 years, took him to several places all over the world to collect specimens, investigate geology, and observe nature. Darwin kept careful notes of his observations and made theoretical speculations throughout. The observations and these initial theoretical speculations were the basis of his groundbreaking evolutionary theory as described in "On the Origin of Species," which was written after almost 30 years (!) of reflection.

In contrast, my journey lasted nine months and in total I reflected almost four years on it. The insights will not change the world like Darwin's insights did, but they can certainly be helpful for those who want to develop or use games with a serious purpose. They make it at least possible "to know the road ahead"...

A number of notes related to the book

1. A movie and a playable demo of *Levee Patroller* can be found on a website that accompanies this book. This website also has information and documents about the workshop based on this philosophy. It further includes links to games that are mentioned throughout this book. See http://triadicgamedesign.com
2. I played most of the games in this book, except for those that I could not buy or download. The screen shots are made by me while playing. For those games that I could or did not play, I requested a screen shot.
3. A standard for citing games has not been established yet. Based on the citation style for movies, computer software, and scholars in the field, I have decided to cite games as follows: "Developer(s). (Year). *Title* [Hardware platform]. Place: Publisher." Games which are very old or of which the origin is unclear, I did not include in the bibliography.
4. The subdivisions of this book consist of "levels" rather than chapters. In Level 1 I will explain why.

Delft, the Netherlands

Casper Harteveld

Acknowledgements

My work is a game, a very serious game—Maurits Cornelis Escher

If writing a book creates many debts, then creating a game *and* writing a book about this process creates many more debts that need to be acknowledged. This turned out to be the case when I started to make the list of people to whom I am grateful. Being overwhelmed by the immensity of the list and the amount of contributions, which is a source of awe and gratitude in itself, I decided to dedicate a separate part of the book to acknowledge all of those that helped me.

To start off with, I want to thank those that made contributions to the progress from manuscript to book. These concern: Hans de Bruijn, Tineke Ruijgh-van der Ploeg, Rafael Bidarra, Harald Warmelink, Sebastiaan Meijer, Rens Kortmann, Arthur van Bilsen, Qiqi Zhou, Alexander Verbraeck, Wim Veen, Ethan Kennerly, Jacco van Uden, Pamela Kato, Yuen Yen Tsai, David Crookall, Ellen Schuurink, and Emanuel Blum. Special mention goes out to my colleague Geertje Bekebrede. Over the years, she has helped me tremendously in getting my thoughts straight.

I would like to have another special mention for my mentor Igor Mayer who taught and made it possible for me to take games more seriously. If I did not run into him as a young and naive student, being unaware of the potential power of games, I may have never been involved with games academically.

For publishing the book, I want to thank the people at Springer, and in particular, Beverley Ford, Helen Desmond, Natasha Harding, and Catherine Moore. Writing your first book is not an easy task. Their encouragement and believe helped me to overcome the obstacles and gain the necessary focus to write something that would be valuable for others to read.

When it comes to the development of the game, I could not have dealt with the world of Reality without working closely with some of the subject-matter experts at Deltares. My thanks go out to Arno Rozing, Cor Zwanenburg, Jan Heemstra, Jan Blinde, Michiel van der Ruyt, and Huub de Bruijn. Similarly, I would like to thank the experts from one of the participating water boards, "Het Hoogheemraadschap van Delfland": Meindert van Dijk, Rob den Dulk, Martijn de Jong, Sandra Junier, Roy Nolten, Rob Nouse, Arie van Schoonhoven, and Jan-Willem Tanis. Each of them enthusiastically played the game and gave me useful feedback for improving it.

I am also thankful for the support and critical observations of the crisis coordinators of all the participating water boards. These are: Margreet Bosker, Eef Janssen, Han Paree, Niels Robbemont, and Kees Rood.

But most of all, I am indebted to the Deltares Game Team. Without them, *Levee Patroller* would not have been such a success. They were able to translate my ideas into a great looking and working product, criticized me when needed, and helped me out when I lost track of things. My story is just as much theirs. It is impossible to thank them enough, so I will stick to a simple "thank you." The following people have been part of the game team (in alphabetical order): Rens van den Bergh (level designer), Arne Bezuijen (modeler), Rui Guimarães (lead programmer), Micheline Hounjet (project manager), Almar Joling (programmer), Jos Maccabiani (project initiator & manager), Raymond van der Meij (project manager), Arjan Peters (programmer), Monique Sanders (content development), Matthijs Schaap (modeler), Sander Smit (modeler), Tom Thé (programmer), Marco Tolman (programmer), Bas Wenneker (programmer), Maarten Wesselius (programmer & interface design), and Maarten van Zomeren (programmer). Of these people, I want to thank Almar, Arne, Matthijs, and Rens additionally for their contributions to this book.

Aside from the game team, I am grateful to Deltares for supporting my "crazy" plans and gaming in general. Not many organizations would allow for such experimentation and innovation, especially when it is not their core business. The game team has now slowly but unmistakenly become part of the organization. Since *Levee Patroller* a number of other games have seen the light and some others are in the pipeline. In addition, I would like to thank the organization for continuing to support me by funding my Ph.D. research, which is about evaluating the use and effectiveness of *Levee Patroller*.

Last but certainly not least, I would like to thank my parents and "little" sister for their endless support. I also want to thank them for reminding me that other things in life are important as well. Being devoted to work let me forget this at times.

The book is a much rewritten, expanded, and elaborated account of my master's thesis as submitted in February 2007 for the partial fulfillment of the requirements for the degree of Master of Science in Systems Engineering, Policy Analysis, and Management at Delft University of Technology. A synopsis of the book was published as "Balancing reality, meaning and play: the design philosophy of Levee Patroller" in *Simulation & Gaming* with the co-authors Rui Guimarães, Igor Mayer, and Rafael Bidarra (in 2010, *41*(3), 316–340).

The book is further the first scientific publication as part of the Games and Learning Alliance (GaLA). GaLA is a Network of Excellence on "serious games" funded by the Eurpean Union in FP7—IST ICT, Technology Enhanced Learning (see http://www.galanoe.eu). GaLA gathers the cutting edge European research and development organizations on "serious games," involving 31 partners from 14 countries. Delft University of Technology is one of the partners.

Contents

Level 1
Press Start

One of the most difficult tasks people can perform, however much others may despise it, is the invention of good games—Carl Gustav Jung

When we try to do something new, we do not know what we are doing. That is the biggest challenge—Jeffrey Kalmikoff

It takes two to tango, but it takes three to design a "meaningful game." For "games with a purpose" to dance, three different worlds need to be balanced: the worlds of Reality, Meaning, and Play. In a nutshell, that is the message of this book. Simultaneously, it is the summary of my experience in designing a "digital game" for training professionals. Both aspects, the theory as well as the practice from which it derived from, are at the core of the following pages.

My journey into the worlds of Reality, Meaning, and Play started in early 2006. Back then I was asked to design a game. The assignment, however, was not to design *any* type of game. They needed a game from which people would actually learn from. At the start of this journey, I was packed with (a) no knowledge or understanding of the subject matter at hand, (b) a basic understanding of the workings of the human brain and how people learn, and (c) little knowledge of games beyond playing them. Consequently, I found myself in quite some "challenging" position. Especially, since the "client" also had no experience with these types of projects at all.

I did not give up. Instead, I consulted experts with various backgrounds, read many books and articles, rooted in psychology to game design, and critically analyzed (and played) several games, from entertainment to serious ones. Looking back I can conclude that the experience was sometimes frustrating and sometimes a bit boring. On occasions, it took many hours, days, or even weeks before I figured out how to deal with a design dilemma. At other times, I was busy translating design documents, writing help files, and doing other activities that are not the most fun imaginable (for me at least). Nevertheless, the project kept me going: I was in a "flow."

C. Harteveld, *Triadic Game Design*,
DOI 10.1007/978-1-84996-157-8_1,

Part of what kept me going pertains to the "instant feedback." Every deliberation resulted a few moments later in an addition or modification of an actual product. Creating a game is hard work. To see ideas develop and come alive is, therefore, extra rewarding. This is similar to the rewarding feeling of defeating an end-boss or retrieving a special item in a game. Playing games—although it is commonly seen as a trivial activity—is hard work too. But to keep on seeing improvements or, in game-specific terms, "to go to the next level," it is often not sufficient to simply use a "trial-and-error" method. Critical "reflections" are necessary to achieve this: what works and what does not?

Throughout and after the journey I have made these sorts of critical reflections as well to understand what it means to design games that are applied for serious purposes. These reflections are written down in this book. This makes what I am about to tell very personal, yet the message of this book, the balancing of three different worlds, goes very much beyond my original assignment to come up with an educational game. The idea of *Triadic Game Design* (TGD), as set out in this book, can be applied to any type of game. In this first level, I will give a glimpse of what this design philosophy is all about. But before I really get to this, I have to provide some necessary background information.

The Background Story

In games a so-called "background story" is given, either textually but nowadays mostly audio-visually, that introduces the game elements and the goal of the game. Quite often this story is irrelevant or uninspiring. It is stereotypically about saving princesses or defeating evil monsters that are terrorizing planet earth. For this reason, many players mostly skip this after they pressed start to play a game. I, however, recommend not to skip this background story, because unlike in most games this information is critically important. This information is necessary to understand where the idea of TGD comes from and how it fits into the larger picture of what goes around in the world of games.

Digital Versus Analog

First of all, about what kind of "objects" am I talking? Obviously games, but these artifacts are quite versatile. They can range from a game of *Chess* to the "Massively Multiplayer Online Role Playing Game" (MMORPG) *World of Warcraft*. To be clear, this book is about *digital games*. I prefer this term over "computer games" and "videogames," as these terms refer in a strict sense to either PC-based games or console games (i.e., games played on Playstation, Xbox, or Wii), respectively. The term "digital" includes all games with a computerized backbone. Additionally, it is the perfect antithesis of analog.

Nevertheless, the distinction between digital and analog is not clear-cut. Many analog games are computer-supported. They use spreadsheets or "simulations" that calculate the input from players and give them feedback about this input. Also, many of them are digitalized. We can play *Chess*, for instance, on a computer. On the other hand, digital games can be "analog-supported." During and in between playing a game, players can use real maps or have "real life" meetings with each other. The distinction is thus more of a continuum of the intensity and extent in which is made use of computer technology rather than one in which it is either/or.

The "intense" use of computer technology can make a difference. Juul (2005) explains that (a) due to the possibility to automate procedures, digital games allow for more complex rules and more detailed fictional worlds, (b) when a digital game is played, a focus is placed initially on the appearance of the game as a fictional world rather than a set of rules to manipulate fictional elements, and (c) because digital games are immaterial, they can depict fictional worlds more easily than analog games.

Therefore, the affordances of computer technology allow for different types of games, more complex, detailed, audio-visual, and so on, and this makes designing such games "slightly" different. Slightly, because the same principles of design can be applied to all sorts of games, from card, party, and gambling games to digital games and virtual worlds (Schell 2008). For this reason, while I focus on digital games, the insights offered can be applied to analog, computer-supported, or analog-supported games as well. They may even help in designing a "meaningful" party or gambling game.

Meaning of Meaningfulness

I mentioned "meaningful games," but all games can be perceived as meaningful to some extend (Jones 2008). Additionally, games can have a profound effect on the society at large in, for instance, our attitudes and ways of thinking and working according to Beck and Wade (2004), Herz (1997), Prensky (2001), Tapscott (1997), Veen and Vrakking (2006) and many others. They more or less argue that the generations that are growing up digitally, who—amongst many other names—are referred to as the Net Generation, the Digital Natives, the Homo Zappiens, or simply the Game Generation, will fundamentally change (or demand) the way we work. Whether this will happen and to what extend remains to be seen.

Nonetheless, the facts that show that more and more people—and not only children and teenagers (cf., Yee 2006)—play games and do so anywhere and anytime, from playing a game on a cell phone during a subway ride to spending a stolen moment at the office by playing *Solitaire*, bring to mind that games have become more deeply embedded in the fabric of our everyday lives. As with everything, this will not come about without any consequences for our society as a whole. This means that the phenomenon of games as seen from a macro-perspective or from a sociological perspective are quite meaningful. They have an impact on our society.

The meaningfulness of games can also be looked at from a different angle: from a micro (or psychological) rather then macro-perspective. Numerous authors have argued that people learn from playing games (Gee 2004; Johnson 2005; Prensky 2001). For example, it has been found that players can improve their visual, motor skills (Achtman et al. 2008; Green and Bavelier 2003; Feng et al. 2007), and leadership skills (Yee 2006), or increase their knowledge about history (Egenfeldt-Nielsen 2007), civilizations (Squire 2004), and urban planning (Adams 1998; Gaber 2007). It also has been found that this learning is useful in practice, as surgeons who play games perform better during actual surgery (Rosser et al. 2007). This makes playing games meaningful beyond the game itself.

Although some proof exists, it can always be questioned whether this learning is useful *outside* the game environment, while *inside* the game environment learning is simply *necessary*.[1] Games are intrinsically "learning environments." Most games start with offering relatively easy and simple challenges and become more difficult along the way (Juul 2005; Koster 2005). To proceed, players have to get the necessary knowledge and skills of how to play the game. They are learning.

Therefore, when players indicate after defeating an enemy that they "beat it," they are actually saying that they "learned how to defeat the enemy." But to be able to do this, the environment itself, the game, needs to be meaningful. Players need to understand that they are required to defeat the enemy to proceed and they need to know how to do this. If the game does not allow for any of such understanding, it becomes incomprehensible and, therefore, unplayable. This means that in fact *any* game *must* be meaningful to be played at all.

While a game must be meaningful in itself, when I refer to "meaningfulness," I actually mean any meaning beyond the game. In other words, a meaningful game is one which has an impact on real world activities. Such a game may or may not have been designed with this "purpose" in mind.

Games with a Purpose

I also mentioned "games with a purpose." Of course, any game (or even any artifact) is designed with a certain kind of purpose in mind, financially for sure, and artistically probably as well. What is mostly meant by a game with a purpose, however, is that they have a non-entertainment purpose (Sawyer 2002). Such purposes can range from building a game to make people aware about the conditions in development countries (see *Ayiti: The Cost of Life*), to recruiting people for a job (see *America's Army*), to even improving search engines (see *The ESP Game*). Tons of other examples are available for various domains (Bergeron 2006; Michael and Chen 2006). When it comes to applications, the sky really seems the limit.

---

[1]People even have to learn how to play games in general similar as to being able to read books. This requires quite some knowledge and skills and has been labeled as "video game literacy" (Gee 2004).

To make things even a bit confusing, while lots of games have been made with an entertainment purpose in mind, they are sometimes used for serious purposes (Van Eck 2009). Games like *Civilization* and *SimCity*, which are employed in classrooms to teach about history and urban planning, respectively, immediately come to mind. More intriguing concerns the use of games as a "social lubricant" for supporting communal activities, in, for example, libraries (Adams 2007). An entertainment game such as *Guitar Hero*, which is sort of a game-like karaoke with fake instruments, can, for instance, be used to bring people together and to get know each other. This gives the impression that it is about the *activity* rather than the artifacts themselves.

Activity or artifact, both need to be designed. With "designed" I mean that the initiators have *consciously* thought of how to develop, modify, or use a game within a certain setting to achieve a specific purpose that extends beyond the game itself. It needs to be thought of how *Ayiti: The Cost of Life* raises awareness, how *Civilization* can be used in the classroom, how *Guitar Hero* could serve as a social lubricant, and so forth. For games with a purpose, the game or the activity involving a game needs to be designed to bring forth value to an individual (e.g., training or education), a group or organization (e.g., collaboration or forecasting scenarios), or a system (e.g., political structures or databases).

To distinguish "a purpose" from the achievement of these real world values, I will continue to speak of "games with a serious purpose." It further *depends* on the specific "serious purpose" if designers are able to use existing (entertainment) games or have to design complete new ones. This brings me to the next notion.

COTS or Not?

I have to stress that when taking existing games—or "Commercial-Off-The-Shelf" (COTS) games as they are referred to—one needs to be careful.[2] Although many entertainment games, like for example *Civilization* or *Sim City*, correspond to meaningful topics, their designers created them with the goal of developing first of all a fun game about a serious topic.

As such, the connection of these games to reality is lost or at least arbitrary (Shaffer 2006). They can still be useful for learning to think about certain aspects in reality as some studies have shown (Adams 1998; Squire 2004). However, because the aspects are not appropriately embedded, it would be difficult for an effective "transfer" from a game to reality to occur. For this to happen, the game should have been built around teaching players to think in a way to solve problems in reality, not in the game. Shaffer explains why this is needed:

[2]In the world of analog games, the term COTS has a different meaning. COTS are games that can be applied to many situations, while "tailor-made" games are specifically developed for one type of situation (Duke and Geurts 2004).

> . . . the focus of a game matters in the end, and in the most extreme cases, commercial games can give dangerously inaccurate portrayals of the way things work in the real world. (p. 177)

Of course, when designing a complete new game, designers run the risk of creating a "dangerously inaccurate portrayal" as well. But the initial intention of those designers and the resulting process of designing the game are aimed at preventing this from happening. In the end, this can make a significant difference.

Despite this warning, it still comes down to the following two words: "it depends." Sometimes it is not necessary to be accurate. Sometimes it is not about the content, but about the activity. Sometimes an existing game just perfectly fits the specific serious purpose people have in mind. The important thing is to be able to make these considerations and judge what to do. For this, TGD may offer a way of thinking and a framework to hold onto.

Babel Problem

Generally, people need a label for everything. This makes life practical. It is much more useful to say "hand me the salt" than "hand me that thing." This requires not only that "things" are labeled, but that others also understand those labels. A shared understanding or agreement about terms and definitions is necessary. If a person does not know what precisely "salt" is, he or she may just as well hand over the pepper.

Aside from accurately naming "things," the problem lies exactly in this agreement about labels. People from different communities and cultures may label differently and this may cause some to not understand the meaning of a label anymore. And if we are thinking about a "Babel problem" or a "rant on terms and definitions," this is exactly what has been happening in the area of games with a serious purpose. Aldrich (2009) mentions a list of terms that are used. Besides naming them "games," he encountered the terms virtual experiences, simulations, social impact games, practiceware, game-based learning, immersive learning environments, educational simulations, serious games, and sims. I want to add to this: epistemic games, edutainment, edugaming, simulation/gaming, simulators, persuasive games, virtual training environments, and so on. The list is endless.

Of this endless list, the two foremost candidates for agreement are "simulations" and "serious games," because these are by far the most widely used and are not specifically restricted to a certain domain. Although the first, simulations, clearly indicates that the artifact needs to have a connection with the world of Reality, I dislike the term for its clear connotation as well with what I call "hardcore simulations." These are dynamic graphical calculators that assist decision makers in solving complex problems. They require no participation of human beings, except for providing some input at the beginning of the calculation process. Additionally, the term *is* a game genre. It is a type of game.

The second, serious games, nicely indicates that we are talking about games and those that are very serious indeed. However, the term is an oxymoron. How can something be both serious and a game? The two seem mutually exclusive. And does this mean that entertainment games are not serious? If players spend over 20 hours on their games, we would assume they would take their games very serious. For these and other reasons (cf., Bogost 2007; Klabbers 2009), not everybody agrees on using this term, although it is by far the best common denominator to let others understand about what we are talking.

What to do with this war over terms with no clear winner? For this, we may find an answer by going back to the label "salt." We can use salt *for* various purposes. Generally, we use it for cooking and food. But we can also use it for getting rid of red wine stains from clothes or for drinking cocktails, like tequila. While it has several purposes, we do not call the first "food salt," the second "stain salt," and the third "cocktail salt." We just call it salt and describe for what we are going to use it. That is what people tend to do in life. If there is not an appropriate term, at least one with which there is not an agreement on, we simply describe what we mean.

Translating this to our problem here, it means that we should talk about games and explicitly state with what purpose we use it. In specific cases, we could still shorten it to, for example advergames, educational games, training games, or exergames, but when we generally speak about games that need to achieve something beyond the game itself, we would need to stick to either "games with a serious purpose," "games with an non-entertainment purpose," or "games with a meaningful purpose." I know this is quite cumbersome and for that reason, whenever I talk about "games" I refer to these types of games. Whenever I need to make a distinction between these games and entertainment games, I will specifically mention this in the text by fully describing—as I just did—the specific purpose.

A History Pop-Up Screen

In games, pop-up screens may appear with additional information about the game after the background story has been told. Before we get to TGD, I have to do this as well, because the idea of using games for serious purposes has unlike what many tend to believe deep historical roots. Over the years (and even centuries) it has appeared in many shapes and forms. It is valuable to be aware of this. History teaches us a lot. It also enables us as Isaac Newton put it so modestly to "stand on the shoulders of giants," and therefore, build upon the knowledge and experiences that are already out there. For this reason, I want to shortly sketch the history of this quickly expanding field. This sketch is by no means all-conclusive. Let us start from the mere beginning when we just began to walk on our feet.

Precivilized Times

Once upon a time we humans came into existence. We do not have any specific evidence of the significance of games in those times, but if we have to belief

Huizinga (1938/1955) play or playfulness has had a significant function to human development from the moment we began to walk on our feet. He writes for instance:

> Play is older than culture, for culture, however inadequately defined, always presupposes human society, and animals have not waited for man to teach them their playing. We can safely assert, even, that human civilization has added no essential feature to the general idea of play. Animals play just like men. We have only to watch young dogs to see that all the essentials of human play are present in their merry gambols. They invite one another to play by a certain ceremoniousness of attitude and gesture. They keep to the rule that you shall not bite, or not bite hard, your brother's ear. They pretend to get terribly angry. And—what is most important—in all these doings they plainly experience tremendous fun and enjoyment. (p. 1)

In his book "Homo Ludens"—the playful human being—he elaborates how play has contributed to sacred institutions, such as rituals and ceremonies, as well as to law, war, poetry, philosophy, and the art. According to Huizinga (1938/1955), the contribution of play is particularly evident in the earlier phases of human civilization. As he puts it, "the more highly organized forms of society, religion, science, law, war and politics gradually lose touch with play" (p. 119). Only in poetics and especially music playfulness is still very recognizable (see also Nachmanovitch 1991).

Formally, playful activities (including games) stand quite consciously outside "ordinary" life. They take place in a "magic circle," a temporary secluded place from reality where a random child can be a doctor or a pilot for a day, and he calls them, therefore, "not serious." Contrary to this, throughout his book he shows and also clearly states that "play can very well include seriousness" (p. 45). This seems a paradox, but it is just an apparent one. In Huizinga's words: "In play there is something 'at play' which transcends the immediate needs of life and imparts meaning to the action. All play means something" (p. 1). While many scholars take Huizinga's work as a point of departure for showing that play cannot be serious, his whole book tries to show that this "not serious" play matters and to such a degree that it has helped to establish something very serious: a civilization.

From this, we can retrieve that from the beginning of times humans (and also animals) have been "playing" and with benefits beyond the enjoyable experience itself. Let us now take a look at the civilized times, the times in which we could find some clear evidence of the use of games.

Civilized Times

During the civilized times evidence suggest that the first actual games were being used. The Egyptian board game *S'n't*, later known as *Senet* or *Senat*, is claimed to be the oldest.[3] It was found in the 2686 BC tomb of Hesy-re and can be seen as a

[3]Besides *Senet*, *The Royal Game of Ur* and the African stone game *Mancala* are frequently mentioned as one of the oldest games (Parlett 1999). Of the first, four complete sets were discovered

precursor of contemporary *Backgammon* and *Parcheesi*. A number of First Dynasty (3100 BC) *Senet* board hieroglyphs indicate that the game may even be older (Piccione 1980). The game was originally strictly a pastime, but it gradually—as the Egyptian religion evolved—transformed into a simulation of the netherworld, with its squares depicting major divinities and events in the afterlife. Even back then "entertainment" games were repurposed for serious causes.

Another interesting old game concerns *Go*. This game is considered to be the oldest "unchanged" game that is still played up to today.[4] Its origin is disputed, because unlike *Senet* its oldest claim traces back to a legend (Fairbairn 1995). This legend holds that the Chinese emperor Yao (2337–2258 BC) designed it to improve the intelligence of his dull-witted son Dan Zhu. The "serious purpose" attributed to the game stands in stark contrast to one of the oldest references found. It is a remark made by Confucius in his "Analects of Confucius," a compilation of his work by his disciples some time after his death in 479 BC. He asserts that playing *Go* is just one step ahead from gluttony and idleness.

Aside from this familiar comment in the light of the discussions about games today, other claims of origin are quite serious as well. Some say that *Go* may have originally served as a forerunner to the abacus. Others think it may have been a fortune-telling device, with black and white stones representing Yin and Yang. Finally, a number of theories suggest that the game was derived from Chinese tribal warlords and generals, who used pieces of stone to map out attacking positions (Masayoshi 2005). As for the latter, insofar the speculation is justified, *Go* has certainly less strong associations with warfare in comparison to another ancient game: *Chess*.

Chess is conceived to originate from India in the 6th century. From there, it spread to, for instance, Europe, where it was modified around 1475 to the version as it is essentially known today (Hooper and Whyld 1992). Its affiliations with warfare are manifest with a board consisting of two opposing armies composed of rooks, knights, and kings. In the Middle Ages and during the Renaissance the game was part of the noble culture. It was used to teach war strategy and was looked upon as a "gentleman's game" (Vale 2001). Similar to *Senet*, *Chess* was also often used as a basis of sermons on morality (Olmert 1996). Criticism about the usefulness of the game can also be heard from that time, for example by Castiglione (1528/1997):

> ...for who ever will be excellent in the playe of chestes, I beleave he must beestowe much tyme about it, and applie it with so much study, that a man may assoone learne some noble

---

in 1926–1927 by Sir Leonard Woolley in royal tombs in what is now Iraq that date back to more than 2500 BC. This suggests that the game could be 6000 years old. As for the latter, paleontologist Richard Leakey found some boards in Kenya that he dates to Neolithic times. Why *Senet* is nevertheless considered the oldest is probably based on the overwhelming amount of evidence that it was played back in those days (Piccione 1980). It may also be that non-board games, such as games of dice, are even older. These games are, however, less well documented. This is thus mere speculation.

[4]Nowadays modern versions of *Senet* can be played. However, unlike *Go* which has never ceased to be played, these versions have been reconstructed based on extensive research. No one knows the actual rules, because instructions have never been found.

> scyence, or compase any other matter of importaunce, and yet in the ende in beestowing all that laboure, he knoweth no more but a game. (pp. 27–28)

The quote is an early instance of critiquing the "validity" and the "effectiveness" of a game. It basically questions whether people will actually learn something useful from *Chess* beyond the game itself and whether it would not have been better to invest in something else. The later Benjamin Franklin (1779) thinks otherwise. He asserts that there is a lot to learn from the game "for Life is a kind of *Chess*." He claims that by playing we may learn certain qualities, like foresight, circumspection, and caution. Although *Chess* is still promoted as educational or intellectually challenging, the representational meaning has become completely lost for today's players. According to Parlett (1999) this is true for many games:

> We think of *Chess* as abstract because, although we are aware of its origins as a war game, we no longer think of the pieces as elements of a medieval army when we actually play it ... [while] *Chess*, to its inventors and earliest players, was as representational as our relatively modern game of *Monopoly*—more so, in that they regarded it as being of educational value in the basics of warfare. Nearly all the traditional games we now regard as abstract were in their day considered representational, or at least symbolic. The simplest process of moving pebbles round a circuit of holes in accordance with the throw of dice was universally perceived as representing a real-life race, while the precursor of *Snakes & Ladders* was a game of moral instruction. Conversely, when playing *Monopoly*, we forget the deficiencies of its representational aspirations—the ancient scale of values, the simplistic purchase of public utilities, the irrelevance of enjoying birthdays and winning second prize in a beauty contest—and slip automatically into the habit of thinking of moves and transactions in abstract terms. (p. 6, italics added)

Many of the games in civilized times were very meaningful to the people in those times. Some may have considered it as a pastime, but others certainly ascribed more value to games. It is hard for us to perceive this, because while the rules have remained, the meaning has disappeared as games are apparently extremely cultural-historically sensitive and dependent. When we now play one of these games we just manipulate the rules, while a couple of centuries ago these were actually seen as games with a meaningful purpose.[5] Let us now jump to the modern times and see what gaming has brought us in the 20th Century.

Modern Times

Early 20th century, in 1910 to be precise, an interesting board game called *Pank-a-Squith* appeared (Fig. 1.1).[6] The game took its name from political opponents

[5] Another way of looking at it, is to use Baudrillard's (1981/1994) concept of simulacra. These are copies without a clear reference to the original. This may mean that due to the many copies over time, the reference to the original intentions of these games disappeared, and hence their representational meaning.

[6] *Pank-a-Squith* was part of the exhibition "Pastimes and Paradigms: Games we Play" by the Division of Rare and Manuscript Collections of Cornell University in 2004. Among the col-

Fig. 1.1 Striving for woman's suffrage in *Pank-a-Squith*. The illustrations show the difficulties encountered by supporters in the suffragette movement. Image provided by Division of Rare and Manuscript Collections of Cornell University

in Edwardian England—the suffragette leader Emmeline Pankhurst (1858–1928) and Herbert Asquith (1852–1928), Prime Minister from 1908 to 1916. Much similar to *Game of the Goose*, the goal of the game is to go from the starting point, where a woman is taking care of her children and her home, and reach the ending point, the House of Parliament, the pinnacle of achievement for the campaign for woman's suffrage. The latter is represented by the picture in the center of the board. In between these two points, illustrations show the difficulties the supporters of the suffragette movement encountered, like police officers who say "How brave I am fighting women," and give an idea of the position of women at the time, as for instance shown in a picture in which a tax collector says "What we do with your money that is no affair of yours madam." From this we see that already at that time, games were being used as rhetorical devices.

Despite some exceptions, like *Pank-a-Squith*, the larger emphasis of using games in the early 20th century was on what is referred to as "war gaming" (Brewer and Shubik 1979; Shubik 1975). While the connection between games and war has been historically laid by for instance *Chess* and *Go*, its extensive use can also be explained logically. The reason to create and use games about war is that people need to be prepared to engage in combat. This preparation can be physical, tactical, or even strategic. It is deemed necessary as it can give a considerable advantage over competitors when a real war arrives and war, as we know, has enormous consequences, so one would like to be prepared for something like this.

---

lection of this exhibition were games that deliver political messages, promote (moral) principles, preserve identity, and are used for education. This collection can be visited online at http://rmc.library.cornell.edu/games/.

Although war gaming really took a flight in the first half of the 20th century, its inception is said to be in 1824, when Lieutenant Von Reisswitz modified his father's work on sand table-top games and produced a map game at a scale of around 8 inches to the mile that was suitable for military training (Brewer and Shubik 1979; Shubik 2009). On viewing the game, Von Meuffling, Chief of Staff of the Prussian Army, commented:

> It is not a game at all. It is a training for war; I shall recommend it most emphatically to the whole army. (as cited in Shubik 2009)

Whether they perceived it as a game or not, gaming has taken an important place in the military. The extent to which gaming is taking serious and the large scale of it can be seen with the "Millennium Challenge," reputedly the most expensive war game exercise ever conducted (Gladwell 2005). The game was used to test modern warfare methods and involved both computer simulations and real-world exercises. To test this, one team, the Red team, represented an unnamed Middle Eastern rogue state and only had the old means of warfare available. They were commanded by retired Marine Lt. General Paul Van Riper. The other team, the Blue team, was able to use the new modern warfare methods.

In the first few days of the exercise, Van Riper kept numerous computer-generated boats and planes, many of them civilian, around the virtual Persian Gulf. As the US fleet entered the Gulf, Van Riper gave a signal which could not be intercepted as it was a coded message broadcast from the minarets of mosques at the call to prayer. The pleasure crafts and planes changed into deadly suicide weaponry that destroyed sixteen ships, along with thousands of marines. By using surprise and unorthodox tactics, Van Riper sank most of the US expeditionary fleet in the Persian Gulf, and in fact won the game. If this would really happened, it would have been the worst naval disaster since Pearl Harbor.

Although it was set up as an objective experiment, the facilitators, faced with an abrupt and embarrassing end to the most expensive and sophisticated military exercise in the US history, pretended the whole thing had not happened. They brought the dead troops back to life and "refloated" the sunken fleet. They further scripted the game to ensure a Blue team victory. They were essentially "cheating." Van Riper got so fed up and refused to play anymore:

> I am angered that, in a sense, 250 million was wasted. But I am even more angry that an idea that has never been truly validated, that never really went through the crucible of a real experiment, is being exported to our operational forces to use. What I saw in this particular exercise and the results from it were very similar to what I saw as a young second lieutenant back in the 1960s...The computers in Saigon said we were winning the war, while out there in the rice paddies we knew damn well we were not winning the war. That is where we went astray, and I see these new concepts potentially being equally as ill-informed and equally dangerous. From an interview with Van Riper by Willis (2003)

Although the Millennium Challenge 2002 has been poorly executed, it does show the potential power and the possibilities of gaming, and its importance for the military. It further reminds us of what makes games different from computer models and simulations: the input of human beings including their ability to use surprise and creativity which creates for unexpected outcomes. Such input is incredibly important, because as Van Riper asserts, computers themselves can led us astray.

In this century gaming did not remain exclusive to the military. In fact, according to Mayer (2009), if we accept the Von Clausewitz (1832/1873) theorem that "war is a continuation of policy by other means," war gaming can be seen as one of earliest forms of what he calls "policy gaming." The transfer from war gaming to other forms of policy gaming was a step-by-step process of trial-and-error and institutional learning. Mayer observes that just after World War II a rationalization process culminated in the field of policy making which became later known as the "decision sciences." In the vein of this movement policy makers tried to "optimize" the complex problems they faced with tools, which range from formal modeling to hardcore simulations.

Similar to Van Riper's conclusions, in the 60s and 70s scholars encountered the limitations of the formalization and use of computer simulations to solve these complex policy problems (Mayer 2009). Public policy making is not neat and rational but chaotic and messy and to account for this a move was needed to more human-centered approaches which were also responsive to the socio-political complexity. A number of less formal and more interactive methods were investigated and among these concerned the use of gaming. With games the "political actors," the participants of a policy process, be it governments or companies, could be included into the process and by means of a "multilogue," the simultaneous dialogue between multiple actors, a greater understanding could be achieved of each other and the topic at hand (Duke 1974; Duke and Geurts 2004).[7]

One of the better known policy games concerns *Hexagon* (or *Hex*), which was originally developed by Dick Duke for UNESCO in 1975 as a tool for governments in developing countries to learn how to allocate resources (Fig. 1.2). In this game, participants are challenged to take on the role of national, regional, or local leaders of a developing country plagued by structural shortcomings. Their task is to ensure the well-being of their population and they can achieve this by allocating resources, like cash, food, housing, infrastructure, efficiently among and between different groups. This requires communication within groups and between different organizational levels. And if this was not already difficult enough, external events, like a huge disaster, can happen.

Parallel to the developments in policy making, the use of games emerged in the business and management sciences and contexts, although in this domain the usage has remained primarily for educational purposes. In fact, similar to policy gaming, gaming transferred from war gaming to what is now known as "business gaming" (Faria et al. 2009). This can be dated back to 1932, when Mary Birshtein who while

[7]Mayer (2009) further argues that the use of gaming is most fruitful when a simulation model is used in interaction with real participants. If only the model is used, it neglects the social-political context. Humans are reduced to factors. If only the participants play a role, it can easily degenerate "into a rather one-sided, superficial venting of desires and viewpoints" or it may lead to "negotiated non-sense": a political compromise or consensus that is not supported by scientific evidence or can even be in conflict with the physical-technical complexity. To prevent this, a "reality-check" is needed and a hardcore simulation model can provide this.

Fig. 1.2 The game *Hexagon* by Dick Duke. The upper platform symbolizes the national level of the developing country, the middle platform the regional level, and the lower platform the local level. Picture by Pieter van der Hijden

teaching at the Leningrad Institute got the idea to adapt the concept of war games to the business environment. She realized that similar to recreating or experimenting with war scenarios, games make it possible to emulate features and characteristics of an organization's routine, so participants can exercise the skills that will be required in the real organization without exposing these real organizations to any direct risks. Her first business game simulated the assembly process at a typewriter factory and was used to train managers on how to handle production problems. From that moment on Mary developed more than 40 similar games with her team until the World War II broke out and interrupted her work (see also Dzhukov et al. 1993).

Similar to policy gaming as well, in the 60s and 70s the use of games took a flight (Faria et al. 2009). In 1962, a survey of 107 business schools reported that 71.1% used business games (Dale and Klasson 1962). Additionally, in 1980, 228 business games were reported to be in use (Horn and Cleaves 1980). The popularity of business games can be subscribed to the close fit with the world of businesses and games: decision making, team work, thinking of strategies, and being able to learn from mistakes while being confronted in a highly competitive and dynamic world requires certain skills, cognitive as well as social, and games are able to provide the sort of settings in which such worlds can be enacted and in which the desired competencies can be learned. Nowadays, the use of business games is quite common at schools. But a lot more has happened as well, so let us now take a look at the developments in our contemporary society.

Contemporary Society

From the 20th century we can see that gaming was already applied in a variety of domains, in politics, military, policy, and business, and used for a variety of purposes, persuasion, assessment of strategies and equipment, exploration of policies, and education. In our contemporary society the use of gaming has certainly extended to a huge number of other domains, from health to advertising, and to a larger variety

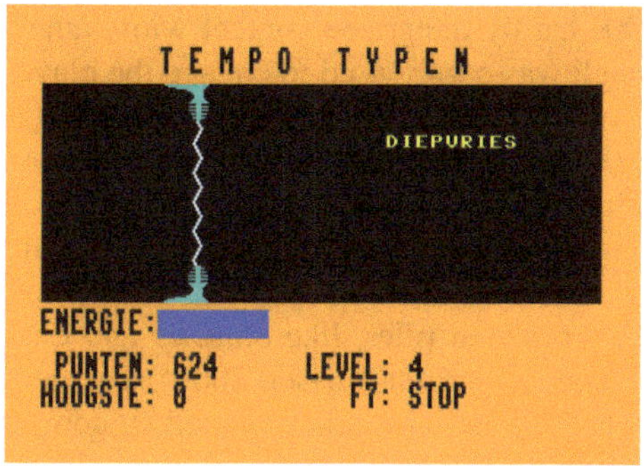

Fig. 1.3 Typing words before they get electrocuted in *Tempo Typen*. The word "diepvries" moves to the left and needs to be typed otherwise it gets electrocuted and the player loses energy. The blue bar indicates the amount of energy left. ©1984 Radarsoft. Used with permission

of purposes, from data collection to attitude change. The most important difference concerns, however, the paradigm shift from "using the computer" to "playing on the computer." In the early 20th century, the computer was used to *support* the game. In contrast, with "digital games," the computer is at the center of what is being played.

Despite that the use of "digital games" has really taken off since the early 90s, the idea of it was incepted precisely around the time that analog games became popular with policy analysts and business schools. Various claims and debates are still taking place about what exactly the first digital game is, but it remains a fact that in between 1947 and 1972, several attempts have been done to create something like a "digital game." In 1972 *Pong* was released and from that moment on many other digital games followed. With the introduction of the PC and several "game consoles," a computer specifically dedicated to playing games on, the digital games market grew out to one of the biggest entertainment industries, if not the biggest by now.

It actually did not take long before some developers started to think of how to utilize these types of games for serious purposes. For example, I found a game from a Dutch company called Radarsoft who created a game in 1984 to learn how to type (Fig. 1.3). This game, called *Tempo Typen* (which can be translated to "Rapid Typing"), requires a player to type the words that appear in the screen and which move from right to left. If the player does not type the words in time, the words are electrocuted and the player loses energy. When the "energybar" is depleted, it is game over. When a player does well, after every level the "electrocuting device" moves to the right so it takes less time before words hit it. This makes the game increasingly harder as the player progresses.

Along with *Tempo Typen* many other educational games were being developed. The sole alibi for the development of these games back then over other educational software was the engaging power of games, the ability to keep players connected to the game for hours (Egenfeldt-Nielsen 2007), which was shown by Malone (1981). Although some interesting games were being developed, such as *Rocky Boots*, in which players have to design simple digital logic circuits, *The Oregon Trail*, in which players follow the footsteps of early American settlers and learn about the American pioneer spirit, and Chris Crawford's *Balance of the Planet* and *Balance of Power*, in which players learn about environmental and international relations problems, respectively, the educational games that dominated the scene in the 80s and

90s hardly integrated content with gameplay (Egenfeldt-Nielsen 2007). The game shell was purely used to engage the player with the content—something which has been referred to as "sugar-coated learning" or "chocolate covered broccoli" (Laurel 2001). Additionally, the games were mostly low-budget, centered upon pre-school children and early school age, and covered basic areas, like arithmetic, reading, typing, and spelling. These types of games have become known as *edutainment*.

Due to the dominance and bad reputation of edutainment, the more educationally oriented titles, like *SimCity* and *Civilization*, were never marketed as educational (Egenfeldt-Nielsen 2007). The developers did not want to be affiliated with edutainment and rather wanted to compete with the commercial titles. The label "education" was not used anymore. Over the years the links of the games industry with edutainment disappeared, and while edutainment titles still appear up today, they are currently seen as "educational software" rather than games.[8]

This "death" of edutainment as a game movement does, however, not indicate the death of games with a meaningful purpose. At the beginning of the 21st century, scholars started to argue for the use of entertainment techniques for non-entertainment purposes (Bergeron 2006; Michael and Chen 2006). The idea was to be innovative, use the state-of-the-art of the industry, and avoid the common pitfalls like separating the content and gameplay. This "new" movement was especially marked by a paper by Sawyer (2002) in which he reintroduced the term "serious games"—Abt (1970) used this much earlier—and described why the field of policy making could benefit from the games industry:

> Given the importance of models and simulations in public policy making, and the need to improve their effectiveness, the governmental and non-governmental model and simulation building communities should be striving to explore and build on other existing model-building practices. Some of the most interesting work being done is within the interactive entertainment industry. (p. 1)

Of course, the military preceded the idea of using game technology. The US military, for example, used a modification of the game *Doom* called *Marine Doom* back in 1996 for training. But besides the domains of the military and public policy, at this point in time almost any domain imaginable started to experiment with the use of game technology for a wide variety of purposes. This led to the emergence of a quite significant global industry, in which games are developed to help lose weight, engage with the news, criticize governmental policies, and raise awareness about problems in development countries amongst many other applications.

All of this may be another "hype" and might be forgotten in a number of years from now, but the difference with previous times is that aside from (a) the much broader range of domains and purposes, (b) the wider availability of game and media technology, at which with high performance and affordable costs non-commercial parties can develop games, and (c) the pervasiveness of games and the digital generation that is entering schools and businesses, and who do not know any better than playing games, it is above-all the ever increasing growth of researchers, practitioners, and users of games with a serious purpose that make it seem that they are here

[8]For a comprehensive overview of the history of educational games, see Egenfeldt-Nielsen (2007).

to stay and will have a considerable impact on what we do in the nearby future. And one of the "critical success factors" to make this happen concerns the "design" of these games. That is where this book aims to contribute to.

The Goal of This Book

Games have clear *goals* and a book should have that too. While players need to know whether they need to "save the princess," "collect as many items," or "solve the puzzle," readers need to know what they can expect. To clarify the goal of this book, it is worthwhile to first describe the academic field surrounding games. At first glance, gaming touches in one way or the other on every imaginable discipline. It stretches from computer science, psychology, media studies, to even philosophy. Even if disciplines, such as mechanical engineering or chemistry, may not be directly involved with games, they are sometimes used as a domain to which gaming is applied to.[9]

Not all of these disciplines have been preoccupied with games over history. In fact, the field is still continuously shifting and in development. For this reason, the academic field of games can be seen as a "kaleidoscope" (Klabbers 2006). Like a kaleidoscope the field has different colors and shapes that can be seen. This makes it difficult to grasp it. It is very much dispersed. One can find a journal article about a game in the journal of Pediatrics (cf., Kato et al. 2009) or an article in the Journal of Geography (cf., Adams 1998).

Attempts have been made to unify the different strands into a discipline on its own.[10] Resistance against such unification can also be found.[11] Opponents stress that the field of gaming is not only dispersed, it is *inter-disciplinary*. To study (digital) games, one has to draw upon many different fields. Some even argue that gaming is *trans-disciplinary* as it integrates different disciplines into a new whole: that of a game.

Whether mono-, inter-, or trans-disciplinary, it is possible to identify some specific streams of game research that are being pursued. I have labeled these streams and positioned their importance to the field of games with a serious purpose:

- **Games as object**: the first stream of research concentrates itself by examining games purely theoretically. It is foremost descriptive and explanatory. Much of the

[9]Coller and Scott (2009) used a game to enhance student's understanding of mechanical engineering and the game *Foldit* by the University of Washington is used to contribute to the science of (bio)chemistry. In both instances the disciplines do not directly contribute to the science of games but a link is nevertheless visible.

[10]The emerged field of *game studies* or *ludology* is an example of the unification of studying games. The proponents argue that games are significantly different from other phenomena and demand a discipline on its own.

[11]The last chapter in Bogost's "Unit Operations" (2006) is devoted to arguing that games demand to be studied in an inter-disciplinary setting and do not call for a discipline on its own.

sociological, philosophical, and media studies related research departs from this stream. Well-known works of this stream are by Aarseth (1997), Jenkins (2006), and Juul (2005). The field benefits from this research by getting a better understanding of what games are.

- **Game usage**: researchers in this stream are concerned with the gameplaying experience and behavior. They can look at this psychologically, by measuring, for example, the heart rate and transpiration and thereby getting an idea of the player experience, or they can look at it more sociologically, by describing ethnographically how, for instance, player communities emerge and sustain over time (cf., Taylor 2006). By understanding how games are experienced and used, new ideas may appear for serious purposes and existing ones may be improved.
- **Game effects**: the third stream is concerned with the effects of playing games (cf., Ritterfeld et al. 2009). Research into player motivations, learning effects, or even violence is affiliated with this stream. The research is often experimental in nature, but it can use a plethora of qualitative methods as well. The latter is especially true when researchers look into the cultural and societal effects of gaming. With the insights into the effects of games, the design and application of games with a serious purpose can be improved.
- **Game technology**: the fourth stream looks into the "technology" behind games. This can relate to the creation of a gaming script, a scripting language especially suitable to programming games, to the Artificial Intelligence (AI) of game characters or of the game itself, to the procedural generation of content in games, and so on. Without any doubt, the field of computer science is strongly involved in this stream. With advances in technology, new possibilities arise for the development and application of games with a serious purpose.
- **Game design**: this fifth stream, which has close affiliations with the general "design sciences," is preoccupied with how to create something that is called a game. Researchers are concerned with what is referred to as "gameplay," level design, narrative construction, and any other ingredients that make up a game. Scientifically, this leads to the establishment of systematic principles, procedures, and theories of designing games. This output can be used by designers of games with a serious purpose.
- **Games as tool**: the final stream has a clear affiliation with games with a serious purpose, because in this stream researchers look into the possibilities of harnessing games as a tool to achieve something. They may use a game to extract data in respect to a research phenomenon, for instance strategic behavior (Kuit 2002) or supply chains (Meijer 2009), or to improve search engine results (Von Ahn and Dabbish 2004). This stream is methodologically oriented.

As with all sorts of categorizations, these streams are not set in stone. More importantly, the different streams overlap and influence each other, just like what we would expect from a kaleidoscopic picture. For example, game technology opens up possibilities for game design: when it became possible to create 3D games, other types of games appeared. Also, when new technological ways arrive in which players can engage with a game, as shown with the Wii, game usage will most likely change and the way we look at games may change as well (Juul 2009). But most importantly for games with a meaningful purpose, if we have a poorly designed educational game, we can expect poor learning effects. On the other hand, insights in the results enable us to know what works and what does not and from there it becomes possible to improve the design. It works both ways. Generally speaking, to bring the field to "the next level," research should take place in every stream.

With this in mind, it becomes possible to position this book and explain its goal. As the title suggests, the idea of TGD is in particular affiliated with "game design." The aim is to contribute to the field by laying out a new way of thinking, a "design philosophy," for developing games. Although the philosophy can be applied to any game, it is foremost meant for games with a serious purpose. This means that this book is further affiliated with the stream "games as tools."

Why is this philosophy needed? Have we not been designing games, even games with a serious purpose, for decades if not centuries? While this is certainly true, it has occurred without a clear idea of what it means to design such games. Knowing how to build a game is not enough for this field. It requires much more, from a proper consideration of what the game needs to achieve to how it corresponds to the physical world, and this makes this field highly inter-disciplinary (if not trans-disciplinary), as all these considerations cross many disciplines.

TGD may help in making these considerations. It provides a basic theoretical sense of what games with a serious purpose are and how they need to be approached when designing them. As such, with TGD as a frame of reference we are able—but I cannot give any guarantee of course—to develop better games. By means of a "tutorial" I will now explain the concept of TGD further.

The Spoon Tutorial

Spoons have a special place in philosophical discussions, tricks, and puzzles. An example of a philosophical discussion is a scene from the movie *The Matrix*, in which a boy shows the protagonist Neo how to bend a spoon with his mind.[12] This mind binding spoon trick is only possible in "The Matrix," not in the real world. He explains to Neo that he can have "superpowers" inside the Matrix by having a "belief." This belief is symbolized in the now famous quote "there is no spoon." When Neo beliefs, he is not dealing with a spoon, but with zeros and ones, the fundamental building units of which the Matrix exists, and is able to bend the spoon (and manipulate many more things inside this "virtual world"). Philosophically, these notions relate to indicating that the beliefs that people have about their "reality" matter. You see what you belief.

Interestingly, and the script writers may have been inspired by this trick, the paranormalist Uri Geller has a similar yet "real" mind bending spoon trick that even has become his trademark. Critics say Geller actually uses magician tricks instead

[12]*The Matrix* is produced by Joel Silver and directed and written by Larry and Andy Wachowski. It was distributed by Warner Bros. Pictures in 1999.

Fig. 1.4 The initial setup of the puzzle. Picture by Almar Joling

of supernatural powers, such as by creating the illusion that the spoon is bending by gradually revealing the bend, by pre-bending the spoon (for example by heating it), or by applying chemical substances so that the spoon weakens and bends in time. The most interesting part is that even though critics unmasked Geller's tricks, people still want to belief it. For some reason people seem to be drawn by mysticism and a belief in the supernatural. Others are more rational and do not believe it right away, while they actually have no understanding of what occurred. In sum, with paranormalists like Uri Geller the essence is inverse to *The Matrix*. It is in this case about "Do you belief what you see?"

Now I have a puzzle about spoons to further introduce the idea of TGD. This puzzle is unlike *The Matrix* and the Uri Geller examples not philosophical or mystical in nature. In fact, it has a simple and clear answer. To solve it, a belief is needed that it is solvable. Many people give up, because they think it is a trick. It is not. I can guarantee this. Of course, "seeing is believing," but when it is solved "you will belief what you see." The setup, rules, and goal of the puzzle is explained below:

1. Take three more or less identical cups and tablespoons.
2. Put the three cups upside down into an (equilateral) triangular shape. The distance between each cup should be exactly one tablespoon (Fig. 1.4).
3. The cups cannot be moved from this moment on.
4. Now the goal is to place *any* object in a stable position *above* and *in-between* the three coffee cups.
5. To solve the puzzle only the three spoons can be used. No other form of assistance is allowed.
6. Do not continue reading until the puzzle is solved!

The answer to this puzzle can be found in Appendix A. The solution shows that each spoon supports and is supported by another spoon. If done well, a stable situation is created that is firm enough to hold relatively heavy objects. But important to acknowledge is that the puzzle cannot be solved without one of the three spoons. This way, this puzzle holds close to an interesting phenomenon in mathematics: the

Fig. 1.5 The Borromean rings. The removal of one ring will result in two other unlinked rings. 3D model by Arne Bezuijen

Borromean Rings (Fig. 1.5). Borromean Rings are three rings that are linked to each other. If one of the rings is removed it results in two unlinked rings. All three rings are needed to remain connected. In other words, with the puzzle as well as the Borromean Rings a *triad* is needed: a set of three similar things that are interrelated to each other.

This book is about another triad, that of Reality, Meaning, and Play. This triad is at the core of games with a purpose beyond entertainment. Each component relates to a different world and needs to be somehow, like the spoons in the puzzle, integrated into a whole. If this is done succesfully, a stable construction arises. Like the spoons that are able to hold an object, the game construction is able to reach something beyond the game itself. To achieve this, all three members of the triad are needed, otherwise the game becomes disconnected like the Borromean Rings. It also requires a "belief." A belief that "there is no spoon." With creative thinking and a vision that reaches further than each of the separate worlds, designers are able to mix and blend the different worlds into a desired shape.

If this is done succesfully, players (subconsciously) accept this new (virtual) reality, much similar to the people living in *The Matrix*, and something "magical" happens. Like Geller's spoon believers, "they belief what they see." They get mystified and in the process they themselves, an organization, and/or a system may benefit from it. It seems like magic when people play a game, but it is not. It is a trick. Games are just as Uri Geller's mind bending spoon trick staged and thought of upfront. They are *designed* like the construction with the three spoons in the puzzle. The "trick" is of course, how can this magic be created? That is where TGD can play a role. I will now continue to explain what each world within this design philosophy is all about.

The Worlds of Triadic Game Design

According to TGD, designing a game revolves around *three* "worlds." It consists of three and not two, four, or five worlds, because when we talk about games with a serious purpose, we talk about games that are based on and/or should have an impact on the real world. It is, however, not sufficient to only consider our "reality." It is also required to consider how such an impact can be achieved. The game should have some "meaning" beyond the game itself and for this to happen, designers have to think about how this could take place. Finally, the third world has to do with the medium itself. A game is a tool or medium that is constituted by "play." It involves make-believe, competition, engagement, rules, and all other aspects that are characteristic to games and not to other sorts of tools or media.

The three, Reality, Meaning, and Play, are called worlds, because each one of them is inhabited by different people, disciplines, aspects, and criteria. Due to this, we can speak of different "worlds" that each shed light on a game in another way. To stick to the world-metaphor, it would be best to say that each of them has a different *Weltanschauung* on how to accomplish a game. To elaborate on these worlds specifically, a short description of each world is given below:

- **Reality**: games have always—how abstract they may be—a relation with the real world. If it is about games with a serious purpose this connection *should* even be tighter, because in the end the real world needs to be affected by the game. Reality could be represented by stakeholders (with their expertise and opinions) from the real world or can be seen as a representation of the real world inside the game. The world Reality thus represents the real world and its model representation—the "model of reality"—in a game. It is grounded in the disciplines related to the subject matter. For a game about the Israeli-Palestinian conflict (e.g., *PeaceMaker* and *Global Conflicts: Palestine*) this would be diplomacy and international relations, while for a game about managing a university (e.g., *Virtual U*) this would be public policy, management, and higher education. Aspects that are part of this world concern the problem that has to be dealt with, the factors involved, and their relationships, and the process of how these relationships evolve over time. Criteria include flexibility, fidelity, and validity. People affiliated with this world are subject-matter experts and consultants.
- **Meaning**: no game can be considered "meaningless." Games, like other media, can have a profound effect on society at large and can be seen as cultural expressions in their own right. Players will also definitely learn something in each game, whether hand-eye coordination skills, visual-spatial skills, or an idea of how ancient Rome may have looked. However, to intentionally achieve a meaningful effect beyond the game experience, something that is useful in the real world, a more elaborate consideration needs to be made of how this can be achieved. The world of Meaning is concerned with this creation of value. It is related to disciplines, such as the learning sciences, psychology, and semiotics. In creating a "value proposal," it incorporates aspects, such as the purpose of what the game needs to achieve, the strategy of how this purpose is going to be achieved, the

concrete operations that aim to achieve this purpose, and the context in which the value creation needs to take place, while among its criteria we can recognize motivation, relevance, and transfer. It is the world of teachers, storytellers, and—depending on the purpose—other people that know how to achieve a certain value.

- **Play**: aside from being related to a real world and having meaning, games are first and foremost a specific tool (or medium). Each tool has its own specific characteristics. When we think of games, we think of highly interactive and engaging tools that immerse people into a fictive situation. This can range from simple point-and-click adventure games and platformers to grand-scale virtual worlds with thousands of players. In creating a game, designers have to think of the goal of the game, the gameplay as in the challenges players face and the actions they can take to overcome these, the gameworld in which it takes place, and the technology to develop and play the game. Its designers strive to fulfill criteria as engagement, immersion, and fun. The idea behind games, and the creation of a "game concept" that expresses what a game is about, belong to the world of Play. This world is affiliated with disciplines as media studies, game design, and human-computer interaction. This world is related to game designers, artists, and media theorists.

For designing a good game, TGD stresses that each world is equally important. This requires designers to "balance" the three worlds. This act of *balancing* is what makes the design process so *difficult*. The idea of balancing is to position the worlds in such a way that they support one another to create a single whole: a game that is able to achieve its serious purpose. This is comparable to the spoon tutorial. The puzzle cannot be solved with one or two spoons. All three are needed. Additionally, the spoons need to be placed in a way that they support one another to be able to carry an object. But most importantly, all three spoons need to be considered at the same time. Similarly, to balance a game all three worlds need to be considered (more or less) at the same time.

Balancing a game is difficult, because in finding a configuration that works, tensions may arise, within or between three of the worlds. When this occurs, designers are confronted with a *dilemma* (or even a *trilemma*) that needs to be resolved. These tensions need to be resolved, since in the end the "ultimate criterion" of TGD, *harmony*, needs to be fulfilled. Without harmony, the game is "out of balance" and it may very likely not be able to create the leverage to support something else—with the spoon tutorial this concerned any other object, with a game this concerns the purpose for which it is designed.

To deal with the challenge of designing a game with a serious purpose, TGD may help by offering a *way of thinking*. It is a way of thinking and not a way of working, because it does not exactly and in much detail prescribe what needs to be considered and in what order. Also, although I touch upon "what" aspects and criteria need to be considered throughout the book, these are more illustrative and not conclusive to what could be taken into account. Other aspects and criteria may play a role as well. The important idea of TGD is "how" the aspects and criteria need to be considered. For this reason, TGD is more of a *design philosophy*.

This is only a glimpse of what TGD is. In the remaining parts of the book this design philosophy is further illustrated, substantiated, and elaborated. This is largely done with the help of the educational training game that I needed to design back in 2006. This game was eventually called *Levee Patroller*.

The Avatar Called Levee Patroller

In games the user's representation is referred to as the *avatar*.[13] It is what the user controls on the screen, whether it is a ball or an actual character. The term, which has been derived from the Sanskrit language, literally means "embodiment" or "incarnation." The avatar of this book concerns the game that I designed: the game *Levee Patroller*. Throughout the book this game forms the main thread onto which the ideas of TGD are explained. This way, it embodies TGD by making it concrete. Many other games make their appearance as well, but as *Levee Patroller* takes such a central role, I will give a short description of how this game came into being and what it is like.

To understand the context of why *Levee Patroller* was developed, try to imagine a country where a significant amount of the land lies below sea level. Natural barriers ensure the land does not get washed away. Unfortunately, these barriers do not provide enough guarantee as history painfully taught this country. To minimize the risk of flooding in the foreseeing future, the government decides to strengthen the natural barriers and build artificial barriers.[14] Despite these measures, the risks keep existing. The barriers are like any material sensitive against extreme conditions, in this case against extreme weather circumstances, such as drought or heavy rain. These conditions can cause a barrier to fail. To prevent failures from occurring, a number of people in this country are trained to find signals that indicate a possible failure of a barrier.

The imagined country actually exists. It is called the Netherlands. The barriers to protect the Netherlands from flooding are referred to as "levees" (or as dikes/dykes).[15] The people who inspect these levees regularly and in case of emer-

[13]Related to digital games, the term "avatar" first appeared in the game *Ultima IV* in 1985. It was further popularized by Neal Stephenson in his cyberpunk novel *Snow Crash* from 1992. Nowadays the term is commonly used in digital games as well as in Internet forums and other ICT services.

[14]Of course, more possible measures to minimize the risk of flooding exist. For example, the Netherlands developed a complex irrigation network to guide the huge amounts of water to some extent. Additionally, regions can be put under water when the water levels start to rise. For reasons of scope I decided to exclude these options.

[15]Formally, dikes or dykes, which are derived from the Dutch word "dijken," are used to refer to the large barriers, those that protect the land from the rivers and the sea. The smaller barriers are seen as levees. The total length of dikes sums up to 17,500 km (i.e., 10,874 mile). On top of that, several ten thousands of levees exist. Out of simplicity I use levees as an umbrella term for all these types of barriers.

Fig. 1.6 The small settlement in my hometown. The red line shows how the levee is moving inwards (away from the water and toward the land)

gencies are referred to as "levee patrollers."[16] A levee patroller is basically a first responder, similar to a fire fighter or a police officer, although these latter types of first responders are much more familiar to the general public. Most people do not even know that levee patrollers exist. In fact, before I started the assignment to design the game I had never heard of it myself.

Part of the explanation of this ignorance is that actual levee failures do not occur that often. Estimates of failures with enormous consequences are about once in the 1250 or 10,000 years (at least, they should be according to the Dutch legislation).[17] Smaller incidents can occur "more often," but are in fact rather rare in themselves as well. An example of such a small incident actually happened in my "backyard." During my domain research I discovered that a levee was about to breach in my hometown, while I did not know anything about it at the time. Due to some excavation activities the levee became unstable and started moving inwards. This can be seen by the small settlement on the top of the levee in Fig. 1.6. It was easily solved back then, because people observed the signals in time.

However, generally speaking, how is it possible to prepare for something that rarely happens? To prevent a rare event, people first need to recognize it. This recognition relies on being able to distinguish subtle cues, "signals," from the environment and make sense out of them on the basis of knowledge. We can separate a banana from an apple, because we know what makes a banana and what makes an apple. Awareness is further needed. If we are not looking for bananas and apples, we are most likely not going to find them. And if we find them, we need to know what

[16]The concept of "levee patrollers" is not unique to the Netherlands. It differs per country how it is organized and who is responsible.

[17]The once in the 1250 years is a rate that has been attributed to most Dutch rivers, while the 10,000 rate is used for most sea levees. Both have been firmly described in a Dutch law. Every four years the levees need to be checked whether they fulfill this demand. It has been suggested in several reports that many levees are not well maintained and, as such, do not fulfill the legal guidelines. In contrast to the Dutch standards, most other countries, including the USA and the UK, hold on to a failure acceptance rate of once in the 100 years (although this is currently changing due to the increasing danger of flooding).

Fig. 1.7 A levee breach has occurred that floods the whole region

to do in addition. While we practice eating (apples and bananas) everyday, levee patrollers have not such an ability for dealing with failures.

Game technology was deemed as a promising solution for this problem. It would enable levee patrollers to practice in a safe environment how to find, report, and deal with (virtual) failures. This way, they could learn how to make sense of failures and what procedures are necessary. But how to design such a game? That is where I came into the picture and my journey in designing games started.

In the eventual game users have to find (random) failures and report these. I like to think of it as a three-dimensional *Pac-Man*, in which the user has to "eat" levee failures instead of yellow dots. No ghosts are present, but if the failures are not eaten well, it could lead to a levee breach that floods the whole region (Fig. 1.7).[18] A seemingly simple idea, yet to actually develop this game many tensions had to be resolved. But before I get to how *Levee Patroller* was balanced, I will first explain some more about TGD.

Walkthrough of the Book

In this introduction level, I made clear that this book is about the design of (especially digital) games with a serious purpose. These are games that try to achieve a certain value beyond the game itself. I further showed that the use of these games has a long and very rich tradition. While this is the case, the field could certainly benefit from a basic theoretical sense of what these games are and how they need to be designed. The idea of Triadic Game Design (TGD) tries to fulfill this gap. This idea can be summarized in one sentence: in designing a game, designers need to balance the worlds of Reality, Meaning, and Play.

In the remaining parts of this book this idea is further illustrated, substantiated, and elaborated. The next level, Level 2, delves into its foundations. I have only

[18]It is worthy to mention that when most players play the game, the first thing they want to see is a levee breach.

slightly touched upon what TGD is and in this level I will explain where the idea is based on, what its implications are, how it relates to the player, and how it differs from other approaches. This level also gives a broad and rich description of the current state of games with a serious purpose from the perspective of TGD. Based on this, it will become clear why it is so difficult to categorize games.

The subsequent levels, Levels 3, 4, and 5, go more in-depth into the worlds of Reality, Meaning, and Play, respectively. Each level gives a detailed explanation of what this world consists of and how it looks at the design process. The levels foremost discuss the aspects and criteria that designers need to take into account according to each world. As each world is affiliated with different disciplines, I am referring to literature, examples, and so on that are strongly coupled to specific fields. I have tried to find a "balance" so the text would appeal to laypeople as well as experts, but it is unavoidable that some parts may be too detailed for some and too superficial for others.

Level 6 deals with the issue of "balancing." It specifically addresses how this was done with *Levee Patroller* and it uses concepts from the previous levels to explain this. This is, therefore, the sort of level in a game in which players need to apply everything that they have learned in the previous levels. The final level in this book, Level 7, gives—as is usual with endings—an outlook to the world beyond the worlds of TGD and this book.

In writing the book I have tried to apply the idea of TGD as well. I wanted to write a book about my experience in the real world which would be valuable for others in an enjoyable and playful manner. The use of the label "level," a term normally devoted in games to describe their discrete subdivisions, instead of the more conventional label "chapter" is just one of many attempts to achieve this.[19] Also consistent with this, the book does not need to be read linearly, although I do recommend reading Level 2 after this. I further think that Level 6 makes more sense when all the levels before it have been read. With this being said, we have "walked through" the book, and are now ready to jump "linearly" to the next level.

Bibliography

Literature Bibliography

Aarseth, E. J. (1997). *Cybertext: perspectives on ergodic literature*. Baltimore: John Hopkins University Press.

Abt, C. C. (1970). *Serious games*. New York: Viking.

Achtman, R. L., Green, C. S., & Bavelier, D. (2008). Video games as a tool to train visual skills. *Restorative Neurology and Neuroscience*, *26*(4–5), 435–446.

[19]The interchangeability of the labels "level" and "chapter" can be quite strongly seen in games. Games like *Professor Layton* use the label chapter for indicating their subdivisions instead of levels.

Adams, P. C. (1998). Teaching and learning with SimCity 2000. *Journal of Geography*, *97*(2), 47–55.
Adams, S. S. (2007). The case for video games in libraries. *Library Review*, *58*(3), 196–202.
Aldrich, C. (2009). *The complete guide to simulations and serious games: how the most valuable content will be created in the age beyond Gutenberg to Google*. San Francisco: Pfeiffer.
Baudrillard, J. (1981/1994). *Simulacra and simulation*. Ann Arbor: The University of Michigan Press (S.F. Glaser, Transl.).
Beck, J. C., & Wade, M. (2004). *Got game: how the gamer generation is reshaping business forever*. Boston: Harvard Business School Press.
Bergeron, B. P. (2006). *Developing serious games*. Hingham: Charles River Media.
Bogost, I. (2006). *Unit operations: an approach to video game criticism*. Cambridge: The MIT Press.
Bogost, I. (2007). *Persuasive games: the expressive power of videogames*. Cambridge: The MIT Press.
Brewer, G., & Shubik, M. (1979). *The war game: a critique of military problem solving*. Cambridge: Harvard University Press.
Castiglione, B. (1528/1997). *The book of the courtier*. Eugene: R.S. Bear at University of Oregon (T. Hoby, Transl.).
Coller, B. D., & Scott, M. J. (2009). Effectiveness of using a video game to teach a course in mechanical engineering. *Computers & Education*, *53*(3), 900–912.
Dale, A. G., & Klasson, C. R. (1962). *Business gaming: a survey of american collegiate schools of business*. Austin: University of Texas.
Duke, R. D. (1974). *Gaming, the future's language*. Beverly Hills: Sage.
Duke, R. D., & Geurts, J. (2004). *Policy games for strategic management: pathways into the unknown*. Amsterdam: Dutch University Press.
Dzhukov, R., Mikhaylushkin, A., Gagnon, J. H., Wolfe, J., & Crookall, D. (1993). In memoriam: Marie Mironovna Beershtain (Mary M. Birshtein) 1902–1992. *Simulation & Gaming*, *21*(1), 6–8.
Egenfeldt-Nielsen, S. (2007). *Beyond edutainment: the educational potential of computer games*. London: Continuum Press.
Fairbairn, J. (1995). *Go in ancient China*. http://gobase.org/reading/history/china/. Accessed 6 October 2009.
Faria, A. J., Hutchinson, D., Wellington, W. J., & Gold, S. (2009). Developments in business gaming: a review of the past 40 years. *Simulation & Gaming*, *40*(4), 464–487.
Feng, J., Spence, I., & Pratt, J. (2007). Playing an action video game reduces gender differences in spatial cognition. *Psychological Science*, *18*(10), 850–855.
Franklin, B. (1779). *The morals of Chess*. http://www.metajedrez.com.ar/franklineng.htm. Accessed 6 October 2009.
Gaber, J. (2007). Simulating planning: SimCity as a pedagogical tool. *Journal of Planning Education and Research*, *27*(2), 113–121.
Gee, J. (2004). *What video games have to teach us about learning and literacy*. New York: Palgrave Macmillan.
Gladwell, M. (2005). *Blink: the power of thinking without thinking*. New York: Little, Brown.
Green, C. S., & Bavelier, D. (2003). Action video game modifies visual selective attention. *Nature*, *423*(6939), 534–537.
Herz, J. C. (1997). *Joystick nation: how videogames ate our quarters, won our hearts, and rewired our minds*. Boston: Little, Brown.
Hooper, D., & Whyld, K. (1992). *The Oxford companion to Chess* (2nd ed.). Oxford: Oxford University Press.
Horn, R. E., & Cleaves, A. (1980). *The guide to simulations/games for education and training*. Beverly Hills: Sage Publications.
Huizinga, J. (1938/1955). *Homo ludens: a study of the play-element in culture*. Boston: Beacon Press (R.F.C. Hull, Transl.).
Jenkins, H. (2006). *Convergence culture: where old and new media collide*. New York: New York University Press.

Johnson, S. (2005). *Everything bad is good for you: how today's popular culture is actually making us smarter*. New York: Riverhead Books.

Jones, S. (2008). *The meaning of video games: gaming and textual strategies*. New York: Routhledge.

Juul, J. (2005). *Half-real: video games between real rules and fictional worlds*. Cambridge: The MIT Press.

Juul, J. (2009). *A casual revolution: reinventing video games and their players*. Cambridge: The MIT Press.

Kato, P. M., Cole, S. W., Bradlyn, A. S., & Pollock, B. H. (2009). A video game improves behavioral outcomes in adolescents and young adults with cancer: a randomized trial. *Pediatrics*, *122*(2), 305–317.

Klabbers, J. H. G. (2006). *The magic circle: principles of gaming and simulation*. Rotterdam: Sense.

Klabbers, J. H. G. (2009). Terminological ambiguity: game and simulation. *Simulation & Gaming*, *40*(4), 446–463.

Koster, R. (2005). *A theory of fun for game design*. Scottsdale: Paraglyph Press.

Kuit, M. (2002). *Strategic behavior and regulatory styles in the netherlands energy industry*. Delft: Eburon.

Laurel, B. (2001). *Utopian entrepeneur*. Cambridge: The MIT Press.

Malone, T. W. (1981). Toward a theory of intrinsically motivating instruction. *Cognitive Science*, *5*(4), 333–369.

Masayoshi, S. (2005). *A journey in search of the origins of Go*. Santa Monica: Yutopian Enterprises.

Mayer, I. S. (2009). The gaming of policy and the politics of gaming: a review. *Simulation & Gaming*, *40*(6), 825–862.

Meijer, S. A. (2009). *The organisation of transactions: studying supply networks using gaming simulation*. Wageningen: Wageningen Academic.

Michael, D., & Chen, S. (2006). *Serious games: games that educate, train, and inform*. Boston: Thomson Course Technology PTR.

Nachmanovitch, S. (1991). *Free play: improvisation in life and art*. New York: Tarcher.

Olmert, M. (1996). *Milton's teeth and Ovid's umbrella: curiouser & curiouser adventures in history*. New York: Simon & Schuster.

Parlett, D. (1999). *The Oxford history of board games*. Oxford: Oxford University Press.

Piccione, P. A. (1980). In search of the meaning of Senet. *Archaeology*, *33*, 55–58.

Prensky, M. (2001). *Digital game-based learning*. New York: McGraw-Hill.

Ritterfeld, U., Cody, M., & Vorderer, P. (Eds.) (2009). *Serious games: mechanisms and effects*. New York: Routhledge.

Rosser, J. C., Lynch, P. J., Cuddihy, L., Gentile, D. A., Klonsky, J., & Merrell, R. (2007). The impact of video games on training surgeons in the 21st century. *Archives of Surgery*, *142*(2), 181–186.

Sawyer, B. (2002). *Serious games: improving public policy through game-based learning and simulation*. Washington: Woodrow Wilson International Center for Scholars.

Schell, J. (2008). *The art of game design: a book of lenses*. Burlington: Morgan Kaufmann.

Shaffer, D. W. (2006). *How computer games help children learn*. New York: Palgrave Macmillan.

Shubik, M. (1975). *Games for society, business and war: towards a theory of gaming*. New York: Elsevier.

Shubik, M. (2009). It is not just a game! *Simulation & Gaming*, *40*(5), 587–601.

Squire, K. D. (2004). *Replaying history: learning world history through playing Civilization III*. Unpublished dissertation, Indiana University, Bloomington, IN.

Tapscott, D. (1997). *Growing up digital: the rise of the net generation*. New York: McGraw-Hill.

Taylor, T. L. (2006). *Play between worlds: exploring online game culture*. Cambridge: The MIT Press.

Vale, M. (2001). *The princely court: medieval courts and culture in North-West Europe, 1270–1380*. New York: Oxford University Press.

Van Eck, R. (2009). A guide to integrating cots games in your classroom. In R. E. Ferdig (Ed.), *Handbook of research on effective electronic gaming in education* (pp. 179–199). Hershey: Information Science Reference.

Veen, W., & Vrakking, B. (2006). *Homo zappiens: growing up in a digital age*. London: Network Continuum Education.

Von Ahn, L., & Dabbish, L. (2004). Labeling images with a computer game. In E. Dykstra-Erickson & M. Tscheligi (Eds.), *ACM CHI 2004 conference on human factors in computing systems* (pp. 319–326). Vienna: ACM Press.

Von Clausewitz, C. (1832/1873). *On war*. London: Trübner (J.J. Graham, Transl.).

Willis, S. (2003). *The immutable nature of war: interview with Paul Van Riper*. http://www.pbs.org/wgbh/nova/wartech/nature.html. Accessed 6 October 2009.

Yee, N. (2006). The demographics, motivations and derived experiences of users of massively-multiuser online graphical environments. *Presence: Teleoperators and Virtual Environments*, *15*(3), 309–329.

Game Bibliography

Alcorn, A. (1972). *Pong* [Atari 2600]. Sunnyvale: Atari.

Blizzard Entertainment (2004). *World of Warcraft* [PC]. Irvine: Blizzard Entertainment.

Bungie Studios (2001). *Halo: Combat Evolved* [Xbox]. Redmond: Microsoft.

Crawford, C. (1985). *Balance of Power* [PC]. Novato: Mindscape.

Crawford, C. (1990). *Balance of the Planet* [PC]. Novato: Mindscape.

Darrow, C. (1935). *Monopoly* [Board]. Salem: Parker Brothers.

Deltares, & Delft University of Technology (2006). *Levee Patroller: The Levee Inspection Simulator* [PC]. Delft, the Netherlands: Delft GeoSystems.

Duke, R. D. (1975). *Hexagon* [Board]. Ann Arbor: University of Michigan.

Enlight Software (2003). *Virtual U* [PC]. Portland: Woodrow Wilson Foundation.

Firaxis Games (2005). *Sid Meier's Civilization IV* [PC]. Hunt Valley: 2K Games.

GameLab, & Global Kids (2006). *Ayiti: The Cost of Life* [Web]. Seattle: Microsoft.

Harmonix Music Systems (2006). *Guitar Hero* [Playstation 2]. Sunnyvale: RedOctane.

id Software (1993). *Doom* [PC]. Mesquite: id Software.

ImpactGames (2007). *PeaceMaker: A Video Game to Promote Peace* [PC]. Pittsburgh: ImpactGames.

Kramer, C. (1984). *Tempo Typen* [PC]. Alphen aan den Rijn, the Netherlands: Radarsoft.

Level-5 (2007). *Professor Layton and the Curious Village* [Nintendo DS]. Tokyo, Japan: Nintendo.

Marine Corps Modeling and Simulation Management Office (1996). *Marine Doom* [PC]. Quantico: Marine Corps.

Maxis Software (2003). *SimCity 4* [PC]. Redwood City: Electronic Arts.

MECC (1982). *The Oregon Trail* [PC]. Concord: Softswap.

Microsoft (1981). *Solitaire* [PC]. Redmond: Microsoft.

Namco (1981). *Pac-Man* [Atari 2600]. Sunnyvale: Atari.

Origin Systems (1985). *Ultima IV: Quest of the Avatar* [PC]. Austin: Origin Systems.

Robinett, W., & Grimm, L. (1982). *Rocky's Boots* [PC]. San Francisco: The Learning Company.

Serious Games Interactive (2007). *Global Conflicts: Palestine* [PC]. Copenhagen, Denmark: Serious Games Interactive.

University of Washington (2008). *Foldit: Solve Puzzles for Science* [PC]. Seattle: University of Washington.

U.S. Army (2009). *America's Army 3* [PC]. Washington: U.S. Army.

Von Ahn, L., & Dabbish, L. (2004). *ESP Game* [Web]. Pittsburgh: Carnegie Mellon University.

Level 2
Foundations

He who has not first laid his foundations may be able with great ability to lay them afterwards, but they will be laid with trouble to the architect and danger to the building—Niccolo Machiavelli

An imitation of an action must represent one action, a complete whole, with its several incidents so closely connected that the transposal or withdrawal of any one of them will disjoin and dislocate the whole. For that which makes no perceptible difference by its presence or absence is no real part of the whole—Aristotle

In a very simple "game" called *September 12th* an anonymous Middle Eastern town is depicted with civilians, dogs, and terrorists (Fig. 2.1).[1] In the game the player controls a crosshair which can be moved around freely. Clicking the mouse button fires a missile which after a short delay destroys everything in the near vicinity of where it hits. The game does not provide any instructions of how to play it, but given the tool—the ability to shoot missiles—it seems rather logical to kill the terrorists. When I played it the first time, after observing the town for a while, I simply started to shoot the terrorists.

There is, however, a catch to it. When civilians are killed, others gather around and weep, and become terrorists themselves. It is nearly impossible to kill all the terrorists without hitting civilians, especially due to the time lapse between hitting the mouse button and the impact of the missile, and so we enter a loop in which the situation only degrades instead of becomes any better. When realizing this, we may understand that the game is a criticism on the "War on Terror" and on the use of long-range precision warfare.

This game nicely illustrates that games are *systems* (Salen and Zimmerman 2004). A system is generally defined as "a set of interacting elements that form

[1] The designers of *September 12th* stress that it is not a game. They call it a simulation. They did this to emphasize that their product really mimics a process in the real world and that its message should be taken seriously.

C. Harteveld, *Triadic Game Design*,
DOI 10.1007/978-1-84996-157-8_2, © Springer-Verlag London Limited 2011

Fig. 2.1 Shooting terrorists in *September 12th*. I just fired a missile and had to wait until the crosshair does not color red anymore. ©2003 Newsgaming.com. Used with permission

an integrated whole with a common goal or purpose" (Fullerton et al. 2008, p. 132) and games can be seen as a set of such interacting elements that work together on the basis of rules in providing players, the participants of a game, an experience. With *September 12th* we see that with a number of simple game elements, a crosshair which shoots missiles and civilians, dogs, and terrorists that walk around in a Middle Eastern Town, and with a number of simple rules that facilitate the interaction between these elements, a system is created with a purpose of explaining a political message. For reaching this purpose, the designers needed to consider and understand how the set of elements work together.

For this, it helps to know what the "complete whole" is and what "several incidents" should connect to it. Otherwise, as Aristotle argued, the "transposal or withdrawal of any" of the needed incidents "will disjoin and dislocate the whole." If citizens do not react to the death of another citizen by becoming a terrorist, the whole idea of *September 12th* would fall apart. It further helps to see what incidents are relevant and what are not. If incidents are "no real part of the whole," they can be neglected. *September 12th* does not include a wide variety of long-range missile weapons, simply because its message could already be shown with the use of one of them.

In making sure a game is designed well, to get a "complete whole," considerations have to be made of what to include and exclude and how everything needs to relate to each other. Creating such a balanced system is quite difficult, even for a seemingly simple looking game as *September 12th*. To assist in this, Triadic Game

Design (TGD) offers a way of thinking. To elaborate on this way of thinking, my attempt in this level is to get into the details of this idea by explaining its *foundations*.

I will first elaborate on the idea in general (see "The General Idea of Triadic Game Design") and then continue to discuss each world separately (see "The World of Reality," "The World of Meaning," and the "The World of Play"). From there, I discuss how it relates to the player (see "What About the Player?") and to other approaches (see "And What About Other Approaches?"). With all of this the foundations of TGD are laid down.

The General Idea of Triadic Game Design

TGD is as its name suggests about "game design." Game design involves the *art* and *craft* of constructing specific artifacts called "games" (Rollings and Adams 2003). It concerns an art, because as with most "designs," it involves inspiration, originality, creativity, innovation, and many other aspects that make it an art. On the other hand, with designing games, it requires similar to designing a watch or a shoe, a certain skill. The more we practice, the better we become at it. This makes it also a craft.

In designing games, nobody wants to reinvent the wheel or make mistakes that could have been prevented and everybody wants the practice to improve over time. For this reason, it helps to consider certain methods, techniques, principles, procedures, theories, and approaches. TGD concerns such a "game design approach." It is an approach specifically oriented at games with a serious purpose. To further distinguish it from other approaches, it must be seen as a *design philosophy*. A design philosophy does not offer clear and detailed steps that designers need to take to design their artifact, but gives them an overall "way of thinking" of how they need to look at their practice.

This design philosophy stresses in particular two issues. It gives an indication of *what* the design of a game with a serious purpose consists of (see "Finding an Optimum") and it tells *how* designers need to deal with this (see "Designing Concurrently").

Finding an "Optimum"

The name "Triadic Game Design" more or less indicates about "what" the design of games with a meaningful purpose consists of. It involves a triad that consists of the worlds of Reality, Meaning, and Play. Each world has its own people, disciplines, aspects, and criteria.

Yet, the worlds are inherently connected to each other. They are even interdependent on each other. If the world of Meaning is not related to Reality than what the world of Meaning tries to pursue becomes meaningless, as what is derived from playing a game cannot be applied outside the game. If the world of Play does not have some representation derived from the world of Reality, it becomes unplayable.

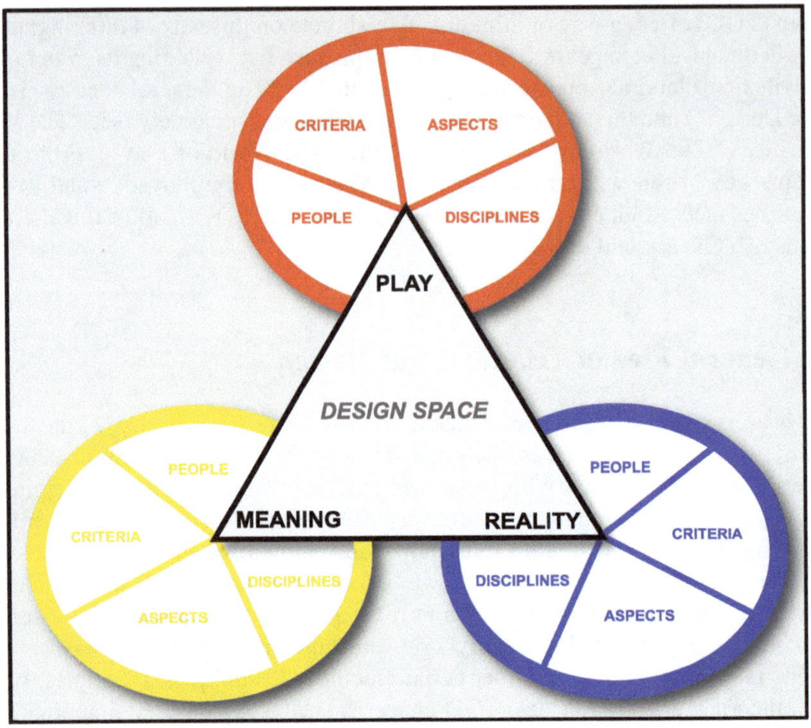

Fig. 2.2 The design space of TGD

Without a representation, nobody can relate to it. Furthermore, if the world of Play is not related to the world of Meaning than no value will be derived from playing a game. This makes the worlds of TGD similar to the Borromean Rings (see Level 1). If one world is missing, the game collapses.

All three worlds are, therefore, equally important and they constitute the *design space* of developing a game (Fig. 2.2). The term "design space" is introduced by Simon (1969). It involves an imaginary place from where the design is created from. For games this means that the imaginary place is inhabited by three overlapping worlds and designers (consciously or unconsciously) consider these when creating a game.

Such creation does not come without any difficulty, because aside from solutions, the design space is also occupied by problems (Krishnamurti 2006). According to TGD, with games design problems can be related back to each of the worlds, because designing is mostly about solving tensions within and between the worlds that inhabit the design space.

Solutions to these problems can also be found in the design space. Solving tensions requires to "balance" the three worlds. Ideally, this means that a solution should be sought for that is most satisfactory for all worlds, but it often means a choice should be compensated with something else. In other words, to deal with the tensions designers have to make many *trade-offs* within and between the three worlds.

For example, to play *September 12th* is not much fun. The designers compensated the world of Play, however, by creating a comical fictional world. Additionally, Reality has been much traded off against Meaning and Play. The game has a simple message and simple game mechanics, and so the complexity of the situation had to be reduced to a model of reality in which resorting to violence under any circumstances causes more violence in response.

If a game turns out to be unbalanced, which means that one of the worlds is favored too often, the danger is that the ultimate criterion of *harmony* may not be reached. If this happens, it is unlikely that the game achieves for what it is designed for. It might be inappropriately linked to the real world, not create the value that goes beyond the context of playing the game, and/or it might not be engaging and enjoyable enough for players to devote their time to.

I consider *September 12th* to be a balanced game, as all three worlds are nicely reconciled with each other. It can, however, certainly be criticized. Costikyan (2003) argued, for instance, that it gives the idea that "terrorists are perfectly peaceable people who toddle around until nasty, evil Western imperialists destroy them and half of their neighbors through indiscriminate missile attacks." This shows that the model of reality is to a large extent imperfect. But to deal with this imperfection, it would severely affect its message, even if it is a bit simplistic, and cause the game to be unbalanced.

Based on the previous, it should become clear why designing games with a serious purpose is so difficult. Designers have to be equally concerned about the worlds of Reality, Meaning, and Play. This makes designing games a "multi-objective problem" rather than a "single-objective problem." Single-objective problems always have a single optimal solution: they have one goal and can be optimized toward this goal. For example, if in a tender proposals are judged on costs, then the decision can be optimized by simply choosing the proposal with the least amount of costs.

For multi-objective problems an optimal solution does not exist. To solve these problems, people have to look for the best solutions, the ones that are "satisficing" to most of the criteria. In looking for these solutions, people may find multiple "optimal" solutions. By taking the tender example again, if proposals are judged on quality next to costs, a trade-off has to be made, because a better quality leads to more costs. Those who submit a proposal as well as the ones who make the final decision have to consider how they will deal with the "space" that is constituted by quality and costs.

According to TGD, in developing a game designers have to deal with the design space that is constituted by the worlds of Reality, Meaning, and Play. In finding an "optimum" in this space it is important that they take the second issue into account: to design "concurrently."

Fig. 2.3 Designers should act like jugglers by designing their games concurrently. Drawing by Rens van den Bergh

Designing Concurrently

To look for "optimal" solutions within the design space we hit the second issue related to TGD, which follows logically from the first. If designing a game involves balancing three equally important worlds, then it follows that these worlds should be considered *at the same time* in *critical parts* of the design process *as much as possible*. If this does not occur, designers run the risk that one or two of the worlds are prioritized too much and this will make the game unbalanced.

Considering the worlds "at the same time" involves to *concurrently* look at several aspects, criteria, and other relevant elements for designing a game and not separately. The need for *concurrent design* also follows logically from the idea that games are systems (Fullerton et al. 2008; Salen and Zimmerman 2004). Games consist of tightly coupled interacting elements that work together in providing an experience. This means that changing any of the elements will affect the "complete whole," the system at large. And a small change can have big ramifications.

A well-known example of such small change with big consequences concerns the game *Counter-Strike*. This game is very similar to other shooters, like *Quake III Arena* and *Unreal Tournament*, but unlike these games *Counter-Strike* is not a mindless action game. It is rather a more team-oriented game and this has been the result of just some minor changes in the game system:

> Unlike *Quake III Arena*, *Counter-Strike* is famous for its team-oriented gameplay, but since there a no rules in *Counter-Strike* that tell players to "play team-oriented," the question is, what makes *Counter-Strike* a team-oriented game? *Counter-Strike* only adds a few varia-

> tions on the team-based modes of *Quake III Arena*: Players do not respawn[2] during a round, there are goals that can win an entire round for a team, and players move more slowly and are much more vulnerable. As it turns out, these variations completely change the game to be more oriented toward team play. Since the player has only one life per round, death becomes something to be avoided at all costs. This makes it very important for players to work together. In even a simple skirmish, being in a group is much better than being alone. Having your back covered becomes important. Communication therefore becomes important. In this way, very simple rule changes can completely change the gameplay of a game. (Juul 2005, pp. 89–90)

To perceive the effects of a design choice, the game system as a whole should be considered. With *Counter-Strike* we clearly see that small changes led to a complete different game—the system as a whole changed. And with this game Juul (2005) only looked at it from the world of Play. If we would also look at it from the world of Reality, it could be said that while it is still an entertainment game, it has become far more realistic compared to real combat situations. Additionally, if we would look at it from the world of Meaning, a clear emphasis shift is made from learning eye-hand coordination skills and training reaction time toward collaboration and communication skills. From this we see that games are so tightly coupled that small changes in a game system have an effect on all three worlds.

To make sure that all three worlds are appropriately taken care off, designers should act like a juggler in creating their games (Fig. 2.3). They have to keep three "balls" going and up in the air. Doing this requires to pay attention to all three balls "at the same time." The three balls represent, of course, Reality, Meaning, and Play.

Designing concurrently contrasts with *procedural design* approaches. These approaches emphasize that design takes place in steps or phases. This means that design issues are not considered at the same time, but in a certain sequence. TGD and its concurrent design is, however, not completely incompatible with these approaches. In fact, they can be used next to each other.

Take the approach by Duke and Geurts (2004), which draws heavily upon the initial work by Duke (1974). It consists of five phases with in total 21 steps that designers can use to anticipate each phase from the outset. This approach for the design of tailor-made analog games, specifically in the area of policy and management, has been tested and developed for over a period of 40 years and is depicted below.[3]

Phase 1: Setting the stage for the project—complete the essential preliminaries.
Step 1: Administrative set-up—organize the project.
Step 2: Define the problem—what prompts this project?

---

[2]When players die in a game, and the rules allow for this, they can "respawn" somewhere. This means they appear alive somewhere in the game environment and are able to continue playing.

[3]I made some adaptations to the approach by Duke and Geurts (2004). They speak, for example, of the creation of "policy exercises" or "policy games" which are participatory methods for actual policy and decision making. I renamed this to "games," because I think their approach goes beyond the creation of these "policy exercises." I also renamed phase 5 from "Implementation" to "Deployment," as implementation has a different meaning in the context of digital games. Last but not least, I further adjusted the steps in such a way that they are understandable to any reader and can be easily related to the aspects mentioned in this book.

Step 3: Define the purpose of the project—what are the primary objectives?
Step 4: Relate objectives to different possible methods—is a game appropriate?
Step 5: Specifications—constraints and expectations.

Phase 2: Clarifying the problem—define both the focus and scope.
Step 6: Defining the model of reality—content, boundaries, interrelationships.
Step 7: Displaying the model of reality—create a lucid depiction of this model.
Step 8: Negotiating the focus/scope with the client—set a clear target.

Phase 3: Designing the game—create a blueprint.
Step 9: Translate the model of reality to a game—make a model of a model.
Step 10: Definition of gaming elements—describe each part of the game.
Step 11: Repertoire of techniques—do not reinvent the wheel.
Step 12: Select a format—what style is appropriate?
Step 13: Game concept—document the idea.

Phase 4: Developing the game—make sure it works.
Step 14: Build, test, and modify a prototype—put the pieces together.
Step 15: Technical evaluation—ensure an efficient and effective tool is created.
Step 16: Graphic design and printing—develop a professional presentation.

Phase 5: Deployment—ensure proper use by the client.
Step 17: Integrate the game into the context—make it fit.
Step 18: Facilitating the game—practical use of the game.
Step 19: Dissemination—deliver or publish the game.
Step 20: Ethical and legal concerns—protect the design.
Step 21: Final report—ensure proper closure.

This approach can to a large extent very well co-exist with TGD, because designing games does indeed consist of certain phases and steps. As for the phases, at the start, for example, no discussion should take place about what the rules of the game are. The discussion should be about defining the problem and purpose. In addition, a game cannot be tested if no design exists. And finally, it is simply impossible to deliver a game while also designing it. The phases, therefore, make sense.

As for the steps, designers cannot do research into the topic of the problem they are dealing with, while at the same exploring, for example, learning theories and thinking about specific game mechanisms. They do this in separate steps. And although in practice this might be different, it would be a logical first step to think about the problem and then define the purpose of the project. For this reason, taking steps when designing a game, such as depicted with this approach, is unavoidable.

TGD delineates, however, from procedural design approaches in how the development of the *core of the game* is depicted. With this, I refer to what the game system consists of: what are its elements and how do they relate to each other? In developing this system, integration takes place—a synthesis has to be made. Findings from the topic of the problem are combined with insights from the exploration of learning theories and with ideas about game mechanisms. In this "critical part" of the design process, designers should think concurrently—they have to think of how they combine the elements of the worlds of Reality, Meaning, and Play together to get a balanced game.

Such concurrency and integration can hardly be derived from the approach by Duke and Geurts (2004). It more or less suggests that designers first have to take care of the world of Meaning by only defining the purpose, subsequently delve into the world of Reality by developing a "model of reality," and when this is done, concentrate fully on the world of Play. While each and every world is certainly and in many occasions during the design process looked upon separately, in the critical parts of the process designers have to consider all three worlds simultaneously "as much as possible."

I mention "as much as possible," because in practice it is often not possible to take everything into account at the same time. Some potential problems may not be known upfront and as is often with systems, especially the more complex ones, the effects of changes cannot be entirely known upfront as well and these changes, as seen with *Counter-Strike*, can have enormous effects. Without having a clear picture of the whole, decisions are difficult to take in creating the core of the game.

To deal with this, *iterative design* is needed (cf., Boehm 1988; Fullerton et al. 2008). Such design suggests to progressively develop a games based on a cyclic process of prototyping, testing, and evaluating the results. Based on the results of an iteration, changes and refinements are made. This repeated cycle of prototyping, testing, evaluating, and refining continues until the requirements are satisfied—that is, a balance has been found within and between the three worlds.

From this, we see that with "designing concurrently" I do not mean that everything should be considered at the same time. This is impossible. Steps and phases remain part of the design process. Iterations are also needed, because it cannot be expected that designers get it right the first time around and they may not have a clear idea of what they need to consider. What I do mean by designing concurrently is that within and between certain steps and phases, and especially in the critical parts of the design process, where the core of the game is developed, designers should act much like a juggler by taking various elements into account at the same time.

But to be able to juggle it is necessary to know with what to juggle. For this reason, I will now delve into each of the worlds that constitute the design space. I will start with the world of Reality.

The World of Reality

Most games are in some way connected to the physical world. They involve many "fantasy elements," such as no gravity, not being able to die, or having three lives. Nevertheless, there are always "things" that are recognizable and to whom we can relate to in reality (whether fiction or non-fiction[4]). If not, a game would not be

[4]Games may also refer to (other) fictional "things" from reality, like movies, cartoons, or books. For example, some games, like *Levee Patroller*, borrow the concept of "teleportation" from the *Star Trek* series which is the ability to disappear at one location and appear at another in a split second (and to which the catch phrase "Beam me up, Scotty!" is related to). Of course, these fictional "things" bear also some connection with reality. This makes games a copy of a copy whenever they refer to these other fictional "things," or, in the words of Baudrillard (1981/1994) a "simulacrum."

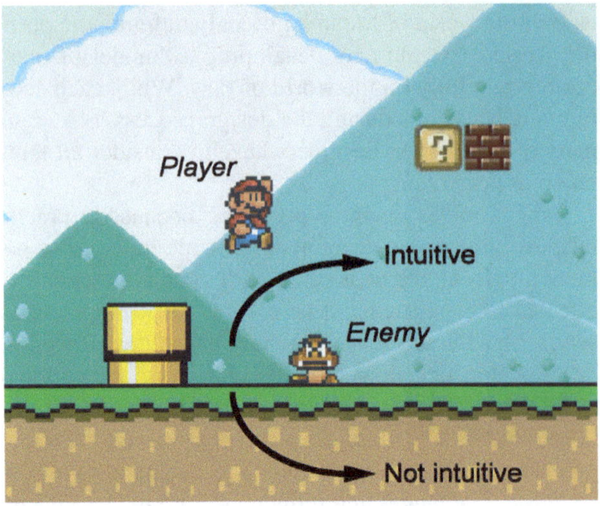

Fig. 2.4 Intuitive behavior in games as *Super Mario Bros.* Screen shot is taken from a Flash version of the original game. ©1985 Nintendo

meaningful to us and we are unable to play it. For example, I do not know any game in which players have to avoid an enemy by "jumping" underneath it (Fig. 2.4). Players always have to jump "over" the enemy, because that is how things work in reality as well. Of course, players cannot jump that high in reality. In fact, it is even unlikely that they will ever encounter the types of enemies in reality (ever seen a "poison head crab"?[5]). The point is that despite all the fiction a game may contain, it always maintains some connection with reality to make the experience intuitive and understandable.[6]

The "connection" between a game and reality suggests that games contain an underlying *model of reality*. The latter says what it is: a representation (of parts) of reality.[7] When a game is developed, designers—consciously or unconsciously—consider aspects of the real world, like people, organizations, objects, variables, and relationships, and put these together into this model. This can be as simple as representations of familiar objects like a car (together with for example Newtonian

[5]A poison head crab is one of the enemies players can encounter in *Half-Life 2*. According to Lamar (2008) it is the second most terrifying game enemy of all time.

[6]Some games, in particular *indie games* (i.e., games developed by independent developers), make actually use of creating an experience that goes against people's intuitive behavior. *The Path*, for example, only becomes interesting when the player wanders around instead of complies with the explicated goal of the game which is to walk from A to B. *Braid* is another game that requires players to reconsider their own logic of how the world on their screen unfolds.

[7]Instead of "model of reality" some scholars call it the "simulation model" and reality the "reference system" (cf., Peters et al. 1998). I opted instead for "model of reality," because aside that this term clearly refers to the world of Reality, the other term, "simulation," can cause confusion. Simulation can also refer to the artifact itself, to a genre of games, or to a traditional tool (in operation research) which uses computer models to calculate possible scenarios and which have little to no association with games, whereas I just wanted to refer to something that is part of every game. For this reason, I chose to use a term that is less contested.

physics of how objects move) to such elaborate representations as a political system (with political parties, issues, and secret agendas). It depends very much on the type of game and its purpose how elaborate, realistic, and valid this model needs to be.

To illustrate, a game to promote fitness may be satisfied with simple statistics that indicate how many calories people burn per type of activity, while a game about educating medical students about the human body needs to contain every "nitty-gritty" detail.

Developing a model of reality requires domain-specific knowledge. If the game is, for example, about computer viruses, expertise on cybersecurity is needed. To retrieve this domain-specific knowledge, *subject-matter experts* are indispensable during the development of a game (although it may well turn out that they cannot give any clear answers or they may not be willing to share information). They can help in determining what the crucial aspects of "reality" are and can also help in how these need to be represented.

The eventual model of reality, and this I need to emphasize, is not the game itself. The model of reality is a blue print, a *conceptual model*, on which the game is partly based. The model co-evolves during the development. When certain changes are made, they may very likely affect the underlying model of reality.

Something else that needs to be stressed is that any model of reality is a subjective depiction of reality. Reality is interpreted, constructed, and translated into a model by a group of designers in collaboration with others and it may well be that another group may achieve a completely different model. This can happen amongst many other reasons due to contrasting theories on the topic, different information sources, different design choices, ambiguous or equivocal information, knowledge gaps, differences in scope, budget, and purpose. It is thus very unlikely that two teams come up with the same model.

What we, however, can observe is the sort of *domains* for which games are being developed. With domains, I refer to specific fields in which games are applied to. Below I discuss some of the domains (in an alphabetical order) and the games associated with them to give an overview of games with a meaningful purpose from this world. The domains, as with everything else in this book, are by no means conclusive. It is simply one way of organizing.

Business & Management

The use of games in business and management has a long history (see Level 1) and are also referred to as "corporate games" (Michael and Chen 2006). Many business games are educationally oriented. They are used within business schools or in the businesses themselves. Although less prominent, for quite some time games have also been used as organizational interventions to evaluate business programs, tools, or let employees get used to new ways of working and thinking. Currently, businesses are considering the usage of games because the generation that grew up with Super Mario is entering the workplace and may require another

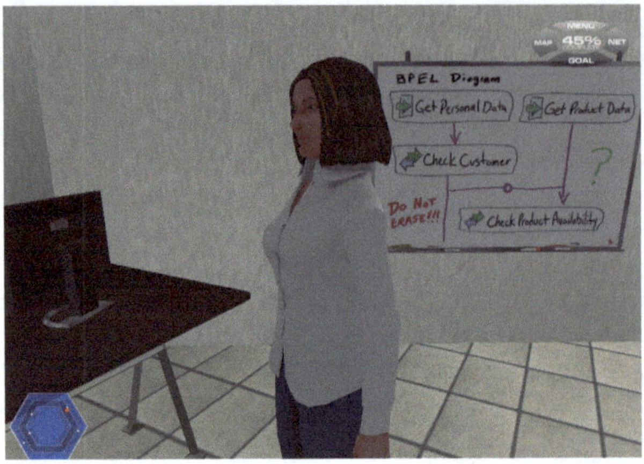

Fig. 2.5 Finding statistics for starting a business process management evaluation in *INNOV8*. Logan just found the call statistics at the IT department and now needs to look for the resource costs at the financial department. ©2007 IBM. Used with permission

way of working (Beck and Wade 2004; Herz 1997; Prensky 2001; Tapscott 1997; Veen and Vrakking 2006), and a number of organizations are experimenting with increasing the productivity of employees by using games (Edery and Mollick 2009).

To give an example of game in this domain, let us consider a game that has been developed by a business itself for business schools. Playing the game *INNOV8*—a game developed by IBM—should give a better understanding of how effective "Business Process Management" (BPM) impacts an entire business ecosystem (Fig. 2.5). BPM is a management approach focused on understanding, managing, and improving business processes. To achieve this, the approach stresses the supporting and enabling managerial possibilities of using technology for optimizing processes by making it possible to design, model, and monitor them.[8]

To learn about BPM, the game features a fictional call center agency, "After Inc.," who has a process model that is functioning sub-optimally. As the protagonist "Logan," a young female business analyst, players must discover the current model (the "as-is model"), find out why it is under-performing and then optimize it to meet the demands of the market (the "to-be model"). In essence, players must first find and collect the separate elements that make a model, such as resource costs, performance data, and other statistics, by visiting the departments within the corporation that are responsible for this, like human resources, finance, and the IT department. After that, players can start revising the as-is model and simulate the to-be model by changing variables and looking at the performance indicators. *INNOV8* thus actually offers playing with a hardcore simulation model within a game environment.

A game that has been played for a much longer amount of time within business schools concerns *The Beer Game* (Sterman 1989). This game does not involve or promote beer drinking, but is rather about supply chain management. Teams of players take up the roles of retailers, wholesalers, distributors, and factories, and need

[8]In the glossary of *INNOV8*, BPM is defined as "a structured, often cross-functional approach—combining management methods with information technology—to improving business process over time or adapting them to meet new customer or market needs."

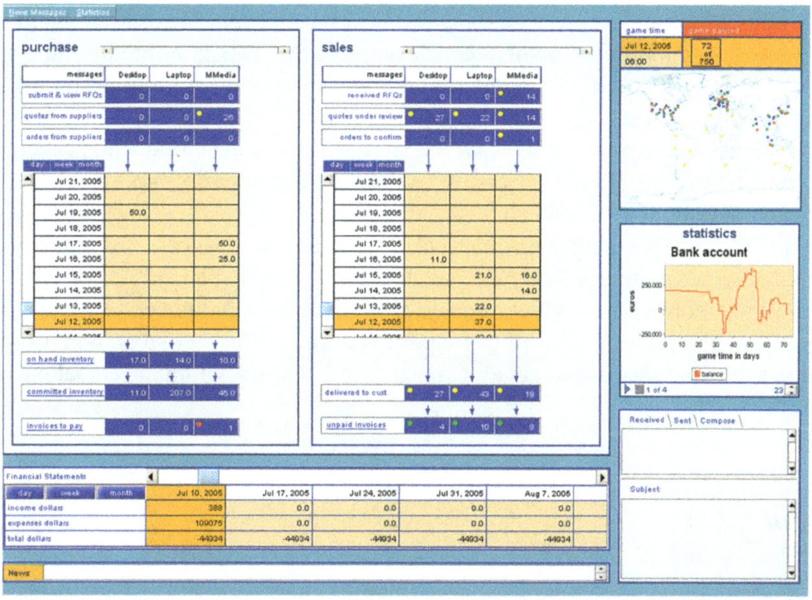

Fig. 2.6 Interacting with a spreadsheet and other players all over the world with the *Global Supply Chain Game*. ©2005 Delft University of Technology. Used with permission

to work together to deliver beer to the customers while minimizing the costs and avoiding out-of-stock situations.[9]

In the aftermath of this game, many other supply chain games have been developed. A quite interesting one concerns the *Global Supply Chain Game* (Corsi et al. 2006). This game is a "distributed game." It can be played simultaneously with players all over the world, in the same vein as most Internet-based games. In one session, the game was, for example, played with teams from business schools from China, France, the Netherlands, and the USA. Another striking point to be made is that this game, like many others, is essentially an *interactive spreadsheet* (Fig. 2.6). Players can adjust variables like they would if they are sitting behind their desk and using the tools they would normally use, like Microsoft's *Excel*, to make decisions. Playing these games lets players, therefore, also learn of how to work with spreadsheets (and potentially other tools).

An example of using games to increase productivity can be found in the work place of Microsoft (Edery and Mollick 2009; McDonald et al. 2008). To catch as

[9] *The Beer Game* was originally built to research and educate the occurrence of the "bullwhip effect": when the inventory levels of the retailer decline, it is followed in sequence by a decline in the inventory of the other roles, the wholesaler, distributor, and eventually also the factory. When inventory falls, players tend to increase their orders. Faced with rising orders and large backlogs of unfilled orders, the factory eventually brews and ships huge quantities of beer, and inventory levels surge. Using a very simple game, in which players only have to place orders, this effect can be demonstrated.

many bugs as possible before launch, the Windows Defect Prevention Team tries to get as many employees involved with bug testing. This is normally quite hard. People are busy and will not volunteer as easily unless they are required to. This changed when the team first set out to create a simple "game," *The Beta1 game*, in which players could earn "letters" which were visible to everyone who participated on a score board. Installing the version would earn players a "b," voting it a "e," and running it overnight a "t," and so forth.

With this game, participation quadrupled and due to this success, the team created immediately a follow up, *The Beta2 game*. This game expanded the original one by awarding points for a wider variety of activities, including prizes, and giving away physical representations of game participation, such as wristbands. This was a success again and shows that games can very well be used within the actual business processes themselves.

Health

A domain that has found a widespread use of games, for consumers as well as professionals, concerns "health." For consumers, we see a huge influx of games to motivate people to be healthy, by for example motivating them to exercise or take medication. The first is known as "exergaming," and is becoming more and more popular, in households as well as in fitness centers. These games "force" players to perform exercise movements to play the game. These exercises can be mapped one-to-one to real world exercises or they are needed to support something completely fictional.

For example, in *Wii Fit*, one of the exercises involves hula-hooping and requires players to make circular body movements to ensure that their virtual alter ego's hula hoop keeps on going and does not fall onto the ground. In another exercise, however, players have to shift their balance to get balls into holes. It can be expected that exergaming becomes gradually more popular when the techniques to infer player movements become more precise.

As for medication adherence, although not so many have been developed compared to exergaming, one quite successful one, the game *Re-Mission*, comes to mind (Kato et al. 2009; Tate et al. 2009). In the game, which is aimed at enhancing the physical health and psychological well-being of young people with cancer, players control a nanobot Roxxi and enter the bodies of teenage cancer patients to investigate symptoms, destroy cancer cells, eradicate bacteria, stop metastases, and manage treatment effects (Fig. 2.7). The way this is done is by means of shooting. Roxxi is a fully armed warrior and the idea is that players use her arsenal to fight cancer colonies. Study results show that those who played the game, even if only for an hour, adhere much more to their medication intake than those who played some other game.

Part of these results can be explained by another result. It was found that players' "self-efficacy," a belief in their own ability to control and cope with something, in this case with cancer, improved. In other words, playing the game gave players the feeling that they were able to deal with their own disease. This psychological effect is probably in particularly instilled by the strong metaphor of fighting cancer cells in someone's body. The resulting sense of agency and power was confirmed by one of the patients: "It feels like you have control over your own destiny" (Tate et al. 2009, p. 30). Others expressed a visceral sense of revenge while destroying cancer and its side effects.

On the professional side, games are used to treat patients. With *SnowWorld*, for instance, burn patients explore an ice world and shoot snowballs at snowmen, robots, and penguins to alleviate their pain (Hoffman et al. 2007). The same technique is also used to treat phobias and Post Traumatic Stress Disorder (PTSD). As for the latter, *Virtual Iraq*, is an environment for treating veterans by simulating sources of combat stress. The interesting aspect of this project is that it does not only include auditory and visual stimuli, such as images of wounded civilians and the sound effects of gunshots and bombs, but also olfactory, like the smell of burning rubber, diesel fuel, and spices, and tactile ones, such as the vibrations that one feels when sitting in a jeep. The idea behind the treatment is to gradually re-introduce victims to the experiences that triggered the trauma, making the memory more tolerable in this way. Early results show that this approach is very promising (Gerardi et al. 2008). For example, one patient indicated that after four sessions of 90 minutes, he no longer needed to "keep thinking about" the identified trauma.

But for health professionals themselves, games are also used. In fact, according to Bergeron (2006) this is a huge market, because there is a need for physicians, nurses, and other clinicians to amass a number of continuing medical education (CME) credits every year to maintain their licensure. They can attend lectures, take tests, or—nowadays—play a game (if it is approved for CME credits). The types of games range from teaching how to handle surgical equipment (cf., Rosser et al. 2007) to teaching how to operate and deal with patients in general.

Military

In Level 1 I discussed how important gaming is to the military and how much they are on the forefront when it concerns the use of new technology. The game *America's Army* is another example that the military is pushing the state-of-the-art (Fig. 2.8). This game, of which at the moment the third version is released, is an enormous success. When the first version was released, in 2002, it was conceived and openly publicized as an Army recruiting and communications tool. In the first six months, over a million users registered. Currently, it has 9.5 million registered users and is considered one of the most popular online games.

In the game, players first have to go through training before they can enter the combat missions and earn medals of honor (Zyda et al. 2003). In this training, it becomes immediately clear that although the game looks and feels much similar to most entertainment military games, it is much more realistic, and more importantly, it forces players to abide by the rules of warfare. If players do not, the game is merciless.

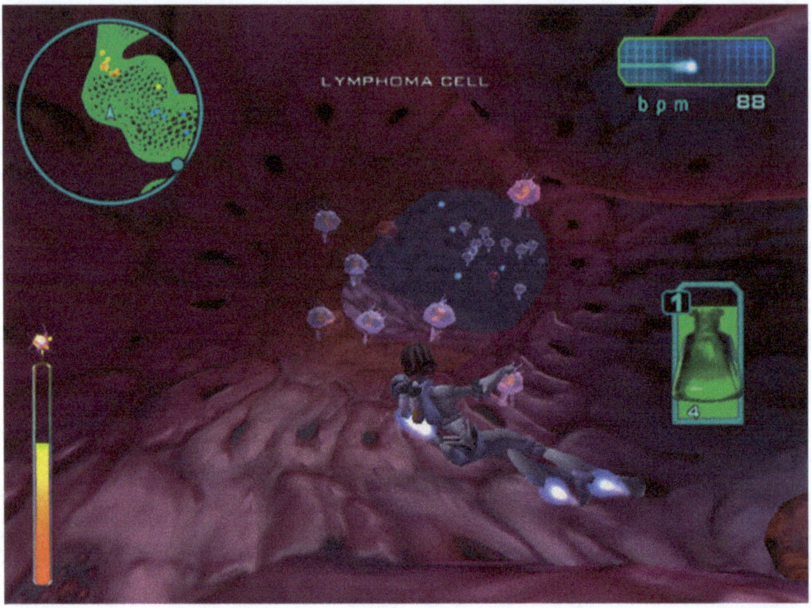

Fig. 2.7 Fighting cancer cells like the lymphoma cell inside a patient's body with *Re-Mission*. ©2006 HopeLab Foundation. Used with permission

For example, if players point their gun toward their drill sergeant in the training, they find themselves in a cell and they need to completely restart the game to play again. After continued violation of the rules, players are even eliminated from the game. They need to create a new account, which means that they have lost everything that they literally and figuratively speaking have "fought" for. This way, the game enforces players to learn and stick to the rules.

On the professional side many forces all over the world make use of *Virtual Battle Space 2*. This game environment makes it possible to flexibly create scenarios and re-enact these with soldiers under the guidance of facilitators who can adjust the scenarios in real-time and role-play some of the characters in the game. I once had the opportunity to play this game and I was amazed how much our group—consisting of people with no military experience—learned in just half an hour in terms of strategy, collaboration, and engagement rules. Where at first all of us ran around in an open field like chickens with their heads cut off and as a result were being shot by just one sniper, we subsequently first grouped together, thought of a strategy, discussed how we would communicate, and moved in two teams slowly and cautiously alongside the houses, so we would not be easily shot by snipers.

Military games are not necessarily only about combat. I already mentioned *Virtual Iraq* which can be considered a military game as well. Another game concerns *Tactical Iraqi* (Surface et al. 2007). This game teaches soldiers Arabic and local cultural customs. Often, language and culture can cause a problem when soldiers have to engage with local people. They can use an interpreter but these are not always there when needed. This game teaches in such circumstances what to say,

Fig. 2.8 Shooting the instructor is not a clever idea to continue playing *America's Army*. ©2009 U.S. Army. Used with permission

how to say it, and when to say it. Whereas other methods only focus on spoken vocabularies and pronunciation, this game also covers practical cultural knowledge, sensitivity, and awareness—including non-verbal gestures, etiquette, and norms of politeness—that are critical for successful communication.

In the game, players have to interact with virtual humans and by means of speech recognition technology, which interprets the words and pronunciation of the players, the virtual humans become trustful and cooperative, and provide the information players need to advance if they speak and behave correctly. Otherwise, the virtual humans will obstruct them from advancing. It turned out that in as a little as a week, players become quite proficient and due to this success other versions have been made that focus on the Dari, French, Indonesian, and Pashto language.

Politics & Society

Expression by means of games clearly occurs in the domain of politics and society. Right after "Joe the Plumber" was mentioned by John McCain a number of times in his race for presidency against Barack Obama in 2008, a game appeared on the Internet with was titled as *Joe the Plumber Game*. In this case it was just merely politically framing an existing game format of connecting pipes from one end to another, but it was political nonetheless.

In other instances, games can be found surrounding political and societal events that go much further. Oftentimes, these games, which are also referred to as "news-games," are developed by young individuals. Supported by game authoring tools, these technological savvy youngsters create rather simple games that support, criticize, and make fun of politics and societal events. And oftentimes as well, these games spark great controversy. One such game, *Super Columbine Massacre RPG!*, concerned a re-enactment of the school shootings at Columbine High School in 1999 and was developed in six months by Danny Ledonne who was 22 years old at the time.

But also companies and institutions employ games to support, criticize, and make fun of politics and societal events. *The ReDistricting Game* can, for instance, be seen as a critique on the American political system in which in most states the state legislators themselves are able to draw the lines of voting districts, making it vulnerable to a wide range of abuses and manipulations (Fig. 2.9). The game offers five different missions, each with a different objective yet a similar game mechanism which simply comes down to drawing and redrawing districts. By exploring how the system works, the game allows players to see how one of the most important aspects of the American political system is open to abuse and how it can possibly be improved.

Aside from criticizing a political system, *The ReDistricting Game* is also educationally oriented as the concept of redistricting is not so well understood by citizens. This educational empowering of people is reflected in many more interesting games. Another game, called *PeaceMaker*, is about one of the most difficult political conflicts of the past decades: the Israeli-Palestinian conflict. This game puts players in the shoes of the leader of one of the sides (Fig. 2.10). Players can view information about stakeholders, such as Hamas, look at polls, to see how well they do on economy, leadership, and sympathy, and take a variety of actions, political, security, construction, or generic ones. Throughout the game, in which they must try to overcome the zero sum game by balancing the needs and concerns of multiple perspectives, they can be faced with all kinds of events that may require the player to take another course of action.

Last but certainly not least, although certain politicians pursue a crusade against games, a number of them make increasingly use of games themselves, for advertising and campaigning. *The Howard Dean for Iowa Game* was, for example, created to let supporters understand the process and power of grassroots outreach and to encourage them to participate in pre-caucus campaigning in Iowa or in their local area (Bogost 2007). All of this was, of course, in support of the presidential candidate Howard Dean for the U.S. 2004 elections.

The goal of the game is to get as much supporters as possible for the Iowa caucus. This can be done by strategically placing campaigners on a map of Iowa who will recruit other supporters and promote the campaign. The effectiveness of each of the new supporters that are placed on the map is determined in mini-games that represent three typical campaign activities: sign-waving, door-to-door canvassing, and pamphleteering.

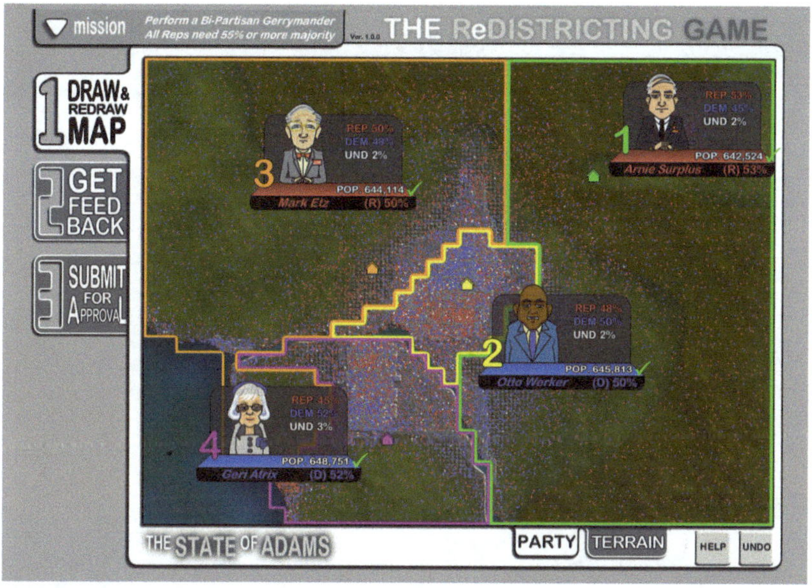

Fig. 2.9 Drawing lines for creating favorable voting districts in *The ReDistricting Game*. The blue and red dots represent Democrat and Republican voters, respectively. ©2007 University of Southern California. Used with permission

Public Policy

Similar to business & management and military games, public policy has a rich history with gaming as well, in particularly when it comes to analog games. However, in the wake of *SimCity* many policy oriented digital games, also referred to as "governmental games" (Michael and Chen 2006), have been developed. These games, like *Virtual U*, are in concept very similar to *SimCity*. They put players in a helicopter mode—also known as the "god mode"—which gives them a complete overview of what is going on and enable them to take particular actions to influence what they see. With *SimCity* actions pertain to urban planning by deciding where to place roads, houses, and industries, and with *Virtual U*, this concerns allocating budgets and making decisions on faculty members, courses, admissions standards, facilities, and so on. By playing these games, users will get an elaborate understanding of the intricate relationships of the various variables that are important in the domain of public policy.

Such an understanding or "awareness" is also used to educate the public about the difficult dilemmas that the government is struggling with and to engage the public with the debate. The designers of *Budget Hero*, a game oriented at the federal budget of the USA, have attempted this. As a citizen it might be easy to complain about why the government does not spend X on Y and by playing this game they may understand why. In fact, they may not spend X on Y considering the limitations of the budget and other hard pressing issues either. An additional value of games

Fig. 2.10 Considering diplomatic actions in *Peacemaker*. The security actions are shown, like police and army coverage, checkpoints, travel restrictions, and extreme measures. ©2007 ImpactGames. Used with permission

as *Budget Hero* is that they offer governments insights into the choices the public makes.

This "participatory model" of engaging citizens in the public policy debate can be extended to the public policy "arenas" or "rounds," the places where policy is made. Public policy can be characterized as being faced with multiple stakeholders, like governments, companies, and citizens, who have their own mental models, interests, values, and so on (Mayer 2009). This dealing with stakeholders could take place in a game. By putting them together in a game environment, the different interests and perspectives can become known and a "solution" can be sought for.

Although not many digital games have done this so far, actually one of the first "next generation" games with a serious purpose, those that use digital game entertainment techniques, applied this "multi-stakeholder approach." This game called *NitroGenius* was developed specifically for a conference on nitrogen, in which scientists, policy makers, researchers, and industry leaders gathered to discuss nitrogen's role in the environment. This discussion was needed, because regarding global warming and the release of gases, nitrogen often failed to be mentioned, while it has disastrous effects on the environment and health. The idea was to learn and discuss about the complexities of nitrogen pollution through a game.

In the game, players take up the role of the government, industry, agriculture, or society and get specific objectives. The government needs for instance to support economic growth and guard public health, while industry should aim to maximize profits. Every round players can make decisions regarding certain policy options, like investing in research or reorganizing the company, and others may be able to cancel certain choices. By doing this, in a simple way the complex relations within the nitrogen pollution situation become known and an optimal policy which reduces pollution while maintaining the lowest costs with the fewest negative impacts on society can be sought for.

Safety & Crisis Response

Although safety and crisis response is an important governmental responsibility, the extent to which gaming has been applied in this area has been so enormous that it can be considered a domain in and of itself. Additionally, safety and crisis response is not solely exclusive to governmental institutions. Many companies are concerned about this issue as well.

Oil companies are, for instance, very much concerned about safety and crisis response. On drilling sites many hazardous situations can occur and to train employees in recognizing such situations, they are exploring the use of game technology. For exploring its potential, a prototype game was developed called *Supervisor*, in which the player is supposed to handle hazardous situations on a drilling site, by taking care of health, safety, and environment regulations and by carefully watching personnel. It could happen that personnel is not paying attention and position themselves at unsafe locations when, for instance, a truck is unloading its load (Fig. 2.11). In that case, the player should respond by directing the worker to a safe area.

Most games that can be affiliated with this domain pertain, just like *Supervisor*, to the operational level. This is the level where professionals need to deal with the situation directly. Such professionals range from police officers, fire fighters, emergency medical personnel, to even, of course, levee patrollers. The reason why gaming has found such a widespread application in this level is that using games enables these professionals to get experience in a relatively safe environment.

On a tactical or strategic level much less games are being developed. *Incident Commander* is, however, one of such games. Multiple scenarios can be trained, like school hostage-taking, chemical spills, terrorism, and severe weather, with up to 16 players simultaneously who can assume different roles. The game can also be customized to create specific scenarios that the users have in mind. Like in *SimCity*, players look at the game from a helicopter perspective and they are challenged to coordinate a multi-agency (fire, police, public works, logistics units, and more) to respond appropriately to the situation at hand by taking the right actions and communicating effectively.

Similar to the other domains, safety and crisis response games can also be oriented at the public at large. It is extremely helpful if citizens stay aware of the risks and try to minimize these themselves to some extent. The game *FloodSim* demonstrates this potential. It aims to raise awareness to issues surrounding flood policy and government expenditure and to increase citizen engagement in this matter.

In the game, players need to make decisions regarding what to invest to make the UK safer against flooding. Interestingly enough, the game is developed by one

Fig. 2.11 Supervising personnel and regulations in *Supervisor*. Notice that one of the workers should be directed to a safe area. ©2009 Delft University of Technology. Used with permission

of UK's largest insurers. The 2007 floods cost the UK's insurance industry approximately £3 billion, and with the climate change, the chances of similar floods occurring are higher than ever before. For this reason, and this is stated at the game's website, flooding is a big issue for the insurer and it is important to keep flooding high on the political agenda.

Science & Education

The use of games for education is the most common association people have with games. A game is seen as one of the tools to teach kids and students. Some consider it even as "the tool" for education, since games fit quit well with the educational philosophy put forth by John Dewey (1938) and many others who stress that education should be grounded in experience. Whereas most text books are rather abstract and dry, a game can make a topic come alive and let kids and students learn and apply the knowledge and skills in settings where they are actually needed (Shaffer 2006).

With this in mind, it is not strange that two of the topics for which games are mostly developed for concern either physics or history. The first is one of the, if not the most abstract topic that students are confronted with. If we talk about molecules, atoms, or even quanta, we refer to "things" that we cannot see with our own eyes. Games, like *Supercharged!*, can enable students to critically engage with such scientific phenomena by forming and testing hypotheses. For instance, in this *Supercharged!*, students need to navigate a spaceship in a three dimensional environment of electromagnetic mazes by first placing charged particles and then controlling the electric charge (either positive, negative, neutral, or dipole) of the ship. The goal of

Supercharged! is to help learners build stronger intuitions for electromagnetic concepts and findings suggest that it is effective in achieving this (Squire et al. 2004).

The reason why history games are so popular is not strange. We cannot easily visualize what it must have been like back in the days. Sure we can visit a museum or ruin, but this just gives us a tip of the iceberg. With a virtual environment we can completely step into the worlds of Cleopatra or Christopher Columbus. This appeal is quite strong, and not only educationally, because many entertainment games are set in historical settings. Aside from *Civilization* one of the better known historical games used in the classroom concerns *Europa Universalis*. In this game, players need to explore, trade, make ware, and be diplomatic in the period of 1453 and 1820.

As for "science," the use of games is much more limited, although an exciting development is taking place in which games are contributing to science (cf., Bainbridge 2007). Take *Foldit* (Fig. 2.12). In this puzzle game, players have to fold proteins, the workhorses in every cell in every living thing, by configuring the shape of a protein (Cooper et al. 2010). These shapes are important, because in the end they determine what function a protein has. For example, a protein that breaks down glucose for releasing energy, will have a shape that recognizes glucose and binds to it, much like a lock and key.

The first purpose of the game is to see whether human folders, that is us the players, are better in folding proteins than computers are. This is called "protein structure prediction" and the number of different ways even a small protein can fold is astronomical due to the many degrees of freedom. To figure out what the best structure is, concerns one of the hardest problems in biology. *Foldit* attempts to harness the puzzle solving intuition and competitive nature of human beings for this problem. Aside from the free labor, if it turns out that humans are better folders than computers, they aim to teach human strategies to computers so they can fold proteins faster.

The second purpose, and this is not pursued yet, is "protein design." In that case, players will try to create proteins to disable a virus or scrub carbon dioxide from the atmosphere. This means that players are inventing solutions to help prevent or treat important diseases, like Alzheimer's disease, cancer, or HIV/AIDS.

To Conclude

Many more domains can be thought of that use games, such as law, religion, art, energy & environment, transport & logistics, and ICT. Besides this, games can frequently be cross-categorized. For example, *Foldit* can be related to the domain of health and to science & education. The point to be made here is that every game is related to at least one type of domain, whether it is public policy or health. Recognizing this relationship is important, because each domain is affiliated with certain disciplines and people that need to be involved when developing a game. Based on the information from the domain and the scope and purpose of the game, a model of reality can be developed.

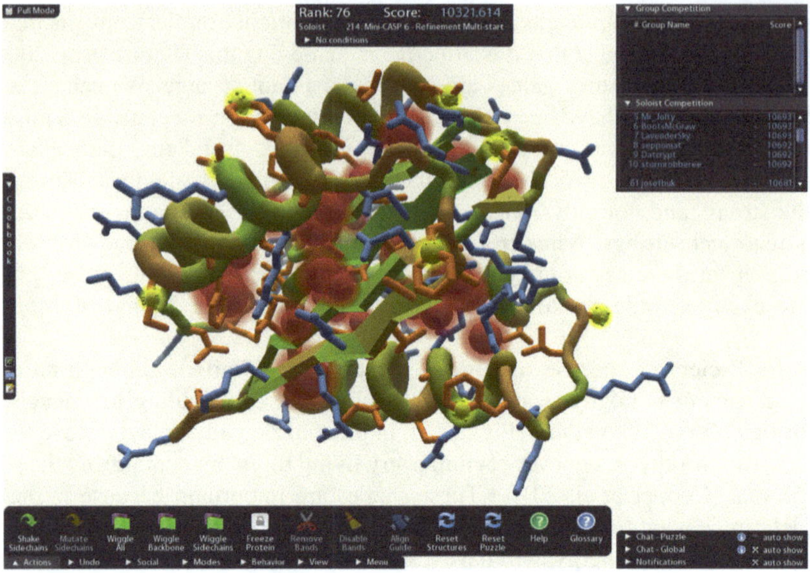

Fig. 2.12 Solving puzzles by folding proteins in *Foldit*. Players need to optimize the structure by dragging the constituents of the protein or using any of the actions at the bottom. The "red balls" indicate a local suboptimal configuration. ©2008 University of Washington. Used with permission

The world of Reality involves more than just retrieving information, the "content", and using this to develop a game. It also involves "dealing" with the real world. This dealing can be considered in two ways. First, it is about working with the different *stakeholders*. Depending on the business model and the type of game, a project may involve one or even more clients. It is not unlikely that these clients have different interests, opinions, and ideas about how they want to make use of the game. These deeper differences will be reflected in their suggested requirements and in their judgments of design documents and prototypes.

But also the subject-matter experts and the eventual users have to be considered. Aside from providing information to develop the game, these stakeholders can be used to judge the game as well. They will undoubtedly do so from a perspective which is very reality oriented. This can be noticed when they give comments like "this does not work like that in reality" or "the game looks nice but I am missing the stripes on the uniform of the game characters."

Second, it is about considering the types of *criteria* that are relevant to this world. With "criteria" I refer to guidelines, rules, characteristics, or dimensions that the game must satisfy in order to be called a "good game." From the world of Reality the criteria "flexibility," "fidelity," and "validity" can be retrieved. The extent to which these criteria are important depends on each individual project and the choices the designers have made throughout the process. It also depends on the consideration of the other two worlds.

The World of Meaning

What does the world of Meaning "mean"? This seems a rather silly question but I can assert that this world is everything but self-explanatory. Let us first take its opposite: can a game be "meaningless"? The answer is a clear "no." Any game, from small to big, from bad to good, has meaning. Of course, players may neglect partly the game's meaning and just play it to spend their time, but the game itself is undeniably full of "signs." First, it contains signs of what the game is about (is it in the past or the future?) and what players need to do (shoot enemies or solve puzzles?).

Second, many of these signs can relate to reality (whether fiction or non-fiction) as I just explained with the world of Reality. Moreover, games could have an underlying message, such as a moral or a criticism on the real world, that the players can take "home." Sadly, most entertainment games do not even surpass the average children's book when it comes to this. At most times it is something like "we have the good and bad guys and the good guys should defeat the bad guys."

But there is something more to (even entertainment) games than we might think. My favorite example of a possible underlying message that is not as obvious at first, concerns an analysis by Bogost (2007) of *Grand Theft Auto: San Andreas* in which a player plays the role of a gangster called CJ (Fig. 2.17):

> Whereas previous iterations of the [*Grand Theft Auto*] series favored stylized representations of historico-fictional times and places, San Andreas takes on a cultural moment steeped deeply in racial and economic politics... [in the game] the player-character must eat to maintain his stamina and strength. However, the only nourishment in the game comes from fast food restaurants... Eating moderately maintains energy, but eating high-fat-content increases CJ's weight, and fat gangsters cannot run or fight very effectively. Each food item in the game comes at a cost, and the player's funds are limited. Mirroring real fast food restaurants, less fattening foods like salad cost more than high-calorie supermeals... The dietary features of *San Andreas* are rudimentary, but the fact that the player must feed his character to continue playing does draw attention to the limited material conditions the game provides for satisfying that need, subtly exposing the fact that problems of obesity and malnutrition in poor communities can partly be attributed to the relative ease and affordability of fast food. (pp. 113–114)

This representation of the world leaves the player with two possible meanings. Either, as Bogost (2007) suggests, *San Andreas* exposes "the social forces that drive the poor and working-class residents of the inner city to consume fast food habitually" (p. 115), or it seems to be a "textbook example of moral strength" as it allows "the player to overcome the social conditions of poverty and poor nutrition through hard work" (p. 116).[10] Whatever meaning players attribute, they "might leave the game and make new observations about the world around them" (p. 116). Therefore, even *Grand Theft Auto*, one of the most criticized game series, can be considered "meaningful" beyond the context of the game itself.

---

[10]The "hard work" that players have to perform in *San Andreas* relates to going to the gym and performing violent crime. The gym leads directly to more stamina and strength. Crime leads to money which can be used to buy the more "healthful" but more expensive salad meals at the restaurants.

However, as Bogost (2007) also outlines, it is unsure whether the game designers intended this or not. This brings me to the third possible meaning production of signs in games: meaning is in "the eye of the beholder." With this I mean that players attribute meaning to the signs based on their own perception, ideas, and experiences. To one player the burger symbol in *San Andreas* could represent a symbol for "food in general" whereas another could see a social critique of society. And some people really do attribute the most fascinating and intellectually challenging meanings to certain games. Look at Murray's interpretation (1997) of *Tetris* (Fig. 2.19):

> *Tetris* is the perfect enactment of the overtasked lives of Americans in the 1990s—of the constant bombardment of tasks that demand our attention and that we must somehow fit into our overcrowded schedules and clear off our desks in order to make room for the next onslaught. (pp. 143–144)

It is obvious that we cannot expect that every single person would make such an interpretation. It is even very unlikely that the original designers, Alexey Pajitnov, Dmitry Pavlovsky, and Vadim Gerasimov, who created *Tetris*, had this idea in mind, because they created it between 1984 and 1986 and are Russian. Murray's interpretation relates to her own world but is nevertheless perfectly acceptable. The point is that sometimes the meaning that people attribute to games is not necessarily intended by the designers.

In sum, meaning can be looked at in different ways, as in what the game is, to what it relates, and how the player relates to it. These meanings—which are present in any type of game—can affect player's lives. Even in situations when the underlying message is difficult to retrieve, such as in *San Andreas*, player's behavior may *unconsciously* be altered. Therefore, games in general, like other media (McLuhan 1964), can have a profound effect on society at large in, for instance, our attitudes and ways of thinking and acting (Beck and Wade 2004), and can be seen as cultural expressions in their own right which make us think about the world around us (Jones 2008).

Now consider games with a non-entertainment purpose. They are intentionally designed to create a meaningful effect beyond the game experience, something that is useful in the real world. Some sort of *value* needs to be achieved and at best this value is measurable. Aside that this requires to understand how "meaning" can be created by playing games, more carefulness and consideration is needed to consider meaning to ensure that the intended value is achieved.

Similar to the discussion of the domains, I will give an overview from the world of Meaning by discussing the types of values that can be pursued when using games. I first highlight values that are aimed at the player. To distinguish these, I use an often applied distinction in knowledge, skills, and attitudes (Wickens et al. 2004).[11]

[11] The distinction of knowledge, skills, and attitudes (KSA) is slightly related to the frequently referred to Bloom's taxonomy (Bloom et al. 1964) which distinguishes a cognitive, psychomotoric, and affective domain in setting educational objectives. KSA departs from Bloom's taxonomy in two ways: skills can be either cognitive (social skills) or psychomotoric (physical skills), and knowledge is a subcategory within the cognitive domain. KSA is sometimes also referred to as knowledge, skills, and abilities which to me seems awkward because I think skills and abilities are similar to each other.

After these, four types of values are discussed that are not aimed at the player but at something else.

Knowledge

"What is knowledge?" and "how do we acquire knowledge?" are just some of the questions that an important branch of philosophy called "epistemology" is devoted to in answering for already quite some time. Answers relate partly to how we see the world. Does truth exist or is that what we "believe" is true, is what we need to call "truth"? Whatever is "true," our society is without doubt a knowledge society in which people have to learn "things"—whether they are based on actual truths or beliefs. This learning is partly about acquiring knowledge (the other concerns "skills").

Some have equated knowledge to "information" and "data," but it is nowadays generally believed that we should separate knowledge into explicit knowledge on the one hand, and implicit knowledge on the other hand (cf., Dienes and Perner 1999). Explicit (or declarative) knowledge can roughly be considered similar to information. It is what we can make known to others and of what we are conscious about. It can be subdivided into semantic and episodic knowledge. Semantic knowledge is concerned with facts, ideas, understandings, and concepts which are not related to personal experiences, like "Sonic the Hedgehog is a game character." By contrast, episodic knowledge involves events of personal relevance. A memory of where, when, and with whom I played *Pac-Man* the last time is a form of episodic knowledge.

Implicit (or tacit or procedural) knowledge covers the informal and hard to define aspects.[12] People are frequently not aware of this latter knowledge and are unable to verbalize it if they do. The most well-known example concerns grammar. We do not know why and what for, but we just know *how* to apply it. An example with games would be asking a player how he or she is beating other players who then responds something like "I just practice a lot."

People acquire these types of knowledge in different ways: reading, listening, imitating, or simply on the basis of experience. A wide variety of theories, methods, and tools are applied to make sure people acquire knowledge as efficiently and effectively as possible in our knowledge society. Games can be seen as such a method or tool. Affordances of games, such as that they are motivational, experiential, situational amongst many others (cf., Gee 2004; De Caluwé et al. 2008), are reasons

[12]Here I do not make a difference between implicit and tacit knowledge. However, it needs to be kept in mind that often the first is seen as all the information that has not been articulated, while the latter is considered to be information that cannot be articulated. I also do not make a difference between implicit and procedural knowledge. However, similar to tacit knowledge, procedural knowledge also cannot be articulated. It is further much more concerned with "knowing how" and in this way it is closely affiliated with the concept of skills, while implicit knowledge covers aspects as conditioned responses and reflexes as well.

Fig. 2.13 Persuading a Soviet officer by quoting Karl Marx in *FF56!*. ©2006 Lauer Learning. Used with permission

why teachers and trainers consider games.[13] In fact, games have been used for already quite some time to provide people knowledge. In this context, they are often referred to as "educational games," or "training games."

To illustrate the use of games for providing explicit knowledge, let us have a look at *FF56!* (Fig. 2.13). This game blends rich, historically-accurate narrative with first person gaming. Players are dropped into the streets of Budapest during the revolution period of 1956. They have to struggle alongside characters that fight for Hungary's freedom. The game offers a mix of fictive and real experiences based on actual events and personal accounts from people who experienced the revolution.

By getting immersed into this specific historical situation, in which players have to deliver medical supplies, rescue the wounded, battle soviet soldiers and the dreaded secret police, gather items, and wrestle with moral dilemmas, players get an understanding of what happened during that pivotal moment. By experiencing it themselves episodic knowledge of playing the game gets supplemented with semantic knowledge of historical facts.

---

[13] In my view, games are specifically good in providing for "system knowledge." This subtype of explicit knowledge is about "knowing the big picture." As games are systems, they enable to understand how the little pieces of a "system" fit together, over time and under different circumstances. It is about seeing the overall structures, patterns, and cycles, rather than seeing only specific events. A system can be anything, from a human body (how does the heart respond to different medicines?) to an economic market (what strategy will make our company survive in the longer term?).

For providing implicit knowledge much less is known when it comes to using games. However, it can be hypothesized that games are very good tools in doing this. Although implicit, acquiring this knowledge includes or starts with acquiring explicit knowledge. When we learned grammar, we also had to learn words and certain rules of how these words need to be combined to make up a sensible sentence. For example, we had to learn that IF "he" or "she" is used as a pronoun THEN a "s" needs to be added to most but not all verbs. Now we apply this rule without thinking about it.

In games, this "proceduralization," learning such IF-THEN-DO constructions, happens all the time. At first it requires conscious effort on behalf of the player—IF I press SHIFT, THEN I will fire—but quickly, after some rehearsal this becomes a habit, a response: IF an enemy is observed, THEN I will automatically press SHIFT. With games, like *Supervisor*, it could happen that players slowly but unmistakenly get implicit knowledge of what to do when they encounter subtle cues that indicate that a possible problem is about to occur. Therefore, games seem to allow for the creation of such knowledge, which according to Anderson (1983, 1993, 1995) is needed for becoming an expert at something.

Skills

Generally, knowledge is regarded as something that is learned, while skills are the abilities to apply what is learned. It is quite difficult to separate the two, especially because in practice they are used and needed at the same time.[14] The difference can nevertheless be clarified by hypothesizing what would happen if somebody is skillful but not knowledgeable (enough). In that case a person might be very good in performing some action but when the situation changes this person is unable to cope with it and quite likely makes a mistake. This is often the case with airplane accidents in which pilots automatically perform actions, whereas they should have acted otherwise.

The other way around, if someone is knowledgeable but not skillful is when we "know" how to do it but still cannot manage to actually do it in practice. We may know how to score a goal in sports, how to make a Windsor knot with our tie, or how to drive a car, but still have difficulty, at least at first, to actually put this to practice. For this, skills are needed.

The latter points out another difference. We know something or not, but skills can be endlessly refined. We can continuously improve how to score a goal, how to tie a

[14]Besides knowledge, skills, and attitudes another term that is frequently applied, especially in the field of Human Resource Management (HRM), is "competences." Some say competences include knowledge and skills, others add also attitudes to it. The term is generally used to indicate requirements that people need to have to perform a job. Although this term nicely integrates aspects that on many occasions are linked to each other, I prefer to use the separate terms, because clearly some games are more aimed at knowledge, while others are more aimed at skills and attitudes. By using the separate terms, these differences in emphasis become clear.

Windsor knot, or drive our car, and so on. Of course, we can improve our knowledge as well yet this would mean we have more information, explicit or implicit, about something, whereas with skills we have gained or strengthened certain abilities.

As for the types of skills, similar to knowledge they can be classified in innumerable different ways. Aside from the more specific task-dependent types of skills, four generic types of skills can be separated:

- **Cognitive skills**: these refer to the "intellectual" abilities that make it possible for us "to know." In other words, when teaching cognitive skills it is about learning how to learn. They relate, for example, to reasoning, memorization, planning, and interpretation.
- **Perceptual skills**: relates to the five senses of sight, hearing, touch, smell, and taste. Improving our skills means being able to distinguish stimuli better by means of one or more of these senses.
- **Motor skills**: movements, such as lifting one's hand, sitting up, crawling, require—how trivial they may seem now—practice and skill too. Most often we need to use our perception as well when performing movements, like in many hand-eye coordination tasks such as grabbing a piece of candy from a jar. When this is the case, we should speak of "perceptual-motor skills."
- **Social skills**: human beings are social creatures and some are better at dealing with other humans than others. The skills to do so, such as collaboration, communication, and negotiation, are what these skills include. This is often also referred to as "interpersonal skills."

Each type of skill can be related to games. In fact, it requires already perceptual-motor skills to use controllers, the keyboard and mouse, or other devices that are needed to play a game. Subsequently, it requires cognitive skills to understand what the goal of the game is and determine what to do. And when it is a multiplayer game, social skills come into play as well. By actually playing a game it is very likely that all of the above-mentioned skills are practiced.

The point for non-entertainment games is how this tool can be harnessed to train a specific skill. It is one thing that games require skill to be played and yet another to play a game to practice a skill that is useful beyond the context of the game. *Tempo Typen*, the old Dutch game to learn the motor skill of how to type, is an example of this (see Level 1). Other examples concern games in which real equipment is connected to a game environment, such as what is being done to train surgeons with laparoscopic equipment and pilots with an airplane dashboard (Bergeron 2006). By using the equipment surgeons and pilots get a feel for it or in other words, they get the needed perceptual-motor skills to use the equipment.

A nice example of training cognitive skills concerns the use of games to train air traffic controllers (Wald 2008). These professionals need to prioritize—according to the available slot availability—airplanes which can be simulated in a game-like environment.

As for social skills, I would like to highlight *Virtual Leader* (Fig. 2.14). In this game, players can practice different leadership styles, such as directing, participating, and delegating (Aldrich 2004). To practice these, they enter several meetings

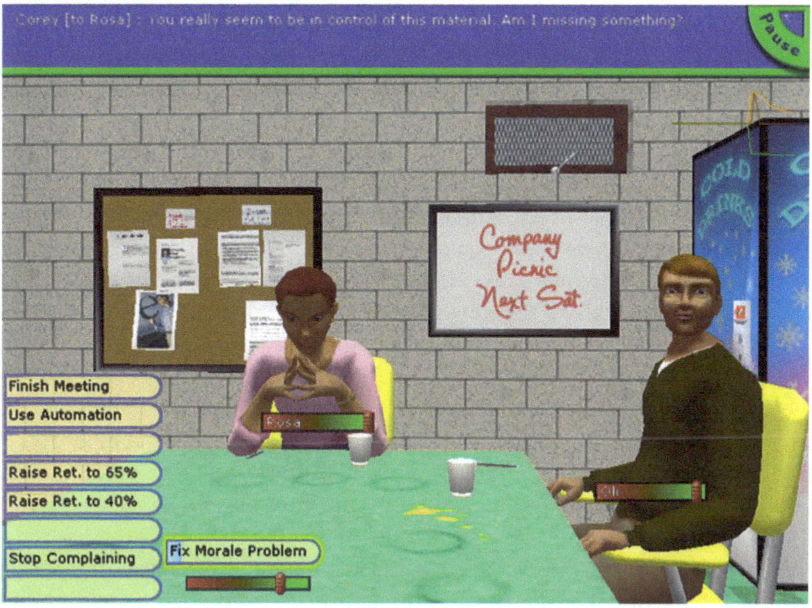

Fig. 2.14 Acting as a leader in *Virtual Leader*. ©2003 Simulearn. Used with permission

which are set in different settings and have a different purpose. Players can introduce, support, or object ideas and can talk to characters by clicking on a slide bar whether they want to react negatively, neutrally, or positively toward somebody. The game characters can also introduce, support, or object ideas and one of the main aspects of the game is to understand the intent of these game characters by observing their body language and interpreting their words.

Virtual Leader and many other games show that games can be used to "practice" skills. For this reason, these types of games are sometimes referred to as "practice-ware," although the more common label of training or educational games can be applied to these games as well.

Attitude

Attitude is a person's "learned predisposition to respond in a consistently favorable or unfavorable manner with respect to a given object" (Fishbein and Ajzen 1975, p. 11). This object can be another person, a product, event, or basically anything else which we could like, dislike, or be ambivalent to. Objects can be tangible and specific, such as the Playstation 3 or Super Mario, or be abstract and intangible, like socialism and computer science. When we judge these objects, we have, implicitly or explicitly, an attitude or "orientation" to these objects.

Quite often, especially if the object is important to a person, judgments are based on feelings and emotions besides the beliefs that one has about the object. Players may like Nintendo, because their first console was a Nintendo and they have fond memories of it, or dislike it because a majority of their games are simply not the type of games they want to play. It is generally believed that attitudes shape people's behavior: a person with a dislike for Nintendo will not buy Nintendo products.

The whole idea of marketing, advertising, and recruitment by companies, politicians, foundations, and others is to make sure people's attitudes judge their "objects," whether a product, service, performance, or something else, positively. And unlike personality, attitudes can change. This can be done on the basis of experience—actually playing some Nintendo games seems to be rather fun—or on the basis of communication—Nintendo's new campaign gives it a new "innovative look" that changes people's minds about the company or of playing games in general (cf., Juul 2009).

The great thing about games is that they can provide both at the same time: games are experiential expressive media. Moreover, games tap into the feelings and emotions of players, because playing a game is not without any (e.g., think about winning, losing, or the frustration of not solving a puzzle). This makes them a powerful tool to "persuade" people.

Bogost (2007) argues that games persuade people by means of *procedural rhetoric*. This is "the art of persuasion through rule-based representations and interactions rather than the spoken word, writing, images, or moving pictures" (p. ix). By seeing how the dynamics of the game world unfolds, players not only experience what happens but also get a message that may influence their attitude to a given object. How this works can be seen in the simple procedural rhetoric of *September 12th* (Fig. 2.1). The way the message of this game is presented to the player is "computational"—not in words but in interacting with a rule-based representation.

Not all games aimed at attitude change apply procedural rhetoric as *September 12th* does. Many games only wrap a theme or visuals around existing game mechanics. I consider this "graphical rhetoric."[15] Look at the Burger King games. Instead of offering the usual toys, this fast food chain started to sell on November 19, 2006, three games that featured their own mascot. One game called *Pocketbike Racer* involves pocketbike racing, another called *Big Bumpin'* bumper-car riding, and the third called *Sneak King* concerns a stealth game in which players have to sneak up on hungry people to surprise them with Burger King food.

None of these games relate procedurally speaking to Burger King but graphically they do.[16] And although users and critics score all three of these games mediocre, the games can be considered successful.[17] On December 31, 2006, "Burger King

[15]The term "graphical rhetoric" is based on the term "procedural rhetoric" and "graphical logic." The latter was used by Noah Wardrip-Fruin to refer to games that only wrap a theme or visuals around existing game mechanics (see Bogost 2007, p. 89).

[16]It could be argued that *Sneak King* does have procedural rhetoric. By sneaking up on hungry people and surprising them with Burger King food, the game says that when people are hungry, we should make them happy by bringing them to Burger King.

[17]I based the mediocre scores of the Burger King games on the meta-scores provided by Metacritic, see http://www.metacritic.com.

announced a whopping (pun intended) 40% increase in quarterly profit" (Edery and Mollick 2009, p. 33). Plus, "the games were not merely a one-time promotion like so many others in the fast-food industry; they were a Trojan horse into the home and make a long-term advantage over might competitors like McDonald's."

Even farther off from procedural rhetoric than graphical rhetoric is *in-game advertising*, such as Barack Obama's Vote for Change advertisements in a number of entertainment games. Results show that even this seemingly minor persuasive effort of placing ads in games has positive effects on attitude change (Glass 2007).

Games aimed at attitude change are generally referred to as "persuasive games."[18] When games are specifically used for advertising the term "advergames" is commonly used and when they are specifically used for social change (such as the games by the UN or the Red Cross), the terms "social impact games" or "games for change" are applied.

Assessment

Assessment is judging systematically the merit or worth of "something." And what could be a better place to judge "something" in a "safe environment" that we call a game? The "somethings" that can be judged in games can relate to organizational structures, processes, tools, instruments, or even people. In job interviews it is not uncommon that people have to perform role-plays or do assignments, because in these sort of situations it can be seen how a person works in practice.

From this, it is a small step toward actual games. In fact, several recruitment agencies or even corporations are already experimenting with this. However, the notion of a "safe environment" becomes in this case a bit problematic. For the applicants the game and their performance in it really matters. If they do not perform well, they may not get the job. Looking at it from the side of the interviewer, however, it is much safer to judge people in a game than to hire the wrong person.

The same line of reasoning can be applied to games in which the performance of people are judged, such as in a game that simulates a crisis or of students whose grade is dependent on their game performance. I have heard quite often that people are unwilling to play a game, because of their status—think of mayors, CEOs, or even presidents—and fear that they may not do well. Students do not really have a choice but it is unlikely that they will enjoy the game as much as they would without

[18]Bogost (2007) introduced "persuasive games" as a substitute to "serious games" or actually as a term that covers "serious games" as well as other types of games, because in his opinion the term serious games does not cover games that "speak past or against the fixed worldviews of institutions like governments or corporations" (p. 57). However, whether this is true or not, in my opinion not all games with a non-entertainment purpose are about "persuasion" in the first place which renders the term useless as an overarching concept. Take games aimed at "data collection" for example. But more importantly, in a strict sense persuasion is aimed at changing or influencing one's beliefs or actions. In other words, it is aimed at "attitude change." These games are thus only related to this value.

being judged. This use of games remains, therefore, a bit tricky but it is without a doubt a way to use them.

When it comes to judging the performance of students, another argument against assessment aside from safety concerns the relationship between learning and performance. While this seems axiomatic, according to many this relationship is weak or nonexistent (Washbush and Gosen 2001). Performance could be based on luck and if it is a multiplayer game, on the performance of other players. Additionally, since people learn from mistakes, it may be a good strategy in terms of learning to make mistakes. Therefore, learning and performance should not be equated to each other. However, as Washbush and Gosen explain, this does not mean we cannot judge people's performance in games:

> In real-world organizations, managers and employees are continually evaluated on performance and rarely on learning. In the university, we usually grade on mastery or performance via test or paper after the completion of a unit rather than a change from one level of understanding, knowledge, or analytical ability to another. Grading on performance is what we usually do, and the caution suggested by these studies is only for those who want to grade on learning only. (pp. 292–293)

At least much less "scary," although the work of many could be at stake, relates to the assessment of organizational structures, processes, tools, or instruments. These can be so to say "plugged into" a game environment and people can start to use them before they are actually used in the organization itself.

An example of such a game involves one which was my first encounter with the development and use of a game for a serious purpose (van Bueren et al. 2009). This was a computer-supported game which evolved around a new financial system that was about to be introduced to the Dutch courts. The players, consisting of court managers and administrative personnel, needed to produce budgets in a number of years for a fictional court. By looking at how players would deal with this new financial system, potential problems, perverse effects, and questions with this system could be dealt with in an early stage. This way, the official introduction of the system would go much more smoothly.

Although the use of assessment in games has some fundamental problems with being safe which need to be investigated further, it has a great potential. And if we think about it, it is not that much of a new or extraordinary application. The newest technologies are frequently applied in competition-like settings. Take for example the solar races in which university teams battle against each other in self-constructed cars that drive on solar energy or the RoboCup Challenge in which teams made up of robots play soccer against each other. Nevertheless, care should be taken when considering this value creation possibility.

Data Collection

With data collection the game is a means to get a certain output which is useful for other purposes. It should not be mistaken for data collection to "improve" the game.

This is something many game companies nowadays do and are able to thanks to the possibilities of the Internet. To apply for this value creation possibility, the collected data should be applied to something outside the game's context. The most simple means of such data gathering are personal statistics, like gender, age, and country of residence. Companies may want this information to see how they could market their products toward people and use a game to acquire this type of information.

Another but rather more sophisticated way of data collection through games concerns "human computation" (Von Ahn 2005). The whole idea behind this is that computers cannot perform the sort of cognitive tasks that humans can do, like recognizing pictures. At the same time, it can be seen that humans spend a major time on playing games. Luis von Ahn, one of the pioneers in this area, argues that while it took 7 million hours to build the Empire State Building and 20 million hours to build the Panama Canal, people spent 9 *billion* hours on playing *Solitaire* in 2003. This means that if it were possible to build both constructions through *Solitaire* the first would take 6.8 hours and the latter a day, respectively! For this reason, Von Ahn suggests to create games that make use of human brainpower "productively" by making sure that the game experience is useful beyond the game itself.

One of the games he designed to implement this vision is the *ESP Game* (Von Ahn and Dabbish 2004). In this game, two players try to reach as quickly as possible a common word that can be associated with a picture (Fig. 2.15). The faster they reach consensus, the more points they earn. The words players reached consensus about can subsequently be stored into a database. This way, search algorithms, like Google uses and which cannot recognize pictures, can make use of the "tags" that people have given to pictures and give more refined feedback to users. According to Von Ahn it is possible to label every image on the Web if only 5,000 people are playing this game for a month. At the moment, many have played the game for over 20 hours a week, and over 20 million image labels have been harvested (Edery and Mollick 2009). This is the equivalent of several million euros of free labor. The earlier mentioned *Foldit* is another example of a game used for human computation (Fig. 2.12).[19]

Exploration

In workshop settings professionals sometimes get together to construct a scenario or simply brainstorm about all kinds of possibilities without having a clear idea upfront. And in research, it is not uncommon that researchers step into or create some environment and just see what happens. In all of these instances people attempt to "explore" a certain topic. This idea can be applied in a game setting as well. A game can be setup with a number of initial conditions and at the end it can be observed what the outcomes are. By comparing different sessions with similar and different conditions a topic can said to be explored within the limitations and context of the game.

[19]For more examples of "human computation" games, see http://www.gwap.com.

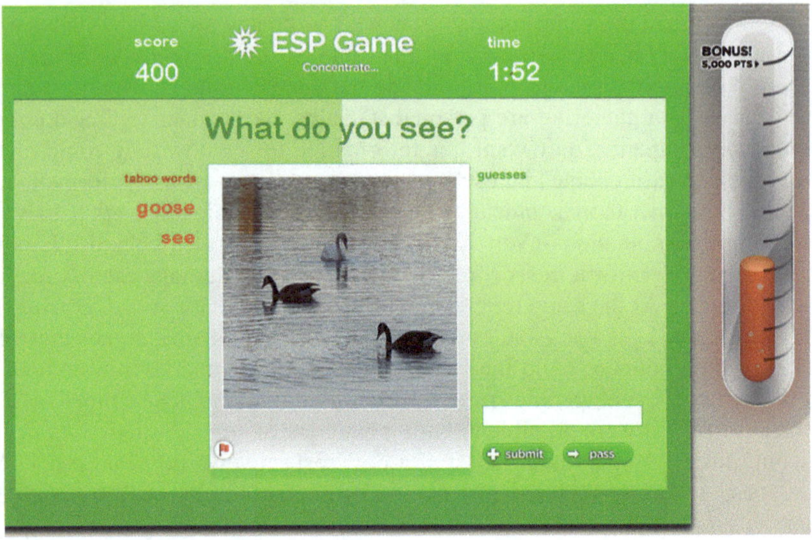

Fig. 2.15 Tagging pictures collaboratively in the *ESP Game*. ©2004 Carnegie Mellon University. Used with permission

The value of using games in this way is similar to and based on other forecasting techniques, such as scenario writing and hardcore simulation models (Mayer 2009). But the use of games should not only be seen as diagnostic tool to predict the future (Greenblat 1980). They can also be employed to understand and explore how historical settings or current patterns have emerged under different circumstances, for example, when it comes to the development of cities (Portugali 2000).

Thc example of a game to explain this value concerns, however, one that focuses on the future. In the Netherlands, the Rotterdam harbor is considered one of the biggest in the world. The government has nevertheless decided to enlarge this harbor to keep up with the economic demands and growth of the rest of the world, and as a matter of fact, they are creating this extension as I am writing these words. To simulate the construction and exploitation of this extension, a game was created called *SimPort-MV2* (Fig. 2.16).

In this game, players have to setup a strategy to construct and exploit this extension. After devising within certain limitations the layout of the extension by appointing industries to locations and setting up a time schedule for construction, they have to allocate clients to the locations within the harbor. At the end of the game, when the time line hits the year 2037, a certain spatial arrangement is achieved with certain costs, profits, and other important indicators to base a score on.

For the players, playing the game allows for understanding the complexity involved with the process of constructing and exploiting a harbor and getting an understanding of what strategies need to be followed to manage it effectively. This is the educational side of the tool. As for the output, the various spatial arrangements and other indicators, they can be examined after a few runs to see if patterns can be recognized.

Fig. 2.16 Building and exploiting a harbor extension in *SimPort-MV2*. ©2006 Tygron Serious Gaming. Used with permission

This is exactly what Bekebrede (2010) has done. She also used different initial conditions, such as whether the game starts with a bad or strong economy which has influences on how clients negotiate contracts with the port authority, to see how this affects the eventual results. This way, by means of a game as an exploratory tool, the construction and exploitation of a harbor extension can be *explored* under different circumstances and by simulating stakeholders in interaction with a physical system.

Using games for exploration has been especially limited for now to public policy and in particularly to urban planning (for other examples, see Mayer et al. 2004, 2005), but its use remains a possibility to pursue for many other domains and with the experiences of these pioneers, it could be "explored" a little bit further.

Theory Testing

In contrast to exploration, games could also be used when people have a clear idea upfront. In this case they would like to "test" if their preconceived notions, based on theories, assumptions, or anything else, hold ground.[20] The game becomes a sort of "laboratory experiment" in which researchers "play" with variables. With tests, it

[20] Scientifically speaking, this distinction can be seen as an inductive approach when it comes to exploration and a deductive approach when it comes to theory.

can, for example, be seen under which circumstances people perform better or how people start to organize themselves given a set of conditions. When a game is repeated sufficiently, the outcomes of sessions (based on criteria set by the researcher) can be used as valuable data to accept or reject a hypothesis.

For instance, the hypothesis of whether gender has an influence on leadership style could be tested by examining the performance of males and females while they play *Virtual Leader*. While in this situation an existing game is repurposed, examples are known in which a game was built from the beginning to test a theory (cf., Meijer 2009).

This idea of using games for theory testing is certainly not new (Brewer 1978; Duke 1974; Gibbs 1974). It simply has not found any common ground because of a number of methodological issues (see also Klabbers 2006). First, we have the problem of validity. Does the game really replicate reality and are we able to generalize to reality? Whatever researchers attempt, this always remains open for debate.

Second, we have the problem of control which is essential to perform experiments. Games are dynamic and open to inventions by players, especially if it concerns a multiplayer game. This means researchers have to control many variables at the same time. Also, it can be expected that every game session is at least somewhat different, which makes it hard to compare.

Third, applying games is in many cases practically cumbersome. It requires a lot of effort to first design a good game and subsequently to setup the experiments. This and more explains why most scholars refrain (so far) from using games to test theories.

To give an example of researchers who did not refrain from this, let us take a look at an analog multiplayer game called the *Mango Chain Game* (Meijer 2009; Zúñiga-Arias et al. 2006). The game is played around a board that represents the mango production and export chain in Costa Rica, one of the countries that exports the mango fruit. Mangoes of different quality are represented as fiches that are harvested by the producers and sold to either multinationals or independent exporters, who on their turn, sell it to retailers. The production, transportation as well as the consumer market is simulated, the rest occurs on the basis of contracts between participants. When a contract is signed, this is represented as a colored elastic band between participants on the board. Colors indicate the duration of the contract.

At first, the researchers hypothesized that because of the low bargaining power of the producer associations and the risk averse nature of people, local farmers with whom they actually played the game with would opt for long-term contracts with its associated higher prices. However, it turned out that mango producers rather have short-term contracts. This gives them the opportunity to remain flexible in responding to changes in the supply they cannot control. In the longer run, farmers may not get the higher prices that come with long-term contracts, but they do not have to disappoint buyers because of bad harvests.

The findings of the study may well have been found by other means of research but the point is that gaming can be seen as another tool by which it becomes possible to research and test theories. It could be used as an environment to further validate observations or as an experiment in and of itself. Moreover, simple game-like features, such as time-pressure, scores, and aesthetics, can be used to "dress up" experiments. One experiment already used the faces of Bert and Ernie from "Sesame Street" to engage young children in an otherwise boring two-choice key-pressing task (Kray et al. 2006). From this, it is a small step to actually use games.

To Conclude

Similar to the world of Reality, the categorizations of this world are exemplary and can also be cross-categorized. In fact, many games will probably already tap into two or more values or could be easily repurposed for other types of values. What needs to be kept in mind is what the primary purpose of the game is. This should be leading in thinking of what value needs to be achieved and in what manner.

In thinking about his, disciplines such as psychology, semiotics, instructional technology, communication studies, rhetoric, and the learning sciences in general, can be helpful and need to be involved. They provide theories, frameworks, and best practices that give direction to how values can be achieved. This part of the development is related to a world that I call "Meaning" and results in a *value proposal*, an extensive description of how a game will impact the real world.

While the world of Reality is related to the stakeholders, this world is affiliated with teachers, storytellers, data mining experts, researchers, or any other "professionals" that have expertise on how to accomplish some value. Although it is certainly not a common practice, it is important to involve such professionals. What type depends of course entirely on the value that needs to be reached. Stereotypical responses of people from this world include "that is not how the point gets across" or "yes, adding flowers to the wall will make the environment definitely more attractive but it will also distract the player."

The world of Meaning is different from Reality. It focuses on the type of value, whether knowledge or data collection, that needs to be achieved and considers this from a whole set of different disciplines and criteria. The criteria part of this world concern, for example, "motivation," "relevance," and "transfer." It also requires to deal with other people, those that know how to create a certain value. Nevertheless, this world needs to be reconciled with Reality, for they are interdependent on each other: without Reality there is nothing to base a game on and apply the eventual meaning to. Both are also interdependent with another world, one that I will discuss right now.

The World of Play

Ask a random person about what a game is and expect to receive random responses. A typical family guy would refer to the cozy times at home of playing *Monopoly*, an intellectual would talk about the great victories at simultaneous *Chess* championships, an athlete would non-stop explain the strategies of his or her favorite types of sports, and a digital native would converse in a for "normal" people incomprehensible manner about the ins and outs of *World of Warcraft*. Games can clearly be found in different shapes, settings, and cultures.

Finding a definition of "a game" is due to this huge diversity quite difficult (Schell 2008; Salen and Zimmerman 2004). In general, however, games are differentiated from "play" by having clear goals and rules. The much more open-ended and free-form type of activities we coin "play," such as *Doctor & Nurse*, also have rules, but these are much less emphasized and rigid compared to games. In *Doctor & Nurse*, for example, the only rule is to behave like a doctor and nurse. That is it. And there is not really any goal in playing it.

Contrast this with *Poker*. In *Poker* every step is dictated by the rules. Not for nothing they came up with the expression "The cards do not lie." It is not the player who determines the outcomes, it is the "rules of the game." The player can only influence the outcomes by manipulating the rules. *Poker* also has a very clear goal. Players win a round when they have the best cards or if their opponents do not dare to compete with them. In the end, the player with the most fiches wins.

Thus, games can be distinguished from the larger concept we call "play" by looking whether it is an activity with goals and rules or whether it is an open-ended and free-form type of activity. This makes games basically a formalized type of play. Although this sounds as if games can be clearly separated from play, in reality this is not always the case. In between *Doctor & Nurse* and *Poker* there are many activities, some which are closer to *Doctor & Nurse* and others which are closer to *Poker*. In fact, many people interchange play with games, probably because the boundary between what is considered a game and what a play is just extremely vague. The confusion rises even higher in other languages than English, since in for example Dutch and German, the word for game and play is identical (i.e., this is "spel" and "spiele," respectively).

For this reason it is better to look at games or other play activities as existing on a sliding scale, a continuum, of being unregulated or having strict rules. Even many more dimensions can be thought of, if we for example want to differentiate "a game of chance," which is structured but does not involve any player effort, like flipping a coin, from "real" games, those that are structured and do require an effort by the player (cf., Caillois 1958/1961; Juul 2005). Nevertheless, I conceive of all these dimensions and their related activities to be part of the "world of Play," especially since real games can contain parts that are mere luck, take for example the throwing of dice in *Monopoly*, and can include some free-form and open-endedness. The latter can, for example, be seen with *SimCity*.

This world of Play needs to be considered if people want to design a game. To develop a game, designers need to come up with a *game concept* which is a detailed idea of what the game is like. It describes what elements are part of it and how they relate to each other in creating an experience. One of the first things designers do is to think of what type of game they are going to design. Although a huge variety of games exist, games can be classified similar to movies and books into certain *genres*.

Not surprisingly, little agreement exist on these genres (Foster and Mishra 2009). One important general tendency can however be noticed: the categories of games are not based on the content, as with books or movies, but are based on the type of challenges (Rollings and Morris 2004). A game with a science fiction theme is not a science fiction game, but is an action, strategy or role-playing game, depending on which type of challenges the game has. Take (again) *The Matrix* movie.[21] Cinematologists would consider this movie to be a science fiction movie, while gamers consider the *Enter the Matrix* game, which is based on the movie, to be an action game, since it involves fighting, button-smashing, and all the other characteristics that make up an average action game.

With this in mind, from my (subjective) point of view I conceive of seven "big" genres: action, adventure, puzzle, role-playing, simulation, strategy, and virtual world games. To provide a perspective onto games with a serious purpose from this world, below a short description of each genre is given. These descriptions are largely based on the work of Rollings and Adams (2003).[22]

Action

Precision, timing, hand-eye coordination, and button-pushing are important aspects of *action* games. For this reason, action games are also referred to as *twitch games*. They tend to be simpler than most other types because there is only so much information and complexity that the average brain can interpret in unit time. Consequently, they do not have a long learning curve. The player just needs to know the right buttons and that is it. If a player asks "Where is the fire-button?" or something similar, then it is obvious that we are dealing with an action game. Other characteristics of action games are:

- **Twitch-speed**: action games are fast-paced. When players forget to pay attention, it is too late, and they have to start over again.
- **Levels**: a level is a specifically defined area in the game arena, in which the objective for the player is to complete a specific task. Action games tend to consist of multiple levels and upon completion the player can go to the next level. Generally, the difficulty will increase with each subsequent level.
- **Lives & energy**: the player gets usually a number of tries to finish the level, or even the game. In some cases the life of a player is depicted with energy. If the amount of energy is depleted, the player looses a life. Lives and energy can be earned in some games by collecting power-ups, game elements that reward the player, or by getting high scores.

[21] *The Matrix* is produced by Joel Silver and directed and written by Larry and Andy Wachowski. It was distributed by Warner Bros. Pictures in 1999.

[22] Compared to the classification by Rollings and Adams (2003) I have made some adjustments. Some genres I conceived of subgenres, like vehicle simulations, and others I conceived as half-breeds, genres that fall between two other genres, such as sports simulations (action and simulation). More information about each of the genres can further be found in their book. I simply made a synopsis of the elements I thought to be most characteristic.

- **Time**: some games have a timer that indicates how much time is left for the player to finish a particular level. When it reaches zero, a major event occurs, such as a levee breach, and the player might need to restart the level. Time is sometimes also used to get a bonus when finishing the level very quickly. Whether a timer is present or not, in every action game time is a critical element. The player needs to accurately and timely respond to events, otherwise it is game over.
- **Score**: a score is an indicator of progress and action games are pretty much centered around it. Most action games have high score tables letting the best players show off to other players.

The designation "action game" covers a wide range of game styles. They do not necessarily involve shooting or fighting. They can be very kids friendly, as in *Super Mario* or *Sonic the Hedgehog*. Subcategories involve "beat 'em ups," "shoot 'em ups," and "platformers." All three of them pretty much speak for themselves: beat 'em ups are about fighting, shoot 'em ups about shooting, and platformers about jumping from platform to platform. Other examples of this genre are *Unreal Tournament* and *Grand Theft Auto* (Fig. 2.17).

Adventure

For *adventures*, the story is central to the whole game. The player has to explore the game world and in the meantime accomplish particular tasks to get to know more about the story. The particular tasks between the storylines can be anything, from collecting and manipulating items, puzzle solving to some combat and action elements, although most adventures have a reduced emphasis on the latter. From a design perspective, the tasks in adventures can be referred to as "mini-games": little games within a game. Not every adventure uses this mini-game approach, some have a very consistent type of task throughout the whole game. The best adventures, such as the *Monkey Island* series make these mini-games fit within the setting and story (Fig. 2.18). The characteristics of adventure games can be summarized as:

- **Story-based**: the story is central to adventure games. Conversations, drama, emotions, humor and other things that make up good narratives should be part of an adventure game.
- **Setting**: the setting in an adventure game contributes more to its entertainment value than in any other genre. The setting creates the world the player is going to explore and to live in, and it is for many players the reason for playing adventure games in the first place.
- **Mini-game approach**: the interactive parts between the stories take a mini-game approach. The player gets different challenges across his path, from decoding a cryptic message, collecting items, doing detective work to (insult) sword fighting.
- **Context-sensitive perspective**: since a lot of things in current adventure games is prescripted, most use a context-sensitive perspective. This means that the camera angle changes in each location to a position that would enhance the story or gameplay.

Fig. 2.17 Eating pizza after some action in *Grand Theft Auto: San Andreas* at "The Well Stacked Pizza Co." Other restaurants in this game are "Burger Shot" and "Cluckin' Bell." CJ stands in the middle with his brand new hair cut and sneakers. ©2004 Rockstar Games. Used with permission

- **Point-and-Click**: most adventures use a point-and-click user interface. With this interface, the player only needs to use the mouse to play the game. The player just points to objects in the screen with the cursor, for example a door or character, and then clicks on the object in order to open the door or to talk to the character.
- **Dying?**: in most adventure games the player cannot die. They are about exploring and not about fighting, so there is not anything that could really kill the player's character. Those adventures in which players can die use ways to inform them very clearly that doing something would kill their character. For instance, if a dragon is in a cave, the designers litter the entrance with bones of earlier adventurers.

Adventure games, like *Zork*, were highly popular in the early days of the computer when graphics did not play a big role. Nowadays the genre gets less attention, but it is a misconception to think that this genre is "dead." Other than *Monkey Island*, *Myst* and *Grim Fandango* belong to this category.

Puzzle

Many games, especially adventures, contain *puzzle* solving. While using puzzle elements, they are not primarily about puzzles. Puzzle games on the other hand are.

Fig. 2.18 Finding adventure in *The Tales of Monkey Island*. The player on the right is conversing with a game character to get a ship. ©2009 Telltale. Used with permission

Quite often these games do not incorporate these puzzles into a storyline or larger goal. The player simply solves puzzle after puzzle until all the puzzles are solved. A puzzle game can be quickly identified when it involves only one screen in which the action takes place. For this reason, they can be considered more static than any of the other categories. Characteristics of puzzle games are:

- **Puzzles!**: well, it is obvious that logical challenges are central in these type of games.
- **Simple rules**: the rules of puzzle games are straightforward and simple. "Get to the exit" or "Get rid of all the balloons" are very clear statements with which the player has to achieve the goal of the game.
- **No story or higher goal**: most puzzle games do not have a story or higher goal. If they do, it is most of the times completely irrelevant. For example, players save the princess after solving ten puzzles in which they have to find an exit in a maze.
- **Single screen**: all the action takes place in a single screen.

Although these type of games do not show off the most powerful graphics, they do belong among the most frequently played games. Who has not played *Solitaire* in his or her life? Other puzzle games are *Tetris* (Fig. 2.19) and one of my favorite games all time, *Puzzle Bobble*.

Role-Play

Role-playing games are derived from pen-and-paper games, such as *Dungeons & Dragons*, and Live Action Role-Playing (LARP) games, and are pretty complex. To distinguish role-playing computer games from their non-computerized forms, they are referred to as "Computer Role-Playing Games" (CRPGs). Characters are central in role-playing games. The player plays one, but frequently more than one character, and during the game these characters evolve. They get stronger and get more abilities. The progress of characters is tracked with "experience points" or some other type of accounting system. The story is, similar to adventures, an important aspect of a role-playing game. However, in general CRPGs can be distinguished from adventures in that they incorporate more action and less story.

- **Configurable characters**: CRPGs are centered around characters that can be configured by players during the game. In some CRPGs players only play one character, in others they can play multiple characters.
- **Story and action**: CRPGs use many action elements, but also use a lot of story elements. Some emphasize one more than the other, but compared to action games they have less action and compared to adventure games they have less story.
- **Fantasy or science fiction setting**: they are frequently set in some Tolkien-esque fantasy or Star Wars-esque science fiction setting.
- **Experience points**: players can gather experience points (or use another accounting system) for their characters to make them stronger or give them new abilities.
- **Inventory**: players carry around all kinds of items, such as potions, weapons and gifts, that they can use throughout the game.

Although Massively Online Role-Playing Games (MMORPGs) have gained a lot of popularity these days, the "normal" role-play genre remains popular as well. Well-known are the *Final Fantasy* series, *Neverwinter Nights*, and *Fable*. In the world of analog games, role-plays are one of the most applied types of games. These do not involve configurable characters or inventories, but simply involve "taking the role" of a person or organization and enacting a situation together with other "role-players."

Simulation

Simulation games could take all kinds of forms, from building cities to controlling a big ship. The way to distinguish them is that they have a closer connection to reality than any of the other genres. Fast-paced action, power-ups or bonus points, fantasy or a story are not part of these games. The emphasis in simulation games is offering the player an idea how it would be like to be a pilot, a mayor, or a theme park owner. They are further more free-form and open-ended than the other genres. Goals are for example in many cases not explicitly stated. Basically, simulations consist of three major characteristics:

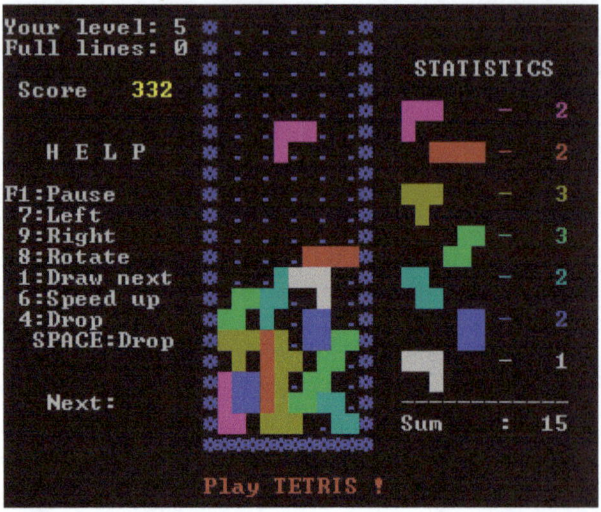

Fig. 2.19 Stacking blocks in the original *Tetris* version. ©1986 Soviet Academy of Sciences. Used with permission

- **Close to reality**: simulation games, as the name suggest, try to stay close to reality. Consequently, this means fantasy has little place within these type of games.
- **No story**: there is no story within simulation games. No background story or overarching story exists that develops as players go along.
- **Free-form and open-ended**: most simulations offer many degrees of freedom and no explicit goals. Players can make up their own goals or just play around with the game.

Roughly a distinction within this genre can be made into "construction & management" simulations, "vehicle" simulations, and "artificial life" simulations. The first subgenre is in many ways comparable to strategy games. They also have a strong emphasis on rules, economy, and resources. Examples of this subgenre are *SimCity 4* (Fig. 2.20), *Railroad Tycoon*, and all other "tycoon games." The second subgenre involves games that model vehicles, such as ships, cars, planes or even bikes, very realistically. Examples of this subgenre are *Flight Simulator*, *Ship Simulator*, and *Gran Turismo*. The last subgenre, artificial life simulations, are those games that involve the player in taking care of one or more virtual characters. *The Sims* and *Dogz* are good examples of this subgenre.

Many games (analog or digital) with a serious purpose are reminiscent of this genre, because the majority stays relatively close to reality, like *Supervisor*. For this reason, a number of scholars frequently label games with a serious purpose as "simulations." This, however, excludes many other types of games, such as *Re-Mission*, while they have certainly a serious purpose. My point of view is that "simulations" are just a genre that designers can choose from the realm of the world of Play (see also Level 1).

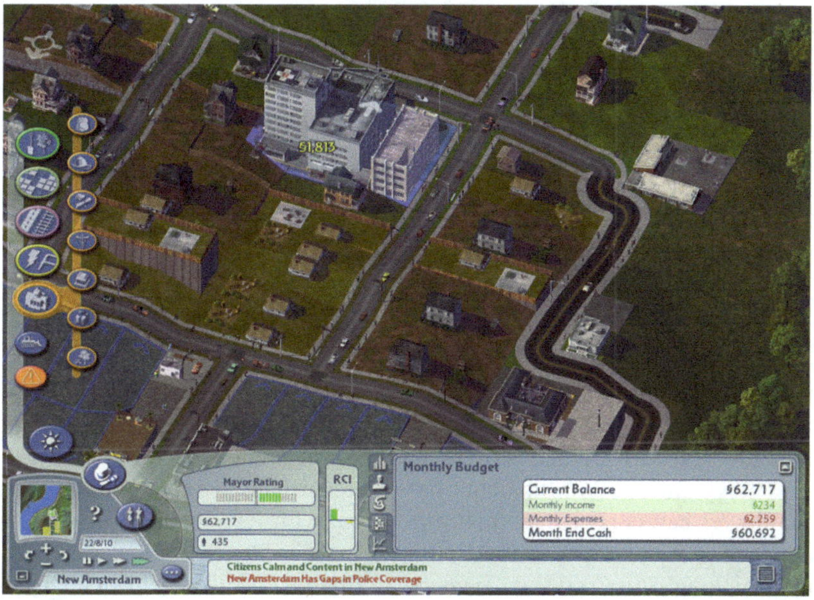

Fig. 2.20 Building a sustainable city with *SimCity 4*. Image provided courtesy of Electronic Arts Inc. ©2003 Electronic Arts Inc. All rights reserved. Used with permission

Strategy

The origin of *strategy* games is rooted in board games, such as *The Settlers of Catan*. They are obviously centered around strategies. The player needs to deploy these to achieve the goals of the game. As in reality, to deploy a strategy people must have a good overview of what is happening in the field, so strategy games use perspectives and presentation layers that support these aspects. The perspective that most strategy games tend to use is the "isometric perspective." This makes the player look at the game world from a diagonally oriented bird's eye view. This is handy, because instead of handling one unit at a time, as with most other games, the player is now able to control multiple units simultaneously.

And managing units to achieve a higher goal is basically what strategy games are all about. Presentation layers differ per game, but in every game they are critical. It can organize and simplify the complexity for the player, and if not handled well, it can make the game overwhelming and confusing. Therefore, important characteristics of strategy games are:

- **Rules**: rules are important in any game, but strategy games are clearly and very visibly centered around them. The rules enable the player to make up their strategies. An example of such a rule could be: "an archer can defeat a knight from a distance, but looses up close."
- **Isometric perspective**: strategy games use this diagonally bird's eye perspective as it gives a good overview of the game.

- **Presentation layer**: strategy games have very characteristic ways of organizing information. This organization is important, as these games are complex.
- **Economy**: every strategy game has some type of economy. Players can trade with other players or non-players to get the resources they need or to upgrade existing resources. When playing well, the player is able to buy more and more and create bigger and better units. In doing this, the player has to balance his incomes and expenditures.
- **Resources**: Any strategy game has some type of resources. It might be just plane money, gold or raw building materials, such as wood, stones, water, grain, etc. With these resources the player is able to get other more refined resources (also referred to as units), such as knights, trains, planes, castles and archers.

Strategy games have a steep learning curve and not surprisingly knowing this, they involve much more complicated systems than any of the other game genres. A distinction within this genre is often made between "turn-based" and "real-time" (RTS) strategy games. With the latter time is a constant pressure. With turn-based games, players can ponder over their moves, but with RTS games everything happens at once. For these games reaction time and quick action are as important as strategic thinking. *StarCraft* and *Command & Conquer* are well-known RTS games, while *Civilization* is a well-known turn-based game (Fig. 2.21).

Virtual World

Over the past few years one genre has received particular attention. This I call *virtual worlds*, but it is also known as "persistent worlds" or "Massively Multiplayer Online Games" (MMOG). Despite the seemingly relatively recent advent of this genre, the historical roots of virtual worlds go completely back to 1978, when *MUD*—later known as *MUD1*—ran on the University of Essex network (Bartle 2003). *MUD* stands for "Multi-User Dungeon" and this term has become synonymous for this early genre.

The games in this genre combine elements of role-playing games, fighting, interactive fiction, and online chat. Players can interact with each other and the world by typing commands that resemble a natural language, similarly to the early text adventures. Nowadays, players can step into gigantic three dimensional virtual worlds inhabited by hundreds, thousands, if not millions of players. For this reason, they are often coined as "massively." Nevertheless, some of these virtual worlds may be massively, but do not have advanced 3D graphics. They can be played on a browser. In general, virtual worlds have the following characteristics:

- **Social**: as hundreds, thousands, if not millions of players can interact by using chat systems or taking up a challenge together or against each other, this makes them inherently social with all the advantages and disadvantages that follow from this. Bonding may take place, but also misbehavior, such as harassment of other players.

Fig. 2.21 Building a civilization in *Civilization IV*. The picture shows my Japanese empire with the pyramids in Edo, a Jewish temple in Kyoto, and a library in Osaka. ©2005 2K Games. Used with permission

- **Community building**: one social element which is particularly unique is being able to join a club, guild, faction, or corporation. These are groups of players that have a shared interest in how they play the game. Players of these groups collaborate to achieve these shared interests.
- **Persistent**: these games simply do not stop. When players stop playing, the virtual world lives on. Producers also continue to build on the world by adding content every now and then. Additionally, time is irreversible. It is impossible to create the exact situation when many players are involved.
- **Leveling**: similar to character development and experience points in role-plays, virtual worlds involve ever evolving characters, space ships, towns, or anything else. Upgrading the game elements is generally known as "leveling" as it is often expressed in what level the player has. With this, players can gain reputation.

Most virtual worlds draw heavily upon the role-play genre. Well-known examples are *World of Warcraft* (Fig. 2.22) and *Eve Online*. These are referred to as "Massively Multiplayer Online Role-Playing Games" (MMORPG). Others, which are often the simple browser types of games, like *Travian* reflect more the strategy types of games.

Apart from these game-like virtual worlds, worlds exists that are more free-form and open-ended and cannot be called games in a strict sense. Some of these worlds, like *IMVU*, are only about socializing. These are basically advanced chat programs. And some, like the infamous *Second Life*, are about socializing but also enable users

Fig. 2.22 Being immersed in a fantasy world with many players in *World of Warcraft*. Screen shot by Eline Harteveld. Permission was granted by all players. ©2004 Blizzard Entertainment

to create games or other activities, like meetings or virtual tours, inside their virtual world. They are more like (development) platforms that enable users to create something on.[23]

To Conclude

The above-mentioned genres are not exclusive nor are they completely comprehensive. Therefore, they should not be taken very rigidly. Many half-breeds exists, such as sports games (action and simulation), combat simulations (action and simulation), and action-adventures (action and adventure). An example of a half-breed is *Tomb Raider* starring the famous heroine "Lara Croft." This is a game in which the player has to (a) jump at certain points from platform to platform, making it a "platformer," has to (b) shoot her opponents to another gameworld, making it a "action" game, and has to (c) solve mysteries and collect treasures, making it an "adventure."

[23] Although "leveling" is not explicitly present in the less game-like virtual worlds, such as *Second Life*, the notion of "reputation" is certainly present. By means of having certain objects or having a "cool looking" and more advanced character, players gain more status.

Other than half-breeds, we even may have games that do not fit any genre. They are sometimes referred to as "weird games" (Griffiths 1996).

Despite these remarks, the genres do give some idea and insight what types of games can be found in the world of Play. Large differences can be seen and designers have to consider what types of games or "game characteristics" fit their purpose. With a type of game in mind, designers can look into a number of aspects that are important for developing a game concept. These concern thinking of what "goal(s)" players have to pursue, what sort of "gameplay" the game offers for reaching the goal(s), and in what gameworld it takes place. Last but not least, the issue of "technology," like what game engine is used or on what platform it is going to be played, has to be taken into account. In dealing with this, designers can draw upon an increasing body of literature from computer science, media studies, and other disciplines interested in the phenomenon called play, and games in particular, to create an interesting game.

Aside from considering the design of the game, designers need to deal with the people that are part of this world. When designing a game, artists, modelers, programmers, level designers, sound engineers, and so on are involved. These people need to know what needs to be made, but may also have their own idea of what makes a game good and this is often different than what subject-matter experts or teachers would think. While of course artistic freedom, creativity, and self-initiative need to be promoted during the development, the ideas of the people from this world need to be aligned with the other two worlds. While sometimes ideas may contribute or overlap, it can happen as well that they are incongruent. Stereotypical responses of people from this world are "but that is no fun" or "I do not find this very intuitive."

In deciding on issues, the world of Play maintains a different set of criteria than the other two worlds. These criteria are mostly related to making sure that the player is "entertained" in whatever form this may be. Three very closely related criteria can be used to judge the "entertainment value." These are engagement, immersion, and fun. In other words, from the perspective of this world a game needs to be engaging, immersive, and fun.

What About the Player?

I have been negligent about a crucial characteristic of games compared to other tools so far: their participatory nature (Murray 1997). Games involve participants which are referred to as "players." This seems rather straightforward, but it is an important point to make as it signals how games differ from other tools, such as hardcore simulations, and, subsequently, how this difference can be exploited and used for non-entertainment purposes.

As I discussed earlier with the world of Meaning, the exploitation and usage of games can roughly be distinguished in two ways. Players can either be an input to achieve an outcome, such as with games for theory testing or data collection, or can be the subject of an outcome, such as an increase in awareness or knowledge about a certain topic. The two possibilities are not incompatible with each other. Both can be applied at the same time. In fact, it is often hard to separate them. It depends on the purpose of the game what possibility is emphasized.

Take again the *ESP Game* (Fig. 2.15). The purpose of this is game is clearly "data collection" by means of human participants (Von Ahn 2005). Nevertheless, the people that play the game are urged to critically think about the pictures they are confronted with. They have to extract visual cues from the picture and elaborate on them by defining what these cues are. As the game uses "taboo words," words that cannot be used, better players are those that have a more richer vocabulary. Additionally, to play the game well, players should be able to "think" what somebody else would guess. This requires empathy. The game, therefore, teaches players some visual, social, and, above-all, language skills. While the main purpose of the *ESP Game* is to use the player as input, the players themselves get something more out of the experience than simply "having a good time."

This discussion about the position of the player relates foremost to the world of Meaning. It is about defining what the game needs to achieve. This is actually just one way of looking at players. It turns out that—based on TDG—we can define three different perspectives to look at a player: the player as person, the player as interpretant (or learner), and the player as player. Each of these roles relate to one of the worlds and are discussed below:

- **Reality—The player as person**: each player is first and foremost a "person." Players have a personality, culture(s) to which they belong to, a social and work environment, attitudes and so on. All of these aspects (and more) influence who the player is "as a person." They also influence how a player experiences and relates to a game. It was, for example, found that the emotional expressions of children differ in playing alone or together and across cultures. Dutch children were far more timid and calm, even when another Dutch child was present, in comparison to Pakistani children, who were extremely loud and emotionally expressive (Shahid et al. 2008).
- **Meaning—The player as interpretant**: people interpret information differently and so do players when making sense of a game. This depends, for example, on the existing knowledge, education, learning styles, and expectations that players have. Players will not make game interpretations, such as Bogost (2007) about *Grand Theft Auto: San Andreas* and Murray (1997) about *Tetris*, if they are not familiar with the American society. Motivation is also certainly an issue. If players do not have the desire to invest in the subject of a game, they will not make an effort. Since not all games are about education, I have opt for "interpretant" instead of "learner." However, when using a game to teach, this perspective can also be formulated as "the player as learner."
- **Play—The player as player**: finally, the player is what it says it is: a player. But no player is quite the same. They differ amongst each other. Players have their preferences in terms of the games they play and how they play them. Bartle (1996) identified, for example, four player types, the "achievers," "explorers," "socializers," and "killers," in how players can engage with a game. Achievers prefer to get the highest score or simply succeed in the game, explorers like to wander off and discover the virtual environment they are in, socializers like to

play together with others and see playing a game merely as a means to meet others, and killers thrive on manipulation, destruction, and competition with other players. Players further have different game skills and experiences that make a difference in how they play a game.

Much similar to the worlds of TGD themselves, the three perspectives are interdependent on each other. How players play the game as a player will be most likely influenced by who they are as a person. The way they play it, will also influence what they will interpret and how. A competitive player will see every other move by a player as a threat, while a collaborative player will take a more positive stance at first. And, of course, culture and other personal characteristics also have a great influence on how information in a game is interpreted.

When designing a game, it is important to keep these three different perspectives in mind, especially since players are crucial (if not the most crucial) element in a game. With these perspectives, we have a way of thinking about players. In evaluating our designs, we can, for example, understand why players "do not get the game," since the game is probably irreconcilable with their real world (Reality). Or it might be that they do not have the basic knowledge that is required to play the game (Meaning). Or it could be that they simply do not have the skills to play it (Play). But in our designs we can already harness these perspectives upfront to make sure it is very unlikely that the target group "does not get the game."

In the rest of this book, I will not specifically address the notion of player and the three perspectives associated with it. It is sufficient to understand how the "player" relates to the idea of TGD as mentioned here and that it concerns an aspect that needs serious attention.

And What About Other Approaches?

Similar to the programming approaches, like object-oriented and procedural programming, multiple game design approaches may exist or come into existence. TGD is simply one way of looking at the artifacts we call games. First of all, an abundant and ever increasing number of books have been written about game design in general (cf., Fullerton et al. 2008; Rollings and Morris 2004; Salen and Zimmerman 2004; Schell 2008). Most of these books provide practical tips and insights in how to design any game. These tips and insights are highly valuable, also for designing games with a serious purpose. One of the worlds that needs to be considered is Play and these books provide the knowledge to consider this world.

This book is, however, above-all about games with a non-entertainment purpose and in this field several attempts have been made to come up with game design approaches specifically for these types of games. In my search for these approaches I found much to my surprise at first that while a good number of them have been independently developed, they are strikingly similar to each other and to the idea of

TGD. This concerns the delivery modes by Aldrich (2004),[24] the four dimensional framework by De Freitas and Oliver (2006),[25] the three design foci by Frank (2007), the simulation movement space by Hall (2009), and the heart of serious game design by Winn (2009). The latter approach parallels TPACK, which stands for "Technological Pedagogical Content Knowledge" as well as for "total package" (Mishra and Koehler 2006).[26] This framework is applied to classroom settings in which technology, such as websites and videos, but also games (cf., Foster and Mishra 2009), are being used.

An overview of all these six approaches and TGD is given in Table 2.1. From this overview, we can retrieve that all these attempts speak of three or include three rather similar cores. It could, of course, be that it is coincidence or that people like to think in threes, but on second thoughts I like to think not. I think that sooner or later, when people get started with designing games, they discover that they have to deal with people, disciplines, aspects, criteria, and so on, that I have related to the worlds of Reality, Meaning, and Play. The reason why I like to think this is that conceptually the approaches are very similar to each other. For example, simulation, context, realism, and content are more or less related to what I call "Reality." The same line of reasoning can be applied to the worlds of Meaning and Play.

The similarities with TGD do not stop here. Frank mentions that the three foci are interdependent and need to be balanced to achieve a well-designed game. He also lists "dimensions" that are part of the foci, such as mystery and validity, that designers could take into account. Even closer comes Winn's the heart of serious game design and Mishra and Koehler's TPACK. They also talk about creating a whole that is more than the sum of its parts by considering three interdependent components, which forces designers to work inter-disciplinary and even trans-disciplinary, and with which tensions or conflicts could arise that need to be resolved by making trade-offs:

> ...a change in any one of the [components] has to be "compensated" by changes in the other two... [Design] is a complex task, often riddled with contradictions and tensions. [Teachers] have to resolve these contradictions and tensions by looking at all the components that

---

[24]The delivery modes are actually three of the six criteria Aldrich (2004) mentions to build a game. I left out the other three, which are systems, cyclical, and linear content, because these content types are provided by the delivery modes.

[25]The four dimensional framework consists—of course—of four dimensions rather than three. I left out the fourth, the "learner," because this dimension is accounted for by TGD and the other approaches implicitly.

[26]In the original article Mishra and Koehler (2006) coined their theoretical framework "TPCK." Later, they changed this to TPACK. This framework is built on Schulman's (1986, 1987) formulation of "pedagogical content knowledge" (PCK). He observed that teachers' subject knowledge and pedagogy were being treated as mutually exclusive in research and education programs and argued that it would be better to focus on the blending of content and pedagogy to get an understanding of how particular aspects of subject matter are organized, adapted, and represented for instruction. For teachers to be successful, they need to deal with C and P simultaneously to make sure the content is (re)presented in the best way possible (by means of analogies, illustrations, examples, etc.). Doing this requires another set of knowledge which Schulman referred to as PCK. More on information about TPACK can be found at http://www.tpack.org.

Table 2.1 Different but comparable approaches to TGD

Triadic Game Design	Delivery modes (Aldrich 2004)	Four dimensional framework (De Freitas and Oliver 2006)	Balancing three design foci (Frank 2007)	Simulation movement space (Hall 2009)	The heart of serious game design (Winn 2009)	TPACK (Mishra and Koehler 2006)
Reality: a paradigm based on elements of the real world (experts or validity) and the development of a model of reality	*Simulation*: selective representation of situations and user interaction. Includes the consideration of technology	*Context*: focuses on where playing takes place. Includes macro-level (historical and political) and micro-level (availability of resources) factors	*Context*: relates to the intended use of the game as well as surrounding factors. For whom, what, and under what circumstances will be played	*Realism*: a game can be placed on an axis ranging from real to surreal	*Content*: relates to items from domain-related areas (ecology or health)	*Content knowledge*: knowledge about the actual subject matter that is to be learned or taught
Meaning: a paradigm based on elements for creating value (teachers or transfer) and the development of a value proposal	*Pedagogy*: methods and tools to ensure that the students' time is spent productively (debriefing or reflection)	*Pedagogy*: focuses upon the processes of learning both formal and informal and the methods and models used to achieve learning	*Training objective*: the primary incentive to create a game. Relates to the scenario, relevancy, and validity	*Functionalism*: an axis that determines the extent of built-in learning mechanisms	*Theory*: theoretical notions that can be integrated in a game (persuasion or flow)	*Pedagogical knowledge*: knowledge about the processes and practices or methods of teaching and learning
Play: a paradigm based on elements for creating playful activities (programmers or fun) and the development of a game concept	*Game*: the provision of familiar and entertaining interactions (puzzle solving or competition)	*Representation*: the mode of presentation, the interactivity, the levels of immersion, and fidelity used	*Engagement*: motivational characteristics are needed to improve training outcome	*Engagement*: axis on which a game can be placed ranging from unadorned content to fun	*Game design*: the practice of designing (programming or storytelling)	*Technological knowledge*: knowledge about standard technologies and more advanced technologies

> play into their design. They have to weigh alternatives and take decisions factoring the differential effects of their choices. (Mishra and Koehler 2006, pp. 1030–1040)

Of course, differences exist. De Freitas and Oliver's context and Frank's context, for instance, also deals with the (educational) situation in which the game is going to be used. This is something that would be part of "Meaning" with TGD. Furthermore, Winn's theory would be applicable to any of the worlds of TGD. Each world has its own set of theories. And while Aldrich's simulation incorporates much (technological oriented) elements that are part of Play, with De Freitas and Oliver's representation it is the reverse. This composes of many elements that I consider to be part of Reality.

But aside from the categorization and linguistic[27] choices, the approaches also differ in what they focus on. Except for TGD and Winn's the heart of serious game design, all the other approaches only focus on education and training. And although Hall's movement space and De Freitas and Oliver's dimensions can easily be used for design, the first has been developed to classify games and the second to evaluate them. When it comes to the design, Mishra and Koehler's TPACK is oriented at designing the activity rather than the artifact itself. It essentially is about integrating *knowledge* about three components to ensure technology is properly used for teaching some content.

Most importantly, however, a quite radical difference exists between TGD and the other approaches. TGD is about three distinct perspectives grounded in different disciplines and affiliated with different people that (should) influence how the eventual game is designed, while those other approaches speak of elements (or axes onto which elements can be placed) that are part of the design and that need to be considered or taken care of. The difference is subtle yet significant. TGD is a "multi-paradigmatic" approach, creating a sense of how to look at games, whereas the other approaches give a pragmatic description of what "ingredients" are needed in "preparing" (or evaluating) a game. TGD, therefore, includes much more and starts from a much higher level of analysis.

These other approaches nevertheless show that what I have found and reflected on during the design of *Levee Patroller* is not something "out of the blue." They provide a slight evidence that the idea of TGD makes sense. This means that whatever designers decide to use, they need to acknowledge that designing a game for

[27] Over time I have been rethinking myself what terms to pick to denote the three worlds. At first, I decided to use "Reality, Pedagogy, and Game." I refrained from the term "Pedagogy" as not every game with a serious purpose is used for training and education. Additionally, the term is derived from the ancient Greek "paidagogos," the slave who supervised the education of slave children. The modern interpretation of pedagogy is the art or science of being a teacher. However, in essence the word "paidia" refers to children, which is why some like to make the distinction between pedagogy (teaching children) and andragogy (teaching adults). To avoid confusion about whether this approach is only directed at children or not, concerned another reason to let go of Pedagogy. As for Game, the reasoning was plain and simple: this term connotes too much the artifact itself and not a "world." After that, I started using more abstract terms, such as "Ontology, Semiosis, and Ludus." Although I liked the terms, I could not see how actual designers would use this in practice.

Table 2.2 Overview of the topics from each world that can be put into the mix

Reality (domains)	Meaning (values)	Play (genres)
Business & management	Knowledge	Action
Health	Skills	Adventure
Military	Attitudes	Puzzle
Politics & society	Assessment	Role-play
Public policy	Data collection	Simulation
Safety & crisis response	Exploration	Strategy
Science & education	Theory testing	Virtual world
Etc.	Etc.	Etc.

a serious purpose involves dealing with multiple elements. And to deal with these elements, they have to act much like a juggler (Fig. 2.3).

Toward Triadic Game Design

In the spirit of Machiavelli who stressed that it is important to lay foundations, this level laid the foundations of TGD. It discussed that designing games requires (a) taking into account a design space of three different worlds, (b) balancing these worlds by making trade-offs, and this works at best when (c) considering these worlds concurrently. It was further discussed of what these three worlds consist of and how they look at the design process. From this, it became clear that from the perspective of the world of Reality we encounter several domains to which games are applied to. From the perspective of the world of Meaning it is possible to conceive of different sorts of values that can be retrieved from playing games. Finally, the perspective of the world of Play showed us that games can be affiliated with a variety of genres. An overview of these perspectives is given in Table 2.2.

From this overview it may become clear why it is hard to categorize games or, in fact, why people do so in different ways. A game can, for instance, be classified as a "first responder crisis game," "operational training game," or "3D first person action game." Each of these classifications relates to one of the worlds: to Reality, Meaning, and Play, respectively. Depending from which world a game is looked at a certain categorization is made. Using TGD the categorizations people make can be traced back to one of the worlds. The types of classification possibilities also show that these games are inherently "triadic" in nature.

The overview can additionally assist in designing games. In creating a model of reality, value proposal, and game concept, it is useful to understand what sort of domains, values, and genres are available and how they can be mixed and put together to get a balanced game: a game with harmony. This requires to see the linkages between them, and most importantly, to have an overview. Designers need to see the "big picture"—the system at large—of what the game needs to become.

With this in mind, they can judge what sort of ingredients they need to add to the mixture. Maybe it needs to be more "spicy" or maybe it needs more "salt." This may obviously ask for some "tasting" as well, for instance by testing prototypes with users, as it is often difficult to judge what is needed.

But to be able to make a proper mixture and juggle with the worlds, the different worlds and how to balance them needs more explanation. This level was simply needed to give the necessary foundations to build on. Therefore, first the worlds of Reality, Meaning, and Play (in this order) are further elaborated on by discussing in detail what aspects and criteria are deemed important by each world. Second, a number of stereotypical tensions are explained that can be experienced while balancing a game. No straightforward solutions are handed over. Instead, a feeling is given of what can be expected and how a designer should think in solving these tensions.

Bibliography

Literature Bibliography

Aldrich, C. (2004). *Simulations and the future of learning: an innovative (and perhaps revolutionary) approach to e-learning*. San Francisco: Pfeiffer.

Anderson, J. R. (1983). *The architecture of cognition*. Cambridge: Harvard University Press.

Anderson, J. R. (1993). *Rules of the mind*. Hillsdale: Lawrence Erlbaum.

Anderson, J. R. (1995). *Cognitive psychology and its implications*. New York: Worth.

Bainbridge, W. S. (2007). The scientific research potential of virtual worlds. *Science, 317*(5837), 472–476.

Bartle, R. A. (1996). *Heart, clubs, diamonds, spades: players who suit MUDs*. http://www.mud.co.uk/richard/hcds.htm. Accessed 31 October 2009.

Bartle, R. A. (2003). *Designing virtual worlds*. Indianapolis: New Riders.

Baudrillard, J. (1981/1994). *Simulacra and simulation*. Ann Arbor: The University of Michigan Press (S.F. Glaser. Transl.).

Beck, J. C., & Wade, M. (2004). *Got game: how the gamer generation is reshaping business forever*. Boston: Harvard Business School Press.

Bekebrede, G. (2010). *Experiencing complexity: a game-based approach for understanding infrastructure systems*. Delft: Next Generation Infrastructures Foundation.

Bergeron, B. P. (2006). *Developing serious games*. Hingham: Charles River Media.

Bloom, B. S., Engelhart, M. D., Furst, E. J., Hill, W. H., & Kratwhohl, D. R. (1964). *Taxonomy of educational objectives: The classification of educational goals: Handbook I: Cognitive domain*. New York: David McKay.

Boehm, B. W. (1988). A spiral model of software development and enhancement. *IEEE Computer, 21*(5), 61–72.

Bogost, I. (2007). *Persuasive games: the expressive power of videogames*. Cambridge: The MIT Press.

Brewer, G. (1978). Scientific gaming: the development and use of free-form scenarios. *Simulation & Games, 9*(3), 309–338.

Caillois, R. (1958/1961). *Man, play and games*. Champaign: University of Illinois Press (M. Barash, Transl.).

Cooper, S., Khatib, F., Treuille, A., Barbero, J., Lee, J., Beenen, M., Leaver-Fay, A., Baker, D., Popović, Z., & Foldit Players (2010). Predicting protein structures with a multiplayer online game. *Nature, 446*, 756–760.

Corsi, T. M., Boyson, S., Verbraeck, A., van Houten, S.-P., Han, C., & MacDonald, J. R. (2006). The real-time global supply chain game: new educational tool for developing supply chain management professionals. *Transportation Journal*, *45*(3), 61–73.
Costikyan, G. (2003). *September 12, 2001*. http://www.costik.com/weblog/2003_10_01_blogchive.html. Accessed 11 August 2010.
De Caluwé, L., Hofstede, G. J., & Peters, V. (Eds.) (2008). *Why do games work? In search of the active substance*. Deventer: Kluwer.
De Freitas, S., & Oliver, M. (2006). How can exploratory learning with games and simulations within the curriculum be most effectively evaluated? *Computers & Education*, *46*(3), 249–264.
Dewey, J. (1938). *Experience and education*. New York: MacMillan.
Dienes, Z., & Perner, J. (1999). A theory of implicit and explicit knowledge. *Behavioral and Brain Sciences*, *22*(5), 735–808.
Duke, R. D. (1974). *Gaming, the future's language*. Beverly Hills: Sage.
Duke, R. D., & Geurts, J. (2004). *Policy games for strategic management: pathways into the unknown*. Amsterdam: Dutch University Press.
Edery, D., & Mollick, E. (2009). *Changing the game: how video games are transforming the future of business*. Upper Saddle River: FT Press.
Fishbein, M., & Ajzen, I. (1975). *Belief, attitude, intention, and behavior: an introduction to theory and research*. Reading: Addison-Wesley.
Foster, A. N., & Mishra, P. (2009). Games, claims, genres & learning. In R. E. Ferdig (Ed.), *Handbook of research on effective electronic gaming in education* (Vol. I, pp. 33–50). Hershey: Information Science Reference.
Frank, A. (2007). Balancing three different foci in the design of serious games: engagement, training objective and context. In D. Thomas & R. L. Appelman (Eds.), *Conference proceedings of DiGRA 2007: Situated play* (pp. 567–574). Tokyo: University of Tokyo.
Fullerton, T., Swain, C., & Hoffman, S. S. (2008). *Game design workshop: a playcentric approach to creating innovative games* (2nd ed.). Burlington: Morgan Kaufmann.
Gee, J. (2004). *What video games have to teach us about learning and literacy*. New York: Palgrave Macmillan.
Gerardi, M., Rothbaum, B. O., Ressler, K., Heekin, M., & Rizzo, A. (2008). Virtual reality exposure therapy using a Virtual Iraq: case report. *Journal of Traumatic Stress*, *21*(2), 209–213.
Gibbs, G. I. (Ed.) (1974). *Handbook of games and simulation exercises*. London: E. & F. N. Spon.
Glass, Z. (2007). The effectiveness of product placement in video games. *Journal of Interactive Advertising*, *8*(1). Available from http://www.jiad.org/article96.
Greenblat, C. S. (1980). *Designing games and simulations*. London: Sage.
Griffiths, M. D. (1996). Computer game playing in children and adolescents: a review of the literature. In T. Gill (Ed.), *Electronic children: how children are responding to the information revolution* (pp. 41–59). London: National Children's Bureau.
Hall, J. S. B. (2009). Existing and emerging business simulation-game design movements. *Proceedings of ABSEL 2009 annual conference*. Seattle: ABSEL.
Herz, J. C. (1997). *Joystick nation: how videogames ate our quarters, won our hearts, and rewired our minds*. Boston: Little, Brown.
Hoffman, H. G., Richards, T. L., Oostrom, T. V., Coda, B. A., Jensen, M. P., Blough, D. K., & Sharar, S. R. (2007). The analgesic effects of opioids and immersive virtual reality distraction: evidence from subjective and functional brain imaging assessments. *Anesthesia & Analgesia*, *105*(6), 1776–1783.
Jones, S. (2008). *The meaning of video games: gaming and textual strategies*. New York: Routhledge.
Juul, J. (2005). *Half-real: video games between real rules and fictional worlds*. Cambridge: The MIT Press.
Juul, J. (2009). *A casual revolution: reinventing video games and their players*. Cambridge: The MIT Press.
Kato, P. M., Cole, S. W., Bradlyn, A. S., & Pollock, B. H. (2009). A video game improves behavioral outcomes in adolescents and young adults with cancer: a randomized trial. *Pediatrics*, *122*(2), 305–317.

Klabbers, J. H. G. (2006). *The magic circle: principles of gaming and simulation*. Rotterdam: Sense.

Kray, J., Eenshuistra, R., Kerstner, H., Weidema, M., & Hommel, B. (2006). Language and action control: the acquisition of action goals in early childhood. *Psychological Science*, *17*(9), 737–741.

Krishnamurti, R. (2006). Explicit design space? *Artificial Intelligence for Engineering Design, Analysis and Manufacturing*, *20*(2), 95–103.

Lamar, C. (2008). *The 10 most terrifying video game enemies of all time*. http://www.cracked.com/article_16247_p2.html. Accessed 6 October 2009.

Mayer, I. S. (2009). The gaming of policy and the politics of gaming: a review. *Simulation & Gaming*, *40*(6), 825–862.

Mayer, I. S., Carton, L., de Jong, M., Leijten, M., & Dammers, E. (2004). Gaming the future of an urban network. *Futures*, *36*(3), 311–333.

Mayer, I. S., van Bueren, E., Bots, P., van der Voort, H., & Seidel, R. (2005). Collaborative decision-making for sustainable urban renewal projects: a simulation-gaming approach. *Environment & Planning. B, Planning & Design*, *32*(3), 403–423.

McDonald, M., Musson, R., & Smith, R. (2008). *The practical guide to defect prevention: techniques to meet the demand for more-reliable software*. Redmond: Microsoft Press.

McLuhan, M. (1964). *Understanding media: the extension of man*. New York: McGraw-Hill.

Meijer, S. A. (2009). *The organisation of transactions: studying supply networks using gaming simulation*. Wageningen: Wageningen Academic.

Michael, D., & Chen, S. (2006). *Serious games: games that educate, train, and inform*. Boston: Thomson Course Technology PTR.

Mishra, P., & Koehler, M. J. (2006). Technological pedagogical content knowledge: a framework for teacher knowledge. *Teachers College Record*, *108*(6), 1017–1054.

Murray, J. (1997). *Hamlet on the holodeck*. New York: The Free Press.

Peters, V., Vissers, G., & Heijne, G. (1998). The validity of games. *Simulation & Gaming*, *29*(1), 20–30.

Portugali, J. (2000). *Self-organization and the city*. Heidelberg: Springer.

Prensky, M. (2001). *Digital game-based learning*. New York: McGraw-Hill.

Rollings, A., & Adams, E. (2003). *Andrew Rollings and Ernest Adams on game design*. Indianapolis: New Riders.

Rollings, A., & Morris, D. (2004). *Game architecture and design: a new edition*. Indianapolis: New Riders.

Rosser, J. C., Lynch, P. J., Cuddihy, L., Gentile, D. A., Klonsky, J., & Merrell, R. (2007). The impact of video games on training surgeons in the 21st century. *Archives of Surgery*, *142*(2), 181–186.

Salen, K., & Zimmerman, E. (2004). *Rules of play: game design fundamentals*. Cambridge: The MIT Press.

Schell, J. (2008). *The art of game design: a book of lenses*. Burlington: Morgan Kaufmann.

Schulman, L. S. (1986). Those who understand: knowledge growth in teaching. *Educational Researcher*, *15*(2), 4–14.

Schulman, L. S. (1987). Knowledge and teaching: foundations of the new reform. *Harvard Educational Review*, *57*(1), 1–22.

Shaffer, D. W. (2006). *How computer games help children learn*. New York: Palgrave Macmillan.

Shahid, S., Krahmer, E., & Swerts, M. (2008). Alone or together: exploring the effect of physical co-presence on the emotional expressions of game playing children across cultures. In P. Markopoulos, B. de Ruyter, W. IJsselsteijn & D. Rowland (Eds.), *Lecture notes in computer science: Vol. 5294. Fun and games* (pp. 94–105). Berlin: Springer.

Simon, H. A. (1969). *The sciences of the artificial*. Cambridge: The MIT Press.

Squire, K., Barnett, M., Grant, J. M., & Higgenbotham, T. (2004). Electromagnetism Supercharged!: learning physics with digital simulation games. In Y. B. Kafai, W. A. Sandoval, N. Enyedy, A. S. Nixon & F. Herrera (Eds.), *The sixth international conference on learning sciences* (pp. 513–520). Mahwah: Lawrence Erlbaum.

Sterman, J. D. (1989). Modeling managerial behavior: misperceptions of feedback in a dynamic decision making experiment. *Management Science*, *35*(3), 321–339.

Surface, E. A., Dierdorff, E. C., & Watson, A. M. (2007). Special operations language training software measurement of effectiveness study: Tactical Iraqi study final report (Technical Report No. 2007010602). Raleigh: Surface, Ward & Associates.

Tapscott, D. (1997). *Growing up digital: the rise of the net generation*. New York: McGraw-Hill.

Tate, R., Haratatos, J., & Cole, S. (2009). Hopelab's approach to Re-Mission. *International Journal of Learning and Media*, *1*(1), 29–35.

van Bueren, E., Mayer, I. S., Harteveld, C., & Scalzo, R. (2009). Van tekentafel naar bestuurlijke implementatie: gamen met bestuurders in de rechtspraak en het Openbaar Ministerie. [From the designers table to administrative implementation: gaming with professionals in the judiciary and the Public Prosecution Office]. *Bestuurskunde*, *18*(3), 47–59.

Veen, W., & Vrakking, B. (2006). *Homo zappiens: growing up in a digital age*. London: Network Continuum Education.

Von Ahn, L. (2005). *Human computation*. Unpublished dissertation, Carnegie Mellon University, Pittsburgh, PA.

Von Ahn, L., & Dabbish, L. (2004). Labeling images with a computer game. In E. Dykstra-Erickson & M. Tscheligi (Eds.), *ACM CHI 2004 conference on human factors in computing systems* (pp. 319–326). Vienna: ACM Press.

Wald, M. L. (2008). For air traffic trainees, games with a serious purpose. *The New York Times*, A17, 8 October.

Washbush, J., & Gosen, J. (2001). An exploration of game-derived learning in total enterprise simulations. *Simulation & Gaming*, *32*(3), 281–296.

Wickens, C. D., Lee, J. D., Liu, Y., & Becker, S. E. G. (2004). *Introduction to human factors engineering*. London: Pearson Prentice Hall.

Winn, B. M. (2009). The design, play, and experience framework. In R. E. Ferdig (Ed.), *Handbook of research on effective electronic gaming in education* (Vol. III, pp. 1010–1024). Hershey: Information Science Reference.

Zúñiga-Arias, G., Meijer, S. A., Ruben, R., & Hofstede, G. J. (2006). Bargaining power and revenue distribution in the Costa Rican mango supply chain: a gaming simulation approach with local producers. *Journal on Chain and Network Science*, *7*(2), 143–160.

Zyda, M., Hiles, J., Mayberry, A., Wardynski, C., Capps, M. V., Osborn, B., Shilling, R., Robaszewski, M., & Davis, M. J. (2003). Entertainment R&D for defense. *IEEE Computer Graphics and Applications*, *23*(1), 28–36.

Game Bibliography

American Public Media, & Woodrow Wilson International Center for Scholars (2008). *Budget Hero* [Web]. St. Paul: American Public Media.

Anderson, T., Blank, M., Daniels, B., & Lebling, D. (1979). *Zork* [Mainframe]. Cambridge: MIT.

Atari Europe (2003). *Enter the Matrix* [Playstation 2]. Newport Beach: Shiny Entertainment.

Big Blue Box Studios (2004). *Fable* [Xbox]. Salt Lake City: Microsoft Games Studios.

BioWare (2002). *Neverwinter Nights* [PC]. Lyon, France: Infogrames.

Blizzard Entertainment (1998). *StarCraft* [PC]. Irvine: Blizzard Entertainment.

Blizzard Entertainment (2004). *World of Warcraft* [PC]. Irvine: Blizzard Entertainment.

Blow, J. (2009). *Braid* [PC]. San Francisco: Number None.

Bohemia Interactive Australia (2007). *Virtual Battle Space 2* [PC]. Nelson Bay, Australia: Bohemia Interactive Australia.

BreakAway, & Department of Justice (2007). *Incident Commander: A Training Simulation for Public Safety Personnel* [PC]. Hunt Valley: BreakAway.

Brøderbund Software (1993). *Myst* [PC]. Mead: Cyan.

CCP Games (2003). *Eve Online* [PC]. Reykjavik, Iceland: CCP Games.
Comedy Central's Indecion 2008 (2008). *Joe the Plumber Game: Layin' Pipe* [Web]. New York: Comedy Central's Indecion 2008.
Core Design (1996). *Tomb Raider* [Playstation]. San Francisco: Eidos Interactive.
Darrow, C. (1935). *Monopoly* [Board]. Salem: Parker Brothers.
Delft University of Technology (2009). *Supervisor* [PC]. Delft, the Netherlands: Delft University of Technology.
Delft University of Technology, & University of Maryland (2005). *Global Supply Chain Game* [PC]. Delft, the Netherlands: Delft University of Technology.
Delft University of Technology, Tygron Serious Gaming, & Port of Rotterdam (2006). *SimPort-MV2* [PC]. The Hague, the Netherlands: Tygron Serious Gaming.
Deltares, & Delft University of Technology (2006). *Levee Patroller: The Levee Inspection Simulator* [PC]. Delft, the Netherlands: Delft GeoSystems.
Enlight Software (2003). *Virtual U* [PC]. Portland: Woodrow Wilson Foundation.
Epic Games (2004). *Unreal Tournament 2004* [PC]. New York: Atari.
Firaxis Games (2005). *Sid Meier's Civilization IV* [PC]. Hunt Valley: 2K Games.
GameBank (1995). *Puzzle Bobble* [PC]. Tokyo, Japan: Taito.
Games-To-Teach Team (2003). *Supercharged!* [PC]. Cambridge: The Education Arcade.
Gygax, G., & Arneson, D. (1974). *Dungeons & Dragons* [Board]. Lake Geneva: TSR.
Hoffman, H. G., & Firsthand Technology (2006). *SnowWorld 3* [PC]. Seattle: University of Washington Harborview Burn Center.
IBM (2007). *INNOV8 2.0: Code: A BPM Simulator* [PC]. Armonk: IBM.
id Software (1999). *Quake III Arena* [PC]. Santa Monic: Activision.
ImpactGames (2007). *PeaceMaker: A Video Game to Promote Peace* [PC]. Pittsburgh: ImpactGames.
IMVU (2004). *IMVU* [PC]. Palo Alto: IMVU.
King Games (2006a). *Big Bumpin'* [Xbox 360]. Warwickshire, UK: Blitz Arcade.
King Games (2006b). *Pocketbike Racer* [Xbox 360]. Warwickshire, UK: Blitz Arcade.
King Games (2006c). *Sneak King* [Xbox 360]. Warwickshire, UK: Blitz Arcade.
Kramer, C. (1984). *Tempo Typen* [PC]. Alphen aan den Rijn, the Netherlands: Radarsoft.
Ledonne, D. (2005). *Super Colombine Massacre RPG!* [PC]. Published independently.
Linden Lab (2003). *Second Life* [PC]. San Francisco: Linden Lab.
LucasArts (1998). *Grim Fandango* [PC]. San Rafael: LucasArts.
Maxis Software (2000). *The Sims* [PC]. Redwood City: Electronic Arts.
Maxis Software (2003). *SimCity 4* [PC]. Redwood City: Electronic Arts.
Microsoft (1981). *Solitaire* [PC]. Redmond: Microsoft.
Microsoft Game Studios (2006). *Flight Simulator X* [PC]. Salt Lake City: Microsoft Game Studios.
MPS Labs (1990). *Sid Meier's Railroad Tycoon* [PC]. Hunt Valley: MicroProse Software.
MTO (2006). *Dogz* [Nintendo DS]. Montreal, Canada: Ubisoft.
Namco (1981). *Pac-Man* [Atari 2600]. Sunnyvale: Atari.
Nintendo (1985). *Super Mario Bros.* [NES]. Tokyo, Japan: Nintendo.
Nintendo EAD (2007). *Wii Fit* [Wii]. Tokyo, Japan: Nintendo.
Pajitnov, A., Pavlovsky, D., & Gerasimov, V. (1986). *Tetris* [PC]. Moscow, Russia: Soviet Academy of Sciences.
Paradox Interactive (2007). *Europa Universalis III* [PC]. Stockholm, Sweden: Paradox Interactive.
Persuasive Games (2003). *The Howard Dean for Iowa Game* [PC]. Burlington: Dean for America.
Play2Learn, Energy Research Centre, & Alterra (2001). *NitroGenius: A Game on Nitrogen Management* [PC]. Wageningen, the Netherlands: Play2Learn.
PlayGen, & Norwich Union (2008). *FloodSim* [PC]. London, UK: PlayGen.
Polyphony Digital (1997). *Gran Turismo* [Playstation]. Tokyo, Japan: Sony Computer Entertainment.
Powerful Robot Games (2003). *September 12th* [Web]. Montevideo, Uruguay: Newsgaming.com.
Realtime Associates (2006). *Re-Mission* [PC]. Redwood City: HopeLab Foundation.

Red Hill Studios (2006). *FF56!* [PC]. Roswell: Lauer Learning.
Rockstar North (2004). *Grand Theft Auto: San Andreas* [Playstation 2]. New York: Rockstar Games.
Rockstar North (2008). *Grand Theft Auto IV* [Playstation 3]. New York: Rockstar Games.
Sierra Entertainment (2004). *Half-Life 2* [PC]. Kirkland: Valve.
Simulearn (2003). *Virtual Leader* [PC]. Norwalk: Simulearn.
Sonic Team (1991). *Sonic the Hedgehog* [Megadrive]. Tokyo, Japan: SEGA.
Square Enix (2002). *Final Fantasy* [Playstation]. Tokyo, Japan: Square Enix.
Systems Dynamics Group (1960). *The Beer Game* [Board]. Cambridge: MIT.
Tale of Tales (2009). *The Path* [PC]. Ghent, Belgium: Tale of Tales.
Telltale (2009). *Tales of Monkey Island* [PC]. San Rafael: Telltale.
Teuber, K. (1995). *Settlers of Catan* [Board]. Stuttgart, Germany: Kosmos.
Travian Games (2004). *Travian* [Web]. München, Germany: Travian Games.
Trubshaw, R., & Bartle, R. (1978). *MUD* [Mainframe]. Colchester, UK: University of Essex.
University of Southern California (2006). *Tactical Iraqi* [PC]. Los Angeles: Alelo.
University of Southern California and Red Hot Learning (2007). *The ReDistricting Game* [PC]. Los Angeles: University of Southern California.
University of Washington (2008). *Foldit: Solve Puzzles for Science* [PC]. Seattle: University of Washington.
U.S. Army (2009). *America's Army 3* [PC]. Washington: U.S. Army.
Valve (1999). *Counter-Strike* [PC]. Paris, France: Vivendi.
Virtually Better, University of Southern California, & Naval Medical Center-San Diego (2005). *Virtual Iraq* [PC]. Decatur: Virtually Better.
Von Ahn, L., & Dabbish, L. (2004). *ESP Game* [Web]. Pittsburgh: Carnegie Mellon University.
VSTEP (2010). *Ship Simulator Extremes* [PC]. Stockholm, Sweden: Paradox Interactive.
Wageningen University (2005). *Mango Chain Game* [Board]. Wageningen, the Netherlands: Wageningen University.
Westwood Studios (1995). *Command & Conquer* [PC]. London, UK: Virgin Interactive Entertainment.
Windows Defect Prevention Team (2006a). *The Beta1 Game* [PC]. Redmond: Microsoft.
Windows Defect Prevention Team (2006b). *The Beta2 Game* [PC]. Redmond: Microsoft.

Level 3
Reality

We have to think of ways to use games not just to escape reality but to re-engage with reality—Henry Jenkins

Even when game designers know a topic well, a representation will always be an interpretation of the world—Simon Egenfeldt-Nielsen

The physical world is represented in many ways and forms. Representations are made for several reasons: to illustrate, clarify, symbolize, simplify, or experiment with something in the real world. We see these representations everywhere. If we step into our car we see "driving signs." These are symbols that represent real world phenomena, such as the velocity of a car or a dead end.

But representations do not necessarily need to reflect the current real world. They can represent the past, such as by paintings of life in the Middle Ages, or the future as in the drawings and models of a new urban region that is going to be developed. Representations "re-engages" us with reality by making it possible to look at it from another perspective.

It is important to realize that although representations are inherently linked with the real world, they are not the real world itself. Nobody has "pictured" this better than René Magritte in one of his famous paintings in which a pipe is depicted. Below the pipe the description "Ceci n'est pas une pipe" is given, which is French for "This is not a pipe." With this painting Margritte wanted to provoke viewers to show that while it looks like a real object it is not. It is just a representation of a real object and as such has its limitations. It cannot, for example, be filled with tobacco neither can it be used to smoke. His point is that no matter how closely we depict an item accurately, we never catch the item itself.

Figure 3.1 shows a virtual reproduction and a game interpretation of this painting. This figure is actually a several printed copies of an animated pipe of a virtual pipe from the *Super Mario* games who are themselves based on pipes—but not the ones Magritte thought of—from the real world (see also Fig. 2.4).

Although representations are restrictive compared to the real object, they can have an important purpose. In fact, sometimes this purpose has a value which we

C. Harteveld, *Triadic Game Design*,

DOI 10.1007/978-1-84996-157-8_3,

Fig. 3.1 Virtual reproduction and game interpretation of the painting by René Magritte from his "The Treachery of Images" (1928–1929) series. The translation of the French inscription is "this is not a pipe." 3D model by Arne Bezuijen and Rens van den Bergh

cannot reach with the real world. Maps are an important example of this. We cannot suddenly get a helicopter view of an environment to determine our location. And to see how we need to go from A to B, it is much easier to look at a small map and see what roads to take than to point in the real world to the direction that needs to be taken. It is even more failure-proof, as people are easily disoriented in the real world.

Yet the value of representations themselves depends on how they are designed. This has been finely pointed out by a Borges (1998) in his "On Exactitude in Science":

> In that Empire, the Art of Cartography attained such Perfection that the map of a single Province occupied the entirety of a City, and the map of the Empire, the entirety of a Province. In time, those Unconscionable Maps no longer satisfied, and the Cartographers Guilds struck a Map of the Empire whose size was that of the Empire, and which coincided point for point with it. The following Generations, who were not so fond of the Study of Cartography as their Forebears had been, saw that vast Map was Useless, and not without some Pitilessness was it, that they delivered it up to the Inclemencies of Sun and Winters. In the Deserts of the West, still today, there are Tattered Ruins of that Map, inhabited by Animals and Beggars; in all the Land there is no other Relic of the Disciplines of Geography. (p. 325)

In this story, maps are perfected and perfected by "the Art of Cartography" that they have become more or less the same as the real world and this renders a map useless. This story shows that although representations can be really powerful, it is important that they are designed well. In designing one of the issues that designers face is "how realistic does it need to be?" If it is too "realistic," the representation can become—similar to the Borges' map—useless. On the other hand, if it is too abstract, the connection with the real world might be lost and it becomes useless as well.

Games, and in particularly the digital ones, are "representational devices." They enable to illustrate, clarify, symbolize, or experiment with something in the real word. The sort of representation or the interpretation of reality "inside" a game is what I call the *model of reality*. Each game has one, from the most abstract games to the most elaborate realistic simulators. In this level I will explain what aspects need to be considered to build such a model.

This concerns first of all the "problem" we are dealing with (see "Defining the Problem"). We do not simply build a game without having a focus. Subsequently, in considering this problem, it is possible to identify certain "factors" that play a role (see "Who or What Is Involved?"). By relating these factors to each other, we get "relationships" (see "Drawing the Relationships"), and when we look at how these relationships change over time, we get a "process" (see "Going Through the Process"). Together, these four aspects, the problem, factors, relationships, and process, deliver the output—the model of reality—of the world of Reality.

This world of Reality is the world of subject-matter experts, consultants, clients, and other stakeholders that need to be considered in translating the real world to a representation inside a game. In doing this designers should also consider the theories and related disciplines of the subject. This is important, because as Egenfeldt-Nielsen (2007) noticed, game designers often do not know the background of their subject very well. This may lead to superficial, generic, or—even worse—faulty representations that may in the end also be delivered up "to the Inclemencies of Sun and Winters."

To prevent this, designers should consider the world of Reality while designing their game, take the four previously mentioned aspects in mind, and think of the criteria that are part of this world (see "The Criteria of Reality"). But before we get to the criteria, let us first start with the first aspect: the "problem."[1]

Defining the Problem

Almost everything can be made into a game. It can be about nuclear energy or about a computer virus. It can even be about "levee inspection." The underlying motive of why a game was created should relate to a certain *problem*. If people hear about a "problem," they immediately think of "big" or "negative" things, such as a crisis or missing a flight. However, with a problem I simply mean that there is something in the real world that needs to be improved: the situation is in some initial state and we would like it to move to some desired state.

This can relate to making people aware about a brand or by teaching children about a subject. In the first case, people did not know of the brand and in the second case, the children did not have the desired knowledge at first. Both I consider to be a problem which *could* call for the design of a game.

I emphasized the word "could," because although everything can be made into a game, not all problems can be solved with a game (Duke and Geurts 2004). Maybe at one day we would get world peace by playing a game, but it seems rather unlikely.

[1] This level is compared to Levels 4 and 5 much smaller in size. This does not mean, however, that this reflects the "reality" of designing a game. I kept this level short, because it involves a lot of content related to the domains I had to deal with, the domains of soil engineering and water management. To most readers, this will not be as interesting and so I have tried to keep the information to a minimum.

This means that when considering a problem, it should be considered whether a game is a solution to deal with it.

Before this deliberation can take place, the problem at hand should first of all be defined. If a problem is well-defined, clear-cut, and relatively easy, this is a rather simple step to take. Unfortunately, many problems are the opposite: they are ill-structured, unclear, and complex. When a problem has these characteristics, it is called a *wicked problem* (Rittel and Webber 1973).

To illustrate this, let us have a look at the underlying problem of some games. The problem behind, for example, *Re-Mission* seems quite straightforward. On this planet, we have numerous children who suffer from cancer and who have little knowledge about their disease and have a hard time adhering to their medicines. This is a clear problem that deserves attention. The problem behind the *ESP Game* is even clearer. It can be summarized in five words: computer algorithms cannot recognize pictures.

In contrast to these previous examples, the problem behind *SimPort-MV2* is of a different order. Its problem relates to how to build and exploit a harbor extension. With such a problem, many variables play a role and many perspectives can be given. Or what about the problem of *PeaceMaker*? The Israeli-Palestinian conflict already lasts for decades and it is everything but clear what has been going on or how it needs to get resolved.

In defining the problem it is further necessary to discuss it with clients, subject-matter experts, and other stakeholders. If all these people say something similar, designers are lucky, since it is more likely that stakeholders have a different *perception* of the problem. This will especially occur when a game design process involves different clients who have their own interests and needs in using a game. For this reason, it is in particularly important to talk to clients, because in the end it is their (perceived) problem that is going to be solved. If the game does not fulfill this, it becomes useless.

Of course, many game design projects are started without clients or do not need them at all. Some games have, for instance, been developed as "a solution in search of a problem." In such a situation, a company designs a game first and tries to sell it later to clients. And quite some games if not most of them are simply developed and placed on the Internet waiting for someone to play it. Nevertheless, even in these instances, a problem definition was considered. It was just done without considering any stakeholders directly.

For *Levee Patroller* we did consider and consult "subject-matter experts" as well as "clients." To give a more elaborate illustration of what defining the problem is about, I will give a synopsis of my conversations with the subject-matter experts and clients, the Dutch water boards, during the development of this game.

Subject-Matter Experts

From the experts I understood that flood risks are despite their rareness much higher than all other industrial risks added together for the Netherlands. It is a densely

Fig. 3.2 The Maeslantkering, one of the defenses to protect the Netherlands from flooding. ©2009 Rijkswaterstaat (part of the Dutch Ministry of Infrastructure and the Environment). Used with permission

populated country and a flood would have a considerable societal impact. Possible consequences have been experienced during the flood disaster in 1953. About 1800 people drowned and over a 100,000 lost their homes. To prevent anything like this again, enormously large defenses have been built, such as the Maeslantkering (Fig. 3.2). Each arm of this defence is about two-thirds of the Eiffel Tower.

Despite all these measures a recent investigation brought to light that 70% of the levees do not fulfill the safety guidelines. Moreover, it is expected that flood risks will increase in the nearby future due to global warming and continued urbanization.[2] After hurricane Katrina hit New Orleans in 2005, the Dutch became worried that considering these environmental developments they might get their Katrina one day.

Compared to such a disaster the most recent failure was, however, considerably innocent (Fig. 3.3). Nobody got hurt. It nevertheless led to enormous costs for repairing the levee and cleaning up the environment. For this reason, it is desirable that even these relatively "minor" failures are prevented as much as possible.

---

[2]Levee failures are in most cases caused by extreme weather conditions, such as drought, heavy rain, high water, or meltwater. Global warming has effect on the rising of the sea level and on the climate. Both lead to extremist situations. Urbanization, on the other hand, leads to less consolidation of the water by land. This causes flood water to spread and accumulate faster.

Fig. 3.3 A "minor" levee failure in Wilnis in 2003. ©2003 ANP. Used with permission

Training levee patrollers to do their job is certainly not the all encompassing solution to this huge "problem." Many other measures can be taken to safeguard the Netherlands from flooding, including further reinforcements, spatial planning policies (e.g., to live with water instead of fight it), and the use of advanced technologies (e.g., to detect anomalies with satellites). These also need to be taken because it cannot be expected than any human being is able to inspect a levee when a hurricane or spring tide is about to hit.

Patrollers are nonetheless part of the chain and a quite important one. They are the "eyes and ears." They are the ones at the scene, the first responders, who provide information to others on which further action can be considered and taken. Making sure they are capable of detecting potential risks could make a difference in whether a levee breach can be prevented or not.[3]

The problem with this is the following: how can we expect patrollers to detect risks if they have never seen any? Failures occur rarely and the only way most could have seen them is by means of lectures given by the experts that I talked to. The experts themselves, however, told me that apart from the little material in terms of pictures and videos that they can show, this lecture does not provide professionals the necessary "experience." Seeing something and acting upon something are two different ways of processing information, where the latter most likely leads to a much deeper processing of it. At least, this is what experiential learning (Kolb 1984), constructionism (Papert 1980), and other learning theories propose (see also Level 4). To understand this a bit more, consider the quote below by Gee (2004).

[3]Some define risk as "possibility of a failure + the consequences of a failure." I, on the other hand, use the more common sense and (Oxford) dictionary definition which states that a risk is "a possibility that something unpleasant will happen."

Fig. 3.4 Shooting other players or computer bots in *Unreal Tournament*. This game can be modified—which is called modding—into completely other types of games, like the virtual demonstration of a Dutch landscape. Eventually, the technology behind this game, the *Unreal Engine*, was harnessed to develop *Levee Patroller*. ©2004 Atari

> While you do not need to be able to enact a particular social practice (e.g., play basketball or argue before a court) to be able to understand texts from or about that social practice, you can potentially give deeper meanings to those texts if you can. This claim amounts to arguing that producers (people who can actually engage in a social practice) potentially make better consumers (people who can read or understand texts from or about the social practice). (p. 15)

If we translate this to the practice of levee inspection, it simply means that if professionals "actually engage" in the activity, they will be more likely to detect possible risks in time and report these properly than when they hear or read about levee failures. Although the experts did not tell me about all these learning theories—they know a lot about soil engineering, not about learning sciences—they did sense and feel that something was needed to give them experience with failures. But how?

A possible answer was found by serendipity. In the summer of 2005 a student worked part-time at the research institute on recreating a Dutch landscape virtually. He used one of his favorite games, *Unreal Tournament*, to do this (Fig. 3.4). This game, like many others today, makes it possible for users to add or use existing content to make their own game environments. It is even possible to make a completely different game. This type of changing or adding game content to an existing game is called *modding* and its derivative a "mod" (Postigo 2007).

The purpose of creating this mod was to show on an exhibition, which was centered on innovation within the water industry, that it is possible to use this tech-

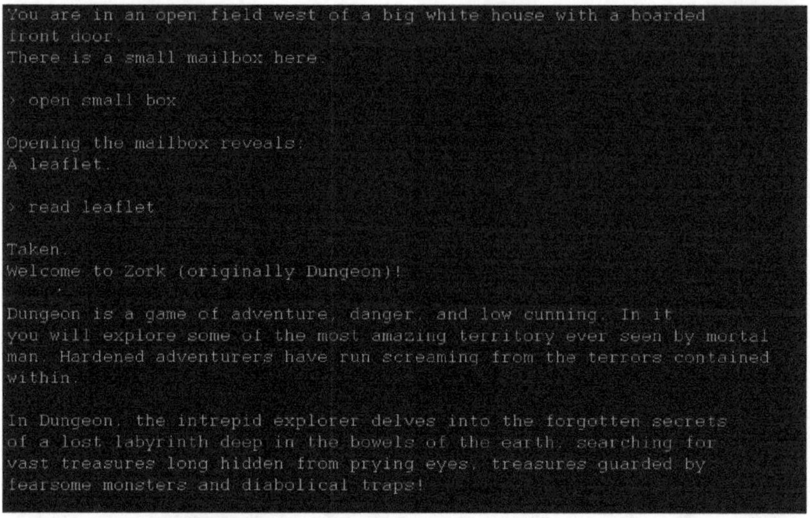

Fig. 3.5 Zork (originally Dungeon), one of the first text adventures. ©1974 MIT

nology. From this virtual demonstration it was a small step—especially considering with what it was made—to consider the use of digital game technology to solve the "experience problem" of levee patrollers.

And although it was found by serendipity, in retrospect the choice of this possibility makes sense. Digital game technology makes it possible to create safe, compelling, and realistic virtual worlds (Gee 2004; Prensky 2001). More importantly, it enables users to get experience with something. As such, using game technology would possibly give patrollers an entertaining as well as a meaningful training experience with levee failures without the occurrence of a flooding in the real world. But how to develop such a game?

The experts themselves had no idea. None of the experts I talked to except for one remembered even playing entertainment games. This expert told me he enjoyed some text adventure from the eighties. Unfortunately, he could not recall the name of it anymore. A lot has clearly changed since then (e.g., see Fig. 3.5). However, funny enough, he was the only one who indicated that the eventual game should also be fun when I asked the experts about their vision. The others only told me it should be realistic and educational.

Back then I also still did not have any clue about the eventual game. After talking to the experts I did have a clear idea of what the problem was. Experience with levee failures is difficult and a game could solve this.

I returned to talk to the experts many times, not only because I needed more information about the world of levee inspection, but also because in the end they would use the game to teach. Using a game to teach requires an extensive understanding of the game (cf., Mishra and Koehler 2006) *and* an approval of the content of the game. Otherwise, the facilitators—the experts in this case—do not want to use it. The experts, therefore, had a double role: they were the experts as well as one of the clients that I needed to take into account.

Clients

The other end-users concern the Dutch water boards. They are one of the oldest institutes in the Netherlands. The boards are currently decentralized public institutes yet financially independent from any other governmental bodies, such as municipalities or the national administration. They get income by raising taxes directly from citizens. Each has their own region in which it operates. Their task has always been to manage the water in terms of quality (think of pollution), quantity (think of a shortage or an abundance of water), and safety (think of the levees). For the latter, they use levee patrollers to inspect the levees.

At the beginning of the project, we only involved five of the 27 existing water boards.[4] We wanted to make sure we had enough funding to start the project, but not involve too many stakeholders as this would probably slow down the design process. The idea was to sell the game later to the other water boards.

Reducing the amount of stakeholders seemed a clever idea, because it turned out that these five already differed widely on a number of issues. This made it difficult to build a general tool that would satisfy each one of them. The list below gives some of the differences that we encountered.

- **Region**: boards operate in different regions. Regions determine the type of water ways (i.e., sea, river, lake, or canal), levees, and the soil. These and other variables affect what type of failures can occur and how they occur.
- **Vocabulary**: each board has its own terminology and conceptions of its practice. Some similarities do exist but overall the differences are striking.
- **Patrollers**: for inspecting the levees some boards use only volunteers, others solely employees or a mix of volunteers and employees. On top of this, and this is not entirely related to whether the board uses volunteers or not, boards differ in the types of responsibilities that they give to the patrollers. At some boards patrollers can, for example, take measures and at others they cannot.
- **Organization**: the organizational setup and procedures surrounding the inspection differ as well. For instance, at some boards patrollers directly communicate to the coordinating field office, whereas at others they do so indirectly. The latter have to communicate to a superintendent who is responsible for a part of the region. This superintendent will further contact the field office.

The above-mentioned differences mattered, because although each board agreed on the problem of not being able to give their patrollers an experience, their perception of what the game needed to cover was not in agreement. And this is a problem of a "problem." Especially, because all of them deemed it to be extremely important that the eventual game was realistic. In fact, most of the water boards rather wanted to speak of a "simulator" than of a "game." According to this vision, we had to stick as closely as possible to the practice of each of the water boards which unfortunately differed to a great extent.

[4]The five participating water boards were Het Hoogheemraadschap van Delfland, Het Hoogheemraadschap van Hollands Noorderkwartier, Waterschap Hollandse Delta, Waterschap Rivierenland, and Waterschap Schieland en de Krimpenerwaard.

Who or What Is Involved?

After the problem has been initially defined, a possible next step in developing a model of reality is to consider more closely who or what is involved. Like any story has its protagonist and any game has its avatar, any problem has its *factors*. With this, I refer to the "objects," whether they are people, organizations, artifacts, or phenomena, that play an important role in the problem. It is important to highlight that in public policy and political science, people and organizations that enact an action in a context are often called "actors," but for simplicity, I call every object related to the problem a factor.

Many factors can exist that contribute to a problem. But not every factor is as *relevant* as others. When looking at the greenhouse effect we have, for example, fuel consumption, the industry production, waste, the number of flights taken, and so on. The *critical factors* are the most important, at least for the problem at hand and how it is defined. If we focus the greenhouse effect problem on the effect of car emissions, then possible critical factors could be cars, drivers, governmental institutes that regulate gas prices and traffic, and even—depending on the boundaries of what is being considered—the companies that produce and deliver gas.

Aside from these factors, we have additional factors, such as the economy (a bad economy may not stimulate environmental considerations), traffic policies (think of road pricing), technological advances (think of the electric car or other alternative energy driven cars), and many others that influence the problem but which are not the focal point. These I consider to be *environmental factors*.

This means that after initially defining the problem, it needs to be decided what factors play a role and to what extent. For a game such as *PeaceMaker* this may seem obvious at first: it would need to involve the Palestinian and Israeli side. However, if we delve deeper, the question appears what parts of the Palestinian and Israeli side need to be involved. Diplomacy has many facets, from military action to humanitarian aids. In all these facets other organizations, people, and elements play a role. The farther one delves into the matter, the more complex it becomes. It is unlikely that this complete complexity needs to be represented in the eventual game. Choices need to be made. It is important to be aware of the choices that are made, since they will reflect the simplifications of the model of reality in comparison to the real world.

For *Levee Patroller* it seems similarly obvious to decide what factors to involve: the patrollers (see "Who Is Involved?") and the failures (see "What Is Involved?"). Nevertheless, as I just argued with *PeaceMaker*, it is necessary to look into both aspects to really see what kind of choices—explicitly or implicitly—are made.

Who Is involved?

If we take it broadly, many people and organizations are involved when it comes to inspecting levees. It goes from the citizens, who can be affected by not detecting

Table 3.1 The different groups within the water emergency response organization

Unit	Tasks & responsibilities
Policy team	Decides about management and very critical issues; develop strategies; accountable
Operational team	Advises policy team about operational procedures; translates decisions policy team to instructions to action center; preoccupied with tactics
Action center	Coordination levee patrollers and construction companies; judge immediate threats; inform operational team; gather information; coordinate measures
Levee patrollers	Inspect levees; communicate findings to action center; assist with emergency procedures; prevent and solve little problems, sometimes with temporary material
Support groups	Implement measures

risks but who can also play the role of "heroes" when they detect failure signals in their backyard and report these to the water boards, to the national government, who coordinates activities in the water chain and needs to decide on structural and far fetching measures when the risks are high, such as inundating an area. In between we have police and fire departments, the military, and municipalities. Nevertheless, the organizations that are mainly responsible for performing the levee inspection concern the water boards.

Within the water boards levee patrollers actually perform the activity. But while they perform it, a complete sub-organization of the water boards, the "water emergency response organization," is closely involved with it and responsible for its execution (see Table 3.1). First of all, generally patrollers communicate their findings to an "action center," a central field office that coordinates the levee inspection. Aside from the patrollers, the action center is in touch with "support groups," such as construction companies, that deliver resources whenever they are needed, like sand bags. These support groups can also be asked to implement the measures.

The action center also informs the "operational team," a group of people consisting of decision makers and experts that decide how to deal with the findings. The operational team, on their turn, are in touch with the policy team if necessary. This team comes into the picture when drastic decisions have to be taken. This policy team is further preoccupied with the development of strategies related to safety and levee inspection.

Normally, organizations outside the water emergency response organization only become involved when the situation gets worse. For example, the military might be called in to help in placing sand bags. It is important to see and understand when and how others become involved when deciding on who is involved with the subject of a game. If we would decide to make the national government a factor, a completely other type of game would eventually be asked for. Even if we decided to only incorporate the water response emergency organization, it would become a different one. It would probably have led to a more strategy type of game in which players have to direct units in preventing a flooding.

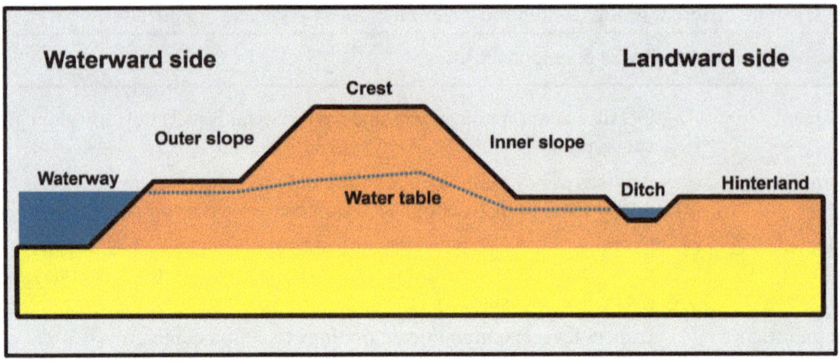

Fig. 3.6 A cross-cut of a generic levee

From the beginning of the project it was clearly stated that the levee patrollers themselves should be the focus, and this has been later acknowledged by the experts and water boards. From the point of view of the tasks of a levee patroller, the strategic and tactical operations by the other stakeholders are not interesting. For this reason, we decided to purely focus on the levee patroller and its interaction with the action center and leave out everything else. The levee patroller thus became our critical factor and the rest were reduced to potential environmental factors.

What Is Involved?

By completely focusing on levee patrollers, it was relatively easy to identify "what" is involved with levee inspection. If, for example, we would have involved the national government, we could have identified amongst many other "whats" international relations and budget considerations. Now it simply came down to what is causing all the problems: the levee failures. This became, therefore, the second critical factor.

Many failures, however, exist. Which would we involve? From the conversations with the water boards we already noticed that some of them have to deal with different failures than others. And we knew that it was sure impossible to implement each one of them. We had to choose. Our first choice was to focus on "green levees." These are levees that consist of soil, grass, and other natural material. They are not made up of technical constructions, such as can be found with sluices, walls made of bricks or concrete, and with the Maeslantkering (Fig. 3.2).

To further refine our choice we needed to get a better understanding of these green levees and how they could fail. Figure 3.6 shows a cross-cut of a generic levee. From this, we see that a levee protects the hinterland from flooding if the water level of a waterway, whether a river or a canal, raises. But unlike what many people would think, such barriers do not obstruct all the water from reaching the hinterland. Waterways remain connected to the hinterland by means of groundwater. The height of this groundwater is called the "water table" (or phreatic surface). The soil below the water table is saturated and the soil above the table is unsaturated. In plain English, everything below the table is wet, everything above it is dry.

Fig. 3.7 A failure with a large settlement at the inner slope of the levee. The area is also very watery, a signal of liquefaction. The mechanism behind this failure is "macro-instability," as a large part of the levee is moving landwards

These types of levees can basically fail in two ways. Either the levee becomes "out of balance" or parts of it are being "worn away." The first has to do with the *stability* of a levee. When the water level changes, the water table changes as well. This affects the composition of saturated and unsaturated soil and could make the levee unbalanced (see Fig. 3.7). If the water level is too low, it could lead to settlements toward the waterward side. If it is too high, settlements could appear toward the landward side. It could also happen that due to the water pressure cracks appear on the crest or slopes, from which the levee further deteriorates.

The second way in which a levee could typically fail has to do with *erosion*. The revetment of a levee, the cover or the most outer layer of a levee on the inner or outer slope, plays an important role in this regard. The revetment, whether hard (i.e., stones or wood) or grass, protects the levee. It makes sure the soil underneath it does not get washed away when water runs over or splashes against it.[5] If soil gets washed away, the levee slowly degrades and loses its function (see Fig. 3.8).

Much agreement exists so far. When going further, however, it turned out to be a big mess. No consensus could be found among theories, experts, water boards in how to name, categorize, and report failures. As a result, we had to come up with our own way of looking at failures. In the end, we decided that a failure consists of one or more signals. Examples of signals are cracks, water outflow, damaged

[5]Grass revetment is less likely to sustain against waves and a strong current than hard revetment, and for this reason hard revetment can be mostly seen around rivers and the sea.

Fig. 3.8 A failure with as signal a damaged hard revetment. The mechanism behind this failure concerns "erosion outer slope." Without protection of the stones, the water will flush away the sand underneath it

revetment, and settlement. We further decomposed the two basic ways of failing into a number of subtypes, like macro- and micro-instability and erosion inner and outer slope, and simplified the situation by deciding that a failure could only have one underlying failure mechanism. Based on this, the regional differences, and the wishes of the different water boards, we chose eight failures and implemented these in close collaboration with subject-matter experts.

Drawing the Relationships

We can draw *relationships* between almost anything. For this reason, it is important to be very explicit to determine *what* the relationships are between the factors of a certain problem when creating a model of reality. To explicate relationships, it is first of all important to know with what factors we are dealing with. Subsequently, it is necessary to consider what the *boundaries* are. Even if a clear focus exists, it is impossible to consider everything. To consider the boundaries, the best way to think about it is to think of an "imaginary box." The relevant factors should be placed inside the box and those that are not outside of it. In other words, this means that the critical and other relevant factors are placed inside the box and all environmental factors outside it. The factors inside the box are called *internal factors*.

With the imaginary box in mind, we have explicated the focus by making clear what is included and what is not. Aside from the environmental factors, the imaginary box has two other external components that have to be looked at: the *input* and *output*. The input of the box is a stimulating factor, something that arouses other factors. To use the example of the greenhouse effect again, the introduction of governmental subsidies for producing environmental friendly cars could be a stimulating event that influences some of the internal factors, such as the production costs of environmental friendly cars. With lower costs to produce environmental friendly cars, it becomes more attractive to consumers to buy them.

The output of the box are factors on which we judge the performance of the interaction between the internal factors. This could be a product or something more abstract, such as quality. For the greenhouse effect example, this could be the amount of carbon dioxide emissions measured in grams per kilometre (g/km). Environmental factors indirectly influence such outputs, as they influence the internal factors. A poor economic situation, for instance, will result in consumers buying cheap cars, cars that are not environmental friendly, and cause production companies to downgrade their investments into research and development. The latter means it is less likely that new innovative technology, which could make a difference in production costs and fuel efficiency, amongst other factors, will be developed.

This may sound logical, but why would drawing relationships be important for game design? For designing a game an overview is needed of the real world situation of the problem at hand. Creating such an overview already takes place when defining the problem and subsequently by deciding who or what to involve. Defining the problem gives the necessary focus to start of with and by deciding on the factors it makes evident which factors within the problem are relevant and on what level (i.e., very detailed or abstract). When drawing relationships, however, it becomes really clear how factors relate to each other and what sort of importance they have on an overall level. Earlier choices may be revised or elaborated on, by being forced to put everything together. This means that by drawing relationships, the "big picture" is retrieved about a real world situation. This systematic overview is needed to properly translate the model of reality into a game.

Sometimes such a model of reality is explicitly visible in a game. This is what I like so much about a game called *Democracy 2*. In the game, players become the president of a country and the goal is to stay president. Sustaining this power position can be done by winning the re-elections and this can only occur when the majority of the population is happy. To make them happy, the motivations, loyalties, and desires of everyone in the country need to be balanced against budget, diplomatic relations, and other political considerations (make an eco-friendly green paradise or a socialist utopia?).

The great thing about the game is that to make decisions, players need to interact with the internal factors that are divided in different "policy arenas," such as justice, economy, transportation, and foreign policy (Fig. 3.9). By rolling the cursor over a factor, for example the Gross Domestic Product (GDP), the player can see what factors relate to GDP and how. The screen will show the relationships with red or green colored lines that are connected to the factor of interest and its related factors. A red line indicates a negative relationship. This means an increase in X will lead to a decrease in Y.

Fig. 3.9 Deciding on policy actions in *Democracy 2*. The different segments represent the policy arenas. In the middle the several societal movements and groups can be seen. ©2007 Positech Games. Used with permission

A green line, in contrary, indicates a positive relationship. This means that an increase in X will also lead to an increase in Y. The strength and direction of the relationships is indicated by how fast the shady squares on top of the connected lines move from the factors to the factor of interest. It is also possible that a relationship is bidirectional. In Fig. 3.9 we can see that GDP is negatively affected by immigration and criminality and positively by air travel and international trade. GDP positively affects air travel and immigration and negatively affects the air quality.

When players want to take measures to influence a factor, say again the GDP, they have to trace back to see what factors relate to it. Depending on whether the influencing factor can be directly manipulated or not, players need to continue tracing relationships by rolling the cursor over these factors to see by what factors they are affected. Players can recognize the direct manipulable factors, because they are colored black while the indirect manipulable factors are colored blue.

For example, petrol tax is directly manipulable. By decreasing this tax, it will positively affect the GDP. Air travel is not directly manipulable. By rolling the cursor over this factor, we can see that it is influenced by "high earnings" which on its turn is influenced by the directly manipulable factors income and corporation taxes. By increasing the taxes, the number of flights—the model assumes that flying is price sensitive—will lower. By going through all of this, players can decide what measures they want to take.

More importantly, by doing this players interact with the model of reality of the game. On the screen all factors are shown and their relationships. Some external influences are given as well, such as news items, but in essence the model is explicitly shown on the screen. Games like *SimCity* or *Civilization* have similar models, but these are not directly visible to the players. In these games, the model and its outcomes are symbolized and visualized on the screen and are not as abstract as with *Democracy 2*.

For developing the model of reality of *Democracy 2*, its designer, Cliff Harris, most likely considered the critical factors of the game. This eventually became the president, its government, the population, and the policy arenas. He further identified what other factors play a role, like taxes, pollution, GDP, and so on. From there he mapped the relationships to all of these factors and made this partly explicit on the screen (i.e., the interface does not show everything, like the precise influence of a factor on another). He left out of the model the local, state, and the real federal politics (and its subsequent dynamics). He basically simplified the political arena to a situation in which the president gets advice by governmental members but eventually decides on all matters by him or herself. This shows that even a quite complex model i greatly simplified with respect to the real world.

Not every game has and needs such an elaborate and complex model. To illustrate this, for *Levee Patroller* we have two critical factors, the patroller and the failures, and a small number of other factors that we considered relevant, such as the weather, the severity of the situation, the types of levees, the types of waterways, the action center, and the occurrence of a flood or not (Fig. 3.10). Although the weather normally influences the severity of the situation and the types of failures that could occur, we reduced the weather to visual stimuli. It can rain or not, but it only affects the visibility of the gameworld. It can, therefore, be considered an environmental factor.

The severity of the situation concerns an input. It determines largely what will occur in the environment. What occurs depends on the types of levees and waterways, because these affect what failures can occur. Patrollers relate to the failures and the action center: they have to find, analyze, and report these failures and communicate with the action center about the severity of the situation and about taking measures. If the failures are not found, they become more serious and could eventually lead to a levee breach. If they are found and properly dealt with, then the environment is saved. The output of the model concerns thus whether a flood occurs or not.

The model of *Levee Patroller* is fairly simple. But even when it is as simple as this, it helps to explicate what it is about. From this, it can be clearly seen what the game will cover and what it will not cover. It gives the "big picture." To develop such a model, it help to create a diagram similar to Fig. 3.10. The limitation of drawing relationships concerns, however, "time." It provides a static image of the model of reality. For this reason, in further developing the model a final aspect needs to be considered: the *process*.

Going Through the Process

In the real world "processes" are abundant. We can look amongst others at software processes, business processes, and evolutionary processes. All of these "processes"

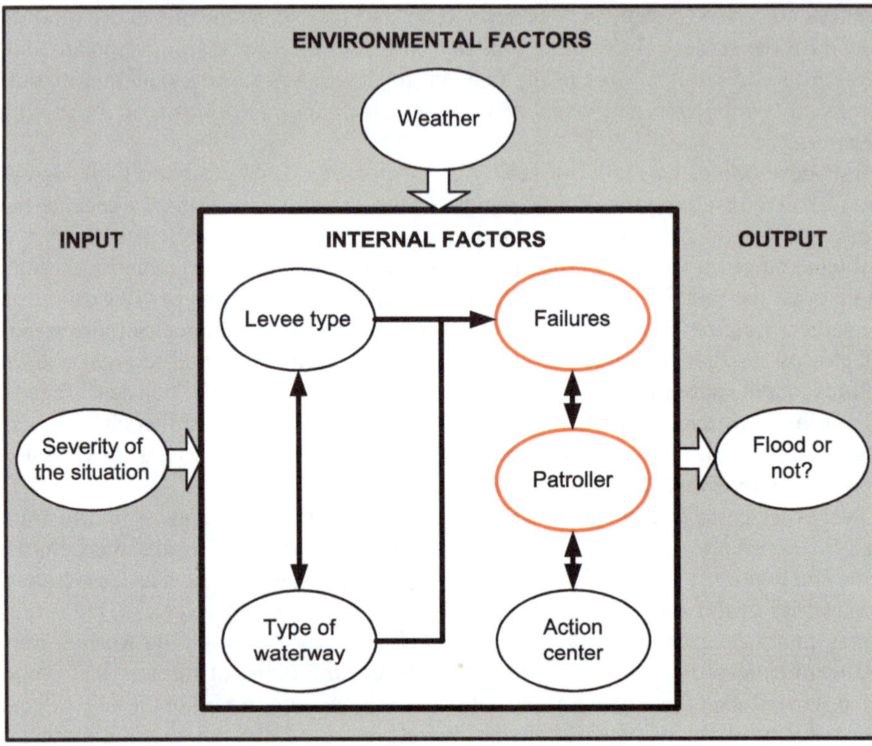

Fig. 3.10 The fairly simple diagram of *Levee Patroller*. The *red colored ovals* are the critical factors

can be considered for a game. What these "processes" have in common—what makes them a *process*—is that they do not depict something at a certain moment in time. In contrary, they describe how "what" gets from A to B and what happens in between. Therefore, a process does not provide one big picture, it gives multiple pictures.

Considering a real world process for a game could be important, because games are by definition "processual" (or "procedural," as some scholars prefer to call it) and this nature can be harnessed. In playing a game, the players starts with an initial condition and continuously reaches other conditions by interacting with the game until the desired or end condition is achieved. This sets games apart from other media (see also Level 5). They are not paintings, which are static, and unlike movies, they depend on the interaction with the user. Playing a game is like entering a process, which changes according to the factors and their relationships of the underlying model.

In games, different ways exist to reach an end condition. It can be by solving a problem, as in "figuring out who murdered Ms. Ratchet" and then the process would consist of collecting evidence to proof this. It can also be a number, as in a game to "find ten rabbits." The game will then continue until all ten rabbits are found. And for some games the process is literally about going from A to B, by needing to go from one location to another. This is the case with most "platform" games. Finally, the end condition can be another state. Like in *Civilization* players change the state of the game by interacting with the system. They start off in 4000 BC with a small town with a few inhabitants and can build up their civilization into a modern society. These state changes are used in game stories as well. By reaching a certain state, a new part of the story will unfold, and this goes on until the end state is reached and the story is completely told.

To harness the power of games it becomes possible for designers to make use of its processual characteristic. It needs to be emphasized that it is not necessary that this "game process" is related to the real world. A game like the *ESP Game*, for instance, does not have a real world process to which it relates to. It has a "process" related to the world of Play, which is actually the *gameplay* of entering words to describe a picture and then trying to see if it matches with the words of another player, and a "process" related to the world of Meaning, which is actually a set of *operations* that enable that a useful database is formed based on the input of players. Games are processual but with process I do not refer to the gameplay or to the operations that create some value. Instead, I refer to real world processes that can be modeled and subsequently simulated into a game environment.

To clarify this, let me give an example of a game in which it is extremely important to implement actual real world processes correctly. In this game called *Pulse!!*, which is aimed at health-profession students and practitioners, players get into a virtual intensive care unit and need to assess, diagnose, and treat the injuries of patients during catastrophic incidents, such as combat or bioterrorism (Fig. 3.11). The game offers a variety of pathologies, patients, settings, and emergencies in a controlled virtual environment. This way, players are exposed to practical experience with rare, life-threatening patient problems. By repetitive practice on reproducible patients it allows for errors to be corrected and performance to be improved—at no risk to real patients. This game is about an actual real world process: the process of treating a patient. To do this well, the game faithfully replicates human bodies with symptoms and presents real-world treatment options with authentic, simulated consequences. In the game, players can click on several virtual objects, such as body parts of the patient or medical personnel, and options appear that can be chosen. After choosing an option, for example using a stethoscope, the player can execute subsequent actions and the patient may respond to this. In case of the stethoscope, the player can click on the body parts where it wants to apply the stethoscope. Players, therefore, have to critically think what steps they take, how they take them, and in what order.

Clearly, if the designers did not faithfully simulate the real world process—if they incorporated wrong procedures, neglected certain steps or represented symptoms and treatment incorrectly—then this could have adverse consequences when players treat real patients. To prevent this, the designers of this game carefully consulted with subject-matter experts to make sure the procedures and representations in the game are similar to those in the real world.

Even in lesser realistic looking games, a process may need to be considered. With another medical game, *Re-Mission*, which adopts a more symbolic rather than real-

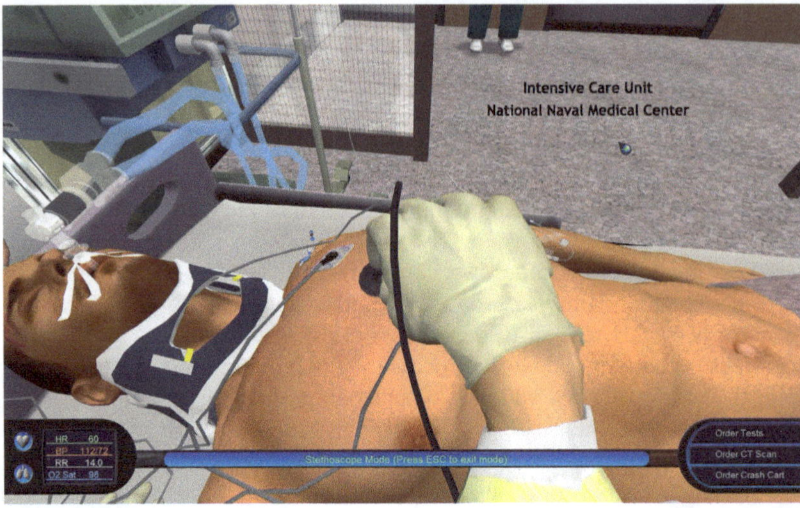

Fig. 3.11 Treating a patient in *Pulse!!*. ©2010 Texas A&M University-Corpus Christi/Office of Special Projects. Used with permission

istic approach, the designers still considered the behavior of tumor cells, bacteria, and immune cells (Tate et al. 2009). When, for example, the in-game patient has skipped his chemotherapy doses, the "chemo-concentrating blaster misfires periodically, allowing cancer cells to escape and become drug resistant" (p. 31). Depicting this process is important as one of the game's purposes is to get better treatment adherence. When patients play the game, they will understand the behavior of cancer cells and the need for chemotherapy.

For *Levee Patroller* we considered two types of real world processes, one related to the procedures that the patrollers need to take (see "Procedural Steps") and another to the development of failures (see "Failure Development"). Both are illustrated below.

Procedural Steps

Unlike fire workers or police officers the task of a levee patroller is pretty straightforward: inspecting levees and that is about it. Fire workers get cats and little boys out of trees, pull cows out of ditches, remove people who are stuck in their vehicles, next to extinguishing fires, while police officers distribute receipts to incorrectly parked cars, guard important people or goods, deal with local quarrels, next to chasing criminals. In contrast, levee patrollers inspect levees, levees, levees and levees.

The comparison with fire workers and police officers is not completely fair. Being a levee patroller is not a 24/7 job. It is not even a daily job. At most water boards, the inspection takes regularly place once a month and if an emergency situation is expected or is happening. Levee patrollers could in this respect better be compared with emergency safety coordinators in companies. Like patrollers, they only take action whenever there is a reason for it.

I was able to decompose the sole task of patrollers into five steps based on the talks with experts and the water boards. The steps are listed below.

1. Finding failures.
2. Reporting signals that make up a failure.
3. Communicating reports to others.
4. Diagnosing the situation.
5. Taking measures when necessary.

The first step is essential. Without finding a failure there is nothing to report or communicate about. Finding a failure is, however, not that easy, because it requires to recognize the *signals* that indicate the possible occurrence of a failure and these signals are frequently very subtle. Upon finding a signal, a patroller needs to report this signal and look for others to get a complete picture of the situation. The procedures for reporting depends on the type of signal that is found. For a crack it is for instance necessary to measure the length, width, and depth.

The next step after reporting a failure concerns the communication of the findings to the action center. When doing this, it is important that patrollers are aware of the failure's location. It often happened that the wrong location was mentioned. This could be dramatic in case a levee breach is about to occur. After receiving the information, the action center gives further directions and these differ per water board. At some boards, patrollers may get the responsibility for diagnosing the situation which involves the determination of the failure mechanism behind a failure and the severity of the situation. They may even take measures. At other water boards the diagnosis and measures are coordinated by the action center. In those instances the patroller does not play a role at all anymore. Instead, construction companies and experts are called to perform these steps.

Although not strictly following the procedures may not directly have as large consequences as in treating a patient, the water boards claimed with much emphasis that they did not want to teach their patrollers anything that is different from their real situation. They were afraid that they would behave according to the game after playing it. This brought us into a difficult position, because what kind of procedure did we need to incorporate into the game without dissatisfying any of our clients?

Failure Development

The second "process" concerned the development of failures. To get insight into this process, we created a "process model" for each of the failures. A process model of a failure is basically nothing more than a description of its development over time and under different circumstances. Take a look at Fig. 3.12 for an example. This figure shows how damage of the revetment by animals could develop over time. If the situation gets worse, a crack can appear from which at later instances water can

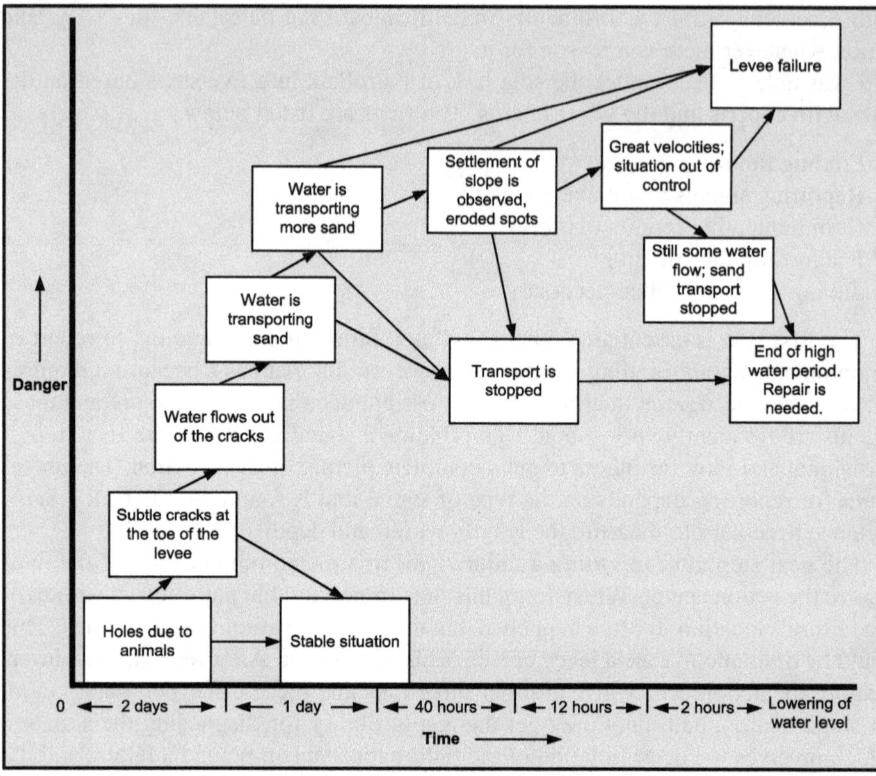

Fig. 3.12 An example of a process model of a failure. It shows how damage of the revetment by animals could develop over time

flow out and even sand. At different moments in time, the failure development can stop by itself. If it does not, it could lead to a levee failure in the end.

Creating these process models proved to be difficult as almost nobody has ever seen the development of a failure in the real world from start to finish, except for a couple of experts who performed large-scale experiments. This meant we were very dependent on a number of specialists to help us in defining what could possibly happen. It also meant little consensus exists about how failures develop. Therefore, it is not strange that the eventual model implementations in the game are criticized until this very day. On the positive side, by creating and implementing the process models we actually contributed to the knowledge base of soil engineering, as they did not exist before.

The Criteria of Reality

When defining the problem, considering who or what is involved, drawing the relationships, and going through the process, designers create a "model of reality."

This model is continuously refined and reiterated during the design until the game is finished. Creating such a model is valuable in and of itself. Although the eventual purpose of the model is to be used for game development, the creation of it has many similarities with what consultants do when they tackle a problem. To come up with a solution, they also analyze the situation as-is and use a variety of modeling techniques to do this.

But aside that the world of Reality is involved with the creation of this model, it has a number of criteria that it puts forth in judging the quality of a game. From my experience, I have picked three criteria that belong to this world and which I discuss below in no particular order. These are "flexibility," "fidelity," and "validity."

Flexibility

The real world is diverse and chaotic. This is illustrated with the development of *Levee Patroller*. The clients of this game, the water boards, differ on a number of fundamental aspects, from the responsibilities they give to patrollers to the failures that can happen in their region. This means it becomes difficult to design a single generalizable game, especially because each board does not want to train their people aspects they do not need to know or which are different from their own practice. In other words, what is asked for is *flexibility*. The clients need the possibility to change the game as it suits them.

The real world is also dynamic. This is another reason to consider flexibility. Not only may interests change in what needs to be trained, new (scientific) findings, procedures, or even failures can be established over time. For example, the failure in Wilnis formed a failure that was not known about before (Fig. 3.3). The failure was caused by drought and not by high water or heavy rain. This never happened before. If the eventual game is unable to cope with these sort of changes or new insights, the game quickly becomes outdated. To prevent this, it is desirable to build the game in a modular way. This way, the game remains flexible for future developments.[6]

A final characteristic of the real world is that it is very rich. Due to this, it is impossible to incorporate everything at once. We decided, for example, to start with eight failures, but these clearly do not cover all the possibilities. For this reason, it is not only relevant to build a game modularly for future developments. It is also smart to make it modular so the game can easily be extended for extra features.

The criterion of flexibility, which considers to what extent the game can be changed on the fly, for future developments, and for extra features, is of less importance when games are developed for a specific event that lasts for a temporary time. Additionally, if the topic of a game is relatively simple, clear-cut, unambiguous, and/or clearly bounded it is not that important as well.

---

[6]In fact, we recently added failures related to drought to the game.

Fidelity

Although each game has some sort of link with the real world, entertainment games are in general more fictional than games with a serious purpose. The latter also need to have a clear link with the real world, because it is based upon it and eventually also needs to affect it. The water boards as well as the experts demanded this link to be seen very explicitly in the game. They told me that the game needed to be "as realistic as possible." With this they meant that the look of the game and what is being done in the game needed to be as *similar* as possible to the real situation. This demand relates to a criterion that is derived from the training literature: *fidelity* (Feinstein and Cannon 2001).

Fidelity can be defined as the "level of realism" presented to the player. It measures the degree to what the game is similar to the real world and according to Hays and Singer (1989) this degree can be measured in two dimensions:

> ... the degree of similarity between the training situation and the operational situation which is simulated. It is a two dimensional measurement of this similarity in terms of: (1) the physical characteristics, for example visual, spatial, kinesthetic, etc.; and (2) the functional characteristics, for example the informational, stimulus, and response options of the training situation. (p. 50, as cited in Feinstein and Cannon 2001)

In other words, fidelity relates to how the game looks and feels (the physical dimension) and how the player and game environment interact with each other (the functional dimension) compared to the real world.[7] The best way to clarify this is by looking at "flight simulators." The types of flight simulators range from computer-based games, such as the well-known *Flight Simulator* series, to a cockpit replica connected to a simulator, up to a full-size cockpit replica mounted on hydraulic (or electromechanical) actuators. In translating the real world, each one of them tries to get every detail right when it comes to the available information, the possible actions, and the consequences of actions. All three types have, therefore, a high fidelity on the functional dimension.

On the physical dimension, however, clear differences between the types can be seen. The game versions have the least physical fidelity, because they are played in a dissimilar environment from the one a pilot normally operates in. The cockpit replica mounted on hydraulic actuators has on its turn a higher physical fidelity in comparison to the simulator which is only connected to a cockpit, because it has "platform motion," a mechanism that creates the effect or feeling of being in a moving vehicle. The feeling derived from this motion creates for a higher fidelity, as an airplane normally also moves and the positioning of the airplane gives important cues to what is happening.[8]

---

[7] Some scholars add a third dimension: the psychological dimension (Kinkade and Wheaton 1972). Psychological fidelity refers to the degree that a player perceives the game to duplicate the look and feel (the physical dimension) and his interactions with the real world (the functional dimension).

[8] It is possible to argue that the addition of platform motion not only increases the physical fidelity but also the functional fidelity. The motion provides extra informational cues and this makes the interaction between player and the environment more comparable to the actual situation.

Other than that the above may suggest, the criterion of fidelity is not sacred. Many studies have looked into the relationship between fidelity and its effectiveness (Feinstein and Cannon 2001). From these studies it was found that a higher fidelity does not necessarily translate into more effective training or enhanced learning. We can—again—best illustrate this by looking at flight simulators. From a meta-analysis of studies into the effectiveness of these simulators, it was shown that "platform motion," which is very costly to implement, has little to no effect on the training results. Thus although platform motion increases fidelity, it apparently does not give an extra added value to the experience (Hays et al. 1992). Moreover, it was even found that a high fidelity can even hinder effectiveness, as it could overstimulate the trainees.

Due to these and other findings, Hays and Singer (1989) stress that a "simulator" does not need to be an exact representation of the real world to be effective. They even stress that it may be necessary to "depart from realism in order to provide the most effective training" (p. 15). This is also something that TGD stresses: a balance needs to be found between the worlds of Reality and Meaning (and also with Play, but in this case it relates foremost to the other two worlds).

Such a balance is above-all needed, because no fidelity at all or too little may make a game also not effective. Therefore, fidelity remains an important criterion for designing games. It is just one, and this is in fact true for all the other criteria as well, for which the importance is dependent on the game that needs to be designed. For example, a game such as *Pulse!!* has placed much more importance on fidelity than *Re-Mission*. We can already retrieve this from just the looks of both games (see Figs. 3.11 and 2.7).

Validity

Closely related but significantly different to fidelity, concerns another criterion called *validity*. Whereas fidelity is about "similarity" in the look and feel of a game, validity is about the *correspondence* of what in the game happens and what it does in the real world. The degree of correspondence between the game and the real world or to what extent it is *isomorphic* is what this criterion measures. But as Peters et al. (1998) explain, this definition is not very useful, as it does not clarify what "correspondence" means. Therefore, they refer to the more utilitarian definition of Raser (1969) who defined, with respect to using games, validity as "the extend that investigation of that model provides the same outcomes as would investigation in the reference system."

A key distinction when investigating the eventual model of reality of the game and the real world has to be made in *internal* and *external* validity (Feinstein and Cannon 2001). In experimental research the first refers to an indication of the reliability of the results. If confounding variables are not ruled out, cause-effect relationships, such as "playing games increases aggression" cannot be made. For example, if playing games leads to aggression at all, it is not very likely that all of them do. The type of a game is, therefore, a variable that also needs to be taken into account.

External validity, on the other hand, refers to whether the results can be generalized to other settings. If playing a game leads to aggression, does this mean that those players are also more aggressive in other contexts, such as at school?

For the design of games the distinction between internal and external validity have a slightly different meaning. Internal validity relates to the content and how it is represented in the logic and structure of the game.[9] It asks the question, "to what extent does a game accurately represent desired phenomena?" For instance, in a game that simulates a marketing department of a product company the specific question could be asked whether advertising expenditures actually contribute to demand. It is an assessment of the model of reality: of its factors, relationships, and processes.

Many types of validity have been termed and defined, ranging from "representational validity" to "content validity." For the purposes of the world of Reality, I would like to propose two types, defined by Raser (1969), that relate to the internal validity and to aspects that have been discussed in this chapter:[10]

- **Structural validity**: a game is valid to the degree that its structure (the theory and assumptions on which it is built) can be shown to be isomorphic to the reference system. It does not need to be similar, but it does need to have congruency. We can think of the types of cancer cells and levee failures. This relates to "factors" and their "relationships."
- **Process validity**: a game is valid to the degree that the processes observed in the game are isomorphic to those observed in the reference system. For processes we can think of flows of information or resources, procedures, or the way a failure develops. This relates, as its name suggest, to the "process."

Like the notion of external validity in experimental research, with games the external validity relates to the performance of the game in relation to other settings as well. It asks the question, "to what extent does a game behave like its reference system?" If a game behaves like its reference system, say a simulated company acts just as the real one, we can make statements, or even predictions, from the game and

---

[9] Another and third construct related to the evaluation of models, simulations, and games is *verifiability* (Feinstein and Cannon 2001). This relates to assessing whether the constructed artifact is operating as intended. It looks, therefore, if it is implemented according to plan. This involves debugging codes and removing other types of errors from the design. Verifiability is an important part of the game design process, but I do not consider it to be part of any of the worlds. Instead, I think it is part of the design process in general.

[10] Raser (1969) defined two other types of validity next to structural and process validity: psychological reality and predictive validity. The latter is similar to the term "external validity" that I use. It relates to the degree that a game can reproduce historical situations, outcomes, or predict the future. The first, psychological reality, is about the perception of the player to what degree the game is realistic. Such a perception can involve validity, as players may recognize correspondences to the real world, but it for sure includes the look and feel of the game. This means psychological reality also deals with fidelity (or, in other words, includes psychological fidelity). To avoid confusion and keep the two closely related criteria of fidelity and validity separate from each other, I do not discuss this type. It is, however, relevant to know that the perceived fidelity and validity by players may differ from other means of measuring these constructs.

Fig. 3.13 Managing a university with *Virtual U*. ©Woodrow Wilson Foundation. Used with permission

apply them to the real world. A game can be said to be externally valid if behavior in the game is similar to behavior in the real world.

To clarify this, take for example the game *Virtual U*, a *SimCity*-like game about managing a university (Fig. 3.13). If it turns out that players make the same sort of management decisions in the same situations as real managers do, or even better, when real managers know how to play better than others, the game can be said to be externally valid "to some degree." To some degree, because it is really difficult if not impossible to say that a game is fully externally valid under all sorts of circumstances. A game incorporates a model of reality and models are always a simplification of the real world. This means it is unlikely that a game always behaves similar to the real world.

Compared to fidelity, validity is much more sacred. A game may have little fidelity, it still must have validity. The knowledge that *Re-Mission*, a low fidelity game, for example, provides about cancer needs to be structurally valid. Only when a game does not need to have a correspondence to the real world, it does not matter so much.

From Reality to Meaning

The world of Reality is about dealing with the real world. Designers may need to talk to clients, subject-matter experts, and to potential users to elicit information about the subject for which they need to develop a model of reality. Or they do not talk to anybody but simply gather information from books, the Internet, or other sources to develop a model. Whatever approach is taken, designers probably try to develop an "objective" model as much as possible unless the point is to be "subjective," by being provocative or voicing an opinion about the subject.

According to Bogost (2006), however, the "objective simulation is a myth because games cannot help but carry the baggage of ideology" (p. 135). Whereas it is driven by ideology or the mere interpretation of the information, the eventual model of reality is without doubt "biased." This occurs "even when designers know a topic well" (Egenfeldt-Nielsen 2007).

The cause of biases relates to the translation of the real world to a model. To give an example of such biases, let us look at those of *SimCity*'s, who have been thoroughly discussed:

> *SimCity* has been criticized from both the left and right for its economic model. It assumes that low taxes will encourage growth while high taxes will hasten recessions. It discourages nuclear power, while rewarding investment in mass transit. And most fundamentally, it rests on the empiricist, technophilic fantasy that the complex dynamics of city development can be abstracted, quantified, simulated, and micromanaged. (Friedman 1999)

What *SimCity* has become or what any game will become is driven by those who design it: the designers and their interactions with each other and with others. Due to this social constructive process it is unlikely that two or more teams with the same assignment will reach the same end result. It is even unlikely that if one design team would hypothetically start all over again, it would lead to the same end result. Games are constructed artifacts and this makes them inherently subjective.

Aside from designer's subjectivity, the user's subjectivity comes into play as well. Players interpret signs from a game and this interpretation process is fueled by as much as what the game includes as what it excludes (Bogost 2006). The inclusion gives a reason to think about something and the exclusion leaves room for interpretations by the players.[11] This is important to acknowledge, because it means that players may not derive the same sort of "meaning" from the same experience.

Such differences may be wanted or not.[12] All of this depends on the consideration of the world of Meaning. This world investigates what values should be retrieved from the game experience. From this world (and also the world of Play), the real world and its model of reality is further (re)considered. If we take *SimCity* again as an example, Starr (1994) says about its model of reality the following:

[11]This idea, as Bogost (2006) explains, "that a sign derives meaning from how it differs from other signs is certainly nothing new; this is the basis of Saussurean semiotics. Saussure understood language as a 'system of differences'—the signifier 'dog' has meaning only insofar as it is not the signifier 'cat." (p. 105). For the same reason, it can be assumed that the interpretation of a game relies as much or more on what it excludes than on what it includes.

[12]For difference in interpretation, Gonzalo Frasca's advice may be helpful: "trust your players and do not worry too much if they read the game differently from what you intended. The fact that they can read it personally means that they can construct with it something that is important to them, and that is the most clear sign that your game has succeeded" (Frasca in Isbister 2006, p. 20).

> The models deliberately exaggerate effects to provide feedback to the player; in real life, the effects of many decisions would be imperceptible. The purpose of *SimCity* is not accuracy or prediction but communication... Asked how he handles controversial choices, like the effects of tax rates on development, Wright [the designer of *SimCity*] dodges the question and says, "We go for game play"—whatever is most fun.

This shows that the world of Reality has been traded-off against Meaning and eventually also Play. It also shows that the design of games forces designers to bias their games: to make them more meaningful or more "fun." But before we look deeper into the interplay between the three worlds, we first have to go from the world of Reality to the world of Meaning.

Bibliography

Literature Bibliography

Bogost, I. (2006). *Unit operations: an approach to video game criticism*. Cambridge: The MIT Press.

Borges, J. L. (1998). *Borges: collected fictions*. New York: Viking.

Duke, R. D., & Geurts, J. (2004). *Policy games for strategic management: pathways into the unknown*. Amsterdam, the Netherlands: Dutch University Press.

Egenfeldt-Nielsen, S. (2007). *Beyond edutainment: the educational potential of computer games*. London: Continuum Press.

Feinstein, A. H., & Cannon, H. M. (2001). Fidelity, verifiability, and validity of simulation: constructs for evaluation. *Developments in Business Simulation and Experiential Learning*, *28*, 57–67.

Friedman, T. (1999). The semiotics of SimCity. *First Monday*, *4*(4). http://firstmonday.org/.

Gee, J. (2004). *What video games have to teach us about learning and literacy*. New York: Palgrave Macmillan.

Hays, R. T., & Singer, M. J. (1989). *Simulation fidelity in training system design: bridging the gap between reality and training*. New York: Springer.

Hays, R. T., Jacobs, J. W., Prince, C., & Salas, E. (1992). Flight simulator training effectiveness: a meta-analysis. *Military Psychology*, *4*(2), 63–74.

Isbister, K. (2006). *Better game characters by design: a psychological approach*. San Francisco: Elsevier.

Kinkade, R., & Wheaton, G. (1972). Training device design. In H. P. Van Cott & R. G. Kinkade (Eds.), *Human engineering guide to equipment design* (pp. 668–699). Washington: American Institutes for Research.

Kolb, D. A. (1984). *Experiential learning: experience as the source of learning and development*. Upper Saddle River: Prentice Hall.

Mishra, P., & Koehler, M. J. (2006). Technological pedagogical content knowledge: a framework for teacher knowledge. *Teachers College Record*, *108*(6), 1017–1054.

Papert, S. (1980). *Mindstorms: children, computers, and powerful ideas*. New York: Basic Books.

Peters, V., Vissers, G., & Heijne, G. (1998). The validity of games. *Simulation & Gaming*, *29*(1), 20–30.

Postigo, H. (2007). Of mods and modders: chasing down the value of fan-based digital game modifications. *Games and Culture*, *2*(4), 300–313.

Prensky, M. (2001). *Digital game-based learning*. New York: McGraw-Hill.

Raser, J. (1969). *Simulations and society: an exploration of scientific gaming*. Boston: Allyn and Bacon.

Rittel, H. W. J., & Webber, M. M. (1973). Dilemmas in a general theory of planning. *Policy Sciences*, *4*(2), 155–169.
Starr, P. (1994). Seductions of sim: policy as a simulation game. *The American Prospect*, *17*, 19–29.
Tate, R., Haratatos, J., & Cole, S. (2009). Hopelab's approach to Re-Mission. *International Journal of Learning and Media*, *1*(1), 29–35.

Game Bibliography

Anderson, T., Blank, M., Daniels, B., & Lebling, D. (1979). *Zork* [Mainframe]. Cambridge: MIT.
Delft University of Technology, Tygron Serious Gaming, & Port of Rotterdam (2006). *SimPort-MV2* [PC]. The Hague, the Netherlands: Tygron Serious Gaming.
Deltares, & Delft University of Technology (2006). *Levee Patroller: The Levee Inspection Simulator* [PC]. Delft, the Netherlands: Delft GeoSystems.
Enlight Software (2003). *Virtual U* [PC]. Portland: Woodrow Wilson Foundation.
Epic Games (2004). *Unreal Tournament 2004* [PC]. New York: Atari.
Firaxis Games (2005). *Sid Meier's Civilization IV* [PC]. Hunt Valley: 2K Games.
ImpactGames (2007). *PeaceMaker: A Video Game to Promote Peace* [PC]. Pittsburgh: ImpactGames.
Maxis Software (2003). *SimCity 4* [PC]. Redwood City: Electronic Arts.
Microsoft Game Studios (2006). *Flight Simulator X* [PC]. Salt Lake City: Microsoft Game Studios.
Nintendo (1985). *Super Mario Bros.* [NES]. Tokyo, Japan: Nintendo.
Positech Games (2007). *Democracy 2* [PC]. UK: Positech Games.
Realtime Associates (2006). *Re-Mission* [PC]. Redwood City: HopeLab Foundation.
Texas A&M University-Corpus Christi, BreakAway, & Office of Naval Research (in development). *Pulse!! The Virtual Clinical Learning Lab* [PC]. Hunt Valley: BreakAway.
Von Ahn, L., & Dabbish, L. (2004). *ESP Game* [Web]. Pittsburgh: Carnegie Mellon University.

Level 4
Meaning

> *A picture is worth a thousand words; a game is worth a thousand pictures—Dick Duke*
>
> *Tell me, and I will forget; Show me, and I may remember; Involve me, and I will understand—Confucius*

Everything in life needs to have some "meaning." It has to have some purpose. Meaning is simply at the very heart of what humans crave. Without it there is a void and that is something we cannot cope with. Danesi (2002) asserted that humans have a "puzzle instinct," an intuitive knack for solving puzzles felt by people across the world. I think beyond this puzzle instinct is a need for "meaning," for understanding the world around us. Puzzles are just one of the artifacts through which we might get a glimpse at or at least have an idea of understanding "something." This is also the hypothesis that Danesi puts forth. According to him, our fascination with puzzles appears to be part of a deep-seated need to make sense of things: to attribute "meaning" to our lives.

How we attribute meaning is very personal and social. The way we look at the world and interpret it is influenced by our own experiences, our assumptions, and our culture amongst many other influential factors. Some riddles illustrate this, and the following one is in particular famous for it. Try to solve it before continuing.

> A father and his son were in a car accident. The father died. The son was taken to the hospital. The doctor came in and said: I cannot do surgery on him, because he is my son. Who was the doctor?

I like the riddle, because it emphasizes how much we look at the world on the basis of assumptions. We have frames and stereotypical images on how the world works and these influence our perception and interpretation of what we see, read, and hear. It is, for instance, known that the riddle is much more difficult to solve for people from some cultures, and especially those cultures in which females still have a backward position in comparison to the other gender and are thus less likely to be perceived as having the occupation of a doctor.

C. Harteveld, *Triadic Game Design*,
DOI 10.1007/978-1-84996-157-8_4, © Springer-Verlag London Limited 2011

But even for people from modern feminist cultures, the riddle seems at first glance strange and unsolvable. Those people also have the stereotypical idea of doctors being males and with the father being dead, the riddle raises some eyebrows. Their stereotype is, however, less strong and with some further thinking they will realize it must have been his mother.

Aside from assumptions, making meaning is strongly related to knowledge. On many occasions it is difficult to understand something if we do not know the context, the background, or simply the facts surrounding something we see, read, and hear. This is what I experience all the time when I go to a comedy club somewhere abroad and they make jokes about local politics or something typical of their culture that outsiders do not know. And speaking of jokes, the following one illustrates the need for this knowledge as well:

Why did Mickey Mouse go to outer space?

It is a bit of a bland joke, but it is good at illustrating that to be able to even answer it, we first of all need to know who "Mickey Mouse" is. In fact, we need to have knowledge about the whole Disney franchise. Although many Western people are very likely to know this, other cultures probably have no idea. Secondly, we have to have some knowledge about outer space and in particularly about the planetary system. Simply put, if we do not know that "Pluto" is a planet as well as the name of Mickey's dog, we would not be able to give the right answer which is "to find Pluto."

But aside from assumptions and knowledge, we can attribute meaning to experiences very differently, especially if the experiences are ambiguous. In life, most inputs are to one degree or another ambiguous and allow therefore for multiple interpretations. This notion that we can look differently at objects is at best illustrated with "ambiguous figures." These are figures who can be interpreted in multiple ways. Try and look at the silhouette in Fig. 4.1. In what specific ways it can be looked at is explained in Appendix A.

In short, we humans are "meaning creators" and we do this amongst other things on the basis of assumptions, knowledge, and the perspective we take on the objects we attribute meaning to. In creating meaning we often make use of all kinds of "sense-givers," devices that give us something to think about, like a poem, a book, a song, or even a puzzle. They are devices that give us a glimpse of understanding "something" and as such they are "valuable." Apart from being a "representational device," and largely because of it, games are also such "sense-givers." With games we can retrieve meaning, for ourselves as players or for the larger good, if we want to test a theory or collect some data.

Similar to the representation, however, to retrieve value, it is still important that a game is designed well and for this we need to look at games from the world of Meaning. In this level I will explain what aspects and criteria need to be considered from this world. It involves taking the "purpose" of what needs to be achieved into account (see "What Is the Purpose?"), thinking about the "strategy" of how to achieve this (see "Think of a Strategy"), realizing how this strategy can be translated into concrete "operations" (see "Operationalizing the Plan"), and finally considering

Fig. 4.1 The silhouette illusion by Akiyoshi Kitaoka. Used with permission

in what "context" the value creation takes place (see "Consider the Context"). When all of these aspects are looked upon, a *value proposal* has been created. Whether this works can eventually be judged by looking into the criteria of this world: "motivation," "relevance," and "transfer" (see "The Criteria of Meaning").

Considering this world involves taking into account the people and disciplines associated with creating meaning. This largely depends on what sort of value needs to be retrieved, but if it is about education, the learning sciences, teachers, instructional designers and so on can play an important role. In this level—and this is a "disclaimer"—I largely look at Meaning from this educational or training point of view, but if one would be involved in a game about advertising or data collection, theories and experts related to this area need to be considered when taking this perspective into account.

But before we get to all these learning theories, let us first have a look at the first aspect which is without doubt critically important if we are talking about "games with a serious purpose."

What Is the Purpose?

Similar to the problems that can be considered for using a game, many types of *purposes* can be thought of. With a purpose I refer to the intention that designers have for developing a game: it needs to have some sort of function aside from entertaining players. Otherwise the game is not *intentionally* meaningful. I stressed the "intentionality" of the creation of meaning through a game, since all games can be considered meaningful to some extent (see Level 2). Only a small portion are, however, developed to purposefully create an added value beyond playing the game itself. The functionalities for using these latter games relate to the "creation of

Fig. 4.2 Typing words to kill zombies with *The Typing of the Dead*. I had to type "absolute" absolutely very fast, otherwise the zombie on the right would have hit me with his hammer. ©2000 SEGA. Used with permission

value." In Level 2 I listed a number of values, such as knowledge, skills, attitudes, assessment, data collection, exploration, and theory testing. When one or more of these values are defined and specified we get the purpose of the game.

For example, *Virtual Leader*, teaches leadership skills (e.g., when to empower or delegate, be directive, or be transactive) and gives the player the ability to acquire these by practicing them in virtual meetings. The purpose of *The Typing of the Dead* is, to give another example, to teach players the physical skills of typing with a keyboard (Fig. 4.2). In this game, which is quite similar to *Tempo Typen*, players have to type as fast as they can to kill the zombies or else they will die at some point. It is "type or die!" In contrast to these value creation possibilities for players, the value of *Foldit* is aimed at collecting data from the game. By solving puzzles, players may contribute to finding cures against HIV/AIDS or cancer.

Many more examples can be thought of. The point is that for a game to be meaningful it first of all has to have some purpose. The second step is to make sure this purpose is translated into a game. This is not that easy as the first educational games, also referred to as *edutainment*, have shown (Egenfeldt-Nielsen 2007). With these games the actual purpose of the game was unrelated to the game. Becker (2008) gives an example of what has become synonymous with edutainment:

> The game starts off as many typical commercial games do, with cool images and some sort of backstory—you are the world's last hope, and must use your superhuman powers to save mankind, and some sort of quest or challenge that must be overcome—defeat the enemy, or recover the lost treasure. But then, when the gameplay reaches a crucial moment, a new

> screen pops up showing what any child over six can identify as an "exercise," and the world-saving task to be accomplished turns out to be solving a quadratic equation. The answer to this equation, for some thinly justified reason, is the key. Even though the resultant number has no connection to the rest of the story, it is some kind of magic number that defeats the enemy. Even worse, this "embedded worksheet" looks nothing like the rest of the game—in fact, it looks very much like the paper worksheet that was used in the same class the year before. This is what has become synonymous with "edutainment." (p. 4)

In edutainment titles the game is little more than a wrapper for the actual purpose; the game is a "chocolate covered broccoli" (Laurel 2001). The visuals and other game elements cover something that is more or less presented in the same way as with any "normal" type of class or training. In this way, the game is used as an *extrinsic motivation* to extract the value. We know from experiments bus also from everyday experiences that *intrinsically motivating* experiences are much more valuable (Malone 1981). Also, the time spent on extras, such as aiming at the right numbers with a gun, may build motivation, in itself it does not create any value. This means the time-on-task can become very small.

Nevertheless, even despite that many edutainment games have been criticized, some of them are still wonderful (Becker 2008; Egenfeldt-Nielsen 2007). And they can also work. Look at the previously mentioned *Typing of the Dead*. This game is in fact also nothing more than a wrapper around which the purpose, learning typing skills, has been built. In addition to this game we can find many fitness related games, games that stimulate us to run, perform yoga, or do other exercises, like *Wii Fit*. The difference with the *Typing of the Dead* and the fitness related games with most of the edutainment games is that although the game might not be a bit more than a wrapper, the purpose is still well *integrated* within the game. For *Typing of the Dead* players actually need to type to kill zombies which is quite something else than first killing zombies with an action button and then doing a typing exercise.

From this it should become clear that integrating the purpose seamlessly within the game is important. In that case, the time-on-task will be almost equal to the amount of time playing the game, and if the game elements are a little more than chocolate, it can also become an intrinsically motivating experience. But before any of this can happen, designers first, as I already pointed out, have to define and specify the purpose of the game. For *Levee Patroller*, which is aimed at training levee inspection knowledge and skills, we defined the following learning objectives:

- **Observing**: to recognize signals of a failure.
- **Reporting**: to report in the correct way the observed signals associated with a failure.
- **Diagnosing**: to recognize a failure mechanism behind a failure.
- **Assessing**: to recognize the different phases and the severity of a failure.
- **Taking measures**: to know how a further progression of a failure can be prevented.

From the list of objectives it is possible to distill that for creating an integrative environment the game clearly needed to involve a player looking for failures and upon finding signals, the player needed to report, diagnose, assess, and possibly take measures. Although this seems rather clear-cut, we still had to come up with a way to make sure the learning objectives would be achieved.

Think of a Strategy

To make sure the purpose of a game is properly integrated into a game, a *strategy* has to be thought of. The word "strategy" normally means something like "to have a plan of action." Such a plan is mostly not some low level short-term plan as "getting a cup of water because I am thirsty right now" but rather an elaborate and systematic long-term plan like "drinking every day at least four cups of water to stay healthy."

With "strategy" in relation to the world of Meaning I refer to setting up or thinking about a plan of action in which game mechanisms can be used to achieve some value in the real world in the best way possible. A setup or way of thinking can relate to existing games or other artifacts which embody some philosophy to create value ("we are going to do it like them") and/or to theories from one of the disciplines that are affiliated with Meaning, like the learning sciences or rhetoric. With these other games and theories in mind, an outline can be made of how the purpose can be effectively translated into a game environment.

For example, when a game is about marketing a person, product, or a company, the purpose of the game is to change the attitude of the player positively toward the person, product, or company. It can also be the other way around when the designers want to make the player aware about the negative sides of a certain person, product, or company.

Whether positive or negative, to achieve the effect designers have to consider how they can "persuade" the player. Like a president preparing his speech to speak to the people, designers of these types of games have to think of how their message gets best across to the players. A president can choose to attack his or her opponents or decide to stick to his or her ideas and defend these. A president can also do both. In addition, the president has to consider what issues to attack or defend and in what order. Whatever the president and the staff eventually decide to, it makes up for their strategy. Similarly, game designers have to think of "how" to involve "what."

This can be illustrated with two games, one which is aimed at a positive attitude change, the other at a negative one. The first, *The Chiquita Game*, was developed to show players that Chiquita, a company which harvests and distributes fruit—not just bananas—all over the world, grows their bananas with "respect" for their employees and the environment. The company pays more than average to the local farmers, builds houses for their employees, and invests in the environment by for example planting trees.

I think that the designers have tried to achieve the purpose by using a strategy that is aimed at *empathy*. Empathy is a sense of shared experience, including emotional and physical feelings, with someone or something other than oneself. It is about "identification." This often happens in response to reading a book or watching a movie: readers or viewers "identify" themselves with the characters and experience the story from their perspective. The aim here is to let players (positively) identify themselves with Chiquita.

The reason why the strategy of focusing on empathy was probably chosen is that most consumers have no idea what Chiquita stands for, except for some of the bananas they eat. Most consumers are simply far off from the actual cultivation of

Fig. 4.3 Sustaining a fast-food empire in a complex network of moral decisions with *The McDonald's Video Game*. This is the restaurant part and it shows a manager who is screaming for help, because he is facing huge line-ups and unmotivated employees. ©2006 Molleindustria. Used with permission

bananas and everything surrounding this process. A game enables to "situate" the player in this process.

The designers of *The Chiquita Game* decided to situate players as a Chiquita manager of a banana plantation. They have to control and simultaneously manage four aspects that surround banana plantations: the cultivation of bananas, the distribution of bananas, the local village, and the local rainforest. To do this well, they have to invest and earn money with bananas, keep the farmers busy, keep an eye on the cultivation process, make sure the inhabitants of a nearby village are satisfied, and also need to preserve and invest in the local rainforest. The ultimate goal of the game is to gain respect. This is emphasized at the beginning of the game:

> Your objective: cultivate bananas and create a profitable plantation by harvesting Chiquita bananas. But be careful, you will need to do it just like we do on our Chiquita farms, by respecting your employees and the environment.

It is quite difficult to fail in the game. It uses game mechanics which are similar to other games that are about planting, growing, and harvesting products as vegetables or fruits and sell these, like *Harvest Moon*. Doing this is a very relaxing and enjoyable experience which contrasts starkly from the fast-paced action games. Players have to wait for the bananas to grow and from there they can harvest and sell them. In the mean time, they have to invest in the local village and rainforest. It seems that the strategy of the designers was to let players empathize with Chiquita by giving them an understanding of what this company does for local farmers and the environment.

The second game, *The McDonald's Video Game*, uses the same strategy but with the opposite purpose (Fig. 4.3). It is what Bogost (2007) calls an "anti-advergame" as it is "created to censure or disparage a company rather than support it" (p. 29). The difference between the two games can already be noted at the beginning. The following message is emphasized at the beginning of this game:

> This game, site, and the creators of them are in no way affiliated with McDonald's Corporation or its affiliates.

Similar to *The Chiquita Game*, players control and simultaneously manage four aspects, this time of the McDonald's production environment. They have to consider a third world pasture where cattle are raised, a slaughterhouse where cattle is made into burgers, a restaurant where the burgers are sold, and a corporate office where decisions are made about lobbying, public relations, and marketing. This is everything but easy. With this game it is in fact quite difficult to be successful. In all sectors players are confronted with moral decisions, like bribing politicians and scientists, bulldozing rainforests to clear space for cattle, using growth hormones to fatten the cows, and so on. The game's rules force players to eventually concede to these business practices as they otherwise have to file for bankruptcy.

For example, to keep up with the demand of burgers, players need to allow for diseased meat to be made into burgers and this spawns complaints and fines from health officers. These people can, however, be bribed through lobbying. All of this relates to the claim of the game: to run a successful global fast-food empire like McDonald's succumbing to immoral practices is "the price to pay."

Playing *The McDonald's Video Game* lets players empathize with the McDonald's corporation but in a negative manner. The game uses a sort of "reverse psychology" by putting the player at the head of the management and experience what the fast-food empire is like. In the end, players will asks themselves "Is this a company I want to support?" Players may recognize that they are part of the problem: the demand side which sets a whole chain of reactions in place and which force the company to be immoral. The game thus exposes the dysfunction of this fast-food empire. The understanding of this problem may lead players to change their attitude and eat a healthy meal instead of a burger at McDonald's.

In politics a particular strategy may work for some but not with others. A speech can divide the public into proponents and opponents or unite them together. Attacking another politician might, for example, be seen by one person as a sign of power, another might consider it a weakness. In making up a strategy these effects have to be taken into account, to either improve the strategy or accept that it may happen.

Similarly, a strategy in a game may not necessarily be successful for everybody. For example, although players like the *The Chiquita Game* (i.e., the world of Play), they questioned whether the message of the game (i.e., the world of Meaning) rings true in the real world (i.e., the world of Reality):

> I played the game and found it funny...yet I question whether Chiquita is really "clean." We hear they are, but is this true in reality? Do employees get a fair wage and are they treated with respect? That is the big question. (Isabel, October 24, 2006, in Heukels 2006, freely translated from Dutch)

Some of the players based this on their own experience:

> From my own observations I can say that Chiquita is not as clean as they say, for their employees as well as the environment. I just returned from Costa Rica and I visited a number

> of banana plantations. There I saw that employees earn just enough to buy food and are unable to leave the plantation, as they will lose their benefits provided by the company, such as their house, free education, and health care. Additionally, due to the use of enormous amounts of pesticides, the environment is severely damaged. I am not going to eat bananas for a while... (Suzanne, October 29, 2006, in Heukels 2006, freely translated from Dutch)

I contacted Chiquita and they told me the game does not misrepresent reality. This is not just a company's perspective on the situation, because Chiquita has won several awards, for example the "Corporate Conscience Award" for its social and environmental initiatives and the "Circle of Excellence Award" for the reduction of the carbon footprint of its supply chain. This means that Chiquita does take care of its social and environmental responsibilities. But to use a game to provide this message, it raises doubts with players (such as with Isabel) or even some anger (such as with Suzanne). Maybe the game is considered a Trojan Horse instead of a Fountain of Wisdom, or maybe players are aware that games can misconstrue reality by providing a one sided picture, and are, therefore, very critical, especially if it does not fit their own ideas about the world. Whatever it is, the point is that the game's strategy is not successful for everybody.

The same can be said about the *The McDonald's Video Game*. Despite the clear warning at the beginning of the game, I talked to players of this game who actually thought the game was made by McDonald's! Other players remarked that this game was "weird," because they were unable to do well. That is of course the whole point of the game, but this did not came across. In the first case, players may become positively affiliated with McDonald's, since it has the capacity to make fun of itself. In the second case, players may criticize the game creators and not McDonald's. Although some of this might be hard to prevent, by looking at best practices and drawing upon proven theories, it is at least more likely that the strategy works.

Back in 2006 we had little to no best practices to look into for developing *Levee Patroller*. We had to resort to other means for thinking about how we could reach a maximum effect of transferring the knowledge and skills of levee inspection. In the end, I decided to resort to the learning sciences to find inspiration for a proper strategy. In my investigation, I first looked at learning in general, and discovered that it is still a mystery to us (see "Learning Mystery"), and subsequently looked into specific learning theories to see what they could tell me about how I could reach the purpose of my game (see "Learning from A to Z").

I have to add that although these findings are specifically relevant for designers of educational games, they are useful for designers of games with other purposes as well. All games are in some way or the other about "learning." For example, even with games as the *ESP Game* and *Foldit* it is eventually important that players learn. This way, their players may label pictures or solve protein puzzles better, respectively.

Learning Mystery

When discussing learning the first issue that needs to be clarified concerns the difference between "education" and learning itself (Knowles et al. 1998). Education involves an activity undertaken and initiated by one or more agents to effect changes in individuals, groups, or communities. It is superimposed on the learners and happens occasionally: when we sit in a classroom, a workshop, or some other educational setting. Learning, in contrary, is a natural process[1] that happens all the time, even when we play a game. This explains why all games involve learning, but that not every game educates.

To conclude, learning is continuous, whether it is experienced consciously or not. This happens, because we use our brain all the time (even despite we sometimes claim that some do not use theirs...). When we use it, little pieces of information called *chunks* are activated, strengthened, created, or even destroyed (Anderson 1983). By activating and strengthening existing chunks it becomes easier to recall these chunks. Even when we do repetitive tasks or things that have become complete routine, we still "learn" by activating and strengthening the chunks associated with the task. In that case, we do not learn something new, but it is nonetheless still learning.

The activation of chunks also explains why while humans learn all the time, we still forget things. The reason why knowledge and skills degrade is basically by not using the associated chunks actively. In some cases the knowledge and skills may even degrade completely, causing someone to redo the whole learning process. In other cases a little rehearsal may be enough to "refresh the memory."

I experienced the latter with ice skating. When I was young I used to do this quite often, but since then I have not done it for at least in ten years. Some time ago a couple of friends invited me to go ice skating in an indoor hall and so I did. The first rounds were uneasy, but after that I quickly processed from a beginner to an average skater.

This "quick recovery" of knowledge and skills only occurs if a person has deeply captured understanding of it. Koster (2005) and Caillois (1958/1961) refer to this deep understanding as "grokking it." If a person "groks" something the associated chunks might get locked far away in the brain if they are not activated for a long time, but it is less likely that the knowledge and skills will evaporate into the universe. When this does happen, the chunks are destroyed.

The gain and loss of in particular knowledge but also skills relates also to the "attitudes" that people have. I defined attitude as a person's disposition to a certain object (see Level 2). These dispositions may change on the basis of new knowledge and/or skills or a loss of it. If we look, for instance, at *The Chiquita Game* and *The McDonald's Game* players may have changed their attitude toward both companies after gaining more knowledge. And if I did not succeed at ice skating, I may have given up on it and start dislike doing it.

In short, humans learn all the time, but also forget all the time, explaining why we do not always wake up with more knowledge than we had the day before. We can

[1] Some scholars conceive learning as either a product, process, or a function (Knowles et al. 1998). I think in the end it does not matter how one perceives it, because functions are needed to have a process and a process is needed to have a product. Personally, I perceive learning as a process, because I think it is important to emphasize that learning is a dynamic activity in which a person engages in.

now define learning as a continuous process in which knowledge, skills, and attitudes (KSA) are gained or (partly) lost. This definition differs from most definitions of learning in that "losing" KSA is included and emphasized (cf., Knowles et al. 1998; Merriam and Caffarella 1999). This choice is made, because to explain how KSA are gained and retrieved, it is also necessary to explain how they can get lost. Additionally, "unlearning" is just as important as learning. When situations change, such as moving to a new place, people need to erase their usual routines and replace them with new ones. This requires unlearning of the old routines and learning of the new ones.

From this definition we can see that learning involves "change" as a result of experience (Knowles et al. 1998; Merriam and Caffarella 1999). The definition does, however, not explain *how* change occurs. This is in fact the part that makes learning still so much a "mystery" to us. Many contradicting learning theories exist that try to explain this.

Learning from A to Z

To look into all of the learning theories would have been impossible: there are just too many of them. But luckily it is possible to classify many of the theories based upon their most dominant traits into a number of different "paradigms" that each have some perspective on how we learn (cf., Knowles et al. 1998; Merriam and Caffarella 1999). For thinking of a strategy, I have only taken these paradigms into account. My exploration is, therefore, certainly not all-encompassing. It has been more an attempt to capture the most important insights of the learning sciences in the past century and see how they can be connected to games. The theoretical paradigms I considered are described below in a somewhat historical order.[2]

- **Behaviorism**: a school of thinking that suggests that behavior can be described and explained without making reference to mental events or to internal psychological processes. Learning is according to this paradigm equivalent to observable behavioral changes. It involves strengthening good behavior by giving rewards and unlearning a habit by punishing unwanted behavior. The environment controls behavior, not some mechanism within the individual. It is based on the works of John Watson (1930), who is generally conceived as the founding father of behaviorism, Edward Thorndike (1932), who became known for a number as laws like the law of effect and exercise for how people and animals make associations between stimuli and responses ("connectionism"), Ivan Pavlov ("classical conditioning"), who became famous for his experiment with dogs that began to salivate in the presence of stimuli that they associated with food, and Burrhus

[2]The labeling of learning theories into paradigms differs—not surprisingly—per scholar. I based my categorization of the theoretical paradigms largely on Merriam and Caffarella (1999). Compared to their overview I subdivided constructivism into "constructivism" and "socio-constructivism" and added "constructionism" to the list.

Skinner (1938) ("operant conditioning"), who believed that all behavior is learned and that we need to reinforce desired behavior and ignore or punish undesirable behavior, amongst others.

- **Cognitivism**: this learning paradigm is a rejection of behaviorism. It posits that internal mental events cannot be ignored. They are according to these theorists actually at the center of learning and do not necessarily reflect themselves in observable behavioral changes. Learning can be seen as a mental process in which new information is attended to and related to previously learned information. This information processing in the human mind does not simply look like a passive exchange-terminal system where the stimuli arrive and the appropriate response leaves. Rather, a thinking person interprets sensations and gives meaning to events. This means the locus of control shifts from the environment toward the individual, or more precisely, the learner's mental processes when looking at learning from this perspective. This paradigm was fueled by insights from Gestalt psychologists, who emphasized to look at the whole rather than the parts of something and at patterns rather than isolated events. Later cognitivists, such as John Anderson (1983) and Noam Chomsky (1968), view the human mind as a computer: an information processing instrument that stores and organizes information.
- **Humanism**: although cognitivists already centered more onto the learner than behaviorists, this was still not enough according to the humanists. They consider learning from the perspective of the human potential for growth. They relegate the perspective of learning not only to behavior and cognitions, but to affective dimensions as well. Not surprisingly, this movement was stirred by no one else than Sigmund Freud who with his psychoanalytic approach started to investigate the influence of the subconscious mind on behavior and looked at concepts as anxiety and drives. Despite that Freud inspired the emergence of humanism, they themselves moved away from the idea that behavior is determined by our subconscious. Instead, they pose that human beings can control their own destiny, are inherently good and strive for a better world, are free to act, and posses unlimited potential for growth and development. Abraham Maslow's (1970) hierarchy of needs and Carl Roger's (1983) learning theory are reminiscent of this paradigm.
- **Constructivism**: constructivists add to the cognitive and humanist learning model that learning is an active social process and something that cannot be separated from the learner's background, culture, and motivation. Learners actively "construct" their own understanding and knowledge by interpreting information and then reconciling it with their previous ideas and experience. The interpretation and reconciliation is depended on the learner's characteristics and the environment. This makes the process of learning different from one to another: each learner is unique. Jean Piaget (1929) with his cognitive development stages is seen as the initiator of this movement (although some consider him a cognitivist). The idea of how people make sense of their experiences and have to be actively involved in this, is in particular emphasized in David Kolb's learning cycle (Kolb 1984), which is quite strongly based on John Dewey's learning-by-doing philos-

ophy (Dewey 1938). This paradigm is sometimes also called "personal constructivism" (to separate it from "socio-constructivism").

- **Socio-culturalism**: this paradigm combines elements from behaviorism and cognitivism. It asserts that both the learner and the environment need to be considered. Behavior is a function of the interaction of the person with the environment: people influence the environment, which in turn influences the way people behave. To explain behavior, the interaction of all these factors have to be studied. For this reason, social-culturalists place an emphasis on the social context in which learning takes place. It considers how people learn from one another, encompassing such concepts as observational learning, imitation, modeling, and mentoring. Other relevant concepts are self-efficacy, self-actualization, locus of control, and expectancy. It further asserts that many higher order functions develop out of social interactions, such as language. Lev Vygotsky (1978) but especially Albert Bandura (1977) have developed the insights of this view on learning. This paradigm is commonly referred to as either "socio-cultural learning" or as simply "social learning" and is closely affiliated with "socio-constructivism" in understanding the importance of culture and the social context. In fact, Vygotsky is seen as one of the founders of socio-constructivism.
- **Socio-constructivism**: this paradigm extends constructivism with the insight from socio-cultural learning by positing that knowledge is socially constructed and negotiated in a dialogic process involving multiple people and/or even communities ("shared meaning"). It contends that learning is "situated": it is contextual and embedded in a social and physical environment. This means knowledge cannot be detached from the situation in which it is constructed and actualized. According to this perspective learning will only become meaningful in an authentic situation and by talking to peers and experts in a particular domain. Familiar concept within this paradigm are situated learning (or cognition), cognitive apprenticeship, communities of practice, and reflective practice. Jean Lave and Etienne Wenger (1991), John Seely Brown et al. (1989), and James Greeno (1998) are important contributors to this learning paradigm.
- **Constructionism**: a (specific) paradigm developed by Seymour Papert (1980) and his colleagues at MIT. It is associated with constructivism but goes beyond it to assert that constructivist learning happens especially well when people are engaged in constructing something external to themselves such as a sand castle, a machine, a computer program, or a book. To Papert, this projecting out of our inner feelings and ideas is a key to learning. Expressing ideas makes them tangible and shareable which in turn, inform and help us communicate with others through our expressions. It is learning by design. Although I will not go into this strand of learning, I do want to emphasize it as it offers many opportunities for learning with games. Quite a number of entertainment games already employ the principles that can be derived from constructionism: from the creature editor of *Spore*, the object creation and manipulation in *Drawn to Life*, to the complete construction of levels in *LittleBigPlanet*, each one them lets players "virtually" construct something external to themselves.

From this overview we can retrieve that the paradigms put a different emphasis on what is important (environment, learner, or both?) and although some overlap exists, they mostly oppose each other. But while they exclude each other, each paradigm enlightened us a little bit about the mysterious process of learning and is backed by an enormous amount of research. Each of the paradigms provide potentially valuable lessons for game design. This potential value is expressed by Hill (1977):

> For most of us, the various learning theories have two chief values. One is in providing us with a vocabulary and a conceptual framework for interpreting the examples of learning that we observe. These are valuable for anyone who is alert to the world. The other, closely related, is in suggesting where to look for solutions to practical problems. The theories do not give us solutions, but they do direct our attention to those variables that are crucial in finding solutions. (p. 261 as cited in Merriam and Caffarella 1999)

I was clearly in search of a solution to a practical problem: to design a game about levee inspection. My strategy in creating *Levee Patroller* was, therefore, to retrieve some basic insights from the different learning theories and try to apply these to my practical problem. To apply these, I had to think about how I would translate the theories to the design of the game. For this, I had to "operationalize my plan."

Operationalizing the Plan

A strategy is a "plan of action." It outlines roughly what needs to be done and how this is going to be done. For implementing the strategy and, therefore, making concrete what happens to reach the purpose, it has to be considered what precise mechanisms are used. A game can have many different or similar mechanisms or even just one mechanism. *September 12th* has, for example, just one mechanism. Players fire a missile and this causes a change in the system depending on where the missile hits. Ultimately, the point is that military actions may cause terrorism to bloom. This is expressed in this one simple mechanism.

With *The McDonald's Video Game*, on the other hand, many similar mechanisms are used to achieve the same purpose of explaining what the business practices of this fast-food empire are. In each of the four sectors, players have to concede in a similar way to immoral strategies. Whereas in one they are forced to use diseased cows and subsequently bribe health officers, in another they are forced to fire unmotivated workers and subsequently bribe politicians who file complaints about labor practices. Each of these mechanisms create together an overall picture of what the game is about.

Such purposeful mechanisms as found in *September 12th* and *The McDonald's Video Game* I call *operations* and this term as well as the idea is based on Bogost's (2006) idea of "unit operations."[3] Operations can be conceived as building blocks

[3] I do not use Bogost's (2006) term of "unit operations," because he differentiates them from system operations. He characterizes unit operations as "succinct, discrete, referential, and dynamic," while he describes system operations as "protracted, dependent, sequential, and static" (p. 3). I do not

that together add value beyond the game itself. These building blocks can consist of the actions the player is able to take or of particular mechanisms that are built into the game, such as characters mourning over the death of a fellow citizen and changing into a terrorist as in *September 12th* or the visualization of the causal relations between factors in *Democracy 2* (see Level 3). Furthermore, operations can take place on different levels. It is, for example, not unlikely that a combination of low level operations can create together a higher level operation.

A convenient example to explain how the latter works, concerns *Portal* (Short 2008). In this game, the players have to solve puzzles by making use of a gun to shoot portals. These portals create a visual and physical connection between two different locations in a three-dimensional space. Objects but also the players themselves can travel through one portal and exit at the other. Aside from shooting portals, the player has a number of other low level operations available, like moving, jumping, pressing objects, and taking objects. Much of the game consists of figuring out how these operations can be combined to create higher level operations which help to solve the puzzle in a particular setting. Examples of higher level operations are dropping objects onto distant enemies, moving from one location to another (also called "teleporting"), and "flinging" oneself across space.

I will use the higher level operation flinging to further elaborate on the different levels at which operations could work. Three specific game rules have to be kept in mind to understand this process. First, players exit a portal in the direction the portal is facing. Second, players exit the portal with the same speed as they entered the entry portal. Third, the game environment is based on Newtonian physics. This means that, for example, gravity applies to falling objects including the player. The three rules in combination with the low level operations of shooting portals, jumping, and moving make "flinging" across space possible by jumping into an entry portal and flying out of an exit portal (Fig. 4.4).

This way of thinking, of thinking about how small independent elements work together and create meaning, helps designers to implement their strategy into a game. And although *Portal* has been developed with an entertainment focus in mind, the flinging and the low level operations certainly create meaning as well. To perform the operation of flinging correctly, players have to get an understanding of Newtonian physics and need to apply some spatial-temporal reasoning. Therefore, small and seemingly arbitrary elements, such as jumping and shooting, force players to critically think about a solution and learn something.

For defining operations, designers could apply two approaches. They can use a "bottom-up" approach, by defining low level operations and seeing how they could work together in creating the desired meaning. Or they can use a "top-down" approach, by looking closely at the purpose of the game and the strategy to achieve this and then defining the operations. For example, the designers of the *McDonald's*

want to make this difference, since games can also consist of system operations and these could bear meaning as well. We can think, for example, of an overarching storyline, which unfolds as players progress through the game.

(a) An in-game representation of how portals are used in *Portal*. ©2007 Valve. Used with permission

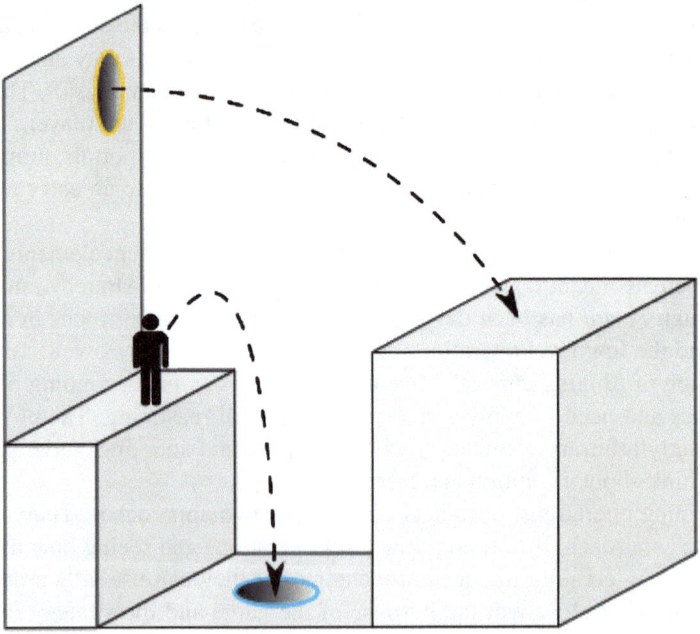

(b) A graphical representation of the mechanics of *Portal*. Picture by a Wikipedia user called "Pbroks13"

Fig. 4.4 An illustration of "flinging." By jumping into the blue portal, the character is launched out of the orange portal and onto the platform on the right

Video Game could have thought of what characterizes the business practices of McDonald's and eventually came up with four relevant sectors. This is a top-down approach. It starts with conceiving what the strategy is and decomposing this into four smaller problem sets.

Or the designers could have thought about how the actions of the player in each of the four sectors would lead the player to understand the message of the game. This is a bottom-up approach. In this case, the designers think from the elementary elements of gameplay, the challenges and the player's actions to overcome these, and how they relate to the overall purpose of the game. Both approaches are feasible (even simultaneously) and lead to what I call "operationalizing the plan." Operationalizing normally means to define an abstract concept in such a way that it can be practically measured. With designing games, however, it means to define the purpose and strategy in such a way that it can be practically played. The mechanisms that facilitate the achievement of the purpose have to be clear.

For *Levee Patroller*, I first conceived bottom-up what possible low level operations were possible, such as moving into a virtual landscape and marking a failure, and subsequently turned to a top-down approach based on my strategy of looking at the different learning paradigms. To operationalize my plan of action, my effort was to find a number of insights from the different learning theories and see how I could translate these to the design of the game.

In total, I found eight insights that I used for defining operations: practice, feedback, chunking, reflection, exploration, experience, guidance, and situatedness. Many more insights could have been retrieved. These are just the ones I concentrated on when developing *Levee Patroller*. I will now continue to discuss how each one of them contributed to operationalizing my plan.

Practice

According to behaviorist theories people learn by associating stimuli with responses. This way, connections are made between chunks of information that can later be retrieved and applied in practice. How exactly the stimuli get connected to the response inside a person's head is something behaviorists are not concerned about. To them behavior is all that matters. Since behavior is observable, the mind does not need to be considered and can be kept a black box. Behaviorists stress a number of factors when it comes down to learning. This brings me to the first insight: *practice*.

Practicing involves being confronted and dealing with chunks till people get enough understanding of the subject. When this happens, they have "grokked" the material and are able to apply and use it for themselves. That is how we learned to write, calculate, ride our bike, and play with our musical instrument. Connections between chunks got strengthened every time we practiced this. This idea is precisely formulated in Thorndike's "law of exercise" (Knowles et al. 1998; Merriam and Caffarella 1999). And as Prensky (2001), who emphasizes the importance of practice when it comes to applying games for serious purposes, explains, this is a slow process and requires a lot of effort. Therefore, much practice is needed. This is also stressed by Anderson (1995):

> ...no one develops expertise without a great deal of hard work...[and] as people become more expert in a domain, they develop a better ability to store problem information in long-term memory and to retrieve it. (p. 273–296 as cited in Merriam and Caffarella 1999)

From this we can infer that operations need to be incorporated into a game environment which make practicing possible. Fortunately, games can be considered "practice environments" in and of themselves. A game can be reduced to nothing more than a test with increasing difficulty that the player has to go through. Wrong means "game over" and right means "the next level." Players have to keep trying till they get it right. The most important concern that designers have to think about is to make sure players practice those things that they need to learn and not irrelevant aspects which often happened with many of the edutainment games Egenfeldt-Nielsen (2007).

A related concern is to consider whether this behavioristic learning principle is enough to build a game around. This depends largely on the purpose of the game. For a game such as *The Typing of the Dead*, it evolves only around practicing the player's typing skills and this seems to work. For games for which a deeper understanding is needed, such as solving math problems, solely using a "drill-and-practice" approach—or what Papert (1980) calls "drill-and-kill"—seems less suitable and designers need to look for additional ways to convey meaning.

Another concern relates to the purpose of the game as well. For some games, it turns out that players do not need to play the game for extensive hours to achieve an effect. According to the developers of *The Chiquita Game* after only five minutes of playing the message gets across (although some have even played it for over 280 hours!).[4] Additionally, an interesting result from the *Re-Mission* study is that one of its objectives, medication adherence, was reached after only one hour of playing (Tate et al. 2009). For both games their purposes have been achieved in relatively short amounts of time, which renders the emphasis on practice less important. I think, however, that practice is particularly less important for games that aim at attitude change, like these two games.

But one thing is certain: when expertise is involved, practice is highly important (Anderson 1995). Because the purpose of *Levee Patroller* was to make players into experts when it comes to levee inspection, we needed to think of what operations we could implement to encourage practicing.

Feedback

When doing something it is not necessarily for granted that it is the right way of doing it. Doing the right thing is especially important for critical jobs such as police

[4] I retrieved this information from the website of These Days, the developers of *The Chiquita Game*.

officers and fire workers, but of course also for students. The way to prevent humans from learning the wrong things brings me to the second insight that behaviorists stress when it comes down to learning: *feedback*. Feedback is critical, since how do we know we did the right thing?

This requires above-all to distinguish right from wrong. Behaviorists believe that by rewarding appropriate behavior and punishing unwanted behavior we are able to "condition" a subject, whether it concerns a human or an animal.[5] This process of reinforcement leads to the strengthening or weakening of connections of chunks which is stipulated by the "law of effect" by Thorndike (Knowles et al. 1998; Merriam and Caffarella 1999). The ability to shape (or "nurture") people by giving feedback is at its most extreme represented in the provocative statement made by Watson (1930):[6]

> Give me a dozen healthy infants, well-formed, and my own specified world to bring them up in and I will guarantee to take any one at random and train him to become any type of specialist I might select—doctor, lawyer, artist, merchant-chief and, yes, even beggar-man and thief, regardless of his talents, penchants, tendencies, abilities, vocations, and race of his ancestors. (p. 82)

To make sure learners correct their behavior on the basis of feedback, it is important that they can relate the feedback to the behavior they exhibited. One way to ensure this, is to provide immediate feedback. This way, learners are able to associate correctly what stimuli belong to what responses. Digital games are thanks to the computational power of processors extremely good at providing "instant feedback." After a player performs an action, the results of it can be immediately visualized.

Other than immediate, feedback should be clear, consistent, and worthwhile. If it is unclear, learners are unable to correct their behavior appropriately. Similarly, if feedback is inconsistent or contradictory with other feedback, learners may get confused which may lead them to reject the experience all together. Finally, a learner can be categorized as a "homo economicus": consciously or unconsciously a learner decides whether they want to attribute attention toward the feedback. If the provided feedback is not worthwhile, a learner will not put any effort in processing this.

When it comes to the sort of feedback, it is known that positive feedback is much more motivating than negative feedback (Rollings and Morris 2004). According to this more of a humanist stance, negative feedback leads to a decrease in self-esteem which is something humans try to avoid in general. This fear of failure clashes with a need to fail to be able to learn. As Schank (1997) points out, failure is needed, because by remembering what went wrong it will not happen again. But how do

[5]Using feedback to condition behavior is called *operant conditioning* and differs from purely learning to associate stimuli with responses. The latter is referred to as *classical conditioning* or *Pavlovian conditioning*.

[6]The statement is provocative, because Watson (1930) was well aware that he could never completely proof this. His point was to raise a voice against many of the "nature" proponents, those that believe everything is inherited. This becomes clear in the second sentence of the quotation: "I am going beyond my facts and I admit it, but so have the advocates of the contrary and they have been doing it for many thousands of years."

Table 4.1 Scoring criteria in *Levee Patroller*

Scoring criterion	Description	Learning objective
Observed failures	The player indicates that he or she has found a failure	Observing
Location accuracy	The player specifies the location of the failure	Reporting
Observed signals	The player reports what signals are part of the failure	Observing
Reporting accuracy	The player fill outs a report for each signal	Reporting
Situation assessment accuracy	The player makes an estimate of how severe the situation is	Assessing
Diagnose accuracy	The player determines the failure mechanism behind a failure	Diagnosing
Measure effectiveness	The player takes an action to prevent the failure from becoming worse	Taking measures

we let people fail without destroying their self-esteem? It is by reinforcing success rather than punishing failure. This means errors are neglected, while if it goes well, it will be rewarded.

Surprisingly (or maybe not), games have captured this philosophy very well. Despite that in-game punishments occur in many games (think of losing lives or energy), most games only reward the player in the eventual end scores and usually with big sizes. Players receive 1,000,000 or even more points after only a couple of tries. It is also never said that the player is a loser. Instead, it is neutrally said that he or she "failed." Upon success, however, words as "master," "hero" or any other superlatives are common to be found. This makes games besides "physically," a "psychologically" safe environment to practice in. Games create what Erikson (1968) has called a *psychosocial moratorium*: a space in which the learner can take risks with little to no real-world consequences.

To provide feedback it is first and foremost important to decide what to give feedback about. When it is an educational game, it seems most logical to give feedback related to the learning objectives. With this information, learners can actively monitor their progress. For *Levee Patroller* we created for this reason "scoring criteria," items on which players have to do well, related to each of the learning objectives (Table 4.1). For two learning objectives, observing and reporting, we created two criteria. For observing we did this, because we wanted to reward players for finding a failure in the first place and separate this from the related signals they eventually find. For reporting we wanted—in consultation with the water boards—to emphasize the importance of reporting the location and so we made a separate criterion for this as well.

Based on the behaviorist theories we know that a game should, next to providing and ability to practice, be responsive: it should give appropriate and just-in-time feedback to the learner to understand how concepts are related to each other. That solely leaning on behavioral theories to design games is sometimes not enough is proved by the failure of the edutainment titles (Egenfeldt-Nielsen 2007). The science of psychology also discovered that behaviorism is severely limited in how it depicts learning. Especially when behaviorists have tried to explain thinking as "covert speech" and language acquisition as conditioning, scientists really began to shy away from disregarding mental states. This led to the emergence of a new learning paradigm from which I derived the next insights: cognitivism.

Chunking

In the late twentieth century cognitivism became the dominant force in psychology, replacing behaviorism as the most popular paradigm for understanding mental function (Gray 2002). According to cognitivists the human mind needs to be the subject of study. Understanding can be achieved by viewing its function as an information processing model. They reduced the human mind to a machine, such as a computer, that receives input from its environment, processes this input and then translates this to some output. With this computational approach, the learner is not viewed anymore as a black box such as with behaviorism.

One of the things cognitivism increased our understanding of is how we store information into our mind. In defining learning I explained that human beings tend to store information into little pieces called chunks and that connections between chunks are established by associating chunks with one another. It is, however, not possible for a human to keep storing information without bringing any structure to it. Cognitivists theorized that humans organize their mind by putting chunks into cognitive structures.[7] Such structures should be envisualized as a network of nodes with links between them. The nodes represent the chunks, the links the associations between them. For example, the chunk rabbit is in most people's brains associated with the chunk mammal, because a rabbit is a mammal.

These cognitive structures reside in our *long-term memory*. Based on the input we get from the environment and to what we direct our attention to, we retrieve particular chunks from our long-term memory and put these in our *working memory* (also called short-term memory), a part of the brain that temporarily stores and manipulates information, to execute a certain action. Any new findings based on this action may get stored through working memory into long-term memory.

Two implications of this process are important for designing games: first of all, chunks need to be accessible if a person wants to apply them in practice, and secondly, working memory is limited which necessitates to make more efficient use of chunks by recoding them in such a way that they take up a lot less space. Both implications relate to a process called *chunking* (Chase and Simon 1973; Anderson 1983). Chunks are units of information and chunking is the process by which these are acquired and organized into more manageable units.

---

[7]Many different names are given to cognitive structures. Amongst others, they are referred to as schemata, mental models, cognitive maps, frames or any reconfiguration of the latter, like mental maps or cognitive models. All of these refer to essentially the same concept.

When it comes to the acquisition of chunks, Ausubel's (1967) distinction between "meaningful learning" and "rote learning" is useful. According to him, learning is meaningful only when it can be related to concepts that already exist in a person's cognitive structure. Rote learning, on the other hand, does not become linked to a person's cognitive structure and hence is easily forgotten. This means that learners have to process information to such an extent that connections are made to existing chunks. It also means that it needs to be ensured that learners are receptive toward information. If they do not have any anchorage, any existing chunks that can be linked to the new content, it will be difficult for meaningful learning to occur.

As for the efficiency in working memory, a lot of research into this area is actually based on a game: the game of *Chess* (Chase and Simon 1973; De Groot 1965). In this game, players have to "read" the board. They have to see and understand the different positions of the pawns, consider how they relate to each other, and think of the possible combinations that may arise in the next couple of steps. It turns out that experts can read the board much faster and are able to see more patterns at the moment and into the future. If given unlimited time, *Chess* players could play a credible game against an expert, but when they have to play a race against the clock, they would definitely lose embarrassingly.

What happens is that expert *Chess* players have more chunks related to *Chess* and are able to hold more elaborate chunks in working memory making it possible to process the situation faster. Humans are only able to hold five to seven chunks of information into their working memory Simon (1969).[8] This means to be efficient, a chunk should be as elaborate as possible.

For example, if we want to calculate "$2+2$", a person unfamiliar with this calculation has three chunks in memory: two twos and one binary operator. From there, this person calculates the answer. When people are, however, familiar with this problem, they will immediately retrieve "$2+2=4$" from their long-term memory. It takes less than a millisecond to retrieve this. Similarly, experts in *Chess* do not have to calculate but just "see it."

Good games should "enable chunking" by taking the process of the development of cognitive structures and the limitations of working memory into account. This can be done by slowly increasing the difficulty and by making sure that new information connects to existing chunks. This way, players will chunk the knowledge, skills, and attitudes and are able to perform actions better and faster. Most entertainment games are already quite good at teaching the player how to play the game, but it remains a challenge to apply this to a game which is not about fighting or shooting and which aims to teach the player something meaningful beyond the game.

[8] Initially, based on Miller (1956) it was thought that the working memory could hold seven $\pm$ two chunks. Many people still refer to this theory, although Simon (1969) showed that it is unlikely that more than seven chunks are handled by a person at any time.

Reflection

Related to chunking, concerns another insight that we can derive from the cognitivists: *reflection*. For grokking to occur, the deep processing of material, it matters *how* information is processed. Cognitivists found that information processing is dependent on (a) the importance of the task, (b) the degree of experience with the particular circumstance, and (c) to what extent *cognitive overload* takes place, a situation which occurs when excessive demands are made on the working memory (Rasmussen 1986; Wickens et al. 2004). Each of these aspects and their interaction play a role at which "cognitive level" the information will be processed.[9]

For a learning environment to be effective, it has to be ensured that the information is processed at some point at a high cognitive level. Otherwise the "grokking" of the material will not be achieved and rote learning (Ausubel 1967) might be the result. To explain this, let us return to the problem "$2 + 2$" and its corresponding response of 4. When this stimuli-response is encoded into long-term memory, people are able to retrieve this instantly whenever the stimuli $2 + 2$ is given. However, if they never understood why $2 + 2$ makes 4, they are not able to transfer the learned rule to, for example, "$1 + 1$." This means that they more or less act like a parrot: they repeat learned patterns without being aware of what they actually mean.

A proper learning process would allow content to be first processed at a high cognitive level, one in which the content is elaborately processed—by reflecting on it. From there, "proceduralization" may take place (Anderson 1983). This involves practicing IF-THEN-DO constructions, such as IF we see a problem set of $2 + 2$ THEN our response is 4. After a while, errors gradually diminish and less to even no thinking is required to execute a response. If this happens, stimuli can be processed on lower cognitive levels.

All of this can be illustrated with the game *Do I Have A Right?*. In this game, the player plays a lawyer who sets up his own firm together with an associate (my firm was called "Harteveld & Forth"). The player's role is to designate clients to the right lawyer within his firm by listening to the client's story and knowing the skills of the different lawyers in the firm. Points (called "prestige") can be scored by winning cases. To win cases, the basic idea is to identify a clear case to fight in court and match this with a skilled lawyer.

To excel in this game, players have to be knowledgeable of the different areas in which law is practiced. For example, my associate Sally Forth started off with expertise in the 4th amendment. This relates to "no unreasonable searches": if someone from the government, like the police, wants to investigate something, they need to have a reason. The first client that entered my lawfirm told me this story (Fig. 4.5):

> My teacher told me to put my hands up so he could look in my pockets for candy, because he wanted to eat some. Did I have a right to say no?

---

[9]Rasmussen (1986) distinguished three cognitive levels: a skill- (automatic), rule- (intuitive), and knowledge-based (analytical) level. This taxonomy is based on and related to the skill acquisition taxonomy of Fitts and Posner (1967) who distinguishes between a cognitive, associative, and autonomous stage (see also Anderson 1983).

(a) Listening to the story of a client. Clicking on the relevant words in the story will result in green happy faces

(b) Managing the lawfirm by connecting clients to lawyers. One client is standing at the elevator, the other sits in the waiting room. The people behind the desks are the lawyers

Fig. 4.5 Bringing cases to court with *Do I Have A Right?*. ©2009 Our Courts. Used with permission

From this story and from the 4th amendment it becomes clear that this client did have a right to say no. By connecting this client to Sally this case can be brought to court and won. This is the essence of the game. The game slowly extends to more areas of law and more and more lawyers and clients are entering the firm. To do well, after learning the law areas and the expertise of the lawyers, players need to proceduralize their knowledge into rules as "IF client's story relates to the 4th amendment and IF the client has a right THEN contact client with Sally Forth," because otherwise the player cannot keep up with all the clients and will lose points for unsatisfied clients (for not being helped, for waiting too long, or for being dismissed while they have a case). In the end, by extensive practicing players may even wind up executing responses automatically.

Although this learning process seems natural, in general games do not stimulate processing material on a high cognitive level. This is due to three reasons. First, because games are relatively safe environments and enable players to make mistakes, they evoke a "trial-and-error" approach. When such a approach is used consciously for hypothesis testing, this is not problematic. Players are in that case like little scientists that try to validate their ideas (Greenfield 1984).

However, when players just keep trying and only remember what works, it is very likely that they do not get a full understanding. For example, with *Do I Have A Right?* I remembered after a couple of times playing which clients I dismissed incorrectly and which ones I did not. Although the order in which clients appear is somewhat random, I could still remember this and improve my scores without being really aware of what I did wrong or right.

Another reason is that games do not offer the player any opportunity to "step back" and reflect on the game. Rather, they muster players to get into their primitive "fight-or-flight" mode with artificial constraints, such as time pressure or enemies that are attacking the player. The human fight-or-flight mode evolved in such a way that less blood flows to the brains, since we need all our energy to fight or run and not to think. Although this system is a bit outdated (see the phenomenon of stress), it is still there and despite that it leads to excitement in games, it undeniably also leads to a less deeper processing of the information.

Do I Have A Right? has a simple solution for preventing the player to get into a fight-or-flight mode all the time. Although the game is certainly based on speed and accuracy given the presence of a timer and the flow of clients, when players talk to either clients or lawyers, they are given unlimited time to think about their response. Besides this, when talking to clients they have to derive the important elements that make it a case from their story by clicking on the relevant words (Fig. 4.5). If players do well, a green happy face appears, and they get points. Otherwise a red sad face is shown. This stimulates players to explicitly think what the story is about.

The third and final reason is that games are very dynamic and rich of stimuli. Game environments consist of static and moving objects that continuously change making it hard for a player to focus on what is important. In addition, the many stimuli also occupy the mind of a player completely. Try, for instance, to ask some questions to a player. Expect to get either a delayed response or—more likely—no response at all. This relates partly to the limited processing capability of humans.

As I explained before, humans are only able to hold five to seven chunks in memory. To deal with this limited capacity, humans filter information by using their *selective attention*: they only pay attention to what they find relevant.[10]

This means to perceive and elaborate on information, we first have to notice something and subsequently direct our attention to it. If our attention filled all our slots in memory with attractive yet irrelevant stimuli, no deep processing of the relevant content may occur. To prevent players from filtering critical information, a game should be designed in such a way that a player can concentrate on what is important by directing his or her attention to the things that matter and leave everything else out of sight.

Based on the cognitivist theories we have a better understanding of what needs to be considered in designing games. The most important insights I derived were a need to enable chunking and a need to reflect[11] the material. Despite these insights, quite similar to behaviorism many scientists also criticized cognitivism. One of the criticisms is that the human brain is holistic. This makes it irreducible to separate components, something the cognitivists attempt. Another criticism is that cognitivism is ignoring the context and as we are "beings in the world" the context does matter. Finally, people criticized the information processing model. It still assumes a rather passive role of the person, whereas many others believe that we actively act on our world. In fact, some argue, we should be active rather than passive as this makes the experience more meaningful. This brings me to another strand of learning: the humanist tradition.

Exploration

According to the humanist orientation humans are essentially good and actively pursue growth and development of their own being. This is at best expressed in Maslow's (1970) concept of *self-actualization*. This concept is part of his theory of motivation based on a hierarchy of needs. At the lowest level of the hierarchy are physiological needs, like hunger and thirst. These must be attended to before one can deal with the next level which deals with safety needs, such as security and protection.

Similarly, if these needs are fulfilled one can go from there to levels that relate to belonging and love, self-esteem, until one reaches the final level which is the need for self-actualization. This need is a person's desire to become all that he or she is capable of becoming. This motivation is intrinsic: a person wants to grow and develop him or herself.

---

[10]Many theories exist about how we exactly filter information, when it occurs—before or after processing information or maybe it does both—, and how cognitive structures drive attention. It goes too far to elaborate this here, but it is definitely worth investigating for designing games.

[11]The notion of reflection is stressed in almost all theories of learning except for behaviorism. I placed it in the cognitivist paradigm as it is foremost a thinking process: a person has to process information on a rather high cognitive level.

People have their own goals in how to self-actualize themselves. To make this happen, freedom and choice, two other important characteristics for learning according to the humanists, are important (Rogers 1983). Learners should decide for themselves what they want to do and how they want to do it. Also relevant are "personal involvement," which stresses that the learner should be actively involved in the process and feel personally related to what is needed to learn, and that the experience is "self-initiated," which emphasizes that the sense of discovery must come from within. These principles and ideas call for "self-directed learning" (Knowles et al. 1998).

It needs to be acknowledged that most games already do a terrific job of incorporating these principles. First of all, since it is a game, a player is actively involved in the process. Of course, the extent to what the player is involved in it differs, but in most games it is the player who decides what happens. Additionally, many of the current games offer players large degrees of freedom.

In *Grand Theft Auto IV*, for example, the player can wander around a representation of New York City which is called "Liberty City." Players can explore this environment on their own: they can go to a park, visit a roller coaster, or just drive around in a taxi and look at the environment. This game and many others also enable different styles of playing. Players can be aggressive and shoot everything that comes into their sight or do nothing and act like tourists that explore an unknown world to them. In games, the players are the "directors" of their own story. Their learning is thus by definition to a large extent "self-initiated."

Even more striking is that many Role-Playing Games (RPGs) *are* about self-actualization. Aside from a story or multiple stories in which the player could get involved in, these games are about developing their avatar, by customizing its looks and skills throughout the game. Players have to decide what types of skills they want to invest in: do they want their character to become stronger or does it need to achieve more speed? In *Eve Online*, for example, players can upgrade their ships and skills in innumerable ways (Fig. 4.6). This game and similar ones are, therefore, about the growth and development of their character (or ship) with which players identify themselves with. This identification process may lead players to become more knowledgeable about themselves (Gee 2004). They grow and develop together with their own character.

From all of this, it is possible to derive a single insight which fulfills some of these humanist visions of learning: make it *exploratory*. By making a game exploratory, players can find out for themselves how they want to play the game, what the game is about, and what it means. But most importantly, it makes the experience self-directed. The experience becomes connected to the own desires and expectancies of the player and this makes it far more motivating than letting players go through a "prescripted" environment. We know, for instance, from the edutainment titles that players skip reading texts or ignore pop-up with information during the game (Egenfeldt-Nielsen 2007) and from the humanist perspective we can explain why. They simply did not ask for this information! It is not self-initiated. Players rather want to look up information when they desire to.

This may also relate to a difference in learning style in generations. Compared to the older generations, today's generation does not read the manual first and then

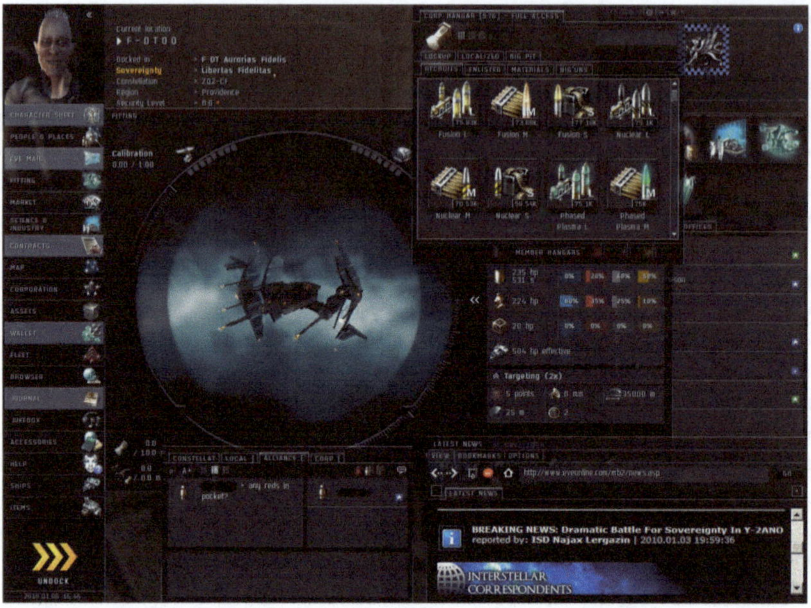

Fig. 4.6 Configuring a ship and the avatar skills in *Eve Online*. Notice the enormous amount of possibilities. The screenshot is taken by Harald Warmelink. ©2003 CCP Games. Used with permission

tries (Prensky 2001). Instead, this generation first tries. When they do not understand something, they look it up in the manual.[12] This "trial-and-error" approach can be detrimental in terms of learning as I just discussed with the insight of reflection. But it does give a sense of discovery, and if players are guided in forming a hypothesis and testing these, trial-and-error may not be detrimental. It may in fact be very effective, because the learning comes from within. These ideas are the basis of Jerome Bruner's (1961) *discovery learning*.

Discovery learning is a constructivist notion of learning and is based on the ideas of Dewey (1938). Learners engage with the material with their own knowledge and background and try to make sense of what they see. From this, we see that the insight of exploration fits the paradigm of constructivism as well. But constructivism teaches us more. It stresses the importance of "experience."

Experience

Throughout history remarkable people, such as John Dewey, Immanuel Kant, Kurt Lewin, Jean-Jacques Rousseau, and many others, have influenced the development

[12]Interestingly enough and probably due to the (increasing) complexity of games, guide books of how to play games are one of the best selling supplementary material of all sorts of media (Johnson 2005). This means that although players do not first pick a manual, they are triggered to find information, on the Internet or with other resources, like guide books.

of constructivism, a view on learning which is inherently closely connected to Kolb's experiential learning (Kolb 1984). The formalization of constructivism is generally attributed to Piaget (1929), who suggested that similar to cognitivist views on learning that individuals construct new knowledge from their *experience*. To put it bluntly, the big difference between the constructivist and cognitivist view is that the first suggests that learners actively construct knowledge, whereas the second merely assumes that knowledge is received.

Actively constructing knowledge means that learners do not passively receive stimuli from their environment. They interact with it. The way this interaction occurs is dependent on the learner's background, culture, and perspective on the world. Each learner is unique and therefore develops his or her own version of the truth. Put in another way, knowledge is a construct. It is developed out of an interpretation of the stimuli by learners in accordance with their worldview. Knowledge is nothing more than a product of what we are and not something that is waiting outside to be picked up by somebody.

The latter indicates a clear break what we have come to see as "traditional education": education in which abstract concepts are taught by teachers to students without any context and experiential basis (Dewey 1938). Prensky (2001) refers to these basic teaching methods in corporations, schools, and colleges as *tell-test education*:

> Boiled down to its core, most of what is billed as training, school, and learning consists of being told information, via lectures or reading, and then taking a test to 'measure' whether the information 'went in'...[it] is especially ineffective with today's younger workers; it just bores them to tears. It is not exactly working great with older workers, either. (p. 71)

The problem with traditional education is that the abstract concepts which the students have to learn are stripped away from all their meaning. They are put inside the learner's head where its meaning can only be related to the upcoming test and nothing else.

According to constructivists, this can be prevented by moving away from a teacher- or content-centered education and move toward a learner-centered education. In such an education learners are put in an active process where they should learn to discover principles, concepts, and facts for themselves. Abstract concepts are meaningless, because concrete experiences need to be related to abstract concepts. To achieve understanding learners have to engage in some activity, reflect upon the activity critically, derive some useful insight from the analysis, and incorporate the result through a change in understanding and/or behavior (Kolb 1984). Kolb visualized this learning process in his well-known experiential learning cycle (Fig. 4.7).

In this cycle, the learning process starts with a "concrete experience." After that, learners have observations and need time to reflect on these ("reflective observation"). In doing so and by drawing up theories, abstract concepts and generalizations are made ("Abstract concepts"). These can be used as an input for experimentation to test whether the newly formed ideas hold true ("abstractive experimentation"). This leads to a new concrete experience from which observations and reflections can be drawn, and where upon new abstract concepts and generalizations can be

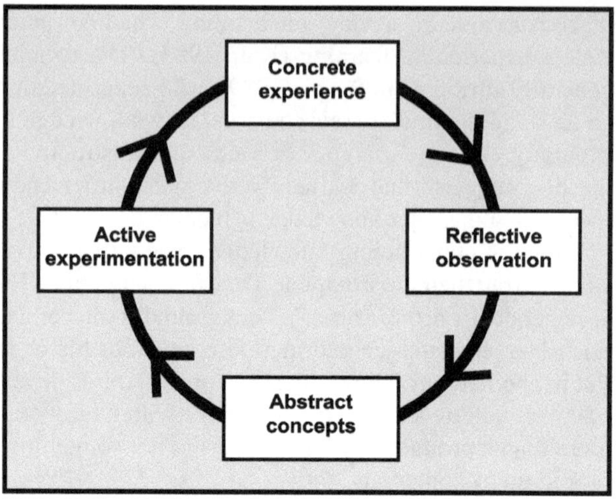

Fig. 4.7 The experiential learning cycle (adapted from Kolb 1984)

made, and so on and on. The cycle continues endlessly and each iteration may happen in a flash, over days, or even weeks.

Experiential learning stresses the importance of reflection (see cognitivism), action (specific to constructivism), and that the learning process must be initiated and sustained by the learners, making it personally relevant and meaningful to them (see humanism). The idea behind this is that this *learning-by-doing* will lead to a better understanding of the material: to a higher probability that the learner groks the material than whenever the learner only reads or hears about the material. The most powerful example that comes to mind concerns an understanding of cultures. We can read about them and the countries affiliated with a certain culture, but we are only able to fully grasp a culture when we travel to a country and "experience" its culture.

From this a line can be drawn to games.[13] Games are "experiential" by nature. They are about doing and as such give a "concrete experience" to its user. And to beat the game, players have to reflect on what they see. If, for example, a rock is blocking the road, the rather simple reflection will be made that to continue, the rock needs to be removed. From here, players conceptualize the possibilities and see if this works. They can pull the rock, try to let it explode, use a magic spell, or maybe try to look for a switch. Therefore, playing a game means iterating through the experiential learning cycle.

This does not mean, however, that the insight of experience is automatically foreseen by deciding to use a game. Not all game experiences are meaningful. The trick is to make sure that these experiences, reflections, conceptualizations, and applications relate in some way to the purpose of the game. This is not as easy as it seems. To make sure players are able to reiterate through a meaningful experiential

[13]In fact, a number of researchers have specifically elaborated and applied Kolb's experiential learning cycle to games (cf., Egenfeldt-Nielsen 2007; De Freitas and Neumann 2009).

learning cycle, another insight is helpful. We learn a lot from others and especially from those that are more "experienced." These experts can give some "guidance" to enable learners to get a full grasp of what the game is about.

Guidance

The concept of using games to achieve concrete experiences is nice, but according to Egenfeldt-Nielsen (2007) learners do not easily translate a concrete experience from a game to a valuable abstract concept. By interviewing players, collecting test results, and other material he noticed that most players were unable to extract meaning, the abstract concepts, out of the playing experience. Based on these results, he concluded that:

> ...games are potentially a valuable tool for providing such concrete experiences through their rich universe, engaging nature and dynamic presentation of information, but instruction is needed to gain educational relevance. (p. 118)

With instruction or *guidance* of the player it is possible to transform the *spontaneous concepts* that players derive from playing a game to meaningful *scientific concepts*. This means that although the use of games in education moves a away from teacher-centered education, teachers remain critically important. The role of teachers only changes. It transforms to one of being a facilitator who guides the learning process which is in itself initiated and pushed by the learner. An example from Egenfeldt-Nielsen's study (2007) with *Europa Universalis II*, a game in which players can relive the history of the times of Jeanne D'Arc and Napoleon by engaging in religious struggles, setting up expedition to claim the New World, and leading their country to prosperity and victory, makes this clear (Fig. 4.8):

> ...a student constantly experienced problems in southern France due to religious turmoil between the Protestant subgroup the Huguenots and the state religion Catholicism. The historical reasons for this conflict were perceived as most interesting by the student. Especially, when [the instructor] suggested that the downfall of the heretics was paramount to France's success and showed the student how he could send missionaries to the infected provinces, change their state religion or the tolerance toward different religious groups...[from this] he could see that religious differences led to rebellion, financial losses and domestic problems. (pp. 205–206)

The idea of guidance is connected to several learning paradigms. It is connected to humanism, because this stresses the need for self-directed learning which automatically calls for a role of instructors to facilitate their learning process rather than drill them about a certain topic. This can be seen from the above-mentioned example. The student is interested in the topic of religion and the instructor helps the student to explore this topic in the game.

It is further and more strongly connected to socio-culturalism, since guidance does not only involve "telling others what to do." Instead, people frequently give an example or show how to do something. From this observation, the student can learn. We can again refer to the above-mentioned example. The instructor *showed* how the

Fig. 4.8 Learning about history with *Europa Universalis III*, the successor of part II. It shows a different take on history. The states of what now is known as the Netherlands are in control of Austria, except for the independent nation "Utrecht" (nowadays an actual province of the Netherlands) which is ruled by David de Bourgogne. Players can amongst many other options declare war or arrange a marriage with surrounding nations. ©2007 Paradox Interactive. Used with permission

player what he or she could do in the game. According to Bandura (1977) "virtually all learning resulting from direct experiences can occur on a vicarious basis through observation of other people's behavior and its consequences for the observer" (p. 392). This means that—unlike what experiential learning may assume—humans can learn from one another without having to go through the same experience. The instructor knew how to manipulate the game and showed it to the student.

The social interaction, the basis of socio-culturalism, and especially the interaction with more knowledgeable people is critical for learning. With the help of others, whether in collaboration or by facilitation, it is possible to achieve a higher level of mastery than whenever people would have learned it on their own. This is, for example, expressed in Vygotsky's *zone of proximal development* (Vygotsky 1978) which is defined as "the distance between the actual developmental level as determined by independent problem solving and the level of potential development as determined through problem solving under adult guidance, or in collaboration with more capable peers" (p. 86). According to this idea, learners should constantly be challenged with tasks that refer to knowledge and skills just beyond their current level of mastery, requiring the aid of peers and instructors to succeed.

In many games, Non-Player Characters (NPCs) are used to perform this task. They explain and show how players need to play the game. And in some multiplayer games, such as *World of Warcraft*, it is not uncommon that expert players help new players. Also, in accordance with the zone of proximal development many games ensure that players learn the necessary skills incrementally by increasing the challenges at the same pace as the players acquire the necessary skills (Gee 2004).

Another and related guidance technique, *scaffolding*, is also used in many games. Scaffolding is the process of supporting the learner and then gradually removing more and more of this support as they become more confident and competent on their own.[14] Many games first let the player wander around, without throwing any challenges at the player or letting the player use complex movements. Then slowly, when the player masters the necessary skills, the game introduces more difficult challenges, which practically means the game removes more and more of its support, because it knows the player is capable of solving the new challenges.

A third guidance technique concerns *articulation*. Articulation is the process of getting the learner to explain—to the instructor, a peer, or on paper—their own reasoning and strategies for solving problems. An example of articulation in a game concerns clicking on the relevant words in a client's story for deciding what makes it a case or not in *Do I Have A Right?*. This way, players "articulate" to the game if they understand why a certain client has a right.

It is important to point out that while many games already apply techniques to guide the player through the game, to let the player reach the end of it, it is questionable whether players, especially when it comes to games with a serious purpose, are able—without any further guidance and elaboration—to fully grasp what the game is about. The study of Egenfeldt-Nielsen (2007) showed that many of the students are not able to do so. Instructors or specific in-game elements are needed to help learners in constructing scientific concepts.

These three guidance techniques, the zone of proximal development, scaffolding, and articulation, relate to socio-constructivism as well. This paradigm stresses the importance of guiding newcomers with little to no knowledge to the center of wisdom of a certain domain by means of "cognitive apprenticeships" or "legitimate peripheral participation" (Brown et al. 1989; Lave and Wenger 1991). To get to this center, newcomers need to be guided by a master and such a master could apply the guidance techniques also. While socio-constructivists are much similar to socioculturalists in this regard, we can retrieve an additional insight from this paradigm: to "situate" the learning experience.

Situated Learning

Constructivists find the context in which learning takes place important, as it shapes our experiences and thought. They leave it at that. It is the learner who acts on

---

[14]The term "scaffolding" is derived from constructing a new building. At first the building may be built to its full height, but cannot stand alone without the structure built around it—the scaffolding—to hold it up. Then, as the full framework of the construction is filled in, it becomes stable enough to hold its own weight, and the scaffolding is incrementally removed.

the environment, interprets the information, and shapes the knowledge. In contrary, social culturalists indicate that knowledge is socially constructed—it is a dialect between the learner and his or her environment. The social construction of knowledge can be exemplified with a clear example by Gee (2004):

> In the world of physics, as an academic area, if you have pushed your stalled car until you are dripping with sweat but the car has not budged, you have done no "work" (given how physicists use this word), but in the world of "everyday" people, people not attempting at the moment to be physicists or do physics, you have worked very hard indeed. Neither meaning is right or wrong. Each belongs to a different social world. (p. 2)

Physicists and "everyday" people belong to a different social world with different meanings about everyday phenomena. Their social context differs and this had led both to have their own sort of knowledge about something.

Socio-constructivists go even further. Aside that they also assert that knowledge is constructed in settings of joint activity, a "community of practice" as they sometimes refer it to (cf., Lave and Wenger 1991), they assert that learning is situated in the activity in which it takes place. Not only the social environment is important, its *physical* surroundings are important as well. According to them, meaningful learning will only occur if it is embedded in the social *and* physical context in which it will be used (Brown et al. 1989).

This means that non-social aspects of the environment play an active role in the individual's learning as well. To really learn something, learners need to be embedded in *authentic* situations and work on *authentic* tasks. Learning is not just a matter of what goes on inside people's heads, or what occurs between people, but it is an activity that is (and should be) fully embedded in a material, social, and cultural world.

This explains some of the critiques on our educational system. What we learn in school is frequently completely detached from the situation we use it in. Research has shown, for example, that while it is perfectly possible to understand Newton's Laws, people are not able to apply them to a concrete case in actual practice to solve a real-world problem (Chi et al. 1981; Gardner 1991). For this reason, much of what we learn in school is useless according to this view.[15]

I will use a classic example to further illustrate the idea of "situated learning." It is about Brazilian street-market children with little formal schooling. These children had to make calculations involving market products in their natural (informal) setting—the street market—and calculations involving market products and abstract problems in an unnatural (formal) condition—at their homes (Carraher et al. 1985, 1987). In the informal condition, problems were given by researchers who represented themselves as customers and the children had to solve them orally. In the formal condition, a follow-up test on the informal condition, the children were given paper-and-pencil to solve the problems.

[15]It is important to mention that not everybody agrees on the socio-constructivistic perspective on learning. It has, for instance, been criticized by Anderson et al. (1996) who take a cognitivistic view on learning. After an academic debate with a proponent of the socio-constructivistic view, James Greeno, a synthesis of the views was published (Anderson et al. 2000).

It turned out that the children solved 98 percent of the context-embedded problems in the informal setting, but only 74 percent of the imaginary, context-embedded items and 37 percent of the abstract items in the formal setting. It was also found that the children applied different mental computational algorithms when presented with problems orally than with the pencil-and-paper test. For example, they decomposed the problem by solving portions of the calculations at a time or they used repeated addition instead of multiplication.

The conclusion of this study was that mental problem solving may be more effective when applied to a real-life context, but also that the strategies (oral or written) invoked are context-dependent. People make use of cues and tools in their surroundings to think and apply their knowledge.

According to social-constructivists, this shows that it is more valuable to engage in an environment where the concepts are actually used in rather than to learn these in isolation. Learning needs to be *situated*. This is an insight for designing learning environments from the socio-constructivistic view. The context in which the game takes place should be more than the chocolate that covers the broccoli to motivate the learner. It should be a critical component of the learning environment:

> In good educational games, narrative events situate the activity, defining goals, constraining actions, provoking thought, and sparking emotional responses as students struggle to resolve complex, authentic problems...From a situated learning perspective, these narrative constraints and possibilities shape action, and become part of students' understanding of a domain in fundamental ways. (Games-to-Teach Team 2003, p. 18)

Other than an insight for designing games, the "situatedness" of learning also explains one of the key appeals of using games. They are the type of tool that Brown et al. (1989) emphasize in their idea of cognitive apprenticeship: "Cognitive apprenticeship supports learning in a domain by enabling students to acquire, develop and use cognitive tools in authentic domain activity" (p. 39). They are the "cognitive tools" or "mindtools" (cf., Jonassen 1999) that accomplishes the context-dependency, situatedness, and enculturating nature of learning by enabling the learner to immerse in an authentic setting. The usefulness of games as a cognitive tool has, for example and to stick with the topic of physics in education, been shown by two different games aimed at educating the player about physics. Both games, called *Supercharged!* and *Physics Geeks*, indicated a significant increase of players' understanding of physics compared to a control group (Squire et al. 2004; Stewart 2009).

To deal with the insight of situating the learning experience with *Levee Patroller*, we started off by creating an authentic situation (Fig. 4.9). The act of inspecting levees is situated in a Dutch landscape that includes the typical windmills, its nature with the many canals and willows, and its animals, like sheep. The challenge was, however, not only to recreate an authentic look. The challenge was to create an authentic situation which not only has the looks, but also the feel of the real setting. The same cues and tools that these people have in their normal practice should be provided in the game environment as well. This is a tough challenge, because games remain a "simulation" of the real world and can, therefore, never completely approach the authenticity that the socio-constructivists prescribe.

Fig. 4.9 Action situated in an authentic Dutch context in *Levee Patroller*

Consider the Context

When designing a game, it is not sufficient to consider the purpose, the strategy of how this purpose can be achieved, and the concrete operations to implement the strategy. Something else that needs to be considered, and this concerns the fourth and final aspect from the world of Meaning, is the *context*. With this I do not refer to the context *in* a game, an issue which has just been discussed with the insight of situating the learning experience. This relates to the design of the gameworld, story, and other game elements that provide a context to the player.

Instead, I refer to the context *of* the game. It matters for example, for whom the game is aimed at (the "target group") and when, how, in what circumstances, and for how long the game is going to be used (the "deployment"). With this "context" I refer, therefore, to everything that surrounds the use of a game and that has an effect on the creation of meaning. To explain why the context is important, let me first elaborate on the *target group* of a game.

Target Group

Potential players are to a large extent unique. They can differ on many variables—from learning styles (Honey and Mumford 1992; Kolb 1984) to playing styles (Bartle 1996). Although each and every player is unique, differences become especially visible between groups of players that differ significantly on one or more of those variables.

Culture is, for instance, such a variable. It heavily influences what players like and dislike and how they interpret information. The strong influence of culture can be seen in the design of the *Mayan Ball Game* (also referred to as the *Mesoamerican Ball Game* or *Pok-Ta-Pok*) and the interpretation of it by the Western culture. This game, filled with ritual importance and considered the first team sport in human history as it likely originates from before 1400 BC (Shelton 2003), involves two teams who pass a bouncing, hard rubber ball to each other without using their hands or feet (but by using their hips, elbows, knees, and occasionally their heads). If a team let the ball bounce more than twice before returning it to the other team or let the ball go outside the boundaries of the court, the other team received points. The goal of the game was, however, especially concerned with getting the ball into one of the rings that were placed sideways at the court. If that happened, a rarity since it was quite difficult, the game would presumably end.

The Mayans thought that the only way to keep the sun shining, crops growing, and people healthy was to sacrifice a "valuable" human being: a ball player. Now from our Western cultural perspective we would think that they sacrifice the losers. Why try to win a game if that means being sacrificed to the gods? Well, the Mayans thought otherwise. It often occurred that the winners were sacrificed. They thought it was an honor to be sacrificed. Players would go straight to heaven, bypassing all other obstacles normal human beings would have to go through.[16]

From this ancient game, we can learn two lessons with regard to the target group of a game. First, people from different cultures interpret situations differently. When asking a Westerner who would be sacrificed, almost every person would say the losers. As meaning needs to be derived from a game, the influence of culture is certainly something to pay attention to.

This is not only true for culture, but also for other influential variables. To give another example, take the age of the target group. For *Levee Patroller*, the average age of patrollers is about 50 years. Not one of these people can be considered a "digital native," somebody who grew up with playing games (Prensky 2001). These "digital immigrants" cannot play a game that is too difficult, otherwise they will not grasp the meaning of it. Similarly, young children should be offered less difficult challenges as they are not as mentally developed compared to adolescents and adults.

The second lesson we can learn from the *Mayan Ball Game* is that designers need to be aware that they have biases, such as their own cultural perspective, and these influence the eventual design of a game. If a Mayan would create a game for Westerners, the latter may not understand it (let alone be fond of it...). To prevent this from happening, it is important to get to know the target group.

To get to know the target group for ensuring the value of a game is retrieved, it may help to think of players in terms of "the player as person," "the player as

[16]Since the *Mayan Ball Game* is such an old game and a variety of versions in different (sub)cultures existed, much unclarity exists about the rules of this game, as well as about the rituals surrounding the game (Shelton 2003). It may very well be that in some of these cultures the losers were sacrificed, while in others the winners were sacrificed. Other than this, it is also important to mention that the game not always ended with sacrificing somebody.

interpreter," and "the player as player" (see Level 2). To do this, it is necessary to think of how players relate to the three worlds of Reality, Meaning, and Play and how all of this could possibly affect the creation of meaning.

Deployment

Not only the characteristics of the target group should be considered in designing the game, the eventual *deployment* of the game matters as well. With this I refer to when, how, in what circumstances, and for how long the game is going to be used. It makes a difference if players play it in a formal or informal setting or when it is part of something else or stands on its own. Although some of this may not require a change of the design of the game, it does require to "design" the environment in which the technology is going to be used.

For example, if classroom hours are 45 minutes, teachers need to consider how they are going to integrate the game within these time slots or whether they should resort to another model of teaching. Additionally, and quite importantly, teachers themselves should be knowledgeable about the use of the game and be able to debrief the experiences.

Aside from the setting in which a game is deployed, a game can become more powerful if it is combined with other material, like books, articles, and excursions, or if it is integrated within some curriculum. From the learning sciences we learned how important "reflection" and "guidance" is. By properly combining with other material or integrating games into a certain context, players may be able to better reflect on their experience and have someone to guide them.

Making a game more powerful could, for instance, be done by using an "Internet forum," a website where the game can be discussed by players, designers, and facilitators. The quite controversial *Super Columbine Massacre RPG!* uses such a forum discussion (Fig. 4.10). This game lets players relive Columbine High School shooting drama near Denver, Colorado, in 1999, by controlling the shooters Eric Harris and Dylan Klebold. It intends to deepen the understanding of the shooting and its possible causes. To achieve this understanding, players are able to express their opinion and views on a forum. This is, for instance, a reaction of one of the players:

> For me, this was one of the hardest games I have ever played. After 20 years of gaming, it is almost natural at this point to try and immerse myself in what I play, but doing so in this case was impossible. If anything, the constant cycle of playing the game versus thinking about playing the game—the association, then dissociation—helped to sharpen the line between game and reality, not blur it. The striking grimness of the contained events, combined with the memory of their transgression, created a very real pathos towards the victims, their killers, and having to deal with consequences for those of us left in the wake. It was certainly not the self-indulgent killfest that many have deemed it. (Dustin SCRMP player n.d.)

Another way to make a game more powerful is to connect players through the game and subsequently have discussions about the differences between players. This

Fig. 4.10 Reliving the Columbine shooting drama with *Super Columbine Massacre RPG!*. Before they armed themselves, they planted a bomb (which did not go off) in the cafeteria. ©Danny Ledonne. Used with permission

has been done in a game called *Budget Hero* (Fig. 4.11). In this game, players can decide for themselves how they would spend the tax dollars on issues such as schooling, health care, and so on. At the end of the game, players have the ability to share and compare their results with others. For making a comparison, it is possible to select players from a certain state, age, gender, income level, or political affiliation. The comparisons show what these groups of people find important and what kind of budget decisions they made. This ability is a great enabler for self-reflection.

After that, players can comment on the game or participate in discussions about the game. The designers foster these latter discussions by providing input. For example, to fuel a discussion, in one post the designers stated the following comment by a Canadian player (Schrenkler 2008):

> Canadian playing here. Its [sic] amazing what your country could become if you dump that big military spending card.

Comments ranged from simple "hell no's" to quite elaborate answers on the question whether military spending need to be cut or not. This way, the game engages the public into a debate about spending tax payer's money.

Admittedly, for both *Budget Hero* as well as *Super Columbine Massacre RPG!* comments are more about the game itself than about what it has to say. The first, especially due to its link with non-profit organizations, received a lot of doubt and criticism about its model of reality, because it creates a feeling that the game is "agenda-influenced" and that it is too "black and white." The second simply received

Fig. 4.11 Deciding on tax payer's money in *Budget Hero*. Each of the skyscrapers represent expenditure areas. The one to the far left represents the military for example. ©2008 American Public Media. Used with permission

a lot of criticism about the quality of the gameplay. Although it is important to discuss the limitations and misrepresentations of the game (world of Reality) and the quality of the gameplay and other game elements (world of Play), these issues may direct the attention away from what the game is trying to say (world of Meaning) and that is a bit unfortunate.

Therefore, we may need to look for other models of how to deploy games to make them more powerful. This goes for all sorts of games that attempt to create some value beyond playing the game itself. I am not providing the answers here. I am merely pointing out that this is certainly something that needs to be taken into account. Best practices and further research should provide us with more insight on this matter.

The Criteria of Meaning

When deciding on the purpose of the game, thinking of a strategy, operationalizing the plan, and considering the context, designers create a "value proposal." This proposal is an elaborate idea of how the value of the game is going to be retrieved. Such a proposal could be a paper-based "living" document, in which the consideration of the several aspects is written down throughout the development of the game. Similar to the world of Reality and its model of reality, to judge the merit of the implementation of this proposal, the world of Meaning has three important criteria that need to be considered: "motivation," "relevance," and "transfer."

Motivation

Next to the law of exercise and the law of effect, the behaviorist Thorndike developed a third law: "the law of readiness" (Knowles et al. 1998). This law relates to the circumstances under which a "learner" tends to be satisfied or annoyed and welcomes or rejects the undertaking. This law stresses, in other words, the importance of whether the learner is motivated or not.

To be motivated, humanists would argue that the learning must come from within. Learners need to be "intrinsically" motivated, by really wanting to learn about a topic, rather than "extrinsically" motivated, such as by getting paid or a grade, to play a game (Malone 1981). Cognitivists, on the other hand, would rather say that information processing takes attention and effort. If a learner is unwilling, the attention and effort is not fully directed toward the game. I could go on and on about how the different learning paradigms look at the subject of *motivation*, but the point here is that it matters for the creation of meaning.

Motivation, whether we talk about an educational game or a game for data collection or theory testing, matters, because in all cases unmotivated players detriment the eventual value that can be retrieved from the game, for the players themselves or for the system at large. For example, somebody who is not willing to get to know the different law areas in *Do I Have A Right?* may play the game in a trial-and-error mode and may not learn anything more than how to proceed in the game. Similarly, if nobody plays *Foldit*, no puzzles will be solved and the game misses its purpose. In short, without motivation, the willingness and persistence to invest time and energy into an activity (Garris et al. 2002), the value of the game becomes limited. This makes it such an important criterion for the world of Meaning.

The importance of motivation is also one of the reasons why games are used. Games can stimulate people and make them motivated (see Level 5). We have to be careful, however, because it is not as simple as putting a "game shell" around the content to motivate players. In the end, the game should make the players enthusiastic about the topic at hand and not only about playing the game itself. Otherwise we are giving chocolate to cover the broccoli. Instead, we should make players like to eat broccoli by showing them how "nutritious" and "special" this vegetable is.

For this reason, I do not like a term such as "incidental learning" when it comes to educational games (cf., Mitchell and Savill-Smith 2004). It may well be that players enjoy the game and without being aware of it "learn something." I rather think that to learn a topic, players need to be consciously interested in it and willing to invest time and energy in it. The game environment may be a great initial motivator to do so in the first place but for continuous and further learning to take place, the player needs to be motivated by the subject in accordance to the play elements, not just by the play elements alone. This means that the learning that takes place is everything but incidental: it is a conscious choice.

This can be illustrated with the exercise types of games, such as *Wii Fit*. Such games motivate and initiate players to do all kinds of exercises. For *Wii Fit*, this concerns amongst many others hula hooping, arm and leg stretching, and breathing exercises. But for players to really persist in doing these exercises, they must have a conscious purpose in mind, as "losing weight" or "keeping my body fit." Otherwise, players may do some of these exercises and after a while get fed up with it, because they see no other reason to continue these exercises and rather play other games or pursue other activities.

While motivation is important, it is also a tough criterion, because motivations are hard to control and differ amongst individuals. Nevertheless, it remains possible to influence motivations and, if necessary, to account for the variability amongst people. When designing a game, see whether players from the target group are meaningfully "triggered"—if they are motivated to contribute to the purpose—by playing the prototypes. If they are, it is at least known that this criterion is taken care off. Now only two other criteria have to be tackled.

Relevance

Other than knowing whether players are motivated to engage with the topic, a crucial element to consider relates to the following question: does playing the game matter at all? It may well be that the value retrieved from the game bears no connection with the original purpose it had. This is quite problematic, because the game was designed to actually reach this purpose. It may seem that it is rather obvious that if a game is designed to achieve something, it also achieves it. The truth is that in practice this may not always be the case. To ensure this connection is made, the criterion of *relevance* has to be looked into.

Something is "relevant" if it serves a means to a given purpose. Therefore, a game fulfills the criterion of relevance if it accomplishes its purpose. To look into the relevance of a game, it is necessary to see how pertinent, connected, or applicable a game is to its original purpose. This can be donc in two ways: the connection with the purpose and what happens in the game and the connection with the purpose and the value retrieved from the game. The first connection concerns the "internal relevance", the second the "external relevance".

As for internal relevance, this relates to the discussion about edutainment games. In these games, the action in the game is often unrelated to the topic at hand. Players may have to shoot, jump, or perform other in-game related activities which are hardly related to the purpose of the game. A way to look at this is to say that the content and game elements are not well integrated. Another way to look at it is to say that the game elements are irrelevant for the topic at hand. The aim for designers is to make sure that the "time-on-task" is as high as possible, meaning that what players do in the game needs to be as relevant as possible to achieve the purpose for what the game is designed for.

Undoubtedly, parts of a game will be somewhat irrelevant. This may concern the time for a player to reach a challenge (the "navigation") or some of the visual stimuli in the game environment. For example, although it could be argued that the duck that swims in the ditch helps to create an authentic setting, I am sure *Levee Patroller* could have done well without it (Fig. 4.12). It bears no strong relevance

Fig. 4.12 The duck that swims in the ditch

for training levee inspection. The central idea for judging the internal relevance is to determine the extent to what the player is really involved with the purpose of the game. This should be at least 75 percent of the time, if not more.

But before judging the internal relevance, designers should first look into the "external relevance." By using the *ESP Game* I will clarify how these two differ. In this game, from the beginning to the end players are continuously involved with tagging pictures. Tagging pictures is the purpose of this game and, therefore, it has a high internal relevance. It also has a high external relevance for a fairly simple reason: it produces tags!

Unfortunately, for other games, especially educationally oriented games, the external relevance is much more difficult to judge, as it is much harder to retrieve and judge its value. We cannot open up the heads of players and see what happened. We can, however, ask players if they found the game valuable—if the game reached its purpose—and, if possible, see if at least *within* the game players improve on the knowledge, skills, and attitudes they are supposed to attain. Experts may also be used to determine this. Nevertheless, to conclude about the difference, external relevance is about whether the game is doing what it is supposed to do, while internal relevance is concerned with how much of the time the game is doing what it is supposed to do.

Another way to look at the two types of relevance is to consider internal relevance as "efficiency," as it is concerned with how much of the game experience players are really preoccupied with the purpose, and external relevance as "effectiveness," as this one is related to whether or not the game really accomplishes its purpose. With this in mind, external relevance seems far more important, but in our times, where people are busy all the time and want to have results as fast as possible, the internal relevance should not be neglected.

The "effectiveness" of a game should not only be judged by its external relevance. If a game accomplishes its purpose, say teaching children simple mathematics such as addition and multiplication, it does not guarantee that it improves the actual real world practice—that it deals with a real world problem. To use the example, accomplishing the teaching purpose does not guarantee whether children are actually able to perform calculations outside the game. Similarly, it does not guarantee whether, in case of tagging pictures with the *ESP Game*, users get better results when they are actually searching for pictures on the Internet. It may be that the tags are not accurate enough in describing the pictures or that people use different words to find than describe pictures.[17]

To judge all of this, we have to look into another criterion, because something could be highly relevant but still not achieve a real world impact. This criterion concerns "transfer" and is about the impact of a game on another environment.

Transfer

The term *transfer* has a bit of a negative connotation nowadays. It is still often used in fields that are dominantly influenced by behavioristic and cognitivistic thoughts, like the field of simulator training. But in fields in which especially (socio)-constructivistic thoughts have taken over, it more or less has lost its merit. I will explain why.

The term was originally introduced as "transfer of practice" by Thorndike and Woodworth (1901). They explored how individuals would learn in one environment and apply what they learned in another environment that shared similar characteristics with the former one. Whereas a wide variety of perspectives and frameworks have appeared since then, all of them share the common principle outlined by Thorndike and Woodworth of how what is learned in one environment affects performance in another (cf., Helfenstein 2005). To affect performance, ideally "what goes in must come out." This means that an ideal transfer is one where the input (what is learned in the learning environment) is more or the less the same as the output (what is applied in the other environment).

Let me elaborate on this by using the game *Do I Have A Right?*. Playing this game is the environment in which individuals would learn, specifically about legal rights. Now the other environment concerns the individuals' daily life, where

[17]It needs to be said that the designers of the *ESP Game* did a great job of increasing the likelihood of retrieving valuable tags by tapping into the social construction of knowledge—players have to agree with each other on the tag to gain points—and by using data mining techniques to compare and validate the results.

they have to judge whether they have a right for something or not. The transfer is knowledge about legal rights, for example the 4th amendment which relates to "no unreasonable searches" (see Fig. 4.5). The designers implemented this and other legal facts, made a game in which players have to apply these facts to cases, and expect that players "pick this up" and use it in their daily lives. As such, a transfer is expected from the game to the application environment.

The negative connotation is caused by two major objections of this picture of learning by scholars from especially the (socio)-constructivistic paradigm. The first objection relates to the idea that information is picked up. According to (socio)-constructivists, people do not simply take up information. They reconcile and interpret it based on their own background and previous experiences. Therefore, it is unlikely that two people will retrieve the same sort of information from a game. What is retrieved from it, concerns not a transfer but a transformation: a construction.

The second objection is about the transfer to the application environment. The socio-constructivists put forward that knowledge is situated. This means that it is unlikely that a (useful) transfer occurs at all. People need to learn knowledge in the social and physical surroundings in which they would perform their actions. When, for example, Brazilian street-market children learn math with market products, they are hardly able to use the same algorithms in another setting (Carraher et al. 1985). What they learned in one situation, is not applicable to another. While games can be considered cognitive tools that enable to situate experiences, they still are simulated experiences and it remains, for this reason, questionable what sort of transfer they bring forth. Players may simply only learn how to play the game.

These objections explain why some scholars are very wary about the term transfer. It assumes that something can be transmitted without being transformed and applied in another situation, like sending mail. While these objections are sound, they are no reason to let go of the idea of transfer. In fact, it would be even problematic, because, as Bransford et al. (1999) put forth, all learning is transfer.

It would also be problematic for games. If games are not able to "transfer," then the whole idea of using games for serious purposes finds basically no common ground. While not all games are educationally oriented, almost each one of them *is* about "transferring" something from the game environment to another to achieve a value, be it attitude change, data collection, or exploration. Only for some games no transfer to another environment is needed. Their usage is immediately apparent. We can think, for instance, of rehabilitation or exercise games. By playing these games, the player's muscles get strengthened right away. The idea of transfer remains, nevertheless, crucial to the success of games and has to be taken "serious" as a criterion.

As for the objections, they merely point out that we have to be careful. Specifically, we have to take into account that players are *unique* individuals. This means it is not likely that all game experiences deliver the same results. Moreover, we have to take into account that *generalization* to another environment can be troublesome. It can be troublesome, because it is difficult to achieve. No clear-cut answers can be given to whether it can be achieved or not, except for saying "it depends." It depends on the problem, the eventual design, the real environment, amongst many other aspects. Some things are simply easier transferred than others and this depends on all of these variables. This is something we have to bear in mind when designing and evaluating our games.

From Meaning to Play

In this level we looked at the aspects and criteria that characterize the world of Meaning. Eventually the consideration of these properties should lead designers to a "value proposal": an idea of how value can be retrieved from playing a game. For my value proposal I delved into the learning sciences. Although all games are about "learning" in one way or the other, these insights, such as practice and chunking, might be less relevant for the development of other games, such as games that aim at data collection or theory testing.

Despite this, the essence of this level is to provide a sense of what types of considerations need to be made when taking this world into account. While for *Levee Patroller* the choice was made to retrieve insights from learning paradigms as behaviorism and socio-constructivism, for another game inspiration could be found in literature about rhetoric, from classics such as Aristotle (1992) and Cicero (90 BC/1954) to a more modern one that even teaches us what Homer Simpson can tell us about rhetoric (Heinrichs 2007). What inspiration is taken depends on the purpose and the strategy to achieve this. This level simply clarified this development process by means of the design of *Levee Patroller*.

Aside that the insights give an idea of how to deal with the world of Meaning, they also provide an idea of why games can be powerful tools. Based on the insights from this level, we can retrieve, for example, that games can be motivating practice environments, are able to provide immediate and extensive feedback, encourage self-directed learning, give concrete experiences, and can situate such experiences, amongst many other things.[18]

As I stressed before, many more insights could be derived from the learning paradigms, to design games but also to explain why they are a powerful tool. To illustrate, one that I did not mention as of yet, concerns *multimodality*. From the learning sciences we can retrieve that information is processed better when it is presented in multiple modes of sensation (Ginns 2005; Mayer 2001). Retention is, for example, improved in case words and pictures are presented together rather than alone.[19] Games make frequently use of multiple modes of sensation. They almost

[18]Gee (2004) mentioned 36 principles that games can offer, from the critical learning principle to the insider principle, in providing an effective learning experience. Most of these principles can be related to the insights that I derived from the learning paradigms. For instance, the "multiple routes principle" relates to the insight of exploration.

[19]The differences in modes and the surplus effect when modes are combined probably relates to the fact that human beings process visual, auditive, and other sensory experiences differently. Our working memory even has two (or even more) different channels, a verbal/text channel (the

always consist of text, images, and sound, and sometimes even have tactile feedback. This ability is probably one of the reasons why Dick Duke asserted that "a game is worth a thousand pictures."

Multimodality is, however, not only valuable from the perspective of the world of Meaning. It also enriches the experience and makes sure players get into it and stay in it. A game without sound is often considered "boring," while a game with sound, if done well, could make players enjoy their game even more. Multimodality is thus important for other reasons as well. These reasons relate to another world, the world of Play.

This third world has much more in common with the world of Meaning. The criteria of motivation and "engagement" for instance. From a Meaning perspective motivation is needed to achieve the purpose of the game. From a Play perspective engagement is necessary to stimulate players to play a game at first, and subsequently, make sure they keep playing (unless this is not needed). Both interests overlap with each other and by dealing with one of them, it may well be that both criteria are satisfied, as they likely reinforce each other.

However, the worlds of Meaning and Play do not always reinforce each other. In fact, they can actually clash with each other. In this level I already pointed out that games hardly give players a moment for reflection. This is crucial from the perspective of Meaning but detrimental from the perspective of Play, as it could break down the flow of the game.

Reflection is just one of many issues that may be encountered during the design of a game that cause a tension within and between worlds. I will illustrate this later on with *Levee Patroller*. We first need to finish the third and final world before we delve into the concept of "balancing."

Bibliography

Literature Bibliography

Anderson, J. R. (1983). *The architecture of cognition*. Cambridge: Harvard University Press.

Anderson, J. R. (1995). *Cognitive psychology and its implications*. New York: Worth.

Anderson, J. R., Reder, L. M., & Simon, H. A. (1996). Situated learning and education. *Educational Researcher*, *25*(4), 5–11.

Anderson, J. R., Greeno, J. G., Reder, L. M., & Simon, H. A. (2000). Perspectives on learning, thinking, and activity. *Educational Researcher*, *29*(4), 11–13.

Aristotle (1992). *The art of rhetoric*. New York: Penguin Classics.

Ausubel, D. P. (1967). *Learning theory and classroom practice*. Toronto: Ontario Institute for Studies in Education.

Baddeley, A. D. (1992). Working memory. *Science*, *255*(5044), 556–559.

"phonological loop") and a visual/spatial channel (the "visual-spatial sketchpad") (cf., Baddeley 1992, 2000). Multimodal information processing affects most if not all of the senses and eventual channels and may, therefore, lead to a better "chunking" of the information.

Baddeley, A. D. (2000). The episodic buffer: a new component of working memory. *Trends in Cognitive Sciences*, *4*(11), 417–423.
Bandura, A. (1977). *Social learning theory*. Englewood Cliffs: Prentice-Hall.
Bartle, R. A. (1996). *Heart, clubs, diamonds, spades: players who suit MUDs*. http://www.mud.co.uk/richard/hcds.htm. Accessed 31 October 2009.
Becker, K. (2008). *The invention of good games: understanding learning design in commercial video games*. Unpublished dissertation, University of Calgary, Calgary, Alberta.
Bogost, I. (2006). *Unit operations: an approach to video game criticism*. Cambridge: The MIT Press.
Bogost, I. (2007). *Persuasive games: the expressive power of videogames*. Cambridge: The MIT Press.
Bransford, J. D., Brown, A. L., & Cocking, R. R. (1999). *How people learn: brain, mind, experience and school*. Washington: National Academy Press.
Brown, J. S., Collins, A., & Duguid, P. (1989). Situated cognition and the culture of learning. *Educational Researcher*, *18*(1), 32–42.
Bruner, J. S. (1961). The act of discovery. *Harvard Educational Review*, *31*(1), 21–32.
Caillois, R. (1958/1961). *Man, play and games*. Champaign: University of Illinois Press (M. Barash, Transl.).
Carraher, T. N., Carraher, D. W., & Schliemann, A. D. (1985). Mathematics in the streets and in schools. *British Journal of Developmental Psychology*, *3*, 21–29.
Carraher, T. N., Carraher, D. W., & Schliemann, A. D. (1987). Written and oral mathematics. *Journal for Research in Mathematics Education*, *18*(2), 83–97.
Chase, W. G., & Simon, H. A. (1973). The mind's eye in chess. In W. G. Chase (Ed.), *Visual information processing* (pp. 215–281). New York: Academic Press.
Chi, M. T. H., Feltovich, P., & Glaser, R. (1981). Categorization and representation of physics problems by experts and novices. *Cognitive Science*, *5*(2), 121–152.
Chomsky, N. (1968). *Language and mind*. New York: Harcourt, Brace & World.
Cicero (90 BC/1954). *Rhetorica ad herennium*. Cambridge: Harvard University Press (H. Caplan, Transl.).
Danesi, M. (2002). *The puzzle instinct: the meaning of puzzles in human life*. Bloomington: Indiana University Press.
De Freitas, S., & Neumann, T. (2009). The use of 'exploratory learning' for supporting immersive learning in virtual environments. *Computers and Education*, *52*(2), 343–352.
De Groot, A. D. (1965). *Thought and choice in chess*. The Hague: Mouton.
Dewey, J. (1938). *Experience and education*. New York: MacMillan.
Dustin SCRMP player (n.d.). *Reaction Super Columbine Massacre RPG!*. http://www.columbinegame.com/. Accessed 12 September 2009.
Egenfeldt-Nielsen, S. (2007). *Beyond edutainment: the educational potential of computer games*. London: Continuum Press.
Erikson, E. H. (1968). *Identity, youth and crisis*. New York: Norton.
Fitts, P. M., & Posner, M. I. (1967). *Human performance*. Belmont: Brooks/Cole.
Games-to-Teach Team (2003). Design principles of next-generation digital gaming for education. *Educational Technology*, *43*(5), 17–33.
Gardner, H. (1991). *The unschooled mind: how children think and how schools should teach*. New York: Basic Books.
Garris, R., Ahlers, R., & Driskell, J. E. (2002). Games, motivation, and learning: a research and practice model. *Simulation & Gaming*, *33*(4), 441–467.
Gee, J. (2004). *What video games have to teach us about learning and literacy*. New York: Palgrave Macmillan.
Ginns, P. (2005). Meta-analysis of the modality effect. *Learning and Instruction*, *15*(4), 313–333.
Gray, P. (2002). *Psychology* (4th ed.). New York: Worth.
Greenfield, P. M. (1984). *Mind and media: the effects of television, video games, and computers*. Cambridge: Harvard University Press.
Greeno, J. G. (1998). The situativity of knowing, learning, and research. *The American Psychologist*, *53*(1), 5–26.

Heinrichs, J. (2007). *Thank you for arguing: what Aristotle, Lincoln, and Homer Simpson can teach us about the art of persuasion*. New York: Three Rivers Press.
Helfenstein, S. (2005). *Transfer: review, reconstruction, and resolution*. Jyväskylä: Jyväskylä University Printing House.
Heukels, F. (2006). *Chiquita lanceert "verantwoorde" advergame [Chiquita launches "responsible" advergame]*. http://www.molblog.nl/bericht/Chiquita-lanceert-verantwoorde-advergame/. Accessed 12 August 2010.
Hill, W. F. (1977). *Learning*. New York: Crowell.
Honey, P., & Mumford, A. (1992). *The manual of learning styles* (3rd ed.). Maidenhead: Peter Honey.
Johnson, S. (2005). *Everything bad is good for you: how today's popular culture is actually making us smarter*. New York: Riverhead Books.
Jonassen, D. H. (1999). *Computers as mindtools for schools: engaging critical thinking* (2nd ed.). Upper Saddle River: Prentice Halls.
Knowles, M. S., Elwood, F., Holton, I., & Swanson, R. A. (1998). *The adult learner* (5th ed.). Houston: Gulf.
Kolb, D. A. (1984). *Experiential learning: experience as the source of learning and development*. Upper Saddle River: Prentice Hall.
Koster, R. (2005). *A theory of fun for game design*. Scottsdale: Paraglyph Press.
Laurel, B. (2001). *Utopian entrepreneur*. Cambridge: The MIT Press.
Lave, J., & Wenger, E. (1991). *Situated learning: legitimate peripheral participation*. Cambridge: Cambridge University Press.
Malone, T. W. (1981). Toward a theory of intrinsically motivating instruction. *Cognitive Science*, *5*(4), 333–369.
Maslow, A. H. (1970). *Motivation and personality*. New York: Harper & Row.
Mayer, R. E. (2001). *Multi-media learning*. Cambridge: Cambridge University Press.
Merriam, S. B., & Caffarella, R. S. (1999). *Learning in adulthood: a comprehensive guide* (2nd ed.). San Francisco: Jossey-Bass.
Miller, G. (1956). The magical number seven, plus or minus two: some limits on our capacity for processing information. *Psychological Review*, *63*(2), 81–97.
Mitchell, A., & Savill-Smith, C. (2004). *The use of computer and video games for learning*. London: Learning and Skill Development Agency.
Papert, S. (1980). *Mindstorms: children, computers, and powerful ideas*. New York: Basic Books.
Piaget, J. (1929). *The child's conception of the world*. New York: Harcourt Brace Jovanovich.
Prensky, M. (2001). *Digital game-based learning*. New York: McGraw-Hill.
Rasmussen, J. (1986). *Information processing and human-machine interaction: an approach to cognitive engineering*. New York: North Holland.
Rogers, C. (1983). *Freedom to learn for the 80s*. Columbus: Charles Merrill.
Rollings, A., & Morris, D. (2004). *Game architecture and design: a new edition*. Indianapolis: New Riders.
Schank, R. (1997). *Virtual learning: a revolutionary approach to building a highly-skilled workforce*. New York: McGraw-Hill.
Schrenkler, J. (2008). *Budget Hero: would you cut military spending?* http://www.gather.com/viewArticle.action?articleId=281474977352111. Accessed 3 November 2009.
Shelton, A. A. (2003). The Aztec theatre state and the dramatization of war. In T. Cornell & T. B. Allen (Eds.), *War and games* (pp. 107–130). New York: Boydell Press.
Short, E. (2008). *The unit is in the eye of the beholder*. http://www.electronicbookreview.com. Accessed 2 September 2009.
Simon, H. A. (1969). *The sciences of the artificial*. Cambridge: The MIT Press.
Skinner, B. F. (1938). *The behavior of organisms*. New York: Appleton-Century-Crofts.
Squire, K., Barnett, M., Grant, J. M., & Higgenbotham, T. (2004). Electromagnetism Supercharged!: learning physics with digital simulation games. In Y. B. Kafai, W. A. Sandoval, N. Enyedy, A. S. Nixon & F. Herrera (Eds.), *The sixth international conference on learning sciences* (pp. 513–520). Mahwah: Lawrence Erlbaum.

Stewart, P. M. (2009). Does the 3d serious game Physics Geeks facilitate learning in conceptual physics students? In M. Goldstein & A. Saravanos (Eds.), *Teachers college educational technology conference proceedings* (pp. 32–34). New York: Lawrence Erlbaum.
Tate, R., Haratatos, J., & Cole, S. (2009). Hopelab's approach to Re-Mission. *International Journal of Learning and Media*, *1*(1), 29–35.
Thorndike, E. L. (1932). *The fundamentals of learning*. New York: Teachers College Press.
Thorndike, E. L., & Woodworth, R. S. (1901). The influence of improvement in one mental function upon the efficiency of other functions. *Psychological Review*, *8*, 247–261.
Vygotsky, L. S. (1978). *Mind in society: the development of higher psychological processes*. Cambridge: Harvard University Press.
Watson, J. B. (1930). *Behaviorism*. Chicago: University of Chicago Press.
Wickens, C. D., Lee, J. D., Liu, Y., & Becker, S. E. G. (2004). *Introduction to human factors engineering*. London: Pearson Prentice Hall.

Game Bibliography

5TH Cell Media (2007). *Drawn to Life* [Nintendo DS]. Agoura Hills: THQ.
American Public Media, & Woodrow Wilson International Center for Scholars (2008). *Budget Hero* [Web]. St. Paul: American Public Media.
Blizzard Entertainment (2004). *World of Warcraft* [PC]. Irvine: Blizzard Entertainment.
CCP Games (2003). *Eve Online* [PC]. Reykjavik, Iceland: CCP Games.
Deltares, & Delft University of Technology (2006). *Levee Patroller: The Levee Inspection Simulator* [PC]. Delft, the Netherlands: Delft GeoSystems.
Filament Games, & Our Courts (2009). *Do I Have A Right?* [Web]. USA: Our Courts.
Games-To-Teach Team (2003). *Supercharged!* [PC]. Cambridge: The Education Arcade.
Kramer, C. (1984). *Tempo Typen* [PC]. Alphen aan den Rijn, the Netherlands: Radarsoft.
Ledonne, D. (2005). *Super Columbine Massacre RPG!* [PC]. Published independently.
Maxis Software (2008). *Spore* [PC]. Redwood City: Electronic Arts.
Media Molecule (2008). *LittleBigPlanet* [Playstation 3]. Foster City: Sony Computer Entertainment America.
Molleindustria (2006). *The McDonald's Video Game* [PC]. Italy: Molleindustria.
Natsume (2006). *Harvest Moon* [Nintendo DS]. Tokyo, Japan: Marvelous Interactive.
Nintendo EAD (2007). *Wii Fit* [Wii]. Tokyo, Japan: Nintendo.
Paradox Interactive (2001). *Europa Universalis II* [PC]. Montreal, Canada: Strategy First.
Paradox Interactive (2007). *Europa Universalis III* [PC]. Stockholm, Sweden: Paradox Interactive.
Positech Games (2007). *Democracy 2* [PC]. UK: Positech Games.
Powerful Robot Games (2003). *September 12th* [Web]. Montevideo, Uruguay: Newsgaming.com.
Realtime Associates (2006). *Re-Mission* [PC]. Redwood City: HopeLab Foundation.
Rockstar North (2008). *Grand Theft Auto IV* [Playstation 3]. New York: Rockstar Games.
Simulearn (2003). *Virtual Leader* [PC]. Norwalk: Simulearn.
Smilebit (2000). *The Typing of the Dead* [PC]. Tokyo, Japan: SEGA.
The Virtual Learning Worlds team (2009). *Physics Geeks* [PC]. New York: Colobmia University.
These Days (2006). *The Chiquita Game* [Web]. Antwerp, Belgium: These Days.
University of Washington (2008). *Foldit: Solve Puzzles for Science* [PC]. Seattle: University of Washington.
Valve (2007). *Portal* [PC]. Bellevue: Valve.
Von Ahn, L., & Dabbish, L. (2004). *ESP Game* [Web]. Pittsburgh: Carnegie Mellon University.

Level 5
Play

We do not stop playing because we grow old. We grow old because we stop playing—Oliver Wendell Holmes

You can discover more about a person in an hour of play than in a year of conversation—Plato

Adults do not play. At least, that is what our common sense tells us. Adults should work, be serious, act responsible, and take care of others. Play is seen as a waste of time, trivial, and childish (Caillois 1961). The negative connotation of play extends to the English language. Consider the following statements:[1]

- "He is just playing around" (i.e., not being serious).
- "He plays with his toys" (i.e., he is like a child).
- "He is a player" (i.e., a heartbreaker).
- "He plays too much" (i.e., not acting grown up).
- "He is playing up to someone" (i.e., fooling or deceiving someone).

Contrary to adults, children do play. Parents even demand them to play. Who has not been told by their parents to go outside and play? It is hard for me to believe that parents demand their children to go out and play simply because they are of the opinion that children should devote their time to trivial activities. Every parent knows, although maybe not that explicitly, that playing is valuable for their children. In fact, the usefulness of play does not and should not stop when we grow old (see the quote by Holmes). The thing is, most adults actually do play! They play in their work and in their private life. Adults only do not (dare) to call it that way.

Take the development of *Levee Patroller*. While working on this game, I noticed that several team members exhibited strong playful behavior when the workday was already over (Fig. 5.1). For example, the lead programmer coded scripts to showcase

[1] I am using the masculine pronoun in these statements on purpose. Based on my (stereotyped) experiences it seems that I have only been hearing adult women say this to adult men, and almost never the other way around.

C. Harteveld, *Triadic Game Design*,
DOI 10.1007/978-1-84996-157-8_5, © Springer-Verlag London Limited 2011

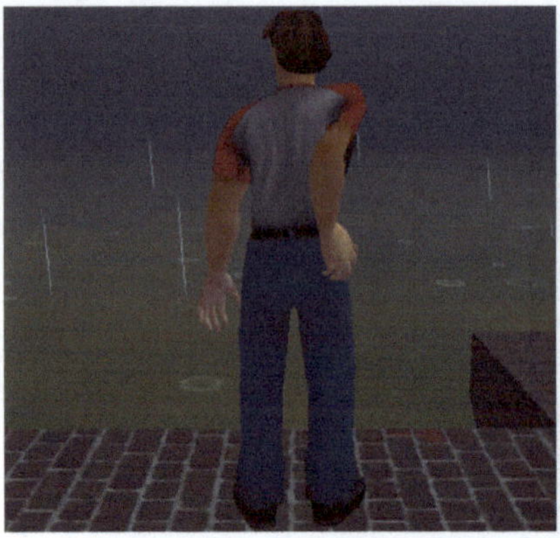

(a) Programmer's fun: an itchy rear

(b) Modeler's creativity: the hidden Dopefish

(c) Level designer's humor: duck hunt

Fig. 5.1 Playful behavior of the *Levee Patroller* design team

some odd behavior when the player-character was not doing anything, like scratching its itchy rear. The working of the scripts could only be shown in a third-person perspective, a perspective in which the player-character is seen from the back, while early on it was decided we would not use this perspective. No player would ever see this. This code was, therefore, not of any use to the project. The programmer was simply "playing around" with the possibilities of the scripting language.

The modelers, on the other hand, were putting effort into creating a graphical object and hiding this in the game. The graphical object they were working on was the so-called "Dopefish." The Dopefish is a historical game object. It first appeared in *Commander Keen 4* back in 1991. Since that moment a complete "Dopefish mania" was released, leading many design teams to incorporate references to the Dopefish in their games.[2] And the modelers were, of course, of the opinion that *Levee Patroller* should have a reference as well. To achieve this, they "played with their toys," their software tools, such as a 3D graphics application to visualize the object, an application tool to export and subsequently import the object to the gameworld, and an editor tool to place and hide the object in the gameworld. To my recollection, no player has ever found this Dopefish.

Finally, I observed that our level designer, the person responsible for creating the gameworld, is a real "player." He plays so many shooter games that he found *Levee Patroller* too boring without any guns. He is not the only one who thinks this. At many occasions, the first thing players of *Levee Patroller* jokingly ask me is "Where are the guns?" To enable this, the level designer imported a gun from another game and changed some of the settings in the editor tool. By doing this, he changed the game into a "duck shooting game." The whole team laughed about this little side project.

These examples of playful behavior seem rather useless, as they are not directly beneficial to the project. Yet, this "playing around" by the design team is everything but trivial. The examples show people very engaged in an activity, willing to commit great amounts of time and energy into this activity, while nobody is forcing them to spend their free time on this activity. Additionally, the team learned and explored the tools they were using to create the game. As such, they retrieved skills and insights that may have been indirectly highly valuable to the project.

Also important to acknowledge is that the behavior exhibited by the team is not much different from the behavior as shown by children who decide to build a shopping mall with Lego on a Saturday afternoon (Rieber 1996). To build this shopping mall, these children also need to be committed and willing to spend their free time on this activity. Therefore, a "homo ludens," a person who plays, be it a child or an adult, is someone who is engaged into a certain activity while concurrently learning about or attributing to something. People who put play away as being trivial either do not realize that what they do is valuable or they do not recognize that they are actually playing.

Play can thus be valuable in and of itself. But to intentionally create an effective playful environment to achieve some real world value is not that easy. One of the activities to promote "playful behavior," aside from make-belief and free form activities, is by using games. Games, as I explained in Level 2, are a subset of play.[3] They differ from other playful activities by being "structured": they have clear rules that guide participants in what happens throughout the activity. This structuredness enables designers to "direct" the experience toward something meaningful. For this

[2]More information on the Dopefish can be found at http://www.dopefish.com, a website devoted to "everyone's favorite fish."

[3]Caillois (1961) called make-belief and free form activities "paidia," while he called games "ludus." These terms are often used in gaming literature. The difference is, however, not that clear-cut. Some games have a lot of "free form" elements and others allow little to no differentiation from what was initially thought of. To my opinion, the difference should rather be seen as a dimension than a categorization.

reason, although other playful activities can be meaningful as well (see the examples of the design team), as a tool for achieving a meaningful purpose, games are the most interesting playful activity. That is why this book is focused on this playful activity and not on any others.

In this level I will elaborate on the design of games from the perspective of the world of Play, the third and final world that makes up TGD. This is the world of game designers, modelers, artists, and programmers, and other creative or technology oriented people. These people look differently at the design process than subject-matter experts, teachers, and storytellers. They borrow insights from cartoons, movies, and music to scientific disciplines as computer science, human-computer interaction, and sociological and psychological studies into the playful nature of human beings. In being involved in this world, I identified four primary aspects and three criteria that are affiliated with it and which almost always need to be considered when designing a game.

The aspects concern the goal of the game (see "What Does the Player Do?"), its gameplay (see "A Series of Interesting Choices"), the game world (see "Constructing an Imaginative World"), and the technology used (see "Choosing the Right Technology"). Together, the consideration of these aspects leads to a *game concept*, a document that describes what the game is about. The criteria for judging the game concept are engagement, immersion, and fun (see "The Criteria of Play").

After explaining the "goal" of this level, what would be a better start than discussing the "goal" aspect of games?

What Does the Player Do?

According to game designer Crawford (1982) the first and foremost question a designer has to answer is "What does the player do?" In determining this, it is important to clarify the *goal* of the game. A goal is an explicit or implicit statement at the beginning of the game that explains what the player needs to do. It defines the sort of objectives, like saving the princess or planet earth, that players need to achieve to reach the desired end-state. If players achieve the goal(s), they succeed. Otherwise they fail.

Defining a goal is not an easy task. At this point in the design, designers basically start from scratch. They may have defined a problem and a purpose, but other than that, they have little to nothing to work with. To succeed, "creativity" is needed and inspiration may be found from existing game genres and daydreaming. But to be able to define a goal, it is first necessary to get a deep understanding of the importance of a goal to games. This has to do with "clarity."

Clarity

Having "goals" is considered one of the most distinguishing characteristics that make up a game (Prensky 2001; Salen and Zimmerman 2004). In fact, when an artifact does not have clear goals, such as *SimCity*, it can be considered less game-like (Juul 2005). Not all games are necessarily about winning and losing, but they are about achieving something. In *SimCity*, players definitely also try to achieve something, like building a grand metropolitan area. The difference is that the players decide what the goals of the game are. These goals are somewhat mediated by the game, because players cannot think of goals like saving a princess unless the game would allow players to do so.

This means that implicitly the game has "some goal." Yet to be a pure game, the goals have to be *clear*. A goal is considered clear when it is known what results are better than others.[4] In *SimCity* this is also up to the player and this makes the "game" a borderline case for being defined as a game (Juul 2005).

The need for clear goals and a clear system of how outcomes are valued, is not only important for an artifact to be a game. It is also relevant to not frustrate players. Playing a game is an emotional experience. Winning and losing are emotional states and achieving "something" in general gives an emotional thrill. Every time I at least finish a puzzle, my body is filled with excitement. If this happens, a sudden burst flows through my body that makes me want to scream "Yes, I did it!"

Next to this emotional layer, players invest time and energy into a game—called "player effort" by Juul (2005)—and they want to be rewarded for it. Although emotionally they would feel terrible if they lose a game, they would accept the loss *if* they lost it in a rather fare and not completely arbitrary way. This is more likely to happen if goals are clear upfront and the outcomes are perceived to be "right" concerning what happened throughout the game. If a player is hit by an enemy and dies, there is no "but."

A game of chance, like flipping a coin, is a good example to further illustrate the acceptance of the outcomes of a game. While such a game *is* rather arbitrary, players still accept the outcomes. They are willing to accept them, because they agreed to the "rules." If players know they are going to flip a coin, they are aware that the outcomes are either heads or tails and that chance predicts what the outcome will be.

Such acceptance is less likely to occur with games with a serious purpose. Such games are everything but arbitrary. They serve something and this something could be highly valuable to the player. If by chance an important part of the results are determined, then it is very likely that players get frustrated and not accept the outcomes—even when they initially agreed on the rules. For them to do accept, it is required that the outcomes make sense.

For example, say a game with a serious purpose uses elements of chance, such as the determination of the demand of a product that players need to sell by a random number. To make sure players accept the outcomes of this, clarity is, again, needed. It needs to be clear why those outcomes are achieved. In this case, it could be explained that demands are fluctuating and that it depends on many variables what the eventual demand will be. The uncertainty surrounding the demand is simply

[4] Juul (2005) termed the criterion to consider whether a game has clear goals "valorization of outcome." This criterion determines whether it is possible to see what results are better than others.

symbolized in the game by drawing a random number and that explains why it has an element of chance. If such a clarification is not given (at the beginning or end), players may find the game to be a "waste of their time."

The point here for dealing with the first aspect of the world of Play, the goal of the game, is two-folded: when designing a game it needs to be ensured that (a) the game has clear goals so the players know what they need to do, and (b) what players do is appropriately valorized in terms of the game's outcomes by making sure the game has clear rules as to how the goals can be achieved. If not, players may very likely reject the game and everything that it tries to achieve. Clarity is thus needed, unless, of course, the game is supposed to be an "open-ended simulation," such as *SimCity*, where the goal of the game and the valorization of the outcomes are on purpose less clear.

Creativity

By now it has become "clear" why the goal of a game is such an important aspect to consider when designing a game. But how to really define one? Sometimes this is a rather easy. This happens when the goal *in* the game is similar to the purpose *of* the game. In the eventual design of *Levee Patroller* this is the case. The goal in the game is to find and report failures while its purpose is to learn to recognize and report failures.

Goal and purpose are not necessarily the same. In fact, they are very different from one another. A goal is an aspect of the world of Play and deals with what the player does inside the game environment. The purpose, on the other hand, is an aspect affiliated with the world of Meaning, relates to what value the game tries to achieve, and goes beyond the context of the game. Despite this, the two are closely linked to each other, because in achieving the goal in the game, the purpose of the game is (hopefully) achieved. With *The Typing of the Dead*, for example, the goal is to kill zombies and by doing this the purpose of increasing typing skills is hopefully achieved.

To think of a goal different from the purpose is obviously more difficult. This requires some *creativity*. To find inspiration, it helps to look into the various existing game genres, like action, adventure, puzzle, role-playing, simulation, and strategy (see Level 2). This helps, because the type of game determines to a large extent the goal a game has. For instance, a puzzle game probably has as goal to "solve the puzzle," a shooter to "kill everybody," a fighting game to "beat the opponent," a strategy game to "conquer enemies or expand territory," and so on.

Deciding on a genre is not sufficient. It assists in finding a goal, but does not completely define it. For this, another inspiration is needed and according to Rollings and Adams (2003) this can be found while "daydreaming." Daydreaming involves experiencing a visionary fantasy while awake. By doing this, designers creatively think of the possibilities of their game. Before I came up with the "seemingly" obvious goal *Levee Patroller* has, I have done this daydreaming. In my daydreams, I took the various existing genres and the purpose of "levee patrollers recognizing and reporting failures" as a starting point. The results of my daydreams are summarized in Table 5.1.

None of the daydreams really satisfied me, as each has a number of advantages and disadvantages. For example, I could immediately eliminate the role-playing and strategy dreams as they are too complex. An average levee patroller would never understand this. The advantage of an adventure, its story, is also immediately its disadvantage. A puzzle game is fun, but limited in what it has to offer, while an action game emphasizes everything except for what needs to be learned. The most obvious choice might have been to go for the simulation genre, but then we would have lost the many possibilities that games have to offer. Aldrich (2004) reached more or less the same conclusion during the design of *Virtual Leader*:[5]

> ...we worried that any of the familiar genres would overwhelm our content, forcing us down a path of greater and greater comprises. By simply putting on a new veneer of linear content and making computational changes to an old framework, we might make the game more acceptable to a business audience, but we really would not be teaching anything substantially different. We came to a conclusion that I believe all [game] designers will have to come to in the near term...we will all have to build completely new genres to populate the world of educational [games]. (p. 64)

From this, we can conclude that to teach "anything substantially different" than what other tools offer, such as books or lectures, we "have to build completely new genres." This is to some extent no surprise. Games with a serious purpose are fundamentally different from entertainment games in that they need to reach a value beyond the context of the game. To achieve this, it may not help to rigidly stick to existing game genres. As Koster (2005) provocatively wrote, current entertainment games solely teach survival skills (e.g., shooting, jumping, fighting, and so on), skills that were useful in the days that humans were still hunting and fishing and not in today's society. Designers can be inspired by existing genres, but by sticking rigidly to them it may lead to failure, as what happened with the edutainment movement (Egenfeldt-Nielsen 2007).

Where to go then? Aldrich (2004) ended up putting simulation and strategy elements with a sip of action elements together in a blender and mix them. The result was *Virtual Leader*, a revolutionary product, as we can firmly state by now. His approach was to "step out of the box" of game genres and look further, but at the same time use the ingredients that make these genres strong. In every meal we add some pepper and salt to make it taste better. Why would this be any different for designing games? We know some of the ingredients of entertainment games work and we can thus derive inspiration from these games in developing the concept of a game with a serious purpose.

In the spirit of Aldrich (2004) I stepped out of the box myself as well, and thought about which ingredients I could put in the blender. In the end, the mix consisted of the following ingredients (in order of importance):

---

[5] Aldrich (2004) speaks in his book of educational simulations. To avoid any confusion I replaced simulation with games.

Table 5.1 Daydreaming about the concept of *Levee Patroller*

Genre	Dream	Advantages	Disadvantages
Action	You are Super Levee Patroller, the one who runs over levees and dismantles failures in a flash with a set of tools as the time is ticking away	Scores and time limits increase engagement; easy to understand and implement	It is about training survival rather than inspection skills; time pressure does not allow for reflection
Adventure	At one day you wake up and you are asked to solve the mystery behind the wet spots in your little town by talking to inhabitants and collecting items	People learn through stories; emphasis on exploration and problem-solving	Difficult to think of a reasonable story that integrates the learning objectives; inflexible; huge effort to implement
Puzzle	Failures are puzzles to the extreme! You get to see one failure at a time. Stop the failure in time or the levee breaches and you loose	Flexible and simple to create; it requires some thinking	Not synchronized with the skills of a real levee patroller; limited in what it teaches
Role-play	Choose for instance Robert, the reporting whizkid, or John, with his laser eyes, and build up the skills of your character, so you can face more dangerous tasks	Configurable characters increase engagement; increasing difficulty is in line with the zone of proximal development	Requires many hours to play, something not everyone is willing to invest; quite unrealistic; complex
Simulation	Take place in a world that looks as real as possible. With some variables set by the facilitator you are ready to go and act as you normally would	Flexible by being able to set up scenarios; realistic	Not very engaging; the high emphasis on realism restricts potentially more powerful ways to transfer meaning
Strategy	You are the commander over one region and need to ensure this region will not get flooded by managing your resources	Many opportunities for deeper learning of the material; easy integration of informational messages	Not synchronized with the skills of a real levee patroller; difficult to implement; complex
Virtual world	You are part of the Waterproof Clan, a group of patrollers that need to protect a region from flooding. Communicate, collaborate, and take leadership to safeguard the whole region	Exchange of information between patrollers; construction of social knowledge	Emphasis on social rather than inspection skills; difficult to implement; a bit unrealistic; complex

Fig. 5.2 Eating little dots while avoiding the ghosts in *Pac-Man*. Screen shot is taken from the Flash version of the original game by Paul Neave. ©1981 Namco

- The realism and flexibility of simulation games.
- The mystery, bewilderment, and the act of solving problems of puzzle games.
- The instant-action, scores, time pressure, and excitement of action games.
- The use of inventories and conversations as seen in role-playing and adventure games.

The only genres I did not add to the mix at all concerned the strategy and virtual world genres, as I did not see any use of their ingredients for this game. The mix can be considered an "action-adventure-puzzle-role-play-simulation" game or as a "weird game," a game that does not belong to really any of the prototypical genres (Griffiths 1996). As this is just a horrible name I tend to refer to the game as an "advanced *Pac-Man*." While in *Pac-Man* the player has to eat all the little dots as fast as possible, the player in *Levee Patroller* has to "eat" all the failures under considerable time pressure as well. This "eating" in *Levee Patroller* can be seen as detective-work, since failures need to be analyzed into detail. This part largely explains for the puzzle element of the game. It is "advanced," because it is situated in a complete three-dimensional environment, has the state-of-the-art computer graphics from the time it was being developed, and involves more than eating dots and avoiding ghosts, whereas the original *Pac-Man* is two-dimensional, has very basic computer graphics, and involves a fairly simple gameplay (Fig. 5.2).

Despite all the "pepper and salt" added to the game, it looks and feels aboveall as a simulation game as it stays quite closely too reality. The goal in the game is even similar to the purpose of the game. But to define this seemingly simple goal, a creative process preceded, in which several (fantastical) possibilities have been looked into. Although creativity is needed in every aspect of a design, the creativeness of designers is especially tapped into for defining what the player does.

When the goal of a game is finally clear, what the player does can be further fleshed out. For this another aspect has to be considered, one that looks into the types of challenges players have to deal with and what players are able to do. This aspect is commonly known as "gameplay."

A Series of Interesting Choices

To achieve the "goal" of the game players face a variety of "challenges." Challenges are basically the obstacles that players must overcome. Rollings and Adams (2003) found a wide variety of challenges in games, from logic and inference, lateral-thinking, memory, intelligence-based, pattern-recognition, moral, spatial-awareness, coordination, reflex/reaction time, to physical challenges. They also assert that the combination of challenges and the "actions" that players can take to meet them, makes up for the most difficult and important task in designing a game: creating the *gameplay*.

Despite the very concrete definition of "challenges plus actions," gameplay seems to involve much more and remains a notion that is difficult to grasp. The only way to really describe it is by telling what exactly happens in the game. This stresses another way of looking of what gameplay is. According to Juul (2005) "it is important to understand that the gameplay is not the rules themselves, the game tree, or the game's fiction, but the way the game is actually played" (p. 83).

How a game is played is very much dependent on the players themselves which makes them a third important element of what comprises "gameplay." Players have their own methods for playing the game. This can be considered the "player's repertoire." Such a repertoire is on the one hand stimulated and demanded by the game and on the other hand interpreted and "filled out" by the players themselves. Similar to how a reader cannot change the words of a book but is able to decide how these words are read and interpreted, a player has some influence on how the game is played.

Another and related reason for the difficulty to grasp gameplay is that it can be considered an "emergent" and "dynamic" property. Gameplay cannot be simply denoted as "defeat monster X" by "either shooting with a gun or kicking him hard." Even when we add a player's repertoire to it, like "I like to continuously jump around so the monster is less likely to hit me," it pictures it as something "static" while in fact gameplay is something dynamic and emerges out of an interaction between the challenges, the available actions, and the player's repertoire. This explains partly why it is so difficult to pinpoint the gameplay in a game. We cannot say "this is the gameplay," because the gameplay is much more than just "this." The gameplay changes over time and is dependent on the interaction of various elements.

The element that connects the various elements, the challenges, actions, and the player's repertoire, are the *rules* of the game. Rules determine what impact an action has on a challenge and determine the solution space of the players and thereby influences their repertoire. For example, if a player shoots, the rules determine that it decreases the life energy of opponents with 10%, whereas if the player would kick them, they would lose 5%. To see how rules can affect gameplay, reconsider the excerpt about two seemingly similar first person shooter games, *Quake III Arena* and *Counter-Strike* in Level 2 (pp. 36–37). From this example we see that small rule changes have a major effect on the game system at large.

Based on these insights, we should reconsider the original definition by Rollings and Adams (2003). In my view, gameplay consists of a continuously changing combination of the challenges players face, the actions that are available to them, the way they execute these actions, and the rules that connect the previous elements. With this in mind, it is no wonder that most people give a very detailed description of their game experience when we ask them to tell about the gameplay of a certain game. With this in mind it is also no wonder why it so difficult to design gameplay. Many elements and their interaction need to be considered. Additionally, it explains why so much playtesting is required to get it "right" (Rollings and Adams 2003).

For designing gameplay the notion of Sid Meier, designer of *Civilization* and many other classic games, that games are "a series of interesting choices" (Rollings and Morris 2004, p. 38) is useful. For a game to be interesting, players should not know upfront what happens. Otherwise they have no reason to play the game. The game needs to have some "uncertainty." But a game is certainly not interesting when the player's actions do not affect the game. Why else would a player put any effort in playing a game? To be interesting, the concept of "interactivity" has to be kept in mind as well. I will elaborate on this latter issue first.

Interactivity

For ensuring "good" gameplay *interactivity* is necessary. This term, which others call "procedurality" (Murray 1997), is a bit mystical, but I think Crawford's (2005) definition is somewhat revealing and to the point: "Interactivity is a cyclic process between two or more active agents in which each agent alternately listens, thinks and speaks" (p. 29). This definition implies that two or more agents, whether it be a computer, human or something else, exchange messages that are related to each other.

Let me illustrate this definition with a piece of experimental software from 2004 which to my knowledge is still unbeaten when it comes to realizing the idea "interactive storytelling" (Crawford 2005).[6] To create "interactive stories," stories must

[6]Other examples are the well-known *ELIZA* piece of software (Murray 1997), developed by Joseph Weizenbaum between 1964 and 1966, and Crawford's 2005 *Storytron* project. The first is not really a game. It is a digital doctor that listens to the complaints and problems of the user. Users can type anything they want. To respond to this, *ELIZA* uses the trick of rephrasing parts of the responses of the user with knowledge of how such conversations normally proceed and this works actually

not be prewritten upfront but be constructed based on the input of the player. This is quite difficult to achieve, because it requires to first of all understand what the player wants and secondly to give a reasonable response. *Façade* is a good attempt to achieve both (Fig. 5.3).

In *Façade* the player enters without having a clear goal a nice apartment as an old college friend of a couple named Trip and Grace.[7] Although no assignment is really given, it quickly becomes clear that Trip and Grace have some relationships issues. Players are able to freely walk around, pick up some object, physically interact with Trip and Grace (e.g., giving them a hug or a kiss), but more importantly, they are able to type anything they want. In most cases Trip and Grace will respond appropriately.[8] This way, an "interactive conversation" is achieved. Consider the following conversation I had with them (I am "Bob"):

BOB: What is that ball you are holding?
TRIP: Oh that—oh, that is just a little joke advice giver toy thing that I like to consult now and then...
TRIP: when I need a little guidance. Ha ha.
GRACE: His mother gave that to him.
TRIP: Oh, Bob, I thought you might like this photo I just put up from our recent trip to Italy.
GRACE: Uhh, it is a beautiful picture of the Italian countryside, of course he will like it!
TRIP: Grace, I know you don't like it, but our friend might.
BOB: It is nice.
TRIP: Oh! Ha ha, ha ha, yeah—
GRACE: Bob, careful, too many compliments can go to Trip's head...
TRIP: Um...uhh, Now, Bob, in one word, what does this picture say to you?
GRACE: Say to you...say to you...yes, good question, good question.
TRIP: Grace stayed behind in the hotel room when I was out taking this picture, so...
BOB: Love.
TRIP: Right! Love! Romance!
GRACE: Romance? Ha, in our marriage, that is just a code word for manipulation.

From this conversation we see how I, the user, give an input, upon which two other active agents, Trip and Grace, respond. Subsequently, I react upon their reaction, and so on. A "cyclic process" was started, in which the exchange of messages

---

pretty well (and is very telling about us humans...). Crawford's *Storytron*, on the other hand, is a project with a huge ambition. It is an engine that enables users to play and create a wide variety of stories in all kinds of contexts. For more information, see http://www.storytron.com.

[7] *Façade* can be considered to a large extent an open-ended simulation. It simulates a daily situation and much similar as in *SimCity* players are allowed to explore the possibilities of the game space. For this reason, it is not surprising that this game does not have a clear goal.

[8] It is more likely that Trip and Grace do not respond appropriately in *Façade* when players do not stick to their role. At the Interactive Drama *Façade* Forum conversations can be read of other people's experiences, such as the thread by an anonymous author at May 28, 2006 called "Trip and Grace do not care about their friends dying...." The transcript of this player's experience describes that he explained to Trip and Grace that he was suffering from a disease that would give him only a couple of months to live and both of them responded rather strangely. Although this can be seen as a limitation of the software, it should rather be seen as an error on the side of the player. This player changed the implicit objective of healing the relationship of Trip and Grace by confronting the storytelling engine with another problem: his own. See http://groups-beta.google.com/group/Interactive-Drama-Facade-Forum/.

Fig. 5.3 Solving relationship conflicts with *Façade*. ©2005 Procedural Arts. Used with permission

occurred more than once. This is prerequisite for something to be called "interactive." If a message would only have been related to my first message, the process should be called "reactive" instead of interactive. Finally, to be interactive, the process needs active agents. This means all agents, in this case me, Trip, and Grace, need to listen, think, and speak for themselves.

This sort of "interactivity" is basically an essential characteristic of computer technology in general and not an exclusive feature of games (Jensen 1999). We also interact with our word processor, our mobile phone, and even with our MP3 player. However, the interactivity among computer technological products differs in complexity: a mouse-click or a simple menu selection is not as interactive as playing a game. Sims (1995) tried to grasp this continuum with his 10-level model for the interactivity between a human and a computer. The lowest level concerns "object interactivity," which involves mouse-activated objects that provide an audio-visual response to "clicks" on the object, and the highest level concerns "immersive virtual interactivity," projecting the user into a completely computer-generated world and providing response to individual movement. Games clearly fit into this higher level of interactivity and this indicates the importance of the concept of interactivity to the development of games.

To create this higher level of interactivity a game should not be, in the words of Costikyan (1994), a puzzle, a story, or a painting.[9] Regular *puzzles*, like a *Crossword*

[9]Costikyan (1994) also poses that games are not toys. He used this metaphor to above-all point out that games possess goals and this is something which toys do not have. This is not related to interactivity and therefore I omitted this statement.

or a *Sudoku*, are, to start with, very static: they do not change at all. A person keeps staring at a sheet with numbers, cells, words, and/or lines and stops filling out the sheet when he or she is done, tired, or frustrated.

While, as Crawford (1982) points out, many games contain "puzzle elements," from figuring out where to go to breaking a code to unlock secret information, and can even be considered "puzzle games," these differ from regular puzzles that they are at least reactive but more likely interactive. A game should continuously change by a player's action: a door gets opened, a treasure is found, or the monster gets defeated.

This makes games dynamic instead of static. Nevertheless, it is better to speak of a continuum rather than a dichotomy, because some games are more puzzle-like than others. Adventure games, such as the *Monkey Island* series are much more static than first person shooters, such as *Unreal Tournament*.

The other negation design metaphor is *story*. Stories are inherently linear, whereas games should be non-linear (Costikyan 1994). Every time we reread or relisten the story, the outcome is still the same. The princess always gets the prince by kissing the frog, Snowwhite always gets rescued by her prince, and Eve always gives the apple to Adam no matter how loud the reader or audience is telling Eve "not to do it" or telling Adam "not to accept it." The reader or listener has no influence on the story. This might actually be a good thing. The author of a story chooses those characters, events, decisions, and outcomes that make up a strong story. Any change to this would not create an interesting story. A Shakespeare story where nobody dies at the end is, for example, not interesting.

Games depend, unlike stories, on decision making. According to Costikyan (1994) these decisions "have to pose real, plausible alternatives, or they are not real decisions." They have to be "interesting." This means that the player should influence the development of the game, and thereby its outcomes. Games make up their own story and the player should decide how. I have already illustrated the influence of players on the construction of such game stories with *Façade*.

Similar to the puzzle metaphor, some games are more story-like than others. These story-structured games are more linear and pose fewer real options, making it less game-like. Take *Grim Fandango* for example, an adventure game which is very similar to the *Monkey Island* games. It has one route through the story, and only one correct solution to every problem. As Rollings and Morris (2004) explain, the player may enjoy it for the artwork, music, or even the story, but in effect it is just a movie that is interrupted by puzzles that the player needs to solve. Every time the player solves a puzzle, the player is rewarded by being shown a little bit more of the movie. *Grim Fandango* and with it many other games are thus quite linear.

The final metaphor concerns a *painting*. While similar to puzzles, paintings do not change, We do not provide any input at all. The artist painted, not us. This makes looking at a painting a rather passive activity. The same reasoning can be applied to movies, television, and theater: we have to sit, watch, and listen. The only thing we actively do is to interpret them.

Contrast this with games. In games players should be able to create their own consequences guided by a set of rules. For instance, in *SimCity* the player decides where to build a primary school, a harbor, and a police department. The city is the player's work of art, not the game designer's. This makes games an active activity.

Being "active" is per definition needed to have interactivity, but games almost never completely consist of "active agents." They always have some "paintings" to decorate the gameworld (i.e., the "artwork") or to provide information to the player. Implementing these "paintings" should be done with some caution, because when playing a game, players do not want to be passive. This was noticed by Egenfeldt-Nielsen (2007) who reported that students found pop-ups with extensive amounts of information largely annoying or they would simply ignore them. Players also do not like reactive responses. I, at least, always found it annoying when playing adventure and role-playing games whenever the agents inside the game environment gave the same response every time I talked to them, like "It is a nice weather today, huh?"

By taking these considerations into account, to not make a game too much of a puzzle, story, or painting, it is very likely that a high level of interactivity will be achieved. This is, however, not enough to have a good gameplay. To achieve this, another concept needs to be considered.

Uncertainty

In reality we like things to be predictable. We do not want to be confronted from one day to the other with things we did not know of or with a complete new situation of which we did not think of before. Ask any CEO in the world and he or she would acknowledge this. However, when we play our preferences change. Suddenly we like unpredictability.

In fact, we actually enjoy it. Would *Monopoly* be fun if every player always takes four steps? It is the rolling of the dice that partly brings the excitement in *Monopoly*, and in many other (chance-based) games: "It is...five! That brings you to...—one, two, three...five—...my hotel at Times Square! Ka-ching! Ka-ching!" The *uncertainty* about outcomes drives our excitement in games. More importantly, the uncertainty makes for an interesting game as it is unknown what will happen.

The reason we do not mind uncertainty when we play is because it occurs in a "magic circle" (Huizinga 1938/1955). It happens in a space (largely) secluded from real life. Maybe we have to pay our friend because we dropped on his or her very expensive hotel at Times Square, but so what? The money, unless the rules of the game have changed, is not worth anything. Except that our friend might make a bit fun of us, there is nothing that will affect our financial situation in "real" life, the life outside the boundaries of the magic circle.

It is nevertheless important to emphasize that the circle is not completely closed off from reality. It has some permeability. It also needs to have this, otherwise any transfer from a game to reality is impossible. This can be a positive transfer, as illustrated at many occasions in this book, or a negative one. It could, for example, happen that if players always lose, it may lower their self-esteem in general. The point of the magic circle in this regard is, however, that the risks are much lower compared to real life, thereby creating a psychosocial moratorium (see Level 4), or in plane terms, a rather safe environment.

With this premise of being in a safe environment we are able to enjoy the side-effects of uncertainty: freshness and replayability (Kramer 2000). Freshness gives us the "aha"-feeling of "it works like this" when we figured out how to defeat an enemy or solve a puzzle. If a game would continuously use the same logic for everything, a game becomes quickly repetitive and becomes less enjoyable to play. All games have some of this repetition, but when games do not have these fresh "aha"-moments at times, players simply lose their interest.

For the other side-effect, replayability, it is important that some uncertainty is created in how the game is build up. If we know the enemy is always hiding just around the corner, it is much less thrilling than whenever we have not got a clue where the enemy is positioned. This creates excitement as we have to concentrate and think about each step we make: one wrong step might be fatal. Therefore, replayability also lessens the feeling of repetition and increases our engagement. It needs to be stressed that many games, foremost the adventure and role-playing types of games, do not allow for replayability. For this reason, players mostly play these games only once (Rollings and Adams 2003).

Creating uncertainty can be very simple. Take *Miss Management* (Fig. 5.4). In this game, the player plays Denise who has become the new manager of Conkling Associates International (C.A.I.). Her job is to ensure that employees get (the right) tasks and do their work on the one hand and are satisfied on the other hand by creating an inspiring working environment, fulfilling their needs (like food, rest, or a chat with another employee), to increase productivity. To succeed, she has to take the individual goals of the employees into account and needs to prioritize the different tasks that need to be done based on their urgency, importance, and the skills and availability of the employees. The game is basically a slightly simplistic yet rather striking picture of what it is like to "manage" people in a company.

In this game, we know that if we assign a task to employees, they will do it. We also know that if we give them rest, they will relax and come back to work with an increased working spirit. These and many other "rules" we can rely on. The uncertainty in this game comes from when tasks arrive on the desk, how fast employees finish them, and how quickly they become fed up with work or are annoyed by the behavior of the other employees. This little "uncertainty" already creates for a challenging "management" job, to make sure everybody, including the player him or herself, keeps on going and the profits eventually increase. Whether this happens, is unknown at the beginning and is dependent on the effort on the part of the player.[10]

The need for uncertainty is neatly summarized by Salen and Zimmerman (2004): "If a game is certain, if the outcome is known in advance, there is no reason to play in the first place" (p. 388). Next to interactivity, good gameplay involves not completely knowing upfront how the actions combined with the player's repertoire have an effect on the challenges that players have to face. While they can take up a

[10]The mechanism applied in *Miss Management* to create uncertainty is similar to the one in *Do I Have A Right?*, a game I discussed in Level 4.

Fig. 5.4 Managing a company with *Miss Management*. Denise, the female to the far left, is getting worried about all the problems with her co-workers who are now sitting at their desks waiting to get work from her and having wants and needs that need to be fulfilled. ©2007 GameLab. Used with permission

challenge, chances are that they may fail, not get enough points, or discover things that they did not know of.

To create this sort of uncertainty and also gameplay in general, another aspect of the world of Play has to be looked into. This aspect deals with how the fiction or the environment is build up. If it is always the same, the game becomes more certain, and vice versa. This aspect is commonly known as the "gameworld."

Constructing an Imaginative World

For playing a game, and thus being involved with gameplay, the player enters a fictional play space also known as the *gameworld*, which is the third aspect of the world of Play. Such a gameworld can according to Rollings and Adams (2003) be looked at from a physical (what space and what kind of scale?), temporal (past, present, or future?), environmental (what sort of appearance and atmosphere?), emotional (what emotions does it need to arouse?), and an ethical dimension (what is right and wrong in this fictional world?). These dimensions can be constructed with graphics, audio, and text. Together they construct an imaginative world that the player sets foot in.

The relationship between the *gameworld* and gameplay has been subject of considerable debate (Rollings and Adams 2003). Some have insisted that games are all about gameplay, since "great graphics" do not make a great game. Plus, it was discovered that players who were initially attracted to a first-person shooter called *Quake III Arena*, would modify the graphical settings of the game to get higher frame rates—which increases the number of images displayed per second and thereby gives faster feedback—at the expense of graphical detail (Juul 2005; Retaux and Rouchier 2002). Skilled players know after playing the game for a while that the graphics, such as the textures on the wall, are not relevant for playing the game. They may actually find all the graphical information distracting (see Level 4) from what they want to achieve, that is, to win the game. For this reason they remove all the detail and focus on what matters. This seems to suggest that graphics are not some chocolate that covers the broccoli, but rather the icing on a cake. After a while, players have enough of the icing and just want the cake by itself.

Aarseth's (2004) claim goes even further when it comes to the contribution of graphics. He says that:

> ...the dimensions of Lara Croft's body, already analyzed to death by film theorists, are irrelevant to me as a player, because a different-looking body would not make me play differently...When I play, I do not even see her body, but see through it and past it.

His claim goes further, because it asserts that not only the detail of graphics does not matter, but also what they represent. In his example, it concerns the main character of the game series *Tomb Raider*, Lara Croft, an adventurous, athletic, and voluptuous woman who goes out treasure hunting in forgotten parts of the world. For Aarseth, he may just as well played with "Carl Trofa," a bald old guy with a beer belly.

This embodiment of the character which does not result in a different gameplay is also nicely pointed out by Juul (2005) who explains that it does not make a difference in *Tekken 4* whether one chooses a small girl or a big muscular guy. Although the representation of both gives the impression that the latter is a much stronger character, the strength of the small girl is on par with the big guy. She hits just as hard.

This seemingly irrelevance of representations and the exposure of it, is shown in another fighting game called *Toribash* (Fig. 5.5). The player controls an abstract ragdoll consisting of some geometrical shapes and needs to fight another ragdoll. Although players are able to dress up their dolls, the game focuses explicitly on the movements, the actions, which is further stimulated by the rules of the game. Players need to click on the various body elements, such as the knees, ankles, elbow, and so forth, and combine these clicks to execute a maneuver. For example, to make a kick, the player must first contract the ankle, then contract the knee and the hip, and after that extend the knee. In this game, players really have to understand the physics behind particular movements—or the anatomy of fighting—to execute them well. More importantly, the game gives the impression that graphics are not that important.

The same goes for the stories, another element which is part of the gameworld, in games. Almost every game has some kind of "background story," a story which explains why the world is doomed and needs a hero to save the day. These stories are, however, only "interesting shading" to the game (Koster 2005). It seems that

Fig. 5.5 Fighting another ragdoll in *Toribash*. Look at the basic yet quite functional graphics. ©2006 Nabi Studios. Used with permission

they do not really matter as well. Players get some information and at certain moments get some more information, for example by "cut-scenes," short movies that break the actual playing of the game. But to put it a bit cynically, when a player holds a gun and a zombie is approaching him with an axe, a player does not need information to know what to do.

This debate about the nature of games is according to Rollings and Adams (2003) not meaningful anymore. Gameplay and gameworld need to work together to produce the total play experience. The interaction between the two is also what makes a game a game according to Juul (2005), who especially made an effort in showing that fiction does matter. He argues that games consist of rules and fiction.[11] The rules cue the player into imagining a world and the fiction can cue the player into understanding the rules of the game. In fact, he asserts that the emphasis on fiction is what makes digital games different from their analog counterparts and concerns the strongest innovation in digital games themselves. We have gone from single screen small fictional worlds, such as in *Pac-Man*, to gigantic environments as found in *Eve Online*, *Grand Theft Auto IV*, and *World of Warcraft*.

With this in mind, the incongruency between rules and fiction in *Tekken 4* may actually illustrate the amazing power of martial arts (Juul 2005). It is not about strength, but how movements are executed. Further, in *Toribash* the fiction which is presented supports the game. The game is about the anatomical elements involved in fighting and it is much easier to see how this works if characters are represented as geometrical figures than if they were represented as realistically looking characters.

[11] Juul (2005) stresses that rules and fiction especially come together at the "level design," the creation of the fictional spaces. The space determines what a player can or cannot do. It determines, for example, where a player can hide. This surmounts to the gameworld *and* to the gameplay.

It sets the player in a state of mind of thinking about the "little" things that make up a movement instead of just pushing one button to execute a helicopter kick or upper cut.

And yes, although many background stories and graphics are not much more than "interesting shading," they do give form and meaning to the experience. In terms of rules, it may not make a difference if we play with a good looking athletic woman or with an old bald man with a beer belly, unless the rules account for this by, for example, making the old man walk slower than the athletic woman. However, in terms of the eventual meaning it matters a lot. The fiction gives meaning to the experience. Although it is pretty self-explanatory when we see a zombie with an axe approaching us, players will definitely (and so I hope) raise an eyebrow if they are confronted with a little baby with a pacifier in his mouth. Similarly, playing *Tomb Raider* with a bold old man would make the experience into something ridiculous, a comedy, instead of the thrilling and exciting experience the *Tomb Raider* series are.

What does this mean for designing games? Juul (2005) gives advice on this as well:

> In the game design process, the game designer must select which aspects of the fictional world to actually implement in the game rules. The player then experiences the game as a two-way process where the fiction of the game cues him or her into understanding the rules of the game, and, again, the rules can cue the player to imagine the fictional world of the game. (p. 163)

This is important to realize, because games with a serious purpose are eventually about bringing forth "some" meaning. For this, the designer needs to think of how the gameplay and gameworld work together in creating "operations" that are in accordance with the purpose of the game (see Level 4), but which are also engaging, immersive, and fun.

For constructing such a gameworld two concepts are in particular important. One has to do with the "aesthetics," the look and feel of the environment, and the other relates to making sure that the several elements that make up the look and feel fit together. The second one is, therefore, about "coherency."

Aesthetics

The gameworld of digital games is similarly to a movie build up out of graphics, audio, and text. Each of these multimedia assets are a key factor in getting people interested in a game. To fully harness these assets, and thereby really spark the interest of players, the *aesthetics* of the gameworld has to be considered. With this, I do not necessarily refer to the game being "beautiful." I rather refer to it as something that arouses the player in a positive way. A game can be considered aesthetically pleasing if it provides sensory experiences that intrigues players—that appeals to them.

As for graphics, usage of state-of-the-art graphics is definitely appealing to many players. This sort of "eye candy" will lure players right into the game. However, a game with simple graphics but with great visual style, such as *Miss Management*, can be visually appealing as well. While the latter may not create a "wow"-effect, the visual style may set the player in a certain mood or may be appealing for its simplicity.

From this we already see that judging the aesthetics is not very clear-cut. In fact, it is not and for two major reasons. The first reason is rather obvious. Simply put, not all games are similar to one another. With this in mind, it would be unfair to judge every game by the same standards. And aside from being unfair, it is actually sometimes impossible. How could we compare a puzzle game to a shooter on their aesthetics?

The second reason involves the subjectivity in determining what is "aesthetically pleasing." What is pleasing for some, may not be pleasing for others. But if something is really of poor quality, it less likely that somebody will ever like it. Aesthetics is not just a matter of taste, it also a matter of quality.

We can relate this to art in a broader sense. With paintings, for example, different "aesthetic movements" exist, from realism to expressionism. It is difficult to compare paintings from different movements, because each style has its own merits and values. It hard to say that, for instance, some baroque painting is better than a classicist painting. We have to judge each of these two paintings by different standards. Additionally, each movement may appeal to someone or not. Some may like baroque better than classicist paintings. This is a matter of taste. However, within a movement and certainly on an individual basis, paintings are constantly judged on their quality.

Within games with a serious purpose, we can roughly distinguish two movements. On the one hand, we have games that adopt a cartoonist style, by depicting the gameworld like a comic strip or a cartoon. On the other hand, we can observe games that adopt a realistic style, by depicting the gameworld as close to reality as possible. But like the aesthetic movements in painting, it would be unfair to compare these two movements. Whatever designers choose to use as a visual style, they just need to make sure it is appealing to the players.

In contrast to graphics, audio is still a much undervalued aesthetic element. This is slowly changing and this change may have been fueled with the arrival of games that focus completely on music, such as *Guitar Hero* or *Dance Dance Revolution*. The first games only had a rather annoying repetitive tune.[12] But nowadays games use a diversity of audio, from ambience music to sound effects, in building up the tension and creating atmosphere.[13]

[12]Funny enough, in the music industry a whole movement—called "chipmusic" — has risen that makes use of the old annoying repetitive game audio.

[13]Different types of audio exist in games. We have "dialog," the audio that tells the story, "music," which gives the emotional tone during a scene, "foley," audio made by human movement and interaction with objects (e.g., footsteps), "ambience," audio that fills the background and gives a sense of place (e.g., the sound of the wind or the river), and "sound effects," audio that is related to specific events (e.g., car smashing into a wall). Due to the scope of the book I put all these types of audio into one big pile.

Fig. 5.6 The train with no sound

The potential power of audio is exemplified in horror movies. For a long period of time, we as the viewers of such a movie do not hear anything at all, except for some heartbeats and footsteps. Then suddenly, we hear a loud noise, somebody may scream or just say "Boo!," and we rise up in our seats with our hands before our eyes. This use of audio is incorporated more and more into entertainment games (and not surprisingly, especially in survival horror games). The power of audio is thus increasingly recognized. To get an aesthetically pleasing auditive experience, the industry devotes specific team members of the design team to audio, establishes collaborations with musicians, and is concerned with audio from the start of the project instead of at the end.

For games with a serious purpose resources in terms of time and budget are much more limited and audio is probably still one of the first elements to fall victim to being cut. For *Levee Patroller* we even had to postpone the issue of audio for the first version. The problem with audio is that if designers decide to use it, they need to use audio for almost everything that would be able to make sound. For example, if we would have decided to incorporate footsteps in *Levee Patroller*, it would be strange if players would not hear the train passing by (Fig. 5.6). If we wanted audio, we had to do it all and this was impossible considering our project limitations. The latest version does have some audio, but it is still not up to a level that would take away all inconsistencies (which makes the game "incoherent").[14]

The third aesthetic element concerns "text." Text can provide information about the gameworld. By leaving "gaps" in the information provision, the interest of the player can be raised. Mystery novels or thrillers make good use of this technique. Take *The Da Vinci Code* by Dan Brown (2003). It is a page turner, because Brown makes sure the reader leaves each section with an unanswered question. This makes readers keep on reading and reading till the book ends.

Although most games use "text" functionally in a useful way, by pointing out the name of a character or the name of an item, they often contain a pretty bad story. The quality is frequently not much better than the worst comics and fairy tales in the world. These stories are nevertheless important, because as I explained before, they can give a context to what happens in the game and keep the player's attention. This means on an overall level stories could be made more aesthetically pleasing. With this I mean that more interesting stories should be incorporated into games.

Making interesting stories could be achieved in two ways. One is quite obvious: write better stories! Like audio, this is slowly changing in the world of entertainment games. In fact, for some games, such as *Halo*, a number of books have been written based on the story universe of the game. This change is probably a result from an understanding that stories can be more than some "interesting shading."

To make stories even more interesting, the second way needs to be considered. This is to integrate story and gameplay by making sure player's actions influence the development of the story. As discussed earlier with the issue of "interactivity," this is difficult to realize as stories are inherently linear. People, like Crawford (2005) and the designers behind *Façade*, are working on achieving this type of "interactive storytelling," but as of yet the technology to completely integrate story and gameplay is still experimental and it remains questionable if it would really work in all sorts of games.

Integrating story and gameplay is difficult to achieve, because to make a story a bit more interactive, it needs to depend on the decisions made in the game and with each decision branches are added to the storyline. Since players make many decisions during a game, a *combinatorial explosion* occurs (Rollings and Adams 2003). It is called an explosion, because with each decision the number of branches grows exponentially. For example, with three decision points in a game and two separate outcomes, the game should already have eight different outcomes.

To prevent such an explosion, designers use a number of tricks aside from simply minimizing the influence of decisions on the story, such as a technique called *foldback*. With foldback players might make a decision, in the end they get to a similar point in the story whenever the player would have chosen something else. This way, the number of branches are kept to a minimum. The game *Star Wars: Knights of the Old Republic* uses this idea.

---

[14] Another reason why we did not prioritize audio is that in the beginning we designed the game especially for being played in workshop types of settings. In these situations, it would be very annoying if everybody has their sound turned up. Using headphones could solve this problem, but in that case social interaction is not stimulated.

Another but extreme way to deal with this is what the designers used in *Dragon's Lair* (Rollings and Adams 2003). In this game, players have to make a split-second decision about what to do and if their decision would lead them from stepping of the "ideal" path they would get killed. This is what Crawford (1982) calls "the game tree of death." This right-or-die approach causes much frustration. Foldback is, on the other hand, not a optimal strategy as well as we are basically deceiving the player to have an influence on the outcomes.

A final possibility is to make use of "quests." These are nested, concurrent and/or serial assignments within a game world with concrete and attainable goals, such as gathering building materials to forge a sword like in *The Legend of Zelda: Phantom Hourglass* (Aarseth 2005). With a quest-system the game basically consists of a series of smaller storylines. This is much easier to manage and gives the player some freedom of choice in how the game is played.

While integrating story and gameplay is tough, these are not the only elements that need to work together. Just for the consideration of the gameworld by itself we already have three elements that need to work together: graphics, audio, and text. And many other (sensory) elements that make up a gameworld could be added, which have not been discussed here, such as olfaction or haptics. To make sure the different pieces of the gameworld fit together another concept needs to be considered, that of "coherency."

Coherency

Games consist of many elements. They consist of gameplay elements, like challenges, actions, and rules, and of gameworld elements, like graphics, audio, and text. In creating a believable, logical, and playable gameworld, these elements, of the gameworld itself and of gameplay, need to be taken into account, as they closely relate to each other. The earlier example of *Toribash* made this clear.

To achieve such a single whole, designers have to think about the concept of *coherency*. This states that in a game the separate elements should meaningfully bond together: it needs to be complete, orderly, logical, and consistent. Incoherency can take place on many levels. It can, for example, only take place graphically. If a game uses different styles in representing the fictional world, then this can be experienced as rather confusing and, therefore, as "incoherent."

Mismatches between elements can happen as well. If cheerful music is used to give an emotional tone to the experience, while this experience is about slaughtering zombies, it can be said to be incoherent, unless the point is to make use of this contrast. Juul (2005), for example, points out that incoherency in games can be used to express something, such as humor. He uses the example of the aforementioned example of *Tekken 4*. He finds the discrepancy between the outward appearance of the fighters and the rules governing their behavior first and foremost humorous.

Similarly, by using a cheerful undertone while engaging in slaughtering, it creates an interesting tension that puts the experience in a completely other perspective—one which makes it a bit ridiculous—if done properly. In such cases, however, it can actually be argued that the game is coherent, because from the perspective of the designers and what they want to achieve, the elements fit together. They just make use of the contrast caused by the different elements to create some interesting effect. For this reason, we should not speak of "incoherency" in such instances, but rather of "incoherent coherency" or "contrasting coherency."

Something else that Juul (2005) points out when it comes down to coherence, is that if we need to resort to describing the rules, props, or the real-world situation where the game was played in explaining what really happened in the game, the game is incoherent. To illustrate this, he gives the example of *Donkey Kong*, a game in which the player controls the most famous plumber in the world, Mario, and has to rescue his girlfriend who is kidnapped by an evil gorilla. For no obvious reasons, the girlfriend is kidnapped every time the player saves her. This means that the whole process of rescuing the girlfriend starts all over again at every level. Even more difficult to explain is why Mario has three lives. This can only be explained for by referring to the rules or by saying that the game would be too hard if players would only have one life.

Many games have such incoherency, but for games with a serious purpose this could have severe implications. For example, we want to avoid situations, in which players of a medical game explain that they as a doctor can only take up to three actions to save a patient's life because that is what the game allows them to take. In other words, we have to be careful if players say something such as "it works like this because the rules of the game work like that." To avoid this, the game needs to be coherent. Or, during the debriefing it needs to be explained why this incoherency is present. For the medical game, for example, it could be explained that time is crucial and actions need to be elaborately thought about before taken. By only allowing up to three actions, the designers hoped to achieve this.

Unfortunately, incoherency is not always easily noticeable. Due to the many interacting elements in a game, it is sometimes difficult to perceive what kind of behavior can "emerge." Sometimes such emergent behavior does not cause a problem. But sometimes it does. Jessica Mulligan, a veteran of the online games industry, told me once a nice anecdote about a problem. She explained that in *Asheron's Call 2*, players needed to get passed a monster which blocked a door to get to some significant content in a certain region of the gameworld. This monster was extremely powerful and it would normally take a lot of effort to defeat it.

However, as unpredictable, or maybe I should call it smart, as players are, they found an alternative way to defeat the monster. The monster was located underneath a cliff and one of the players climbed up this cliff and let his or her character fall down on top of the monster. According to the gravity rule of the game a collision leads to damage and the amount of damage is—quite similar to the real world—dependent on the height of the fall. In this case, the damage was enough to kill the monster.

The game designers did not acknowledge upfront that the monster could be killed in such a fast way. They estimated that it would take players some time to finish off the monster. This estimated time was important, because all the following events in the game were dependent on this time. And so, after the collapse with the monster the other players opened the door, but the game could not respond to this, since the following events were not triggered yet. This caused the game to crash.

In this anecdote, the unexpected combination of game elements to beat the monster was constituted by the game rules, as the gravity rule killed the monster, and the visual space, as it enabled one of the players to get to the cliff and fall down. Such unexpected combination would be perfectly feasible, if it was not inconsistent with the other game elements to unlock the content. The anecdote about *Asheron's Call 2* makes clear that games are complex. Due to this, it is sometimes difficult to foresee if any incoherency occurs.

For a gameworld to fit together, to be a complete, orderly, logical, and consistent whole, every part of the game has to be made explicit and be clearly connected to other parts. All of it needs to make some sense. To create such a "coherent gameworld," the fourth and final aspect of the world of Play has to be looked into, the use of "technology."

Choosing the Right Technology

With computer technology we are able to do everything we want. That is at least the perception of many among us and I do not blame anyone for thinking this. We can see virtual worlds, such as *World of Warcraft*, in which millions of people come together in amazing fantasy worlds, we can see people flirting, dating, having meetings and conferences while they fly in three dimensional virtual worlds, such as *Second Life*, and we see that with one press on a button books can be bought, data can be analyzed, and so on. The possibilities seem endless. Every day new technologies arise that increase our options to do something. From this, it just seems like everything can be done with multiple combinations of zeros and ones.

Not surprisingly, this is everything but true. While computer technology is able to do a lot of things, it is also restricted in many ways. Otherwise fully interactive storytelling games would already exist and Von Ahn and Dabbish (2004) would not need human participants to label images.

Even more important to realize is that *technology*, the fourth and final aspect of the world of Play, is not some objective, external instrument that can be shaped to the wants and needs of its user (cf., Orlikowski 1992). Each technology has certain affordances and influences what designers are able to do. It is thus not just a matter of choosing a technology and deciding how to use it. It goes the other way around as well. The technology influences what is being made. This "expressive pressure" of technology is described by Bogost (2006):

> ...the entire hardware architecture of the Atari 2600 (also called the Atari Video Computer System, or VCS) was crafted to accommodate *Pong*- and *Tank*-like games. the device's memory architecture and hardware register settings provide access to a playfield backdrop, two player sprites, two missiles, and one ball. The VCS is generally considered one of the most difficult platforms to program, and gameplay innovation on the platform required developers to work within its constraints. These constraints are not only physical (a paltry 128 bytes of RAM and 2 kilobytes of game data on the cartridge) but also conceptual:

> the hardware was designed for games like *Pong* and *Combat*, artifacts based on tennislike attributes. While ROM size 2600 carts eventually increased, new game concepts required VCS programmers to manipulate the hardware's affordances to create new play experiences. The VCS offers a striking example of how the structure of a technology platform exerts expressive pressure on the software created to run on it. (p. 59)

The decision what technology to use for developing a game extends, therefore, further than just how detailed objects may look on the screen. It has an impact on the eventual "game concept." We can also see this with entertainment games. If a game is designed, for example, for the Nintendo DS, a handheld device with a dual screen, of which one screen can be touched with either a stylus or fingers to play, designers think really hard how they can make use of the specifics of this type of hardware. This makes Nintendo DS games conceptually quite different from the games that are developed for other devices, even when it is the same game. This means that the choice for technology needs a careful consideration.

To be precise, when we think of game technology, we talk about the hardware on which the game is played (e.g., PC, console, or Internet?), the specific software that is used to create and develop the game (e.g., game engines, editor tools, and visualization tools), what programming languages are used to code (e.g., Java, C++, or Flash?), and what sort of interface is used to interact with the game (e.g., joystick, keyboard, and/or mouse?).

This is, however, a limited view on technology. The sorts of material familiar to analog games, like a board, cards, and other paraphernalia, are technology as well. And in fact, digital games may make use of these analog technologies as well. Thus, when considering the aspect of technology, we should extent our view beyond computer technology, and consider any type of material, from pens to drawing boards, that can be used to create and support the game.

Nevertheless, when it comes to designing digital games and the use of technology, the hardware and software considerations remain the most dominant. While these considerations are important, I will not provide an overview of the possibilities and the trade-offs of what is available today. This has to do with the incredible rapid technological advances in the field of games. I dare to say that games are in many ways the first when it comes to showing off the newest technological possibilities.

Take for example the latest game console by Sony, the Playstation 3. It is one of the first products that uses the Blu-Ray Disc technology, a technology that enables to store up to 50 GB of information on a single disk (to compare, a single layer DVD Disc can store up to 4.7 GB). Due to the incredibly fast advances in gaming technology some even argued that the development of games follows a "quadratic Moore's Law," which basically means that game technology develops much faster than its internal hardware components (Bergeron 2006; Prensky 2001). [15] This also means that everything I have to say about this now will be old news tomorrow.

---

[15]Moore's law indicates the rapidly continuing advance in computing power per unit cost. It actually refers to the doubling of the number of transistors on integrated circuits every 18 to 24 months.

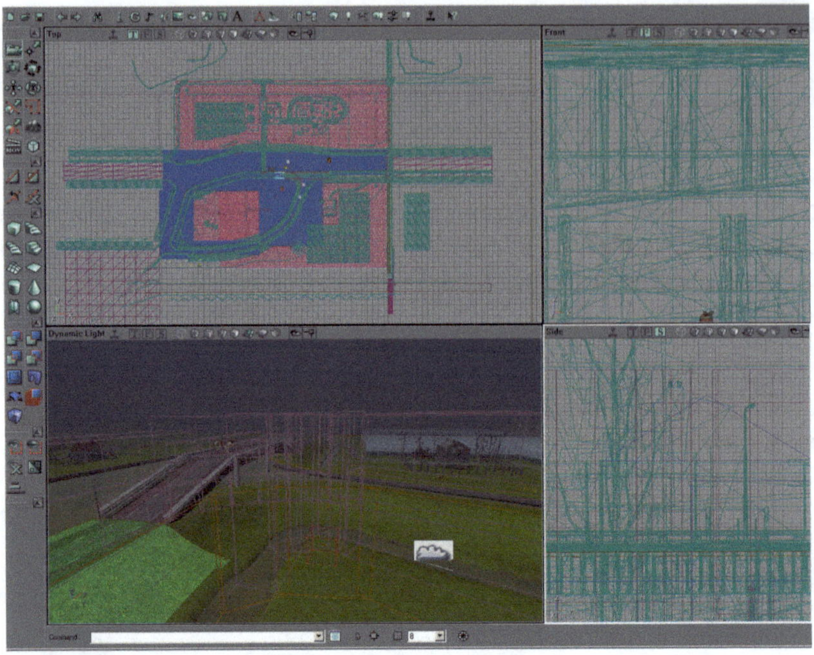

Fig. 5.7 Creating a gameworld for *Levee Patroller* with the UnrealEd

What I can tell is what sort of technology we used to develop *Levee Patroller*. During the development of this game, the choice for technology was more or less already implicitly taken at the start of the project. During the summer of 2005 a student developed a mock-up with the "Unreal Engine 2," a specific game engine that is commercially available (see Level 3). This technology comes with a development suite, the *UnrealEd*, that allows for the easy and rapid creation of gameworlds (Fig. 5.7), has its own programming language, the *UnrealScript*, and takes care of many basic functionalities, like rendering graphics, collision detection, audio, scripting, artificial intelligence, network possibilities, and so on. Since we wanted to go for the state-of-the-art at that time—the Unreal Engine 3 is currently already available—and also did not know any better, our first choice was to stick to this technology and work from there.

The type of hardware was also never a real discussion. Although at the time not all the PCs at the water boards had the right set of requirements for playing a game, the water boards already had this platform. If we decided to go for a console game, they would have needed to buy additional hardware.[16]

[16]Some of the PCs at the water boards did not have a graphics card, which is an absolute necessity to play a game with three dimensional graphics. Nowadays every PC has at least some graphics card so this should not pose a problem anymore. Unless, of course, we decide to upgrade the game to the newest technology of today. Then it requires a much better graphics card and possibly other requirements that call for a better PC.

Despite that we certainly not regret choosing the Unreal Engine 2, in an "ideal" situation it would be better to compare the alternatives. To compare the different technologies and make a choice, "it depends" on what is needed for. It cannot be said that certain technologies are always better than others. What technology should be chosen relies on many considerations, which can be related to the aspects in this book. The problem with the choice for technology is that some considerations cannot be thought of upfront, while a technology is one of the first items that designers frequently decide on. To get as much insight about what is needed as early in the design process as possible, it may help to develop prototypes with simple technologies, such as with pen and paper (see also Fullerton et al. 2008).

The Criteria of Play

From this level we are so far able to derive that according to the world of Play designing a game involves at the very least four aspects: the determination of the "goal", the "gameplay," the "gameworld," and the "technology" to build and play the game. Together, these aspects make up a "game concept," a conceptual description of what the game is like.

Next to the model of reality and the value proposal, this game concept should be the basis for designing the game eventually. Also similar to the outputs of the other two worlds, the concept should be a "living document," one that is continuously updated throughout the design process when changes are made. To judge this document and the eventual game from a Play perspective, I consider three closely related criteria to be most critical. These are "engagement," "immersion," and "fun."

Engagement

An "engagement" is generally conceived as a connection between two objects, at the moment, when two combat forces fight each other, or planned ahead, such as with a wedding. Related to games, *engagement* means something similar. It refers to the "connection" between a player and a game. This connection can be real-time when players are that much intrigued by the game that they keep on playing and playing. They forget about time and before they know it, it is time to go to bed, or even worse, it is way past bedtime.

The other connection is "offline." Players may not actually play the game, but they are thinking about it while "engaged" with something else and/or are willing to play the game anytime soon again. In sum, engagement is about the involvement and commitment in playing games and concerns the first criterion from the world of Play.

This criterion is seemingly similar to the first criterion of Meaning: "motivation." They definitely overlap to some extent and are certainly difficult to separate from each other, especially because they influence one another. Many scholars, therefore, equate them to be the same.[17] I see, however, a fundamental difference. Motivation refers to a willingness and a commitment to learn the knowledge and skills of a subject when it is about education or training, to contribute to a proper experiment when it is about theory testing, and to judge the worth of "something" when it is about assessment, for example. Motivation relates to the value to be achieved from the game.

With engagement, on the other hand, it comes down to a willingness and commitment to play the game. The game itself must be interesting. People can play a game not because they like the subject matter so much, but because they are intrigued by the game itself. I experienced this with *The Typing of the Dead*. I really do not think I need to improve my typing skills, but for some reason the game lured me in and I kept playing despite that I was not interested in increasing my typing skills.

Two frequently referred to theoretical frameworks can account for why people potentially get engaged with a game in this way. The first framework is developed by Malone and Lepper (1981, 1987a, 1987b). They investigated why games are such "intrinsically motivating" activities, and found first four "motivational factors" and added a fifth one later.[18] Here we also see the blur between motivation and engagement. To remain consistent, I rename their following factors to "engagement factors":

- **Challenge**: the activity should be of an appropriate difficulty level for the player. The activity should also have clear goals and have uncertainty about the outcomes. Constructive and encouraging feedback about how the challenges are dealt with is essential for players to keep engaged.
- **Curiosity**: this can be sensory or cognitive related. With the first, beautiful landscapes or interesting objects can draw player's attention and keep them staring at the screen. With the second incomplete, inconsistent, or unparsimonious information keep them engaged as humans havc a desire to understand things.
- **Control**: the player should have the overall feeling of being in control. This is done through creating an interactive environment, in which the player has a high degree of choice and in which the player's actions have significant outcomes in the environment.
- **Fantasy**: this is the world in which the game is played. The represented fantasy can attract players to a game and let them stay engaged. It may also increase

[17] The difference between "motivation" and "engagement" is just a matter of definition. I find it perfectly acceptable that people use the term motivation in relation to just the games themselves. However, for evaluating games with a serious purpose it is important to make a distinction between being motivated to contribute to the value of the game and to play the game.

[18] The fifth factor, interpersonal motivations (which I renamed to "interpersonal engagement"), was added in the latest revision of Malone's original work from 1981. Before this revision Malone's motivational theory focused, like Csikszentmihalyi's (1991) flow theory, on the individual. The concept of motivation is much broader than the concept of flow and that is why Malone, in collaboration with Lepper, added social factors to his theory, while these do not appear in the flow theory. The latter did not happen for obvious reasons, because flow is not a social but an individual process.

Fig. 5.8 The theory of flow (adapted from Csikszentmihalyi 1991)

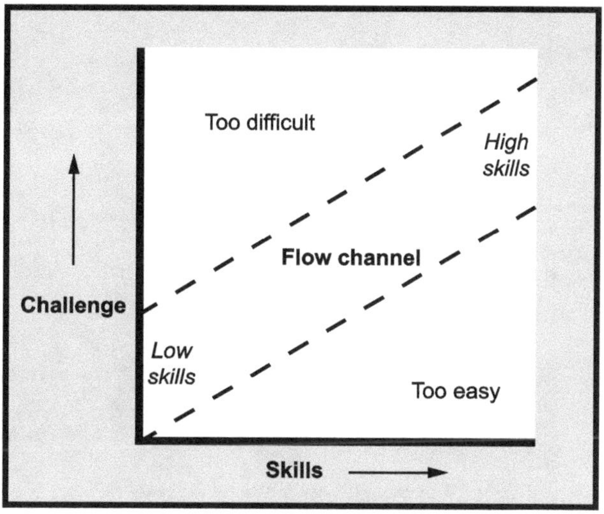

engagement as it enables players to satisfy certain needs which they may not be able to satisfy in their real life.

- **Interpersonal engagement**: this refers to the increased engagement resulting from the social context of a game. For example, competition or collaboration with peers highly stimulates players. The recognition of peers also helps to stay engaged.

With this framework in mind, my engagement with *The Typing of the Dead* could be explained by the challenges it offered, as it still required a certain effort on behalf of my typing skills to kill the zombies, by the fantastical setting and the curious zombies themselves, as they are ugly yet interesting figures that needed to be killed, and by my ability—I was the one in control—to actually kill the zombies. I played it all by myself, so no interpersonal engagement played a role.

The other framework is Csikszentmihalyi's (1991) theory of *flow*. This is a generic theory that can be applied to any activity, from programming code to playings sports. It describes that when people engage in an activity, they can get into a "flow", a state in which they keep on going. To reach and stay in such a condition, Csikszentmihalyi states that:

> ...optimal experience requires a balance between the challenge perceived in a given situation and the skills a person brings to it...To remain in flow, one must increase the complexity of the activity by developing new skills and taking on new challenges...Flow forces people to stretch themselves, to always take on another challenge, to improve on their abilities. (p. 30)

A "non-optimal experience" appears when people perceive the activity as "too difficult." This leads to anxiety—a loss of self-confidence—or frustration. If, on the other hand, the activity is perceived as "too easy" it leads to boredom or disinterest and a non-optimal experience is achieved as well (Fig. 5.8). That is why, as Koster (2005) puts it, games "have to navigate between the Scylla and Charybdis of deprivation and overload, of excessive order and excessive chaos, of silence and noise"

Fig. 5.9 Controlling massive and little ships in *Ship Simulator*. An inland container ship is on its way to bring a load to another cargo area. Screen shot is taken by Pjotr van Schothorst. ©2010 Paradox Interactive. Used with permission

(p. 42) to keep the player engaged. If game designers are able to avoid the Scylla and Charybdis their games will definitely put players into a flow as "games are obvious flow activities, and play is the flow experience par excellence" (Csikszentmihalyi 1975, pp. 36–37).[19]

Interestingly, and strikingly similar to the engagement factors, Csikszentmihalyi (1991) lists a number of elements, such as clear goals, fast feedback, a sense of control, and uncertainty, that make it more likely that people get into a flow when they are engaged with an activity. For example, uncertainty, needs to be present to get into a flow, because there should be a perceived possibility of failure. Otherwise people are not forced to stretch themselves. At the same time, people should have a feeling to be able to complete the given activity: they need to be in control. The idea of stretching oneself by being challenged with increasingly difficult tasks is further remarkably similar to Vygotsky's (1978) zone of proximal development (see Level 4).

With both theoretical frameworks in mind, and by using the example of a game called *Ship Simulator* (Fig. 5.9), I will further explain the relationship between engagement and motivation. *Ship Simulator* is basically what it says. It is a game devoted to being able to control all kinds of vessels, from massive cargo ships to

[19]Even a game is completely devoted to the theory of flow, first designed by Jenova Chen and Nicholas Clark for the PC and later published on the Playstation 3 by their company called "thatgamecompany," with the recognizable name *flOw*.

speedboats, yachts, water taxis to even the mighty Titanic. In the game, the player has to execute a range of missions, from rescue operations, transporting goods and people, to racing and stunting. For professional usage, training objectives can relate to navigation and passage planning, collision avoidance regulations, flag and light communications, search and rescue operations, and fuel efficiency training amongst a number of others.

The game gets contradictory responses from its players. Some give the game a score of 10 out of 10 and praise especially its realism. Others give it a 1 out of 10 and react as follows:[20]

> So BORING! Really not so good environment details, NOTHING TO DO. What you read in description is 100% of the game...nothing left to discover.

From this reaction, we see that this player in particular is definitely not engaged. He is not challenged and his curiosity is not raised. The player may further find it "boring," because except for the speedboat, the vessels move slowly and the missions that need to be executed—from sightseeing tourists with a taxi to rescuing a swimmer—take quite a bit of time and are not very varied. In essence, they constantly involve getting a ship from A to B.

From an engagement perspective, the players that do praise the game feel most likely attracted to the "fantasy" of "controlling" different types of ships. But to have such a specific fantasy, players must have an interest in the subject and have a strong will to learn more about it. In other words, such players have a motivation to play the game. Their motivation reinforces their engagement and the other way around.

Although this is to some extent mere speculation, I have seen something similar with *Levee Patroller*. With this game, players not affiliated with the domain and with no specific interest in the topic, also thought it was too boring to play. Aside that they were not interested in measuring cracks, nothing happened according to them. They quickly stopped playing while the real professionals, the levee patrollers, cannot get enough of it.

Therefore, we must make a distinction between engagement in playing the game and the motivation to be involved with the subject matter. The two can overlap and reinforce each other, but they are significantly different and this becomes especially clear with games with a specific serious purpose that are used for education and training. A great game may initially attract players and keep them engaged, a real willingness to put effort into the value of the game is really needed for it to become effective in the longer term.

For other types of games with a serious purpose, motivation is certainly beneficial to retrieve proper values, but the engagement is what really drives the success of it. For example, with the *ESP Game* I do not believe that people are really into it because they want to improve their linguistic skills. The challenge and the interpersonal engagement are what is driving the success of this game.

---

[20] I retrieved the information about *Ship Simulator* from Metacritic, a website that collects critic and user reviews (see http://www.metacritic.com/). The comment is from a user called "Atef M."

Immersion

The effects of a flow, a sense of timelessness, of being at one, of exhilaration, focus and immediacy, is what people frequently associate with another well-known phenomenon of games and which I consider to be the second criterion: *immersion*. It is even that illustrative for what games achieve that some rather refer to them as "immersive learning environments or simulations" (De Freitas 2006; Wexler et al. 2007).

But as a concept in relation to games it is theoretically not yet fully developed and also not so well understood. For example, the assumption that engagement and immersion are one and the same is understandable but wrong (cf., Calleja 2007). Before I elaborate on this discussion, let me first introduce the meaning of this criterion by using the words of Murray (1997):

> The experience of being transported to an elaborately simulated place is pleasurable in itself, regardless of the fantasy content. We refer to this experience as immersion. *Immersion* is a metaphorical term derived from the physical experience of being submerged in water. We seek the same feeling from a psychologically immersive experience that we do from a plunge in the ocean or swimming pool: the sensation of being surrounded by a completely other reality, as different as water is from air, that takes over all of our attention, our whole perceptual apparatus. We enjoy the movement out of our familiar world, the feeling of alertness that comes from being in this new place, and the delight that comes from learning to move within it. Immersion can entail a mere flooding of the mind with sensation... But in a participatory medium, immersion implies learning to swim, to do the things that the new environment makes possible. (pp. 98–99)

Distilling from the above-mentioned explanation the most simple and straightforward definition of immersion would be "being somewhere else." To stress the virtual nature we could add to this "even when one is physically situated in another" (Witmer and Singer 1998). For this state to occur, players should believe the fictional world surrounding them is real. That is why immersion is related to Coleridge's (1817/1985) phrase "the willing suspension of disbelief." Murray (1997) stresses, however, that "we do not suspend disbelief so much as we actively *create belief*" (p. 110). When it comes to games, players fill in the gaps that the fictional world has and reinforce rather than question the reality of the experience. They actively pursue some belief of being somewhere else while they actually sit in front of a screen.

Research into immersion was fueled by the work of Minsky (1980). He coined the term "telepresence" to refer to the feeling of inhabiting a distant location while remotely (tele)operating robotic machinery inside it. Minsky was concerned with enhancing the "feeling of presence" in designing teleoperating technology. In other words, he was concerned with "being somewhere else":

> The biggest challenge to developing telepresence is achieving that sense of "being there." Can telepresence be a true substitute for the real thing? Will we be able to couple our artificial devices naturally and comfortably to work together with the sensory mechanisms of human organisms? (p. 48)

The issues Minsky (1980) raised became important not only in the field of telerobotics but more generally in the field of *virtual reality*, which focuses on the use of head-mounted displays that put users into another world.[21] With this expansion a community of researchers became dedicated to look into this phenomenon which they called "presence."[22] Although definitional issues can be found between presence and immersion, the two are mostly used interchangeably (Calleja 2007). The first is simply more used in relation to virtual reality, while the latter is more commonly applied to games.

When we relate the idea of immersion to Minsky's (1980) conception of telepresence, we can replace the remotely controlling of a robot with that of an avatar, the character that the player controls. The Holy Grail of scholars interested in immersion (or presence) is, however, the "holodeck" from the Star Trek series (Murray 1997). The holodeck is a futuristic technology that is able to generate a world as real as the world we live in. This world is projected into a room making it able for a participant to move and behave as one would in reality. Another way of framing this is to say that the participant becomes "completely immersed" into the world.

This idea of "complete immersion" or the focus on and importance of immersion when it comes to games, is criticized by Salen and Zimmerman (2004) who consider its consideration "the immersive fallacy":

> The immersive fallacy is the idea that the pleasure of a media experience lies in its ability to sensually transport the participant into an illusory, simulated reality. According to the immersive fallacy, this reality is so complete that ideally the frame falls away so that the player truly believes that he or she is part of an imaginary world. (pp. 451–452)

They stress that players may just as well get "immersed" into a game, like *Tetris*, which is not tied to a sensory replication of reality, as to a rich visual-spatial world, such as *World of Warcraft*. Using Fine's (1983) idea of "double-consciousness," they also stress that players are aware of their different roles: their role as a player controlling an avatar ("player as player") and their role as a person who plays a game ("player as person").[23] During a game, players continuously switch between these two modes. For these two reasons, they oppose to the insistence of "immersion" in designing games. They even find it dangerous for the maturity of the medium.

Calleja (2007) points out that the conception of immersion by Salen and Zimmerman (2004) and many others who have a similar view is one in which immersion becomes synonymous with absorption or "engagement." He further says that "equating immersion to a loss of sense of time makes the term as readily applicable to gardening or painting miniature figurines as it does of digital gameplay" (p. 92), while the

[21]The term "virtual reality" is used very loosely (2007). Here I specifically refer to the use of head-mounted displays. These differ from games in that the latter are visualized on a screen and mediated by means of a controller or a keyboard, while head-mounted displays are directly fed into the senses of the user and frequently enable the user to make natural movements. Although future trends in display technologies are still clearly visible, the use of head-mounted displays has currently lost attraction. Not only do they cost extra, they can be extremely uncomfortable.

[22]The original term by Minsky (1980) was shortened to "presence" to indicate that it is not only applicable to teleoperation but also to virtual reality.

[23]I would add a third (and intermediary) role besides the roles of player and person on the basis of TGD (see Level 2. This is the role of the player as "interpretant" (or learner).

Fig. 5.10 Walking an old lady to a bench in *The Graveyard*. ©2008 Tale of Tales. Used with permission

term incorporates much more than that. He argues that a distinction should be made between "immersion as deep absorption," which is the conscious concentration of being involved with a game, and "immersion as traversable space habitation," which is non-critical—a willingness to suspend disbelief—and unconscious involvement into a game. The first may only happen with *Tetris*, while with *World of Warcraft* both forms may occur.[24]

I conceive of these two forms of "immersion" as one in which the player plays the game and becomes involved with this. This "immersion as deep absorption" I call "engagement." When the player submerges into the world of a game by suspending his or her disbelief and gets involved with this other world, the other form, the "immersion as traversable space habitation," occurs. This I call "immersion."[25]

To explain this distinction further, let me refer to a nice experimental "game" called *The Graveyard* (Fig. 5.10).[26] In this game, the player controls an old woman and the goal is to walk her to a bench somewhere in a graveyard. Like an old woman

[24]In relaxation or "zen games" the emphasis is only on being somewhere else. These games offer little to no engagement and focus just on getting away from daily life. These thus only involve "immersion as traversable space habitation" or what I simply refer to as "immersion."

[25]Calleja (2007) himself decided it would be best to dispose of all the current terms and introduced a new one. He calls this "incorporation." Incorporation has six types of involvement: tactical, spatial, affective, narrative, shared, and performative.

[26]The creators of *The Graveyard* see the game more as a digital poem. It is digital art. For this reason, I put the term game between quotations.

of that age, she walks slowly...very slowly. She even has to use her stick, because she has some difficulty with it. When I played this game and I finally, after a long five minutes reached the bench, I felt tired and sighed. I felt more or less like an old lady who finally reached her destination and is able to sit down.

This game is everything but engaging. It does not offer any challenges and the pace of it is that slow and rather uninteresting—it just involves bringing an old lady to a bench—that any commitment to keep on playing or return to playing it, is close to nothing. On the other hand, the game did make me experience what it is like to be an old woman. During this even still relatively short experience I felt the pain and trouble to even be able to do the most simple and basic movements in life: to walk from A to B. While the game was not engaging to me, it did make me immerse into another reality.

Although I agree with the statement by Salen and Zimmerman (2004) that the notion of immersion is overrated by some, it is in many instances an important criterion to consider. Take the *Ship Simulator* again. If people are trained by using this environment they definitely need to suspend their disbelief about the virtuality of the environment and act accordingly. If they cannot do this, the whole idea of using a virtual environment to partially replace and complement actual training in the real world is a fad. Therefore, obviously depending on many aspects (such as the purpose and the type of game), designers may need to consider how they can ensure that players get immersed into the game.

And when it comes to getting immersed, the role of "player as a person" is important for fulfilling the role of "player as player." For example, I think people interested in ships or who are involved with it do a much better job at getting immersed, because they are able to "create belief" much better than people who do not know anything about ships. The first group are able to fill in the gaps that the virtual environment offers and imagine many other aspects that might play a role, such as the weather, while the game environment may not take this into account.

The second group, the laypeople, just see a ship and water and get quickly bored with bringing a ship from position A somewhere in the water to position B. They are not able to immerse themselves and combined with a possible lack of engagement they most likely disregard the game as being any "fun," the final and next criterion of this world, to play.

Fun

Many claim that games for serious purposes are first and foremost games, and for that reason need to be *fun*, as this is the "ultimate criterion" of designing a game. The general wisdom is that "if it is no fun, nobody will play it." Others, such as Rollings and Morris (2004), are less pronounced about the importance of "fun," but do emphasize to "make sure it is fun." And we have even scholars who point out that for certain games fun is not important at all (e.g., Bogost 2006).

While a clear consensus about this criterion cannot be seen, without doubt it matters when designing a game. But what is this "fun" exactly? In his "Theory of

Fun for Game Design" Koster (2005) helps us out by explaining what fun is and how it relates to games:

> Fun is all about our brains feeling good—the release of endorphins into our system. The various cocktails of chemicals released in different ways are basically all the same. Science has shown that the pleasurable chills that we get down the spine after exceptionally powerful music or a really great book are caused by the same sorts of chemicals we get when we have cocaine, an orgasm, or chocolate. Basically, our brains are on drugs pretty much all the time. One of the subtlest releases of chemicals is at that moment of triumph when we learn something or master a task. This almost always causes us to break out into a smile. After all, it is important to the survival of the species that we learn—therefore our bodies reward us for it with moments of pleasure. There are many ways we find fun in games, and I will talk about the others. But this is the most important. Fun from games arises out of mastery. It arises out of comprehension. It is the act of solving puzzles that makes games fun. In other words, with games, learning is the drug. (p. 40)

In the rest of his book Koster (2005) explains the other things that can make games fun, such as the graphics, the sound, the social interaction with friends or other players, and so on. He stresses however, that fun from games exists above all "out of mastery." After a player finally defeats a monster, finishes a level, or beats his friend in a racing game, the endorphins are released and we experience the phenomenon of fun. The reference Koster uses to "the act of solving puzzles" is not coincidental, because the fun that comes with mastery is exactly what makes puzzles fun as well according to Danesi (2002):

> ...solving puzzles provides an intellectual "kick," which results from discovering the patterns, traps, or tricks they conceal. This is true for people of all ages, as borne out by the fact that puzzles of all kinds appeal to children and adults alike. Needless to say, some puzzles are more intellectually pleasurable than others are. The *aesthetic index* of a puzzle, as it may be called, seems to be inversely proportional to the complexity of its solution or to the obviousness of the pattern, trap, or trick it hides. Simply put, the longer and more complicated the answer to a puzzle, or the more obvious it is, the less appealing the puzzle seems to be. Puzzles with simple yet elegant solutions, or puzzles that hide a nonobvious principle, have a higher aesthetic index...puzzles are forms of intellectual play, based on the same mental plan in which humor is rooted. In both cases, getting to the "punch line" is the source of the pleasure. The less obvious the punch line, the funnier the joke; the less obvious the answer, the more pleasurable the puzzle. (p. 40)[27]

If fun is about "mastery," it explains why Bogost (2006) argues that not all games are necessarily about fun. The games *September 12th* and *The McDonald's Video Game* cannot be mastered. In *September 12th* there is nothing to solve. The only thing what a player can do is to realize what is meant by this experience (or reject it as nonsensical).

---

[27] Another interesting and quite philosophical issue that Danesi (2002) raises but which I find out of place to consider in the main text, concerns the idea that puzzles constitute metaphors for life. Life has many unanswerable questions, such as "what is life?" and "what is the universe?," and puzzles seem to provide a "comic relief" from the angst caused by the unanswerable larger questions. They are "small-scale experiences" of the larger questions that life poses to us. He explains that "since there are no definitive answers to the large-scale questions, we are strangely reassured by the answers built into the small-scale ones" (p. 36). The same effect may be applicable to games as well.

Similarly, players cannot manage the McDonald's corporation. They are doomed to fail. Aside that some of these types of games do have fun elements—destroying a diseased cow with a flame thrower is fun for instance—and definitely have some humor, the fun could also consist, if we really stretch it, to the insight of "discovering" what is meant by the game. This sort of insight thinking is what makes puzzles attractive as well (Danesi 2002).

But I have to agree that we would really need to stretch the meaning of fun and render it meaningless, especially if we consider such games as *9-11 Survivor*. In this "game," the player is put into the building of one of the Twin Towers at the moment the hijacked planes crash into it. Depending on the situation the player is in at the moment of the crash—this is every time the game is started different—the player may be able to leave the building or has no choice but to jump out of the window. Through this experience, the player realizes the role of chance and chaos on that fateful morning. I do not think any endorphins are released during and after playing this game.

Nevertheless, although Koster (2005) acknowledges that other elements aside from mastery can be fun as well, his conception is still rather one-sided. His conception refers especially to what is considered "hard fun" (Lazzaro 2008). This relates to challenge, strategy, and problem solving. Next to this type of fun, Lazzaro observed three other types of fun after an eleven year history of improving player experiences:

- **Easy fun**: this type of fun is not about achievement but about the sheer interaction with and the imagination of a fictional world. Novelty, curiosity, fantasy, exploration, and/or role-play are elements that relate to this.
- **Serious fun**: this happens when players play with a purpose to create something of value outside of the game itself such as to relax after a hard day at work. Players aim to change how they think, feel, behave, or to accomplish real work. Games low on serious fun feel like a waste of time.
- **People fun**: this comes from the social interaction around the game. Competition, teamwork, social bonding, and/or recognition are elements that relate to this.

From these types of fun in relation to games with a serious purpose, "serious fun" seems rather interesting. Aside that it could explain for the type of "fun" Bogost (2006) refers to, it asserts that achieving a purpose, a value beyond the game, can be fun in itself.[28] Lazzaro (2008) gives the example of the *ESP Game* as that the players' enjoyment may actually increase from knowing that they are accomplishing a real world task. Likewise, *Dance Dance Revolution* might be considered (more) fun when it is known that it has extra benefits, like loosing weight.

But what is most important to realize from the model of Lazzaro (2008) is to understand that fun is an *emotion*. It is a response, a reaction to something and in this context this something concerns the playing of a game. Hard fun gives emotions as

[28] Bogost (2006) himself ends up calling the experience derived from games that go beyond mere entertainment *fun'* (fun prime), a kind of alternate-reality fun that entails the social, political, and even revolutionary critique of an art, yet acknowledges that this term is not very useful in practice.

fiero—Italian for the feeling of accomplishment—and frustration, easy fun surprise and wonder, serious fun relaxation and excitement, and people fun Schadenfreude—German for the feeling of pleasure at a rival's misfortune—and amusement. This is what connects fun to engagement and immersion yet makes it also different from it.

We can see, for example, that the four types of fun can easily be related to the engagement factors of Malone and Lepper (1981, 1987a, 1987b) and the theory of flow (Csikszentmihalyi 1991). Hard fun relates to challenge and control and the theory of flow, easy fun to curiosity and fantasy and the concept of immersion, and people fun to interpersonal engagement. The serious fun could be explained for by the motivation criterion from the world of Meaning. When people are willing to achieve a value, this may resonate with the "fun" they experience while playing a game.

The difference between the criteria comes down to this. Engagement and immersion are criteria for experiences that occur over a relatively longer period of time. We are involved and committed to a game for minutes, hours, weeks, or even months and while playing we may wane ourselves into another place for minutes or even hours. The mentioned factors and the theory of flow are theoretical frameworks that assume how we can ensure that players get engaged or immersed. Fun, on the other hand, is not some continuously occurring process. It is an event that is triggered at certain moments in time. If we say "we had fun," it actually means that we had fun at particular occasions. When we play a game, we do not always have fun. This only happens when we defeat the monster, discover the mystery, or get the recognition from a peer.

The resultant effect, however, may influence the further engagement or immersion. It is important to realize that fun does not need to occur for us to stay engaged or immersed. Take a sad movie. This might be engaging, because of its drama, while we hardly experience any fun.[29] In fact, fun could even break the engagement or immersion. This may be wanted, such as a well timed joke in a thrilling movie, to break the tension and give the viewers some relief. Or it could be really disturbing and put people in the wrong "mode." I experience this sometimes in meetings when suddenly somebody starts to get "funny" and while we started well off, we do not seem to get down to any "serious" business at all anymore.

Let me explain this with another experimental game called *I Wanna Be The Guy: The Movie: The Game* (this is the actual full title...). In this game, the player controls a 15 year old "child" that left home to go on a dangerous and epic quest to become "the Guy." The game is best known for its incredibly high difficulty. To get passed the first scene (Fig. 5.11) I died close to 100 times. This game opposes every conceivable idea of how to engage players. Furthermore, it is unlikely that players get immersed into its fairly basic gameworld. And still, people play and like it.

How is this possible? First, this is "hard fun par excellence." This is the Holy Grail for hardcore gamers. The game is almost masochistic but because of this extreme difficulty, it becomes more satisfying if the goal is achieved. Secondly, the

[29] This also relates to the difference between fun and entertainment (Rollings and Adams 2003). Entertainment does not need to be pleasurable. It can be about "drama" as well.

Fig. 5.11 Getting killed frequently with *I Wanna Be The Guy: The Movie: The Game*. ©2007 Kayin Nasaki. Used with permission

game has a sense of humor and manipulates the player's expectations. For example, in the first scene, the apples first drop to the floor, but when the player gets to the platform, they suddenly go upwards. This, together with the most crazy deaths imaginable creates for a sort of easy fun that reliefs the player from all the frustration in dying all the time.

At the moments the game does something unexpected, a subgoal is achieved, or crazy deaths take place, the endorphins are released that ensure, if enough, for players to keep on going with this game. Therefore, this game is fun and this emotion helps in getting engaged, whereas the game mechanics hardly allow for this themselves. For me the fun was not enough. After close to 500 deaths the frustration was too much and the relief too little and I quit early. I am much more into "serious fun" anyway.

I want to conclude this tough and still largely unsolved "puzzle" by saying that while fun matters in general, its relevance is sometimes a bit overrated similar to immersion and even engagement. Other emotions can play a role too and are worth to consider when designing a game (cf., Freeman 2004).

From Play to Balancing

In this level I explained what the world of Play is about, what aspects need to be considered, and finally what criteria can be used to judge the worth of a game from this perspective. Although definitely many more issues can be related to this world—complete books are only devoted to this topic alone—and more research is needed to better understand the delineations between engagement, immersion, and fun and what each of them mean for different types of games, this level should have given an initial strong idea of this paradigm.

It is important to emphasize that to create a game, it is not just a matter of putting the ingredients, as described in this level, together. To get a proper mix, it also comes down to *balancing* the game. A well-known example of balancing the world of Play relates to preventing any dominant strategies from occurring. If this happens, players are not offered "an interesting choice." They will always pick the dominant option. A way to prevent this is to make use of "intransitive relationships" (Rollings and Adams 2003; Rollings and Morris 2004) or "triangularity" (Crawford 1982).

This is exemplified with the children's game *Rock, Paper, Scissors*. The goal of this game is to choose a gesture which defeats that of the opponent. Each turn players swing one hand in a fist up and down on the count of three. On the third count, the players change their hands into one of the gestures that symbolize rock (by keeping the hand into a clenched fist), paper (represented by an open hand), or scissors (by extending and separating the index and middle fingers) and confront the other player with it. The rules to win are simple: scissors cut paper, paper wraps stone, and stone blunts scissors.

From this, we can clearly see that none of the gestures is better than any other. Each choice is equal. This sort of relationships are put into digital games as well, for example in strategy games where people can choose from different units to attack others. Rollings and Morris (2004) mention the example of warrior, barbarian, and archer units where the warrior beats the barbarian, the barbarian the archer, and the archer the warrior. This way, players are forced to think of a strategy rather than only invest into one specific unit that will defeat all others.

According to Rollings and Adams (2003) a balanced game is further one in which "a better player should ordinarily be more successful than a poor one unless he has an unusually long run of bad luck" (p. 240). Concerning this, I remember very well that I played a game called *Bushido Blade*. This is a very "realistic" game. Unlike many other fighting games in which players have an energy bar to show how much damage the player-character can still take, in this game every blow with a weapon would either result into a serious injury that would hamper the player in continuing the fight or it would immediately kill the player.

I liked the game for its new take on the "beat 'em up genre," but I was done with it when a "newbie" came around, sat down, grabbed the controller, did not ask me which button was meant for what, and started to play. While I was attempting my rigorous tactics and strategies to kill this newbie in a flash, the newbie pushed the buttons like a maniac. Unfortunately, this newbie killed me nine times out of ten. My other friends were laughing enormously, because I had been bragging about my

Fig. 5.12 The winning artwork by GundumPanda of "The Cracked Photoshop Contest" about "If video games were realistic"

(a) Scorpion and Liu Kang are ready to fight each other

(b) After one second Scorpion throws a spear at Liu Kang

(c) Liu Kang immediately dies and Scorpion wins a flawless victory

skills for playing this game. There I was, with a game called *Bushido Blade*, which lets newbies beat "professionals." I never played it again.[30]

[30] *Bushido Blade* is actually critically well received. It is considered a classic, mostly because of its innovation in the fighting genre. Maybe I just had "an unusually long run of bad luck" in this case.

The example of *Bushido Blade* also brings to mind that the notion and importance of "balancing" goes much further when it comes to TGD. Not only does the world of Play need to be considered. It involves also the consideration of the worlds of Reality and of Meaning and the interactions between the worlds. The "ingredients" of these two other worlds and their criteria have to be balanced and put into the mix as well.

In *Bushido Blade* we see a potential problem caused by its realism. On the one hand, the idea to not use an energy bar but let every hit count was innovative. We can see this as a synergy between the worlds of Reality and Play. On the other hand, is it any fun to die right away? Is it any fun if an unexperienced player is able to win quite easily? Although the latter is a matter of the world of Play itself, by ensuring that players with better strategies and skills are more likely to win, the first question indicates a clash between the world of Reality and of Play.

Interestingly enough, the "innovation" of *Bushido Blade* and the clash between the worlds of Reality and Play is illustrated very nicely in a winning animation artwork in a contest in which participants had to think about what "if video games were realistic" (Fig. 5.12). In the winning artwork a classic beat 'em up game, *Mortal Kombat*, is shown in which two fighters, Scorpion and Liu Kang, have to battle each other to death. Normally, a fight takes up a considerable time. With each hit the energy bar of a player decreases and when it is empty, the fight is over. However, with the artist's impression, Liu Kang immediately dies after getting hit with a spear similar to the mechanics of *Bushido Blade*. A game session is in this case finished in a second. It seems that "reality sucks all the fun out of the game."

Designing games is about recognizing and dealing with these sorts of design dilemmas. In designing *Levee Patroller* I discovered that these dilemmas can be related to the three worlds that have been discussed in this book and that it requires on behalf of the designer to find a balance. In the next level I will elaborate on this "balancing" by explaining the dilemmas that we were dealing with during the development of *Levee Patroller* and how we tried to find a balance.

Bibliography

Literature Bibliography

Aarseth, E. J. (2004). *Genre trouble*. http://www.electronicbookreview.com. Accessed 22 September 2009.

Aarseth, E. J. (2005). From Hunt the Wumpus to Everquest: introduction to quest theory. In F. Kishino, Y. Kitamura & H. Kato (Eds.), *ICEC 2005* (Vol. 3711, pp. 317–328). Heidelberg: Springer.

Aldrich, C. (2004). *Simulations and the future of learning: an innovative (and perhaps revolutionary) approach to e-learning*. San Francisco: Pfeiffer.

Bergeron, B. P. (2006). *Developing serious games*. Hingham: Charles River Media.

Bogost, I. (2006). *Unit operations: an approach to video game criticism*. Cambridge: The MIT Press.

Brown, D. (2003). *The Da Vinci code*. New York: Doubleday.

Caillois, R. (1961). *Man, play and games* (M. Barash, Transl.). Champaign: University of Illinois Press. (Original work published in 1958).

Calleja, G. (2007). *Digital games as designed experience: reframing the concept of immersion*. Unpublished dissertation, Victoria University of Wellington, Wellington, New Zealand.

Coleridge, S. T. (1817/1985). Biographia literaria. In H. J. Jackson (Ed.), *Samuel Taylor Coleridge: the mayor works* (pp. 155–482). New York: The Oxford University Press.

Costikyan, G. (1994). *I have no words & I must design*. http://www.costik.com/nowords.html. Accessed 20 September 2009.

Crawford, C. (1982). *The art of computer game design*. http://www.vancouver.wsu.edu/fac/peabody/game-book/Coverpage.html. Accessed 3 November 2009.

Crawford, C. (2005). *Chris Crawford on interactive storytelling*. Berkeley: New Riders Publishing.

Csikszentmihalyi, M. (1975). *Beyond boredom and anxiety: the experience of play in work and games*. San Francisco: Jossey-Bass.

Csikszentmihalyi, M. (1991). *Flow: the psychology of optimal experience*. New York: Harper Perennial.

Danesi, M. (2002). *The puzzle instinct: the meaning of puzzles in human life*. Bloomington: Indiana University Press.

De Freitas, S. (2006). *Learning in immersive worlds: a review of game-based learning*. Bristol: Joint Information Systems Committee.

Egenfeldt-Nielsen, S. (2007). *Beyond edutainment: the educational potential of computer games*. London, UK: Continuum Press.

Fine, G. A. (1983). *Shared fantasy: role playing games as social worlds*. Chicago: Chicago University Press.

Freeman, D. E. (2004). *Creating emotion in games: the craft and art of emotioneering*. Indianapolis: New Riders.

Fullerton, T., Swain, C., & Hoffman, S. S. (2008). *Game design workshop: a playcentric approach to creating innovative games* (2nd ed.). Burlington: Morgan Kaufmann.

Griffiths, M. D. (1996). Computer game playing in children and adolescents: a review of the literature. In T. Gill (Ed.), *Electronic children: how children are responding to the information revolution* (pp. 41–59). London: National Children's Bureau.

Huizinga, J. (1938/1955). *Homo ludens: a study of the play-element in culture* (R.F.C. Hull, Transl.). Boston: Beacon Press.

Jensen, J. (1999). Interactivity: tracking a new concept in media and communication studies. In P. Mayer (Ed.), *Computer media and communication: a reader* (pp. 160–185). Oxford: Oxford University Press.

Juul, J. (2005). *Half-real: video games between real rules and fictional worlds*. Cambridge: The MIT Press.

Koster, R. (2005). *A theory of fun for game design*. Scottsdale: Paraglyph Press.

Kramer, W. (2000). *What makes a game good?* http://www.thegamesjournal.com. Accessed 20 September 2009.

Lazzaro, N. (2008). The four fun keys. In K. Isbister & N. Schaffer (Eds.), *Game usability: advice from the experts for advancing the player experience* (pp. 317–343). Burlington: Morgan Kaufmann.

Malone, T. W. (1981). Toward a theory of intrinsically motivating instruction. *Cognitive Science*, *5*(4), 333–369.

Malone, T. W., & Lepper, M. (1987a). Intrinsic motivation and instructional effectiveness in computer-based education. In R. Snow & M. Farr (Eds.), *Aptitude learning and instruction* (pp. 152–188). London: Lawrence Erlbaum.

Malone, T. W., & Lepper, M. (1987b). Making learning fun: a taxonomy of intrinsic motivation for learning. In R. Snow & M. Farr (Eds.), *Aptitude learning and instruction* (pp. 223–253). London: Lawrence Erlbaum Associates.

Minsky, M. L. (1980). Telepresence. *Omni*, *2*(9), 45–51.

Murray, J. (1997). *Hamlet on the holodeck*. New York: The Free Press.

Orlikowski, W. J. (1992). The duality of technology: rethinking the concept of technology in organizations. *Organization Science*, *3*(3), 398–427.
Prensky, M. (2001). *Digital game-based learning*. New York: McGraw-Hill.
Retaux, X., & Rouchier, J. (2002). Realism vs surprise and coherence: different aspects of playability in computer games. In *Conference proceedings of playing with the future: development and directions in computer gaming*. Manchester: Centre for Research on Innovation and Competition.
Rieber, L. P. (1996). Seriously considering play: designing interactive learning environments based on the blending of microworlds, simulations, and games. *Educational Technology Research and Development*, *44*(2), 45–58.
Rollings, A., & Adams, E. (2003). *Andrew Rollings and Ernest Adams on game design*. Indianapolis: New Riders.
Rollings, A., & Morris, D. (2004). *Game architecture and design: a new edition*. Indianapolis: New Riders.
Salen, K., & Zimmerman, E. (2004). *Rules of play: game design fundamentals*. Cambridge: MIT Press.
Sims, R. (1995). *Interactivity: a forgotten art?* http://www2.gsu.edu/~wwwitr/docs/interact/. Accessed 20 September 2009.
Von Ahn, L., & Dabbish, L. (2004). Labeling images with a computer game. In E. Dykstra-Erickson & M. Tscheligi (Eds.), *ACM CHI 2004 Conference on human factors in computing systems* (pp. 319–326). Vienna: ACM Press.
Vygotsky (1978). *Mind in society: the development of higher psychological processes*. Cambridge: Harvard University Press.
Wexler, S., Aldrich, C., Johannigman, J., Oehlert, M., Quinn, C., & Barneveld, A. V. (2007). *Immersive learning simulations*. Santa Rosa: The eLearning Guild.
Witmer, B., & Singer, M. J. (1998). Measuring presence in virtual environments: a presence questionnaire. *Presence: Teleoperators and Virtual Environments*, *7*(3), 225–240.

Game Bibliography

Alcorn, A. (1972). *Pong* [Atari 2600]. Sunnyvale: Atari.
Atari (1977). *Combat* [Atari 2600]. Sunnyvale: Atari.
BioWare (2003). *Star Wars: Knights of the Old Republic* [PC]. San Francisco: LucasArts.
Blizzard Entertainment (2004). *World of Warcraft* [PC]. Irvine: Blizzard Entertainment.
Boon, E., & Tobias, J. (1992). *Mortal Kombat* [Arcade]. Chicago: Midway.
Bungie Studios (2001). *Halo: Combat Evolved* [Xbox]. Redmond: Microsoft.
CCP Games (2003). *Eve Online* [PC]. Reykjavik, Iceland: CCP Games.
Chen, J., & Clark, N. (2006). *flOw* [PC]. Los Angeles: thatgamecompany.
Cole, J., Caloud, M., & Brennon, J. (2003). *9-11 Survivor* [PC]. Published independently.
Core Design (1996). *Tomb Raider* [Playstation]. San Francisco: Eidos Interactive.
Crawford, C. (2009). *Storytron: Interactive Storytelling* [PC]. Jacksonville: Storytron.
Darrow, C. (1935). *Monopoly* [Board]. Salem: Parker Brothers.
Deltares, & Delft University of Technology (2006). *Levee Patroller: The Levee Inspection Simulator* [PC]. Delft, the Netherlands: Delft GeoSystems.
Epic Games (2004). *Unreal Tournament 2004* [PC]. New York: Atari.
Firaxis Games (2005). *Sid Meier's Civilization IV* [PC]. Hunt Valley: 2K Games.
GameLab (2007). *Miss Management* [PC]. New York: GameLab.
Harmonix Music Systems (2006). *Guitar Hero* [Playstation 2]. Sunnyvale: RedOctane.
id Software (1991). *Commander Keen 4: Secret of the Oracle* [PC]. Garland: Apogee Software.
id Software (1999). *Quake III Arena* [PC]. Santa Monica: Activision.
KCE Tokyo (2001). *Dance Dance Revolution* [Playstation]. Tokyo, Japan: Konami.

Kee Games (1974). *Tank* [Arcade]. Sunnyvale: Atari.
Light Weight (1997). *Bushido Blade* [Playstation]. Tokyo, Japan: Square Enix.
Linden Lab (2003). *Second Life* [PC]. San Francisco: Linden Lab.
LucasArts (1998). *Grim Fandango* [PC]. San Rafael: LucasArts.
Mateas, M., & Stern, A. (2005). *Façade* [PC]. Portland: Procedural Arts.
Maxis Software (2003). *SimCity 4* [PC]. Redwood City: Electronic Arts.
Molleindustria (2006). *The McDonald's Video Game* [PC]. Italy: Molleindustria.
MotiveTime (1990). *Dragon's Lair* [NES]. San Jose: CSG Imagesoft.
Namco (1981). *Pac-Man* [Atari 2600]. Sunnyvale: Atari.
Namco (2002). *Tekken 4* [Playstation]. Tokyo, Japan: Namco.
Nasaki, K. (2007). *I Wanna Be The Guy: The Movie: The Game* [PC]. Published independently.
Nintendo (1981). *Donkey Kong* [Arcade]. Tokyo, Japan: Nintendo.
Nintendo EAD (2007). *The Legend of Zelda: Phantom Hourglass* [Nintendo DS]. Tokyo, Japan: Nintendo.
Pajitnov, A., Pavlovsky, D., & Gerasimov, V. (1986). *Tetris* [PC]. Moscow, Russia: Soviet Academy of Sciences.
Powerful Robot Games (2003). *September 12th* [Web]. Montevideo, Uruguay: Newsgaming.com.
Rockstar North (2008). *Grand Theft Auto IV* [Playstation 3]. New York: Rockstar Games.
Simulearn (2003). *Virtual Leader* [PC]. Norwalk: Simulearn.
Smilebit (2000). *The Typing of the Dead* [PC]. Tokyo, Japan: SEGA.
Søderstrøm, H. (2006). *Toribash* [PC]. Singapore: Nabi Studios.
Tale of Tales (2008). *The Graveyard* [PC]. Ghent, Belgium: Tale of Tales.
Telltale (2009). *Tales of Monkey Island* [PC]. San Rafael: Telltale.
Turbine Entertainment Software (2002). *Asheron's Call 2: The Fallen Kings* [PC]. Westwood: Turbine Entertainment Software.
Valve (1999). *Counter-Strike* [PC]. Paris, France: Vivendi.
Von Ahn, L., & Dabbish, L. (2004). *ESP Game* [Web]. Pittsburgh: Carnegie Mellon University.
VSTEP (2010). *Ship Simulator Extremes* [PC]. Stockholm, Sweden: Paradox Interactive.

Level 6
Balancing

What I dream of is an art of balance—Henri Matisse

The world is not dialectical—it is sworn to extremes, not to equilibrium, sworn to radical antagonism, not to reconciliation or synthesis. This is also the principle of evil—Jean Baudrillard

On a daily basis we are confronted with the notion of "keeping balance." We have to balance our diet, our work and private life, our income and expenditures, and so on. We even have to balance standing on both our feet, although we are not much aware of it, unless we get injured and have to use crutches. In some cases we can clearly say if something is balanced or not. The most clear example to even measure balance is in English funny enough called a "balance" (although it is more commonly referred to as a "scale"). With this weighing machine, we are able to get balance even if we do not know the exact weights of the elements. This is the basis of one of the more familiar logic puzzles that circulate around.[1] An example of such a puzzle is described below. Try to solve this puzzle before continue reading. The answer can be found in Appendix A.

> There are 12 identical-looking weights. 11 of these weights are indeed identical, but one is different. This one is either heavier or lighter than the others. Use a balance, of which either side of the sales is large enough to hold up to 12 weights, three times to determine which weight is different.

Although this puzzle is certainly not easy, the point is that it is possible to *measure* with such a system and with some logic behind it. It is deterministic. With other aspects in life, it is much more difficult to tell whether something is balanced.

Take our diet. Hundreds if not thousands of books are written and prescribe what people should do to keep their balance. None of them can precisely point out when someone is in balance other than giving advice like "do not overeat" or assuming we

[1] These puzzles even appear in games. A number of them, differing in difficulty, have to be solved in *Professor Layton*.

C. Harteveld, *Triadic Game Design*,
DOI 10.1007/978-1-84996-157-8_6, © Springer-Verlag London Limited 2011

should not eat more than 100 grams of meat every day. What these books (and the people behind them) do illustrate is a way of thinking about how to approach food. They give a sense of what balance is and how it can be achieved. Most even give the basic steps for people to reach this, although this cannot be guaranteed (despite that many of them pretend and suggest so. . .).

Games belong to the second category, the one in which it is hard to say when a balance is achieved. We cannot put a game onto a "weighing machine" and measure if it is balanced. We can, on the other hand, use all kinds of heuristics to get a better idea of what the game does and if we are satisfied with it (cf., Isbister and Schaffer 2008). Similar to the diet books we can also give advice, assume what is good, propose a way of thinking, and give some basic steps to think about.

Despite that I do not want to affiliate myself with a diet guru, this is exactly what TGD is about. And according to TGD it is critical to achieve a balance between the worlds of Reality, Meaning, and Play. When that happens, we can speak of a "good" game. Unfortunately, similar to the diet books, I cannot guarantee that when this approach is used, it will automatically lead to a successful game. Nevertheless, by being aware of the importance of all three worlds and the need to balance these, it is less likely that failure occurs.

The enormous importance of the act of this balancing process is expressed in the ultimate criterion of TGD. This is not validity, transfer, or fun. This is *harmony*.[2] Harmony extends beyond any of the separate worlds, as it actually stresses that to "live in harmony," to be harmonic, it is important that each world is appropriately taken care off and interacts meaningfully with each other. This requires congruity of the parts with one another and with the whole but is also about making sure that the parts themselves are represented well enough within this whole. Each world has its own aspects and criteria and they need to be considered on their own behalf as well. If this is done successfully, the worlds reinforce and support each other, similar to the "spoons puzzle" in Level 1. The whole becomes, in that case, more than the sum of its parts.

From the previous levels we can see that in quite a number of cases harmony seems to be easily reached. From Level 4 we can derive that games are, for example, inherent learning environments in and of themselves. They concur with many of the ideas I retrieved from the different learning paradigms, such as being experiential and giving fast feedback. This means the worlds of Meaning and Play reinforce each other already. Moreover, when we look at the worlds of Reality and Play, we see that parts of Reality are always represented in games. They already have some underlying model of reality. The same relationship exists between Meaning and

[2]With regard to games, the idea of harmony has also been mentioned by game designer Brian Moriarty (Rollings and Adams 2003). He defines harmony as a feeling that all parts of the game belong to a single whole. I consider this definition too narrow, as it actually refers to "coherency." Harmony goes beyond coherency (and the world of Play) as it involves more than making elements fit together. A bad game can be very coherent. Think of a game with a dominant strategy—the inclusion of this does not relate to coherency but to a poor balancing of the gameplay. For this to change, a balance is needed and this happens if all the elements are appropriately taken care off. If this is done, the game also has harmony.

Reality. If Meaning does not involve aspects of the world of Reality, its output, the value proposal, is "meaningless" a priori. From this, we see that the worlds have a natural tendency to overlap and work together.

Despite this, Baudrillard's "principle of evil" applies to game design as well. The worlds also have a natural tendency to clash, to disagree, and not create an equilibrium or synthesis. In this level I will illustrate the various clashes or tensions within and between the worlds with concrete examples from the development of *Levee Patroller*. These examples are illustrative for two reasons. Firstly, we had to deal with far more tensions during the project. In fact, I believe that game design is about "solving tensions." Secondly, the tensions can be exemplary for other game development projects as they may represent stereotypical types of tensions.

But before we delve into the examples, I will first further elaborate on the idea of TGD with regards to the act of balancing. With this elaboration, a better understanding is achieved of how we can "deal with tensions."[3]

Dealing with Tensions

To reiterate, the idea of TGD stresses that designing games requires (a) taking into account a design space of three different worlds, (b) balancing these worlds by making trade-offs, and this works at best when (c) considering these worlds concurrently. The three worlds concern the worlds of Reality, Meaning, and Play. Each of these worlds are affiliated with different people, disciplines, aspects, and criteria.

The idea of TGD involves, however, much more and this relates in particularly to the act of balancing. For balancing a game it is handy to keep in mind with what sort of tension has to be dealt with (see "Types of Tension"). Additionally, for balancing a game designers do not have a complete freedom. They have to take certain constraints into account (see "Constraints").

Types of Tension

When designing a game, and putting all the different elements derived from the three worlds together, trade-offs have to be made, because within and between worlds *tensions* may arise. To deal appropriately with these tensions, it is useful to know with what "type of tension" we are dealing with. For this reason, based on the idea of TGD I have distinguished three primary types of tension:

- **Within-world dilemmas**: in some cases a situation may arise in which the designer is confronted with a dilemma, a choice between two alternatives that seem equally desirable or undesirable, which is restricted to one of the worlds. This means the dilemmas arise *within* either Reality, Meaning, or Play.

[3]Many of the tension examples have been described in Harteveld et al. (2010). However, based on further insight and reflection some of the examples have been renamed and repositioned.

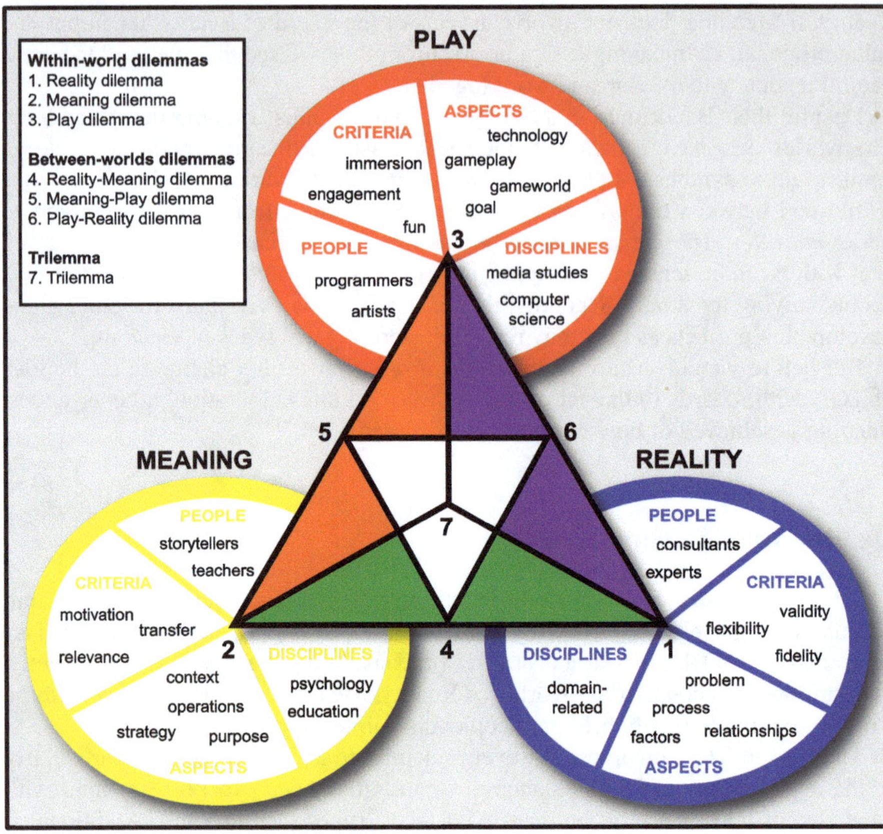

Fig. 6.1 Reality, Meaning, and Play and their tensions

- **Between-worlds dilemmas**: in other cases a dilemma may arise *between* two worlds. Such tensions happen when two worlds are irreconcilable. The two worlds may have a different idea of how something should be implemented and this causes a conflict.
- **Trilemmas**: if a designer faces a tense situation in which all three worlds play a significant role, we speak of a "trilemma." In this case all three worlds can have a different take on the situation.

Based on these three primary types, we can get to a total of seven types when we specifically relate them to the three worlds (see Fig. 6.1). These seven different types are important to keep in mind, because they determine where in the "design space" we have to look for solutions. If, for example, a tension is purely related to the world of Play we do not have to look at the other two worlds.

For each of the seven types of tensions I will give one or more examples from the development of *Levee Patroller*. Although I solely use this game to illustrate the tensions, they are likely to occur in other game projects as well. Tate et al.

(2009) observed, for example, in fact a Play-Reality dilemma during the design of *Re-Mission*:

> An often-recurring issue involved conflict between a proclivity toward dramatic license to enhance game appeal (held most strongly by our game designers) and a preference for "biological accuracy" and "scientific evidence" (held by our health professionals). (p. 31)

To give another example, Winn and Heeter (2006) observed actually a Meaning-Play dilemma during the design of an educational game:

> The game designer initially included levels as an abstract design feature because they provide players with subgoals and a means to gauge their progress through the game. However, levels also create barriers to advancement in the game. If players are unable to beat level 1, they will not be allowed to play level 2. The pedagogy expert deemed this unacceptable. From her point of view, she did not want the game to prevent learners from accessing learning content. Therefore, levels conflicted with the pedagogy perspective, and the feature was eliminated. (p. 2)

But the examples illustrate more than just the seven tension types. They are in and of themselves typical as well. In Table 6.1 an overview is given of all 16 examples from *Levee Patroller*. To each and every one I have assigned a name to indicate that they represent issues that can also be expected in other projects. It is, for instance, not unlikely to expect that another game project will experience a definition or usability tension.

While this may be true, it is important to first of all stress that the tension examples are not conclusive. Many more typical tensions can be thought of. Take the above-mentioned tensions. The example by Winn and Heeter (2006) does not fit any of the tension examples. It could be considered another typical tension, which we could name "accessibility tension."

On the other hand, it could very well be that a tension example fits but involves another tension type. The example by Tate et al. (2009) can be considered a "representation tension," while this one concerns a Play-Reality dilemma and not, such as with *Levee Patroller*, a Reality-Meaning dilemma. Nevertheless, for some tension examples, such as "demarcation tension" and "strategy tension," such change of tension type is less likely. They will always be a Reality dilemma or Meaning dilemma, respectively. With others, like "computation tension," the tension type may change, but it has a natural tendency to involve a particular world. With the computation tension it will, for example, always involve the world of Play.

In resolving these tension examples some aspects and criteria, as discussed in the previous three levels, were more *prominently* involved than others. With the examples of *Levee Patroller* it can be noted that certain aspects and criteria are hardly noticeable (e.g., problem and fun) and some are not even mentioned at all (e.g., context and motivation). This does not mean that these elements were not important. All aspects and criteria mentioned in this book have played a role during the development of the game. They are just less prominent—less visible—in the examples I am about to give.

Table 6.1 Overview of the tension examples experienced with *Levee Patroller*

Tension example	Tension type
Definition	Reality
Demarcation	Reality
Strategy	Meaning
Usability	Play
Guidance	Reality-Meaning
Representation	Reality-Meaning
Stimuli	Meaning-Play
Reflection	Meaning-Play
Uncertainty	Play-Reality
Translation	Play-Reality
Computation	Play-Reality
Scope	Trilemma
Score	Trilemma
Variety	Trilemma
Framework	Trilemma
Story	Trilemma

Constraints

The design space to consider is also influenced by something else, because dealing with tensions does not occur in a vacuum. It is one thing to have a vision about "some" game that might change the real world (a little bit). It is another thing to really implement this game and get it to work. In accomplishing this, it helps to have previous experience in designing games, have an understanding of game design, and/or use a design philosophy such as TGD, but it certainly requires time, budget, skilled and available people, and other resources. When developing a game these latter elements also and in fact are quite frequently influential in deciding on design dilemmas. This becomes clear when team members give comments like "What is easier to implement?" or "We do not have time to do this." This means that in balancing a game certain *constraints* have to be taken into account as well.

Constraints determine what is possible and what is not. They limit or restrict the possibilities in a design process. This means that for finding a "optimal solution" constraints need to be considered. If, for example, from the perspective of aesthetics of the world of Play it is better to use a state-of-the-art game engine to be able to create impressive visuals, this may become infeasible if the costs of using such an engine exceed the available budget. Constraints, therefore, reduce the imaginary design space to a set of solutions that are feasible.

For game design constraints concern especially time, budget, and personnel. Constraints thus mostly involve the available resources to create a game. Other types of resources can also be influential, such as the available software and hardware at the beginning of the project to even the office space in which the game is developed. Other than resources, constraints could be imposed by the environment in which the game is eventually used. If clients do not have very powerful computers to play a game on and are unwilling to buy new computers, then this imposes a constraint on what is possible.

Throughout the project, constraints are not static. They are able to change and whether this occurs is very much dependent on how the project is managed. Developing a game involves much more than just "designing" a game. Acquisition, marketing, human resources management, finances, planning, and so on are all aspects that have to be considered as well. These aspects influence the design process and in particular the constraints on the design space. For example, if new clients have been contracted by means of acquisition, the budget for designing the game will increase.

Although these management aspects that surround the design of a game are incredibly important and very influential, in essence they only bring forth the constraints that the designers have to keep in mind while solving their dilemmas. As these aspects—in a strict sense—do not belong to "game design," I will not further elaborate on them.[4] I mention them here, because it is important to realize how constraints are shaped, as the constraints themselves determine to a large extent how dilemmas are solved.

Due to the importance of constraints I will give a general idea of the constraints that played a role during the design of *Levee Patroller*. First of all, it was decided to develop the game in-house at an institute with no experience in designing games but with much expertise about the subject matter. The advantage of this is that almost all the necessary information to develop a model of reality was easily available. Disadvantages of this choice are that no personnel worked at the institute with experience in developing a game and that no resources other than standard PCs were available.

As for the personnel, at the start of the project a part-time project leader working at the institute as a geo engineering consultant hired three students: a programmer, a part-time modeler, and me. It was, however, quickly decided that this team was not capable of finishing the project with the desired end result in 9 months.[5] Therefore, new team members were looked for and, in the end, about 16 people, mostly students, worked on and off the project. After the first months, on average 8 people worked on the project.

---

[4]It is possible to conceive of a fourth world, the world of "Management," which consists of people such as managers, disciplines like organization science, aspects as finances and planning, and criteria as efficiency and effectiveness. However, as is mentioned in the text, in a strict sense everything related to this world of Management is not part of what is considered "game design." When looking at the development of a game from a much broader perspective, the elements of this world can be considered.

[5]The majority of the people working on *Levee Patroller* were students. Although some of them stayed around and took a part-time job, the lion's share of them had other priorities at a certain point in time and left. While students are cheap labor forces, this is important to keep in mind. Project members who leave the project endanger the continuity, especially if they worked on crucial parts of the project. We experience this up to today in improving the game.

As for the finances, the first version had to delivered with more or less a budget of around 200K euros. The clients, the water boards, financed 50% of this budget, the other half was made available through an innovation funds at the institute itself. At least one fourth of this whole budget was spent on hardware, software, and licenses to even be able to develop the game.

With these constraints in mind, we can now turn to the examples. First I will discuss the "within-world dilemmas" by discussing—in this order—the Reality, Meaning, and Play dilemmas. Following this, the "between-worlds dilemmas" are illustrated, from Reality-Meaning, Meaning-Play, to Play-Reality. Before we conclude this level, a number of examples are discussed that can be marked as "trilemmas."

Facing the Reality Dilemma

When we consider the world of Reality, designers take the problem into account, consider the factors that are part of the problem, and from there draw relationships and outline the processes affiliated with the problem. This happens often and most likely in collaboration with subject-matter experts and clients. In doing this, designers may have to face a dilemma. When they do without having to consider any of the other worlds, we speak of a *Reality dilemma.*

A number of such Reality dilemmas I already discussed in Level 3, like the classification of levee failures which was different amongst clients. In the end, we decided to reconcile this dilemma by coming up with our own classification scheme. This concerned a typical "definition" tension. Another design tension that will particularly emerge from constructing the product of Reality, a model of reality, can be brought back to a matter of "demarcation." I will discuss each of these typical tensions below.

Definition Tension

It does not need an explanation that definitions may differ among people. People have simply different perspectives on phenomena in the real world and/or have a different idea on what is important. The latter, the difference in importance, can be seen in politics. Environmentalists want everything to be "green" and pay much attention to proposals that attempt this, while other political movement groups may find this much less important and prioritize on other issues.

Aside from the classification of the levee failures, we bumped into another *definition tension* when we considered the aspect in which this is most likely to occur: the problem. Although all clients agreed that the game needed to involve levee patrollers and levee failures, differences were found on whether more importance should be given to the "recognition" of failures or the "communication" about failures during the procedure of inspecting. Both do not necessarily exclude each other, but they do stress a different kind of problem. Recognition is a cognitive problem, whereas communication is a social problem. Emphasizing one or the other will in the end lead to a different purpose of the game and eventually also lead to a different type of game. Additionally, an unclear problem definition will lead to an unclear solution. For this reason, we needed to resolve this difference in problem perspectives in one way or the other as soon as possible.

We reconciled this by stressing that to communicate about failures, it is first important to recognize them.[6] Although we could have incorporated both aspects into our problem definition, it would make the project much more complicated, because we would need to take an additional phenomenon into account. For this reason, we explained to our clients that it would be better to first focus on recognition before the communication could be dealt with. The clients who prioritized communication accepted this, but they did tell us that in the nearby future they want to have something about communication, because according to them this is where the "real problem" occurs.

And in fact, the game does deal with "communication" in certain ways. It, for example, presents terms and definitions that relate to levee inspection, like the categorization of levee failures. This way, patrollers adopt an inspection vocabulary which well help them to communicate with each other. Besides, the shared experience which the game offers, also helps in telling other patrollers what they see in practice. Although I have never observed this, I would not be surprised if somebody said "Remember when you played *Levee Patroller* and you see this failure in a ditch? This is what I am currently seeing here." Nevertheless, we certainly prioritized recognition over communication, rendering the latter less important.

Demarcation Tension

Another dilemma that I already slightly touched upon in Level 3 concerned what failures to include in the game. It is simply impossible to represent everything from the real world and so choices need to be made of what to consider, especially when there is no unlimited time and budget.

To keep it manageable, we wanted to include a maximum of eight failures. It was, however, difficult to get agreement onto which eight needed to be incorporated as interests diverged. Interests diverged, because the clients have to deal with different failures in practice. Failures are dependent on the types of levee and the characteristics of the region and these differ per water board. It is no wonder each client had a different priority list with failures that they wanted to be added to the game.

We resolved this by choosing eight failures of which we thought would satisfy most if not all clients. Besides this, we made it possible to easily add new failures to the game (see criterion of "flexibility"). Such choices of what to include and exclude relate to a *demarcation tension*. In some cases, a demarcation can be clear, like the

[6] In this project, the two problem definitions were closely related to each other. It can also happen that stakeholders have a completely different idea of what the problem is. In that case, it becomes much harder to get to a shared problem definition.

Fig. 6.2 Embankments at the levees

choice to only focus on the levee patrollers. In other cases, like this matter on the failures, it is less clear what should be done. And sometimes it becomes clear when testing a prototype that something could be excluded which is included or, as what happened with us, something needs to be included what was excluded before.

This happened with a seemingly minor issue. When we were playtesting one of our first prototypes, levee patrollers remarked that certain levees were not realistic. According to them these levees were missing proper embankments, a kind of wooden wall to protect the levee from erosion (Fig. 6.2). To me this was a little detail, but for them it was a huge deal.

In the end, it is most important to ensure that the critical factors, those that really matter and make a difference, are part of the model of reality and are thus included. Next to this, some factors can make a difference in whether players perceive it to be realistic (Peters et al. 1998). If such "psychological factors" which at first may not seem important are not included, it may make a difference in how players judge the experience. We felt that the embankments were such a psychological factor and just to be safe we added this to our model of reality.

Addressing the Meaning Dilemma

Similar to how the Reality dilemma only relates to the world of Reality, the *Meaning dilemma* only relates to the world of Meaning. In this world designers create a value proposal by considering the purpose of the game, the strategy to achieve this, the operations that support the strategy, and by thinking about the context in which the value creation takes place.

Many types of Meaning dilemmas can take place, but the one I found most symptomatic concerned a trade-off in how the purpose should be achieved. This could happen if several objectives are identified that ask for a different type of strategy. If such a *strategy tension* occurs, designers are forced to prioritize the objectives. This happened in our project.

We defined five types of learning objectives, ranging from observing, reporting, diagnosing, assessing, to taking measures (see Level 4). Behind these objectives we can find the cognitive skills to recognize failures, the procedural skills to report and take measures if necessary, and a conceptual understanding of what failures are and how they behave. The latter two, the procedural skills and the conceptual understanding, are in conflict and I will explain why. Procedural skills relate to knowing how to perform an inspection. To learn this, it is best to situate a person into a situation in which he or she would normally perform. In other words, to achieve this objective it would be better to stay as close as possible to the perspective of the patrollers themselves.

A conceptual understanding of the behavior of failures, on the other hand, would be difficult to achieve from the perspective of patrollers. Patrollers only see the outer side of the levee and not the inside which means they only see a tip of the iceberg. The failures caused by erosion do not have this problem, because they start from the outside. However, for those failures that are caused by the instability of a levee (see Level 3), patrollers can only see the signals that are the result of the processes inside the levee. By using the perspective of the patrollers themselves, they can recognize the signals, but may not understand what is causing them.

Let me explain this with the example of the failure mechanism called "sand boils" (Fig. 6.3). If this mechanism occurs, a "pipe" will be created underneath a levee. If this pipe is sustained and sand is eventually transported, this mechanism can cause the levee to erode from the inside out. On the outside the creation of this pipe, the sand transport, and its mechanism cannot be seen. What can be observed is a water outflow in the hinterland together with some sand—if this is transported. These signals are enough to recognize the failure, but do not explain what is happening inside the levee. To get such a conceptual understanding, it would be much better to centralize the levees and not the patrollers. This is, however, difficult to reconcile with the teaching of procedural skills. This means a choice had to be made of what to emphasize.

Eventually we decided to emphasize the procedural skills. To balance our choice, we added a handbook function in which the failures and their signals are described textually and visually with 2D pictorial cross-cuts, such as can be seen in Fig. 6.3. Although patrollers are not forced to read these descriptions and look at the pictures, they may need to if they are unsure with what sort of failure they are dealing with. This way, they get some conceptual understanding of failures.

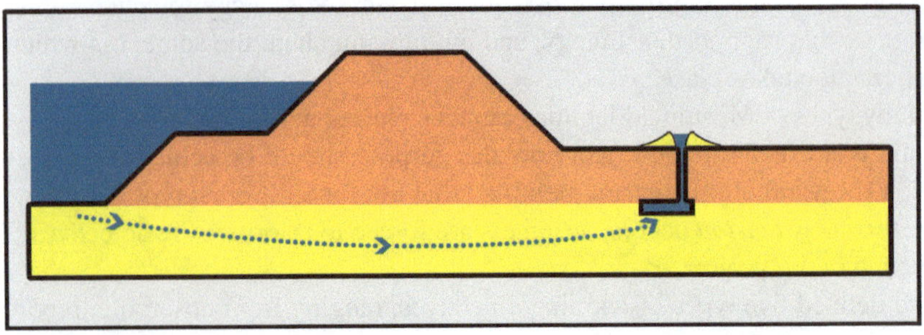

(a) First phase of a failure called "sand boils" with its signals of water outflow which can be seen from the outside

(b) When it becomes worse, soil starts to flow. This transportation of soil is caused by a creation of a pipe underneath the levee. This cannot be seen in the game

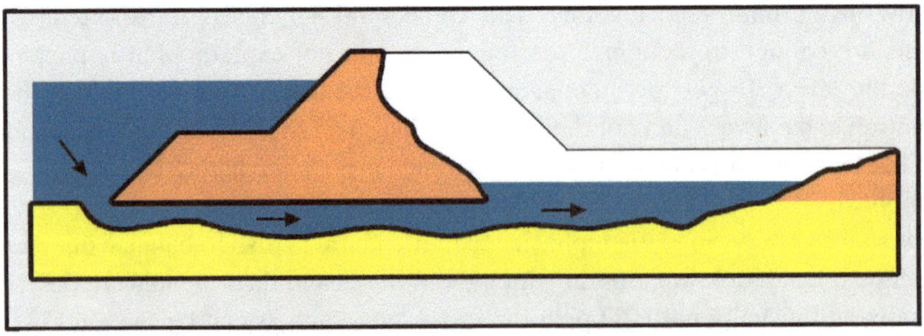

(c) Finally, if nothing is done, the levee collapses like a pudding

Fig. 6.3 Reconciling a Meaning dilemma

Coping with the Play Dilemma

The final within-world dilemma that can occur concerns the *Play dilemma*. This dilemma relates to solely the consideration of the goal of the game, its gameplay, gameworld, or the technology to develop or accompany the game. I want to illustrate one particular Play dilemma that we hit upon. This dilemma has to do with "usability."

The dilemma occurred, because it is a nice idea to use a game to train people, but this automatically assumes that these people are literate in using a computer and in playing games. Considering that the average age of levee patrollers is about 50 years, we know for sure that these users are not the "digital natives" that Prensky (2001) talks about. I was, therefore, not surprised to see from a little survey among levee patrollers that only a few used a computer intensively and that almost none of them played digital games. The average levee patroller is more like a "digital immigrant," a person who did not grow up with computer technology, but who is using it for certain specific purposes.

The little computer literacy that digital immigrants have severely restricts the design options as the game should be relatively easy to understand and playable. To play and enjoy a game, it is first and foremost important that a user must master the controls. The more complex the controls are, the steeper the learning curve becomes, and the less likely that every user may enjoy the game. On the other hand, a simplification of the controls limits the gameplay possibilities. With two buttons, fewer fighting combinations are possible in a fighting game than with four. This means we were coping with a *usability tension*.

From the beginning, we favored the use of a mouse and keyboard. The use of these controls are standard in 3D first-person games, like *Unreal Tournament*, and this is the type of game we wanted to develop. In these types of games, the mouse is used to look (and aim if it is a shooting game) and the keyboard to move. We liked this configuration as looking around is an essential task for inspecting levees and walking is obviously necessary to explore a region. Unfortunately, this configuration is difficult to master for digital immigrants, since it requires the ability to use the mouse and keyboard at the same time. This parallel task is not something digital immigrants are very good at (Prensky 2001).

Alternatives for the combination of keyboard and mouse are using the keyboard *or* the mouse. With solely a keyboard a user would be able to walk left, right, backward, and forward with the arrow keys and would not be able to easily turn, look up, down, or diagonally at the gameworld. It would further require users to use other buttons on the keyboard to perform actions and although we could have used stickers to indicate what buttons they need to use, it is everything but ideal.

With solely using the mouse the same observational restrictions would apply, except that in this case the user is not overwhelmed by the number of possibilities but does risk the possibility to get a wrist injury. Since the game is largely about observing, we wanted this not to be restricted.

A better alternative concerns the "joystick," an interface that most game consoles use. With this, the user is not confronted with a superfluous amount of "buttons" and gets only one apparatus to control the game. However, despite that it certainly simplifies the interface, the disadvantages of the joystick in comparison to the keyboard and mouse combination are that they require an extra purchase on behalf of the clients and the possibility of interface problems, because joysticks are not standard PC equipment.

A simple test with the mouse and keyboard that required patrollers to walk from A to B over a levee showed that while they had trouble mastering the controls, they did persevere, and more importantly, they were engaged with it. We came to the conclusion that although they did not do anything meaningful in this simple test, they were so much attracted to the ability to explore the world of levees that they were willing to invest in learning the controls. These insights led us to decide to choose the keyboard and mouse combination.

But to balance our decision, we made an enormous effort in creating a training stage in which users are made accustomed to the controls (Fig. 6.4). In this stage, we explain step by step what is expected from them in the game. For example, we explain that the arrow keys are their feet and their first assignment is to walk to a certain location. At this location, we tell them that the mouse concerns their eyes and now they are asked to use the mouse and look around to find a love bug.

The next step concerns an assignment in which both skills are combined. They have to go through a maze and by combining the keyboard and mouse they can easily find the exit. The other training steps relate to the specific procedures they need to employ in the game to report a failure, such as measuring the distance and height.

Handling the Reality-Meaning Dilemma

The first between-worlds dilemma concerns the *Reality-Meaning dilemma.* With this dilemma the tension, as its name suggests, relates above-all to a clash between the worlds of Reality and of Meaning. Although such a clash seems unlikely we only have to refer to our education to see that this is not so strange and happens quite often. In school, teachers decide to neglect a part of Reality, simplify it, or change it to ensure that students understand it better. Later, when they receive more information, the students may find out that things work slightly differently. If they did not receive the first basic knowledge in this transformative way, however, they could not have reached this understanding as easily. Teachers decide to trade-off pieces of the real world to provide a clear and understandable message that they can transfer to their students.

For example, when it comes to physics one of the first things we learn is Newton's laws. Later, when we have become more acquainted with physics, we learn about Einstein's relativity theory and actually discover that things are a bit different than what we learned before. To illustrate, when it comes to gravitation, we learn that it is not a force that attracts things that have a mass but that it is a consequence of spacetime curvatures that puts objects into motion. Although Newton's theory has

(a) Find the lady bug with by using the mouse. It is very tiny...At post 2 the maze can be seen in which players learn the parallel use of mouse and keyboard

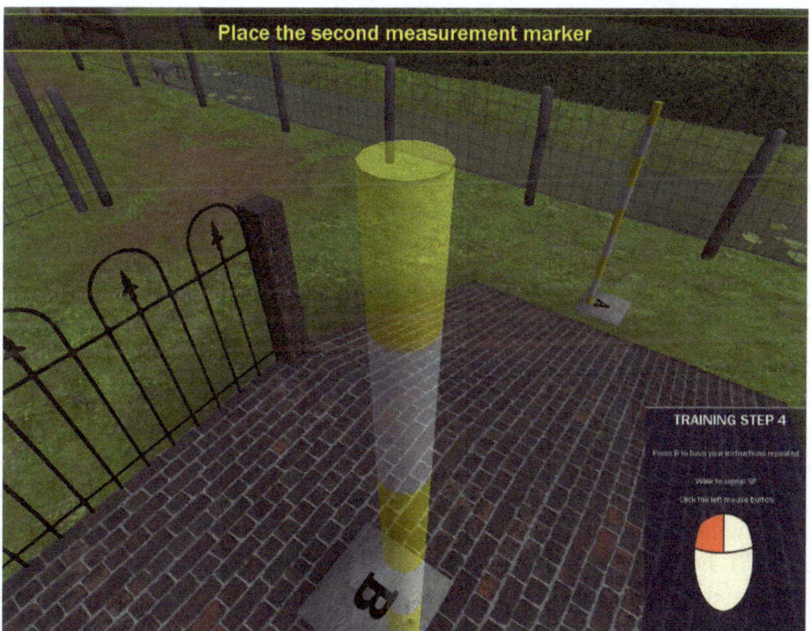

(b) Learn how to measure the distance and height

Fig. 6.4 Two tasks that need to be completed in the training stage

been superseded, it is taught first, as it is a much simpler theory to work with and it still gives sufficiently accurate results for most applications.

But outside school, in our everyday life, we actually make this trade-off often as well. To tell a story or a message we often find ourselves thinking about how we are going to tell this. Sometimes we exaggerate and sometimes we understate the real world facts as we know them or leave out certain details to bring across a story or message. Other than this, we also use examples or metaphors to hopefully make things clearer, but at the risk that the receivers may get the wrong idea of what we are actually trying to clarify.

Here, when it comes to game design, I would like to share two of these types of Reality-Meaning dilemmas that I encountered during the development of our game. The first concerns whether it is better to guide the players according to the procedures of the real world or deviate from this to foster critical thinking (see "Guidance Tension"). The second relates to a problem related to the large distances that need to be crossed. Either a realistic method of traveling could be applied or we could use a futuristic yet unrealistic transportation method (see "Representation Tension").

Guidance Tension

When inspecting a levee, patrollers take a number of steps. First they have to obviously find a failure. From there they have to report the signals that make up a failure, communicate the report to others, diagnose the situation, and take a measure if this is necessary (see Level 3). In taking these procedural steps, patrollers are extensively guided by the central coordinating field office: the "action center." This center tells the patrollers exactly what to do and when.

Another guidance that patrollers have concerns a checklist for reporting signals. If they see a crack, the checklist precisely tells them where to look and what questions need to be answered. Some patrollers told me they do not use the checklist. They immediately call the action center to report that they have seen something and from there the action center guides them through the process. The effect is the same. The patrollers are only used as "the eyes and ears" of the water boards, as an extension of other people who do the actual thinking.

This is how it goes in the real world. The clients finely pointed out to me that they do not want to teach other knowledge and skills then what is needed in their practice. They are the eyes and ears and nothing more. At this point we already hit a dilemma, because the tasks and responsibilities differ per water board (see also "Translation Dilemma"). For example, some water boards allow patrollers to diagnose and take measures and at others this is not allowed. Each water board was afraid that because of the game, the patrollers would get a wrong idea of how procedures work out in the actual practice and would "think too much." In short, from the world of Reality the game needed to be as close to the actual procedures as possible. To guide the players, the experts as well as the clients thought the checklist needed to be part of the

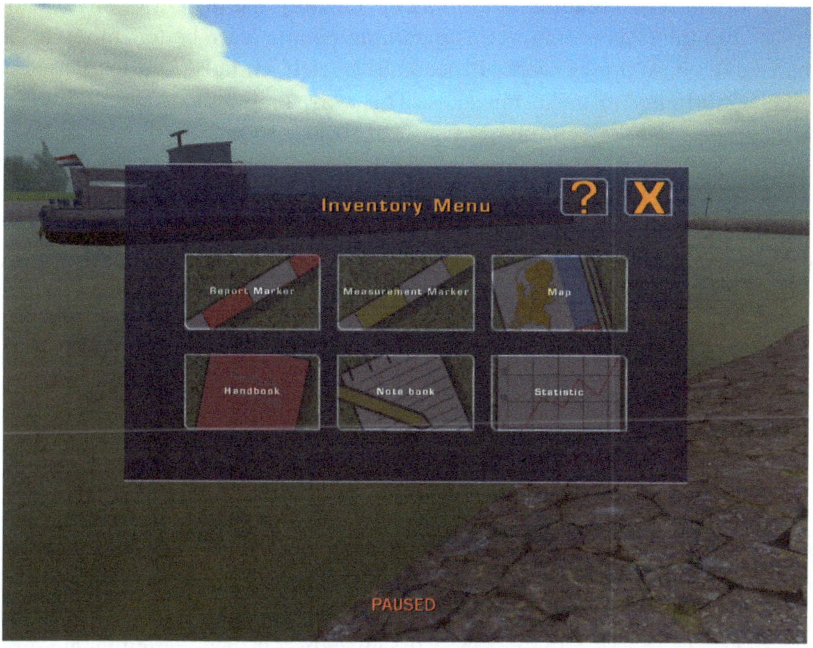

(a) The inventory menu with its tools

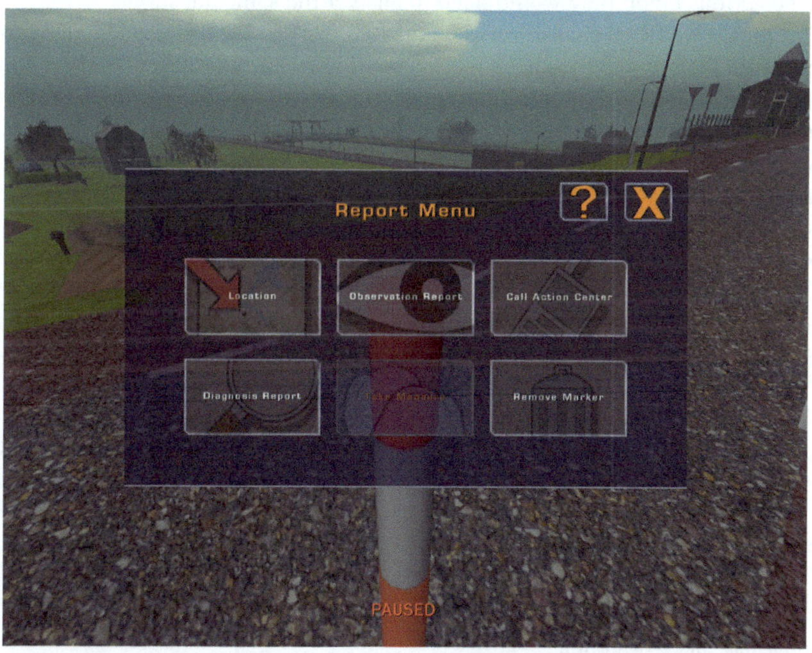

(b) The report marker menu with its tools. Notice the transparency of "Take measure"

Fig. 6.5 The use of inventories

game.[7] The world of Meaning, and more specifically the insight of "exploration," disagrees with this. According to this paradigm people learn better if they discover for themselves how things work. It needs to be self-initiated and learners should have the opportunity to make mistakes. This way, they will understand why and when they need to take certain steps instead to just follow the flow and do what they are asked to do. This enables "critical thinking" and although this may not be necessary in the actual practice, the knowledge and skills that they need to learn for this practice will be better captured if they have an understanding of why and for what reason they need to know this. Otherwise the knowledge remains "abstract" and a mere "association" in the behavioristic tradition. The world of levee inspection stays, therefore, a black box. They see the inputs, the signals, and give an output, a report. Everything in between remains a big mystery.

The checklist exemplifies this black box. With it patrollers do not have to sit down and thoroughly think of what they need to do when encountering a failure. Rather, they just take the checklist and follow its procedures. For each signal, the checklist has a number of particular questions that the patroller needs to answer with "yes" or "no." Depending on the answer, the checklist points to what the patroller needs to do. For example, if they see a crack, the checklist asks if any water outflow can be observed. If this is the case, they should also fill out the signal water outflow. This way, patrollers do not need elaborate knowledge chunks of failures. They just need to pay attention and check the boxes of the checklist. If they communicate directly with the action center, they would need to answer the same questions.

This meant we faced a clash between the two worlds. We balanced them by using the procedural steps and the checklist as a starting point. We subsequently modified the real world situation by not guiding the players too much and by giving more room for exploration. We achieved this exploration by making use of a characteristic element from adventure and role-playing genre: the *inventory* (Fig. 6.5). In the eventual game, players have an inventory from which they can choose particular actions. In this inventory they have (a) a tool to indicate they found a failure (i.e., the report marker), (b) a tool to measure signals (i.e., the distance marker), (c) a map to see where they are, (d) a handbook of levee inspection to look up information about signals and failures, (e) a notebook to write down some information, and (f) an overview of their performance during the scenario. If they choose the "report marker" and place this, they even get another inventory with even more items: (a) a tool to indicate their location, (b) a tool to create reports, (c) a telephone to call the action center, (d) a form to diagnose the failure, (e) a form to decide which measure needs to be taken, and (f) a tool to delete the report marker.[8]

---

[7] Although clients and experts recommended the use of the checklist, they actually did not completely agree with the content of it. During the development many discussions were held about how to modify the original checklist. From this, we see that the game development in itself can bring about "change" in the real world.

[8] From a usability perspective I am aware that the inventory menu and the report marker menu can be confusing. We have thought of many ways to improve this, for example by giving each one a different color. The current version of the game does not have this improvement.

With these inventories, instead that players are pushed through the inspection process, they can decide for themselves what tools they want to apply and when. For example, reporting the location is one of the first things a levee patroller has to mention in the actual practice. Instead that the game asks the player to fill out the location directly upon reporting a failure, a player now has to think what needs to be done and remembers that the location has to be filled out. If the player does not, the action center will remind the player of the mistake by saying "we need to have the location before we can talk any further." This enables to make mistakes and fosters critical thinking.[9]

As for the checklist, this formed the basis of the "tool to create reports" from the report marker inventory.[10] With this tool, players need to choose a signal and fill out a specific report related to this signal (Fig. 6.6). While most of the types of signals and the questions of each specific report are based on the original checklist, we removed all the references to what other steps patrollers have to take. With this removal, players have to think for themselves what the reports actually mean and what sort of further steps they need to take. They need to be aware that if they see a crack that they should also check for water outflow.

To prevent us from prioritizing Meaning too much over Reality in handling this *guidance tension*, we did not give complete freedom to players. They are, for example, not allowed to diagnose before they even called the action center and they are not allowed to take measures if the action center did not agree upon this. In Fig. 6.5 it can be seen that the "take measure tool" is much more transparent than the other tools indicating that it is not available yet. We did this to prevent patrollers from getting the impression that they are able to completely decide for themselves what needs to be done.

Representation Tension

A second Reality-Meaning dilemma related to an issue we encountered during the design. To avoid making the inspection too easy, we developed landscapes that

---

[9]The guidance dilemma is foremost a Reality-Meaning dilemma. However, looking at it from the world of Play I would say that this world would agree by not pushing the player through the game. It would be better, because it is far more interactive, if players decide for themselves what to do.

[10]We translated the checklist into a digital form. The original checklist fits onto a single sheet of paper, but this also means that patrollers see much information about the other signals that they are not concerned about. To reduce this information overload and let them focus their attention, players only see information that they are concerned about at a particular moment. Additionally, we revised the original checklist in a number of ways. We added some signals that were missing from it and also added questions that seem relevant and deleted questions that seemed less relevant or difficult to implement in a digital environment. For example, one question asked the patroller to jump up and down on the levee to see what happens. Although it is not impossible to jump in a digital environment, it would require a lot of effort to visualize the effects that patrollers would see in the real world by doing this. Some experts and clients were of the opinion that these irrelevant questions still needed to be asked. This is an example of a clash between Reality and Play, because if it does not relate to the game why bother implementing it?

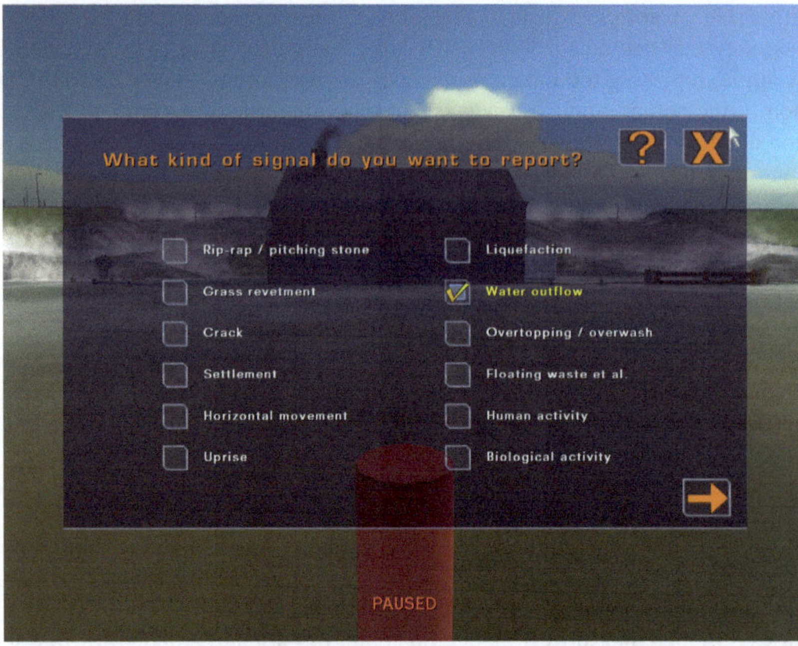

(a) Choosing a signal to report. In this case it would actually be much better to run...

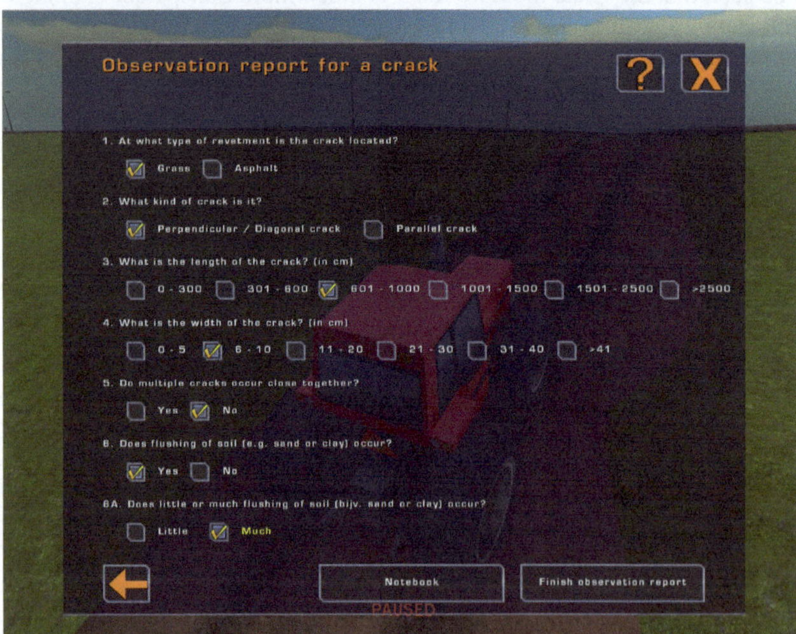

(b) Filling out the report which is based on the checklist. I did this while riding a tractor — one of the game's Easter eggs

Fig. 6.6 Overview of the reporting procedure

would be comparable to a region of 200 by 200 meters. This is far less than the areas levee patrollers normally have to patrol, but even using this limited area it already takes approximately ten minutes to just walk over every virtual levee. Actually inspecting these levees requires even more time as this asks for looking at the environment very carefully. Since we wanted players to return to failure locations to see if they worsened, players would thus spend a large part of their time walking. Besides being tedious, it constitutes a waste of precious time—time that could be used to educate the player.

To solve this issue we looked at the use of powerful metaphors in games that simplify processes or represent some process. An example concerns stealing a car in *Grand Theft Auto*. With a single push of the button the player-character opens the door, grabs the person driving the car, throws him or her out, and sits down. The game takes automatically care of the processes and relieves the player from being involved with uninteresting gameplay. Another representational example is the "medikit." This is an object—a medical kit—that can be picked up to improve the player's health. Instead that players need to go through a medical procedure to heal from their wounds, they walk over this kit and they are magically healed.

In some entertainment games, such as *Metal Gear Solid 3*, the healing process is much more realistic (Baker 2007). In *Metal Gear Solid 3*, if players get a gunshot wound, they have to extract the slug with a knife, then apply disinfectant and styptic, and then a bandage. Broken bones require a splint, cuts require suturing, and burns require salve. This concerns a "tedious" process, because it requires players to scroll through submenu after submenu to select the right medical equipment. And ultimately, it has the same effect as picking up a "magical" medikit.

What designers need to choose to represent real world factors depends on the purpose of the game. If the value of the game relates to knowing the procedures to heal from a gunshot wound versus a burn, it would be important to include the "tedious process." If it does not matter, it would be better to simplify or represent the process, for example by using a medikit.

In our case it was clear that we did not want to let players spend extra time on walking. A solution would be to implement a much used game functionality derived from the "Star Trek" series: "teleportation." This means that players would be able to disappear at one location and suddenly appear at another. The problem with this solution and all other "representational" solutions, like the medikit, is that players need to understand what they represent. Otherwise, the metaphor may be confusing or feel out of place. On the other hand, sticking closely to reality, the game may becomes less efficient in what it tries to achieve. We were thus facing a *representation tension*.

This dilemma was further fueled, because many, even the development team itself, had trouble envisioning the use of teleportation, because it seemed awkward to use a science fiction method within a realistic game. Solutions were sought to create a more believable way of transportation and balance this dilemma, like making it possible for a player to get into a bus or use a bicycle. Besides that these more realistic methods required a lot more work to implement, they were far more "tedious" and less flexible to get a player to a certain location. For a bicycle, the

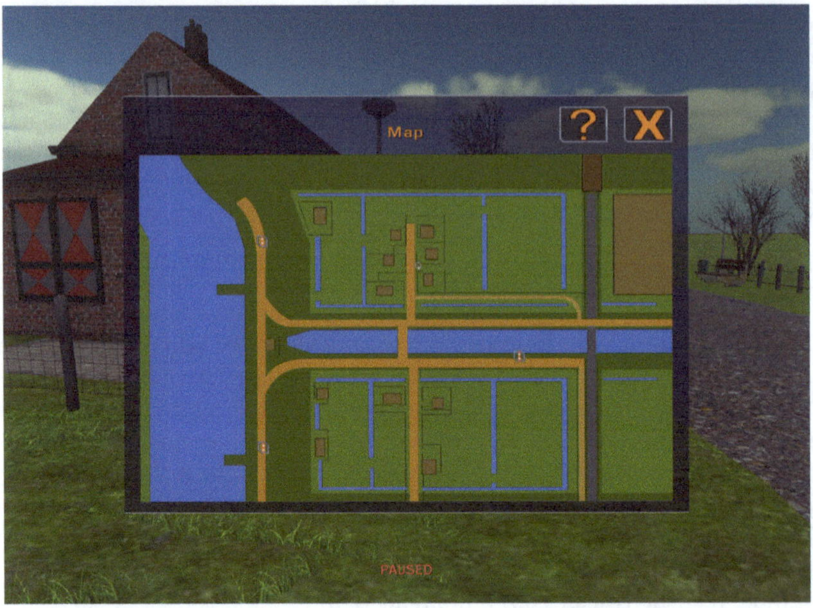

Fig. 6.7 The map and the mini-markers that the player can teleport with

player needs to grab his bike and cycle to it and for the bus, the player needs to go to a bus stop and take the bus (which is probably not even able to get the player everywhere). And ultimately, these solutions have the same effect as teleportation: getting a player from one location to another.[11]

In the end, we decided to keep it simple and chose the world of Meaning over Reality. After finding a failure, the player has to mark the location by putting a marker into the ground. Later the player can teleport to the marked failure by accessing the map tool and clicking on a "mini-marker" that represents the failure (Fig. 6.7).

Treating the Meaning-Play Dilemma

Koster (2005) explained that "fun" is all about learning. When we learn, the same endorphines are released that we associate with fun. If this is true, it shows the enormous potential of games as learning environments and indicates that the world of Meaning and Play can overlap or even reinforce one another. But we learn all the time and so we learn all the time in games as well. In games with a serious purpose it is about what we learn and it could very well be that this specific learning purpose

[11] Another solution to the distance problem would be to let the player run like Steven "Flash" Gordon, a comic strip hero who runs incredibly fast. Besides being more tedious as well compared to teleporting, we noticed that some people could get "cybersick" from playing the game. By being able to run incredibly fast, this cybersickness would probably be further stimulated.

might be interfered with learning irrelevant aspects, like learning how to shoot with a gun in the gameworld.

It is further not uncommon to find that engagement, immersion, and fun can also be detrimental to learning. When it comes to the engagement factors, Malone and Lepper (1987a, 1987b) explained, for instance, that from one perspective these factors can increase students' attention and enhance learning yet from another they may be distracting and thereby decrease the efficiency with which the students are able to learn something. I at least know from my own experience that it is "dangerous" to research games, because before I know it, I am playing for several hours, and it is hard to tell how efficient the time-on-task in the end is.

It is not only a matter of efficiency. It may also happen that the game elements are to such an extent distracting that the actual purpose is not reached. Or it may happen that the designers have completely lost track of the original purpose in constructing the game. In the end, while the game may be great in terms of gameplay and other elements from the world of Play, it does not have any operations that actually allow to accomplish its purpose.

On the other hand, too much emphasis on what has too be reached, may actually cause to not reach the purpose as well. Such a large emphasis could "destroy the game." Players may become unwilling to continue playing or become less willing to invest energy and time into the game if the designers did not take sufficient care off the elements from the world of Play. Aside from efficiency, the effectiveness is, therefore, concerned with these tensions as well.

And when we encounter these sorts of tensions, we are dealing with a *Meaning-Play dilemma*. From the development of our game I picked two examples to illustrate this dilemma, one which is concerned with whether to have a quiet and peaceful setting or a busy and fantastical setting (see "Stimuli Tension"), and another which is concerned with making players reflect on their experience or keeping them in their flow (see "Reflection Tension").

Stimuli Tension

By the standard of many games these days, the gameworlds are very elaborate. *Grand Theft Auto IV* or *World of Warcraft* provide huge worlds that the player may explore. In these worlds, the player's senses are stimulated by all kinds of interesting objects with whom they can interact with or not. Such worlds increase the engagement of players by drawing upon the curiosity and fantasy engagement factor. Additionally, they can increase the immersion, because the freedom and the interesting objects that can be explored could give the feeling that players are somewhere else. In other words, "busy fantastical settings" are wanted from a Play perspective.

The world of Meaning thinks otherwise about this. First of all, everything needs to have some purpose, and more specifically, needs to be related to the "purpose" of the game. If players spend time on interacting with objects that are not related to the purpose of the game, this decreases the time-on-task and can be considered a waste

Fig. 6.8 Detailed objects like windmills amongst "empty" levees

of time. It can be argued that the non-related interactions increase the enjoyment of players and keeps them longer engaged, but why would it not be possible to create engaging *and* meaningful interactions?

This would certainly be preferable, also for the second and closely related reason. This has to do with distraction and with the limited space in working memory. If players play a game they are confronted with stimuli. If some of these stimuli are not relevant than the irrelevant ones take up attention and processing space which could be otherwise spent to meaningful stimuli. It could even be that players are confronted with so much stimuli that "cognitive overload" happens, a situation in which the player is not able to think straight anymore. Therefore, from this world a "quiet peaceful setting" is preferred and this put us into a *stimuli tension*.

Although it formed a dilemma, we solved this relatively easily by stressing that the environment needs to be free from distracting stimuli where the real action and thinking occurs: the levees. Everything else, the nearby houses, the windmills, and so on, have much detail and even could have some animation (Fig. 6.8). Our team really tried to make this part "aesthetically pleasing." This way, we satisfied both worlds to some extent.

Reflection Tension

Not only can games distract players, they can also not give the opportunity to reflect about the experience, which is important according to the world of Meaning. Players

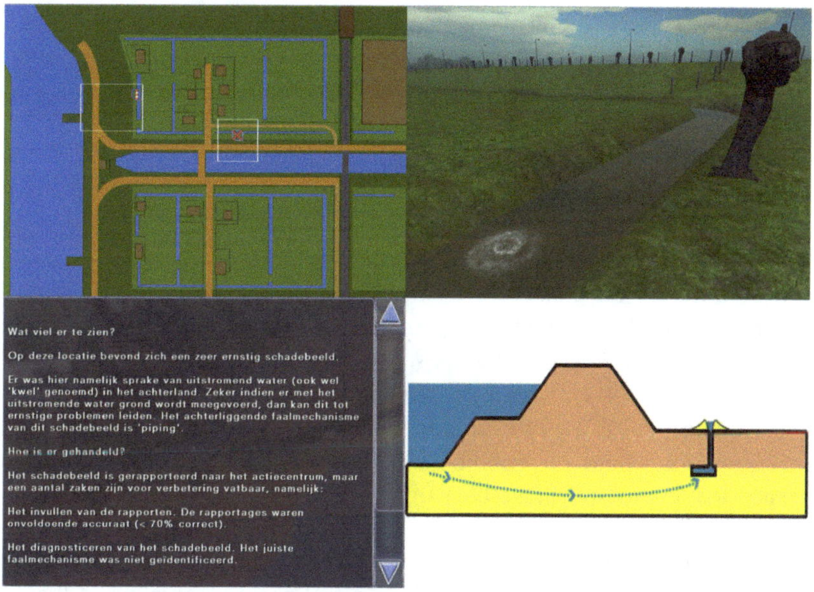

Fig. 6.9 Reflection-on-action with the feedback screen at the end of a scenario

can be so much engaged or immersed with what is unraveling on the screen in front of them that they hardly stop and think about what is happening. This brought us into another dilemma, because for letting players stop and reflect about what they see, we have to break the engagement and/or immersion. We have to tell them to stop "playing" and let them sit back in their chairs to consider the meaning of their experience. This connects them from the gameworld and is thus unwanted from a Play perspective.

Before explaining this further, it is important to stress that we should make a distinction between "reflection-on-action," which is the deliberation after the action occurred, and "reflection-in-action," which is the deliberation during the action (Schön 1983). The first poses not a problem to this dilemma, because it occurs after playing the game. It should be dealt with during the debriefing, the explanation and discussion of what happened in the game (Crookall 1995).

We dealt with "reflection-on-action" by implementing a feedback screen at the end of a scenario (Fig. 6.9). In this screen, which is divided into four sections, players can see on a map what failures were present in the scenario and which ones they found. By clicking on any of the failures, players receive information about this failure and their performance with it. Next to this textual information, players are provided with in-game images and pictorial 2D cross-cuts of the failure to foster further understanding of it. Aside from this possibility for "reflection-on-action," facilitators can also help players in linking the in-game experiences to the real world.

In contrary, the second, "reflection-in-action," does pose a problem, because it requires to interrupt the "flow" of the game and this could possibly negatively affect the experience. This is where the dilemma occurred, not with the "reflection-on-action." It would "break" the game especially as we wanted to increase the excitement by adding an element familiar from action games to it: *time pressure*. Although we decided not to add an actual visual clock, players know that if they are not in time with finding a critical failure, it could lead to a levee breach that will flood the whole region. Bearing this situation in mind, it would be quite weird to sit down and think about the world aside that it decreases the possible excitement created by the time pressure.

Eventually, we decided to resolve this *reflection tension* by building in moments for reflection during the game that seemed to be understandable concerning what needs to be done or that seemed to be part of the gameplay. As for the first, we used the same "trick" as *Do I Have A Right?*. When players enter any inventory menu, the game is paused. This is not so subtle, because we wanted this to be clearly visible to the player (Fig. 6.7). With this in mind, players have a chance to carefully look at the information from their handbook, look at their scores and try to understand them, and most importantly, take their time in filling out the reports. Although this may break the experience to some extent, the pausing is understandable, especially concerning the many questions that need to be considered. This way, players are not put into a "fight-or-flight" mode but still get a feeling of urgency when they leave the menus.

The other implementation is much more subtle. During the conversation with the action center, in which players have to provide their findings, the action center asks them to make a "situation assessment." Players can choose from the following options:[12]

- The situation is not serious.
- The situation is serious.
- The situation is very serious. Measures have to be taken immediately.

This reflection moment is subtle, because it is built into the gameplay. By asking this question, players have to stop and think for a second "Ok, so what is this situation precisely all about?" They have to think about the "meaning" of their observations and this is a type of in-game reflection.[13] This way, we tried to balance our choice, although clearly Meaning was prioritized in this case over Play.

[12]The provided options during the conversation with the action center depend on the "state" in which the player is in (see "Story Tension"). For example, if the player is in the "checking state," he can choose from "the situation is stable," "the situation has become worse," and "the situation has become very serious. Measures have to be taken immediately." The example in the text concerns when the player is in the "reporting state."

[13]The situation assessment question can also be seen as a departure from the world of Reality as such questions are not "officially" part of the levee inspection procedures. Nevertheless, from conversations with patrollers I understood that the severity of the situation is frequently determined during the conversation with the action center. In that case, the action center might indeed ask such assessment questions.

Managing the Play-Reality Dilemma

For a game to become a coherent whole, every part has to be made explicit and connected to other parts. This is exactly where the world of Play may possibly clash with the world of Reality. The world of Play demands structure and predictability (to a large extent), whereas the real world can be chaotic and difficult to capture in algorithms. This is needed, because designers need to know upfront how the game should respond to the player's actions and design a gameworld which is interesting and playable. In other words, while the problems in reality may be ill-defined (Rittel and Webber 1973), the problems in a game environment should be explicit and solvable. A player cannot execute an action and not have an effect (unless the point is to not have an effect).

For example, games have a hard time representing phenomena as love, ambition, and social conflict (Juul 2005), precisely because we cannot really explain how all these phenomena work. How would one fall in love? What is love in fact? These questions can be described and approximated yet it is not as easily captured as describing how to cook an egg. To represent such ill-defined phenomena, designers have to either symbolize them in the gameworld and/or use simple rules to approximate them.

In *The Sims*, for instance, players have to make sure that the long term relationship between two sims is above "80." To do this, players have to make sure that the sims chat, flirt, and slowly go from there to hugging and kisses before making out, and so on. Their "relationships building level" will build up in a couple of days and they are in love! It is that easy.

From this, we see that games represent such phenomena very technocratic, rational, and mechanistic. It needs to work or fit together. But the final between-worlds dilemma, the *Play-Reality dilemma*, can occur with other types of issues as well. To give another example, the world of Play may want to exaggerate or transform aspects in Reality to make the experience more engaging, immersive, or fun, while the world of Reality wants to stay as close to Reality as possible.

In our experience, the Play-Reality dilemma occurred often. Here, I will illustrate the three most striking examples. They range from how to define the goal of the game (see "Uncertainty Tension"), how to translate the real world into a fictional gameworld (see "Translation Tension"), to how difficult it can be to implement a seemingly easy handling in real life into a digital environment (see "Computation Tension").

Uncertainty Tension

At first, the definition of the goal seemed easy and obvious. The game concept involved players finding, reporting, assessing, and diagnosing failures, and if necessary, they could take a measure to prevent a levee breach from occurring. As such, the goal would be to find failures and deal with them to prevent a levee breach from occurring. We initially thought it would be "exciting" to have some "uncertainty" about how many failures reside in the region. More importantly, this is very realistic. In practice, we do not tell patrollers to go out and find five failures. Therefore, we thought the world of Play and Reality were in agreement with each other.

This turned out to be not true. During a number of play tests, players kept asking me if there were more failures or worse, in case they did not find one yet, if there were any failures at all. They already asked this after a couple of minutes of playing the game and in retrospect I can understand why. When playing the game, nothing happens at all unless players hit a failure. Without any further information, the inspection seems pointless in this digital environment, although paradoxically enough, they exactly do this in the real world. It may happen that patrollers go out and inspect levees for a number of hours without finding anything. Due to not knowing how many failures reside in the region, players became less engaged when they did not find one after a while. They stopped playing.

To prevent this from happening, I used an action game trick. Instead of leaving everything unknown to the player until the end, I made everything known to the player. Upfront players know that they have to find for example three or five failures. This little trick works very stimulating, because instead of saying "Pff, I do not think there is any failure here," they would say "@!#$&*, I cannot find that @!#$&* failure." Players became very engaged and, most importantly, they felt challenged. They felt that they really have to find those three or five failures. From this, we decided that to manage this *uncertainty tension* it is better to know than not to know. And we "know" ourselves that this little trick clearly brought us farther away from the world of Reality and closer to the world of Play.

It is further important to stress that players should not keep on saying "@!#$&*, I cannot find that @!#$&* failure." If this happens, the game might be too frustrating. Therefore, by changing a simple "rule," the same game can change from a boring experience to one which is frustrating. Although we could have implemented something, such as an action center that calls the players at a certain moment to tell them that they received information from a citizen[14] who found a failure in his or her backyard, we have not implemented this. From subsequent play tests, we noticed that if a scenario has three or more failures, players are always able to find a failure and do not become too frustrated.

Translation Tension

From the categorization of failures and the decision on what failures to implement initially into the game, we can already derive that the clients differ amongst each other. When it concerned the categorization and the implementation decision, it was

[14] Actually, it happens very often that citizens call the water boards to tell them about a possibility of a failure. The offered suggestion is for this reason not that strange.

a matter of balancing the world of Reality itself. However, when we have to translate the real world to a gameworld, we might hit a dilemma between the world of Reality and of Play. Such a *translation tension* was inevitable, because aside from vocabulary, the water boards differ in their regions (e.g., the types of water ways and levees), patrollers (e.g., the tasks and responsibilities given), and the organization (e.g., organizational setup and procedures).

The dilemma came down to this. Every water board wanted to have a game that fit their organization, while a single game cannot deal with this asked for flexibility that easily, unless we would have decided to create a unique game for every water board. Obviously, creating a unique game was not an option, so we had to look for something else to solve this dilemma. Creating a single consistent and coherent game would definitely not be this solution, because the danger is that the game may lose its connection to the "reality" of any of the water boards and then the clients may not feel affiliated with it anymore, which would render the game useless.

We resolved this dilemma by stepping away from the real world and by creating a fictive landscape that would contain all the important "realistic" elements from the different regions of the water boards. In this way, each client's region is represented.

Other than resolving the dilemma, making it fictive has some advantages. Players will be more critical if the game is a complete copy of their region. They know their region almost by heart and if something is not correct, they probably think the game is not good enough and reject it. Additionally, with a fictive environment designers have almost complete freedom in deciding how to make an interesting world. Therefore, such a fictive environment was desirable from a Reality as well as Play perspective. In creating the landscape we first made a big drawing on a paper and from there we translated this sketch into a digital version and optimized it during several iterations (Fig. 6.10).

To deal with the differences in responsibilities, we developed a *scenario generator*, an option of the game in which it is possible for users to create their own scenario by deciding on the region, the weather, the type and number of failures, and, last but not least, the type of responsibilities (Fig. 6.11). We added this possibility, because those water boards who did not allow their patrollers to diagnose or take measures, were not sensitive to our argument that adding these responsibilities would lead to a better understanding of the inspection process and make for a more interesting game. Games are about making decisions and the most interesting one when it comes to levee inspection is to decide whether to take a measure or not. Nevertheless, we gave in to the world of Reality and made it possible to also play the game without it. In that case, the action center takes measures based on the reports of the player. On the plus side, the option to select responsibilities makes it possible for increasing the complexity of the game along the way. And this possibility concurs with the ideas of the "zone of proximal development" and "scaffolding."

As for the organizational differences, we more or less departed from Reality already by making the game a single player experience. In the real world patrollers often walk in groups of two. We further decided to focus on the most basic procedures which were present in all water boards and further only focused on the interaction between a patroller and an action center. Despite these simplifications,

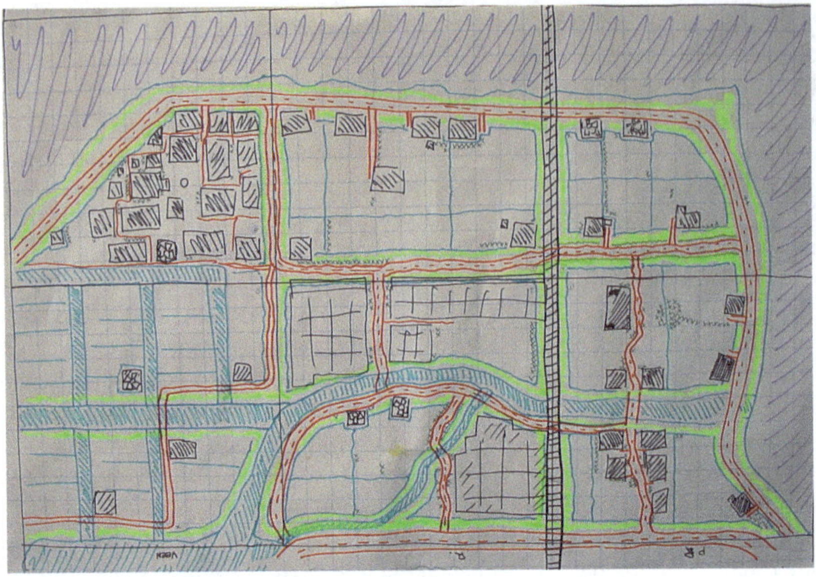

Fig. 6.10 Before digitalizing everything, we made a drawing of the different regions

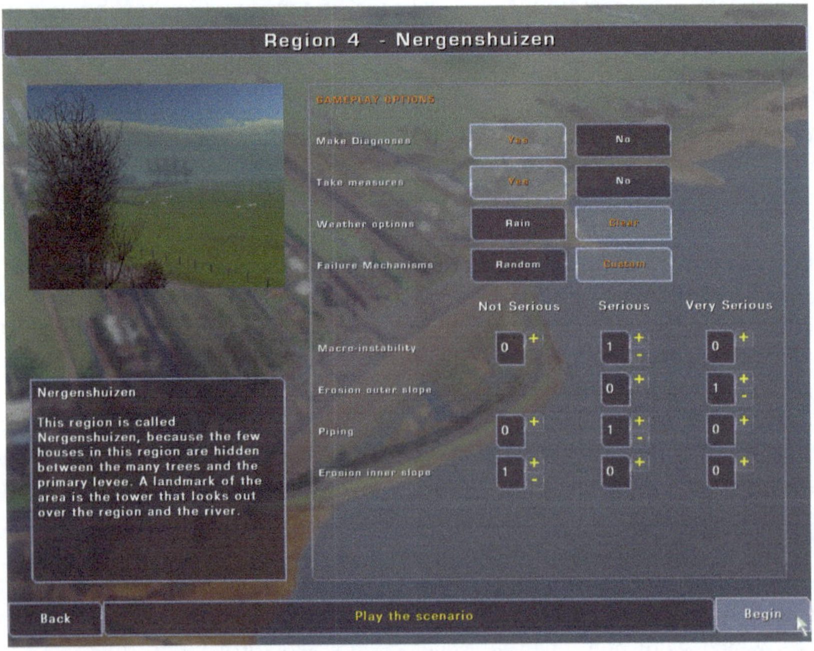

Fig. 6.11 The scenario generator with the possibility to change responsibilities

in general we ensured that the game is flexible and realistic enough to satisfy the clients.

Computation Tension

One of the most difficult design dilemmas concerned a very essential and seemingly simple one. This was to indicate that a failure is found. In the real world patrollers just write down or communicate the location by using street addresses, a description of a well-known object, such as a bridge or building, or they use—in case they are inspecting the levee of a river—the number of a levee segment which can be observed on a post.[15]

In a virtual environment, especially if it represents a fictive environment, this is much more difficult to do. We could have added street addresses, number segments, or ensure that each part would be recognizable by some well-known object. However, this seemed quite cumbersome and either not failure proof, in case players would have to describe the location, or utterly annoying, if players would need to pick the location from a list of possibilities.

But even just pointing at a failure as saying "It is here!" caused a problem. We could not use the mouse for this, because this was already used to look around. Another thought was to change to a mode in which a player could use the mouse to point to a failure, like a "sniper" specifying its target. Although possible, this solution seemed not very intuitive and would make it unnecessary complex.

In other words, letting the game know that a failure is found put us into a *computation tension*. We wanted it to be as natural and realistic as possible yet these realistic ways of indicating a failure—like pointing at it with our fingers—are not ideal or even possible to implement from a Play perspective. The solutions from a Play perspective, are not ideal as well.

In the end we came up with the idea of using a "marker" to indicate a failure is found (Fig. 6.12). These markers are used in reality, not to indicate that a failure is found, but to see if a failure has evolved. If the soil moves or the crack expands, the marker can be used as a bench mark. This solution seemed so natural that nobody ever made a remark that it is not realistic. The solution also nicely reconciles the two worlds. While it is playful to put down a marker, it is a realistic element as well, as it is used in the actual practice.

Unfortunately we had to restrain our enthusiasm, because the solution still had a major issue. Reports and conversations with the action center are linked to the markers. How would the computer recognize which marker he needed to connect to what failure?

Eventually, we came up by dividing the levees in segments in which a failure could occur and only allowed one failure per segment. If players want to place a marker into a segment in which they already placed a marker, they get a message

[15] Like roads, the levees of rivers are divided into segments. Each one of them has a unique number.

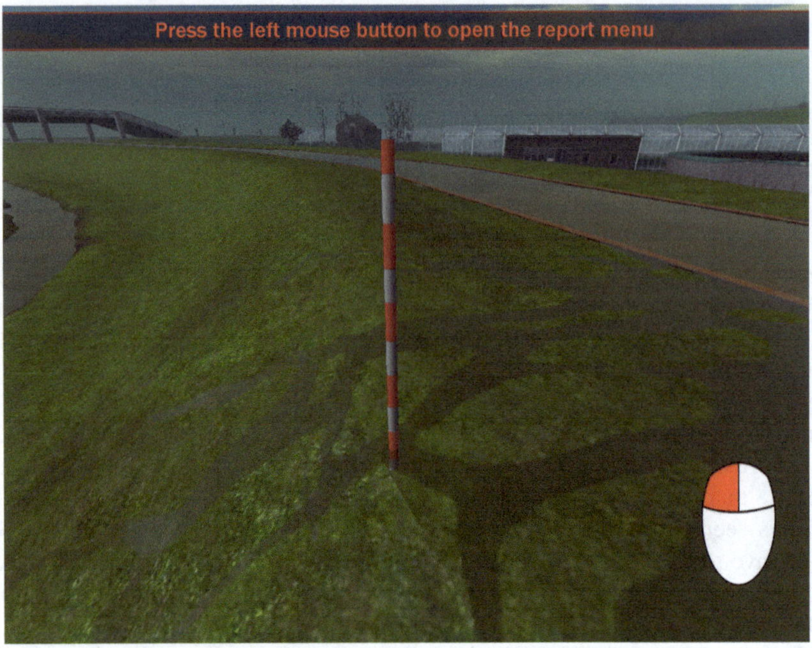

Fig. 6.12 The marker to indicate failures. This is a failure with overtopping

that the new marker is too close to another marker and cannot be placed. This shows that the technology forces designers to restrict reality in certain ways.

Taking Care of Trilemmas

From the within and in-between worlds dilemmas we can already notice that it is difficult to disentangle the worlds as decisions on one dilemma are influenced by or are related to each of the worlds, even though the essential dilemma may only be restricted to one world. With *trilemmas*, however, each world has clearly something to say or contribute.

Trilemmas do not necessarily offer three equally or undesirable options related to the three perspectives. A trilemma simply occurs when from each world a relevant perspective can be given onto a tension. These perspectives may overlap and agree with each other to a certain extent but they do need to shed a unique light onto the tension.

In resolving a trilemma, it may happen that designers are able to satisfy the three worlds equally but it is more likely that two out of three worlds are pleased. If only one world has been favored, then strong reasons should be given for this decision. Normally, such a decision would very likely unbalance the game (unless the designers make other decisions to balance this choice).

To show how we have balanced our trilemmas, I selected five tensions, concerned with measuring (see "Scope Tension"), scoring points (see "Score Tension"), randomness ("Variety Tension"), levee failures (see "Framework Tension"), and integrating story and play (see "Story Tension"), respectively.

Scope Tension

Large and elaborate discussions have taken place around the issue of "measuring." When patrollers find a failure, they need to measure the width, length, and if possible and necessary the depth or height of signals. For example, for a crack the width, length, and depth needs to be measured. From a Play perspective it became immediately clear that this is a rather uninteresting element. It is something that can slow down the flow of the game, concerns a tedious process, and above-all, seems rather pointless. Measuring seems to be a skill that can be better practiced in the real world than in a virtual environment. And if it would be that important to still consider it—to make patrollers aware of the need to do this in the real world—it would be sufficient to give a rough indication, like small, medium, or large.

The water boards and experts, representing the world of Reality, thought differently here. They explicitly wanted a system in which it was possible to make exact measurements. Measurements are important as they indicate the severity of a failure and for this reason, measuring constitutes a relevant part of the inspection process. In addition to this, patrollers all too often make rough estimates of signals, and this is a practice they wanted to discourage. For this reason they did not like the idea of giving a rough indication aside from the fact that they thought it would be difficult to explain what small, medium, or large means for each signal. They rather sticked to the exact measurements.

The world of Meaning also had a bearing on this. On the one hand, it agreed with Play that it would be unnecessary to enable players to measure in the game. Any transfer in the ability to measure cannot be expected from doing this in a digital environment, except for possibly reading scales, but this is certainly not the issue. On the other hand, it agreed with Reality that it would be good to make players aware of the importance of measuring. Next to this, if patrollers are already reluctant in being specific, this awareness should certainly be about giving exact measurements. The idea of using rough indications seemed, therefore, not a good idea.

Another possibility which was suggested was to retrieve measuring information automatically when players are close to a signal or when they indicate that they have found one. This, however, is not a solution that Sid Meier would consider an "interesting choice" (Rollings and Morris 2004). It is hardly interactive. Players are just confronted with information without being asked for it. This also makes it an uninteresting option from the perspective of Meaning, because they get feedback for no effort and it is also not self-initiated.

With inspiration from solving the dilemma of the report marker, we suddenly realized that we could use to same marker (but in a different color) to measure

Fig. 6.13 Measuring the height and distance with two yellow markers. In this case it concerns a small crack with water outflow, an indication of micro-instability

(Fig. 6.13, see also Fig. 6.4). We implemented a system in which players are able to put two markers into the ground to retrieve information about the distance and height. First, they put a marker at the starting point of a measurement and then walk over to the other end to put the second marker into the ground. And voilà, measurement information is retrieved in a game-like and meaningful sense, while it ensures also that players do not have to read scales and so forth. The only type of measurement which remained impossible to accomplish was the measuring of the depth of a crack, but this was something we simply had to accept. Most of it was now taken care off.

So it seemed, because similar to the report marker, a major issue appeared. Although "Unreal units," the measurement units that are used in the Unreal Engine, can be easily converted to real units, such as centimeters or meters, the models were not built by computing the distances beforehand. They were built with some sense of how objects are relatively scaled to each other. Due to this, some of the measurement results proved to be everything but realistic, especially for the smaller measurements.

For example, normally the width of a crack is somewhere around three to five cm; the results with the distance markers were more like around 30 to 50 cm! At this point it became clear to me why "coherency" is important for creating a gameworld.

We "solved" this problem by dividing the smaller measurements by ten. This seems like a very rough solution, but it worked as nobody ever reported any unrealistic measurements so far. Nevertheless, this *scope tension* shows us again that a seemingly very simple handling in reality is not so easy to implement in a game environment.

Score Tension

Every learning paradigm stresses the importance of "feedback." Feedback is necessary to correct behavior and to understand what is going on. In games feedback is given in animations, like seeing how a character is unable to reach another platform and falls down onto a number of heavy spikes, textually by means of words as "game over," and arithmetically by expressing the performance in numbers that we call "scores."

To first of all be able to give feedback at all, we defined a number of criteria that were important for the performance of inspecting levees (see Table 4.1). These are observed failures, location accuracy, observed signals, reporting accuracy, situation assessment accuracy, diagnose accuracy, and measure effectiveness.

From here we faced a problem that every game designer will face when implementing an assessment. It is difficult to decide how to determine the performance of a player, especially on aspects from reality that are hard to quantify. In our case we could luckily determine relatively easily whether or not players fulfilled our criteria.

For example, with observed failures, an algorithm can simply look at how many failures the player found out of the failures that are part of a scenario. With location accuracy, to give another example, it is just a matter of determining whether the given location corresponds to the actual location. In a game such as *PeaceMaker* it will be much more difficult to do this. When are players diplomatic? This is not a matter of right or wrong or counting how many objects the player has found.

The problem with us was mostly with deciding on how to translate the "facts" into a score. We did not want to make all the criteria as important so we had to assign weights to the criteria. Aside from this we also needed to assign some value, some multiplication factor, like "for each failure players find, they get 10 points." This process of assigning weights and values is quite arbitrary to say the least. This shows that assessment is unrealistic by nature, since it is always subjective and controversial. An assessment can, therefore, almost always be criticized. What we could have done, and the world of Reality would have agreed with this, is to just use the criteria, present the facts, and leave it at that. This way, little to no subjectivity would have played a role in the assessment.

From a Play perspective, however, scores work very engaging. They stimulate players to improve themselves and if the game is played in a competitive setting, it would even further foster engagement in trying to become the best. But according to this world scores need to be straightforward and somewhat ludicrous. The seven criteria are too complicated for a scoring system to communicate to a player. They need to be simplified and it would be much better if they are converted to a score with either huge numbers or with a specific rating that makes sense, such as getting a score of between one and ten or a score in percentages.

Fig. 6.14 The scoring system at the end of a scenario. Notice the relative complexity of it

The world of Meaning, which is concerned with the learning objectives, wanted to stick to the seven criteria as they reflect the learning objectives. In addition, according to this world it is important for the scores to be transparent. Players need to be able to distill what they did wrong. With ludicrous scores this is hardly possible. While a score of ten points is simply not as impressive as one of 10,000 points, the first is much easier to trace than the second. Taken together, a "trilemma" emerged between all three worlds.

We reconciled this trilemma by developing a scoring system that shows the facts, converts everything into a single indicator, and is still transparent (Fig. 6.14). The scoring tool in the player's inventory and the scores at the end of a scenario visibly multiply facts, like having found one or more failures, with a certain weight and aggregate the separate scores of the criteria into a single score. The aggregated score is a conversion of the total number of points to a percentage. The choice for a percentage was made, as a score of 90% sounds more impressive and conclusive than one of 90 points.

Together with this score, the scoring system provides a textual description of the performance. We added this, because if a levee breach occurred, we do not want to think that the player has done a good job when he gets a seemingly good score (which is perfectly possible to happen). Unlike entertainment games we decided to not use the word "failed" as this is a bit controversial when used in the context of first responders, such as patrollers. Therefore, we used "insufficient" when players did not perform well and used terms as "good" and "perfect" when they did. Admittedly, this scoring system is not very intuitive at first sight neither does it feel realistic, but it does lead to excitement as well as insight.

Variety Tension

The core gameplay of *Levee Patroller* concerns finding and reporting failures. To make this interesting, it would be important to make sure that failures do not always appear on the same location. Some "variety" is needed to create some uncertainty. Otherwise players will always know that close to that one windmill the failure mechanism "sand boils" may occur.

To prevent this from happening, randomness was needed according to the world of Play. This would increase the "replayability" of the game. And this "replayability" enables users to keep on "practicing" without learning the material like a parrot. Moreover, in the real world we also have some uncertainty of where and when a failure may occur. This means we started off really well with this issue, because all worlds agreed on the need and importance of the randomness of failures.

Our ideal idea of incorporating randomness was to divide the levees into segments in which a failure could or could not occur. To keep it simple we already departed from the real world by deciding that no more than one failure could occur in one of these segments at a time. Aside from simplifying the real world, we were also forced to do this, because of our use of the "report marker" (see "Computation Dilemma"). The game needs to know when a player has found a failure. If we would enable multiple failures into one segment, we would need to "segment" these segments further and this would complicate the situation even more.

From this technological restriction we ran into further restrictions, because not all types of failures can occur everywhere. Of the eight failures, four of them can only occur along the "primary levees," levees surrounding rivers, seas, or lakes, and four of them can only occur along the "regional levees," levees surrounding smaller water ways. While this "problem" would not matter so much from a Play perspective, the world of Reality but also of Meaning were in favor of restricting the failures to those levees that they would normally appear at. Over-simplification might take place and players might associate certain types of failures with regions in which they never occur.

Unfortunately, it turned out that the world of Play had even more restrictions for implementing randomness. For creating a variety of failures in a segment, it was required that at least four failures—and preferably more to accommodate for new failures—could possibly appear in one type of levee segment. When trying to implement this, however, it appeared at first that it would be impossible to put more than one failure into one segment. We put the "failure models," the graphical objects and animations of a failure, *manually* into the levee segments of the gameworld and it turned out that only one failure model could fit a segment without causing visual problems.[16] This restriction severely reduced the randomness. Each region in the game has about 20 segments which means that each failure could appear at only two or three locations.

Luckily, with a later revision of the game we found another solution. With this solution, the regions are not completely built upfront, but are built when starting a scenario. Failure models are not turned on or off. They are literally placed into the levee segments. With this technique, it became possible to have more than one failure into a levee segment and thereby increase the variety of the game. How many failures exactly fit a particular segment is dependent on the levee type (i.e., primary or regional?) and the model of the levee segment. Not all levee segments are identical in the game and it turned out that not every failure model could fit into a certain levee segment.

This *variety tension* shows that although the worlds may even initially agree, with the subsequent implementation it is possible to encounter all sorts of problems that create tensions between the different worlds. In this case, the worlds of Reality and Meaning restricted where failures could be placed and the world of Play restricted us in how failures could be placed.

Framework Tension

The story of *Virtual Leader* shows that it can be quite a problem to implement the subject of a game (Aldrich 2004). No leadership theory or framework was immediately applicable for this game, so the designers had to come up with their own leadership framework to interpret the actions of the player and give sensible feedback. Such a problem may differ for each project, but for our project, it concerned a trilemma around the main subject of the game: the "levee failures."

To implement levee failures into a game environment, the ideas of "interactivity" and "coherency" from the world of Play are important. They stress that failures need to fit into the logical structure of the game to be able to make the interaction with the failures understandable and assign, for example, scores to them. To achieve this, it is necessary to "standardize" the failures. This can be done by developing a "generic failure framework." With such a framework, every failure acts according to a generic pattern and this makes it possible to interpret the interactivity between the player and the failures by the game.

Reality is, however, messy. Failures are hard to categorize—even for the failures individually the experts already disagree on how they develop.[17] When looking at

[16]To place more than one failure model into a segment, it meant the models had to be placed on top of each other. If a segment has four failure models, it would have four layers. Depending on what failure model would be active, a certain layer would be shown. This caused some visual problems. If, for example, the fourth layer would be shown of one segment and the first layer of the segment next to it, the player would suddenly experience a height difference.

[17]In fact, the development process of the game was a learning process for the experts themselves. They continuously revised their mindsets based on the progressions of the modelers in visualizing the failures.

failures generally, failure types are that much diverse that it becomes almost impossible to capture them into a single framework. Creating a generic failure framework would not capture reality but distort it and provide a (simplified) picture with whom not everybody could identify with. The alternative, making each failure unique, would, on the other hand, make it very difficult to create a coherent gameworld.

From the perspective of Meaning, it was desirable to allow players to experience every phase of the development of a failure. Almost nobody has ever seen the creation of a failure from start to finish and from an educational point of view it would be extremely powerful if this became possible. Players would be able to store an elaborate cognitive structure in their long-term memories with which they can make sense of the signals in the real world. This desire clashes with the real world, because when failures are found, preventive measures are quickly taken. This possibility would prevent players from seeing the development of a failure from the beginning to the end.

With this *framework tension* in the back of our minds, we initially decided that we wanted to implement "dynamic failures," failures that develop throughout the game and that allow players to witness a failure from start to finish. But aside that this idea clashed with Reality, it clashed with Play as well. When playtesting we realized that it was impossible to report a failure if it was developing at the same time. Even if we would tackle this, if failures continuously develop, players can make ten if not hundreds of reports. It seemed thus inevitable that we had to put the failures into some "generic failure framework," to make it at least playable.

The alternative would be to get rid of the idea of using dynamic failures and instead use "static ones." In that case, players just find a failure, report and deal with it, and continue. With this option, we would, however, lose the richness of being able to experience the development of a failure and not stress the importance of checking the state of a failure.

We balanced the dilemma by making a generic failure framework in which failures are dynamic in-between three phases but more or less static during the phases themselves (Fig. 6.15).[18] The first phase takes roughly about ten minutes and allows players to have time to find and report failures (see "Representation Dilemma"). The other two phases are much shorter with five minutes per phase, because if players found a failure before, they only have to return to the failures and report the differences. With these three phases, we created some control over the number of times that players need to create reports.

Not coincidentally, the three phases are related to the situation assessment that players have to reflect about (see "Reflection Dilemma"). Each phase indicates a certain severity, with the first phase being less severe than the third phase. If a failure reaches the end of the third phase, a levee breach may be the result unless the player

[18]The failures develop subtly within a phase. This development has no impact on the reports of the players, because we used categories from which the player can choose from in their reports. As long as no new signals appear and the development stays within a category, the reports in a phase do not change. We chose to enable this subtle changes, as this would make the change to another phase less abrupt.

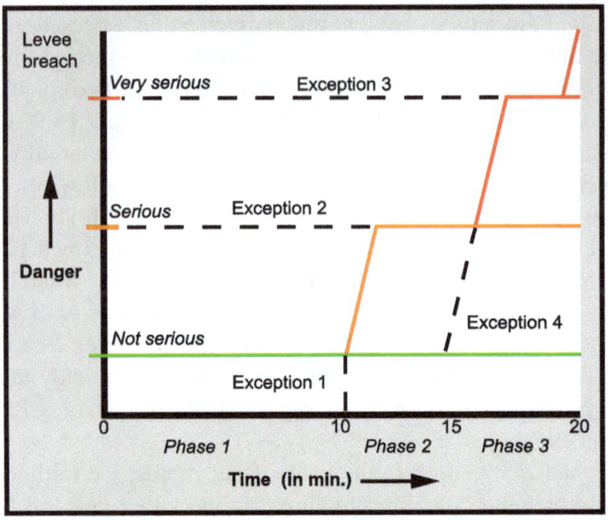

Fig. 6.15 The Generic Failure Framework with its many "exceptions"

has taken an appropriate measure in time. Failures do not necessarily go into the third phase. It could be that they do not develop at all or only develop into the second phase and then become stable. The exact definition of each phase is given below and is illustrated with the failure "macro-instability" (Fig. 6.16):

- **Not serious**: if a failure resides in this phase, a player needs to make a report, and call the action center. The center will tell the player to keep an eye on the situation. In this situation, a failure is not harmful at all, but it is unsure whether it is stable. For macro-instability we can see small horizontal cracks on the crest of the levee in this phase.
- **Serious**: in this phase a failure is to some degree harmful, yet not harmful enough for immediate measures to be taken. If, however, the failure continues to develop, such immediate measures need to be taken. To see whether this is necessary, the action center advises the player to regularly check the failure. For macro-instability the horizontal cracks have become bigger in this phase and a small settlement can be observed together with a horizontal movement around the ditch.
- **Very serious**: if a failure resides in this phase it is considered very harmful. If no measures are taken it will result in a levee breach. After confirmation of the action center, players are able to take the necessary measures. If players do not have this responsibility, the action center takes care of it. In this phase, macro-instability consists of a very large settlement.

With this framework in mind, we tried to fit the eight failures into it. We quickly discovered that this was impossible. Out of the eight failures we already needed to make an exception for four of them. Even more striking is that all four exceptions were different from one another. One exception concerned a failure for which we could not identify a "not serious" phase ("Exception 1"). Two other failures can

Fig. 6.16 Example of the development of the failure "macro-instability"

(a) Not serious phase: two small horizontal cracks

(b) Serious phase: a large crack, small settlement, and horizontal movement

(c) Very serious phase: a very large settlement

occur in an early stage but are serious or very serious from the beginning ("Exception 2" and "Exception 3," respectively). The last exception concerns a failure for which we could identify a not serious and very serious phase but not a serious phase ("Exception 4").

Although it was hard to accept at first that we could not fit the failures into our framework without distorting the real world and providing an incorrect message, the exceptions were actually not that much of a problem at all. The only thing we needed to make sure is that they would not have a negative impact on the gameplay. For example, if exception three, the failure which is immediately very serious, would lead to a levee breach in the first phase, the game could end prematurely and make it too difficult to play.

This trilemma shows how difficult it can be to have an underlying framework that connects to the real world, serves a meaningful purpose, and fits seamlessly with the gameplay and gameworld. But while this asks for quite some effort, it can be very rewarding in the end. As a matter of fact, this framework is now being used to create a digital catalog of pictures of real levee failures and it is even used in the inspection practice itself.

Story Tension

It poses an enormous challenge to integrate a story within an interactive environment (see Level 5). For this reason, we kept the usage of story element initially very simple. We reduced the background story to "You are a levee patroller and need to find failures" and that is it. I did think about creating a story, but aside that it would be infeasible to implement with the constraints we had, it would be difficult to sell to our clients that the game involves, for example, some kind of hero that needs to save the day. It was already quite tough to convince them to build the game in the first place.

Despite that we discarded the idea of using an overarching story, we still had to deal with story elements, most noticeably when the player interacts with the computerized action center to communicate about the findings. Although we did not want to focus too much on communication (see "Definition Dilemma"), this communication is an important part of the inspection procedure and could not be neglected. Next to being relevant from a Reality perspective, we conceived the interaction as an opportunity to provide guidance and reflection, as the action center could be used as a tutor by reminding players what to do and asking them what they have seen. But to have a sensible interaction, we needed to think of how we could integrate this ongoing conversation about the status of failures with the rest of the game.

In thinking about how to achieve this integration, we hit a trilemma. We, first of all, wanted the conversation to be as natural as possible. This is difficult to achieve in a game, as computers have trouble interpreting natural language. Secondly, we wanted the conversation to be dependent on the player's actions. Besides the difficulty of ensuring that the responses of the action center are sensible, it would result in an enormous amount of possible responses. In other words, a "combinatorial explosion" would occur.

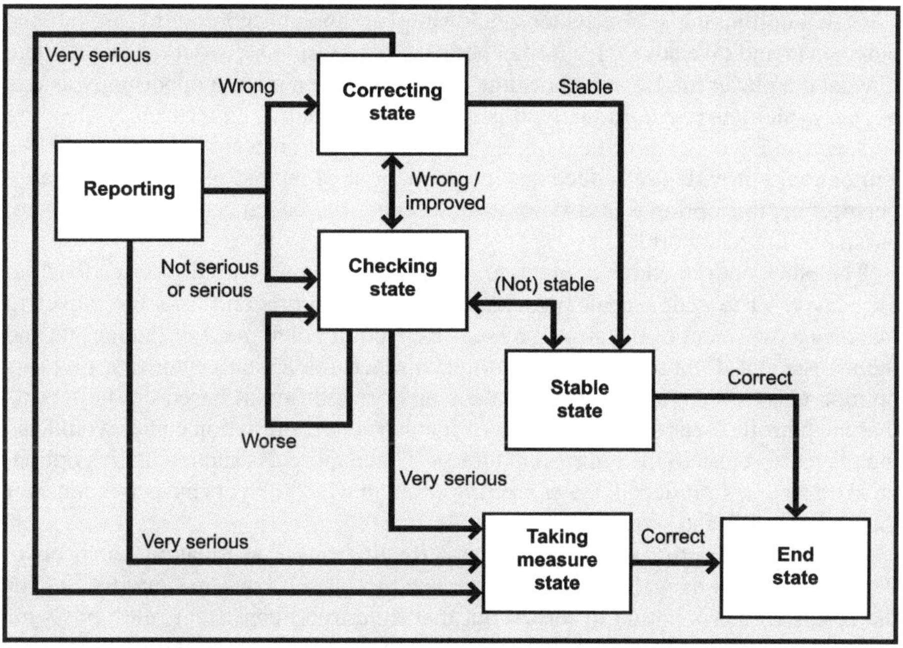

Fig. 6.17 A simplified story structure for the conversations with the action center

Aside from leaving out the conversation with the action center, our least favored choice, we thought of two closely related options for taking care off this trilemma.[19] With the first option we would make the conversation dependent on the state a player is in related to a certain failure (Fig. 6.17). Since the game is about finding failures and returning back to them to see how they developed, we thought of at least four states.

The first state is the *reporting state*. Players enter this when they find a failure. From there players go into the *checking state*, a state in which players have to go back to the failure to see if it is getting worse or if it stays or becomes stable. This happens unless players perceive the failure to be very serious right away. In that case, they enter the *taking measure state*. From the checking state players reach this latter state if it becomes clear that a failure has become worse enough for a measure to be taken. If a failure stays or becomes stable, players enter the *stable state*. If the appropriate measure is taken or if a failure is indeed stable, players get into the *end state*. For each failure in a scenario players are in one of these states.

[19]A third possible option to integrate story and play would be to use symbolic language instead of natural language. *The Sims* uses, for example, "simlish," a language which is not comprehensible but which is supported by symbols above the heads of the sims. This way, users can understand what they think and feel. Although this would diminish our problems with natural language processing, such an approach is only really feasible for big and abstract concepts, like hunger and love, not for very specific issues and findings, like "I found a crack of 20 centimeters."

In this option, the action center would simply respond according to the state the player is in and give advice for further action. These responses would thus not relate to what the player has done in the game. This would be a missed opportunity as it is not very interactive. Additionally, it is not very informative either from a Meaning perspective. Feedback is critical for learning and the action center which can act like a tutor could provide useful feedback on the actions of the patroller. From a Reality perspective, this option was also not ideal, because the action center is certainly not passive in the real world.

The other option, which is much tougher to implement, would give feedback to the players. The action center would interpret the reports and asks the player to make an assessment of the situation (see "Reflection Dilemma"). If the reports and the assessment do not correspond with each other, the action center first gives its opinion and explain why they think the situation is different based on the reports that the patroller sent to them. In case of incongruence, the action center would ask the player to return to the failure and look at it once more. As such, with this option, an extra state is introduced, the *correcting state*, in which players have to reconsider their assessment and/or reports.[20]

Although this option seems great from a Reality as well as Meaning perspective, the interpretation as well as the response need to be valid and meaningful. As for the first, the interpretation, it turned out that little to no consistent rules exists for determining the severity of a situation, while we really needed to know if a crack of 20 centimeters is "not serious," "serious," or "very serious." Some rules of thumb could be retrieved, like IF water is running over the levee and IF the revetment is damaged THEN we have a serious problem, but overall no complete and consistent "expert judgment system" was available that could be adopted for the game.

As for the response, with this option it becomes dependent on the input of the user. Although the usage of states makes it "manageable," by taking all the different inputs into account, over a hundred possible conversations become still possible. And then it also needs to be ensured that the interactive responses are comprehensible.

In the end, we decided to go for the latter option, while we were actually running out of time to finish the project. Some extra personnel was hired to just work on this part of the game. To further make it possible to finish it in time, in consultation with experts we came up with a number of decision rules ourselves to interpret the reports. We also decided that players give a bullet-wise summary of their findings instead of telling their findings in a more natural way. Next to this list, the conversation consists of standard building blocks of which only a part is affected by the input of the player. For example, when players tell the action center where they have found a failure, the sentence always starts with the building block "Hi, action center, I observed damage" and is connected to a textual fragment which is affiliated with the location of the failure in the game. A typical example of a conversation is given below:

[20] If the second time around the assessment of players is still incongruent with their reports, the action center accepts this but not without giving their opinion. This way, the correcting state does not become too annoying.

Action center: Hi, this is the action center speaking.
Player: Hi, action center, I observed damage close to the waterside of the pumping station in Hooge Sluis.
Action center: What are your observations?
Player: The damage consists of one signal: Water outflow. These are the characteristics of the signal:

- The signal is located at the hinterland.
- It has a length of 0–2 m.
- It has a width of 0–1 m.
- The velocity of the current is low.
- The amount of water outflow is little.
- Outflow does not occur at multiple locations.
- Flushing of soil does not occur.

Action center: Thanks for the information. How do you assess the situation?
Player: The situation is not serious. [the player chooses this during the conversation]
Action center: Ok, do return to the damage. Call us after this to tell if the situation is stable or has become worse. Bye!
Player: I will. Bye!

The conversation looks a bit inhuman but it works. With it we created a slightly interactive and realistic yet very meaningful conversation that helps players to better understand what they did.

From Balancing to Game Over?

If after reading all of these dilemmas and trilemmas one thing should become clear, it should be this: everything is related to everything. Decisions on one design problem impact another. Take the "strategy tension." By choosing procedural skills over a conceptual understanding, it is more likely that a first-person perspective will be chosen. And by choosing to reflect-in-action, it is more likely that an interactive conversation with the action center will be chosen. A game is a system and all the elements that are part of it relate to each other and need to interact in a harmonic way to create a realistic, meaningful, and enjoyable experience.

We can also see that although some tensions are restricted to only one world, the other worlds always play a role in the background or are confronted with the decision in another tension. The decision to choose recognition as a problem beyond communication has a subsequent influence on what learning objectives are chosen and what type of game is developed. The three worlds remain under all circumstances tightly related to each other and this tightness becomes clearer the farther the project evolves. When designers look at the problem or learning objectives, they more or less can still view it from one world, but when a translation needs to occur and the actual game needs to be developed, when the initial model of reality, value proposal, and game concept need to be integrated, that is when almost always all three worlds have a significant role.

From this tight interconnection of game elements, we can distill the need for "concurrent design" as discussed earlier in Level 2 when designers are involved with the core of the game. But *literally* designing concurrently by taking "everything" into account at the same time is impossible. Just as with "multi-tasking"—apparently good multi-taskers are people who can easily switch from one task to another—designing concurrently should involve some *switching*. It should involve two types of "switching" to be precise.

The first concerns *perspective-switching*. In designing a game, designers need to have an overview of how the game as a system works. If they have this bird's eye view of the whole, they can decide in a top-down manner what needs to be included and in what way. But to make such decisions, designers also need to go into the "nitty gritty" of the design, to see how specific elements play out and relate to the whole. This means that designers should switch back and forth between a top-down and bottom-up perspective (see also "Think of a Strategy" in Level 4).

Perspective switching does not stop here. Designers need to make sure that they appropriately take care off the worlds of Reality, Meaning, and Play. In designing a game, especially when it concerns the core of the game, each world has some perspective, as I have illustrated with the tension examples from *Levee Patroller*, onto what decisions need to be made. To make sure the game becomes balanced, designers have to switch between the different perspectives that the worlds offer onto design problems. Therefore, perspective switching is not only vertically (top-down vs. bottom-up) but also horizontally (Reality vs. Meaning vs. Play).

The second type of switching involves *decision-switching*. In designing game, many decisions have to be made, from choosing the right technology to thinking of the name of the avatar. As I have just explained, everything is related to each other. Although it cannot be expected that all design decisions can be put next to each other, important design problems that relate to the core of the game have to be considered at the same time as much as possible. This can be done by switching from one problem to the other and making the final decisions for each separate issue when the complete picture is known.

Of course, by means of "iterative design" many wrong decisions can be adjusted. But we have also seen that some earlier decisions, such as with how the gameworld has been built with *Levee Patroller* (see "Scope Tension"), can create a problem for further development, like the implementation of the measurement system. We would have never—even not with unlimited resources—gone back to the drawing board to change the complete landscape. This shows that earlier decisions have a "lock-in" effect. This means that when decisions are made and implemented it is sometimes hard to return and change them.

While this specific problem could be attributed by not having enough design iterations, which would have made it possible to discover the problem earlier, it saves time and prevents potential future problems for sure by realizing upfront as much as possible how the decisions of various design problems relate to each other. We should not completely rely on the "magical power" of iterative design to eventually come up with a "good" game.

Speaking of this, what is actually a "good" game? Is *Levee Patroller* a "good" game? Defining what makes a game good is difficult and very subjective. That is why I have put good between quotation marks throughout the book. But when it comes to games with a meaningful purpose we at least know that they need to "work"—they need to achieve something beyond the game itself. As I have argued throughout the book as well, this requires that the worlds of Reality, Meaning, and Play are all three taken care off. One world cannot achieve the meaningful purpose without the others. All three worlds are needed and this is achieved by "balancing" all three of them.

However, to judge whether a game is balanced is also difficult. In fact, it is even hard to do. Balancing remains sort of an art. Henri Matisse suggested that the art of balance is something to dream of. I interpret this as that it is difficult to achieve balance. Despite that it is difficult to achieve, it does not mean it should not be sought for and that it cannot be approached or even found.

To elaborate on this matter, finding balance is one of the topics of the next level. This is also the final level, because one level remains before it is "game over."

Bibliography

Literature Bibliography

Aldrich, C. (2004). *Simulations and the future of learning: an innovative (and perhaps revolutionary) approach to e-learning*. San Francisco: Pfeiffer.

Baker, C. (2007). *Medikits, power-ups, and cheat codes: in praise of the video-game cliché*. http://www.slate.com/id/2170747/nav/tap3/. Accessed 20 September 2009.

Crookall, D. (1995). *Debriefing: the key to learning from simulation/games*. Thousand Oaks: Sage.

Harteveld, C., Guimarães, R., Mayer, I. S., & Bidarra, R. (2010). Balancing reality, meaning and play: the design philosophy of Levee Patroller. *Simulation & Gaming*, *41*(3), 316–340.

Isbister, K., & Schaffer, N. (2008). *Game usability: advice from the experts for advancing the player experience*. Burlington: Morgan Kaufmann Publishers.

Juul, J. (2005). *Half-real: video games between real rules and fictional worlds*. Cambridge: The MIT Press.

Koster, R. (2005). *A theory of fun for game design*. Scottsdale: Paraglyph Press.

Malone, T. W., & Lepper, M. (1987a). Intrinsic motivation and instructional effectiveness in computer-based education. In R. Snow & M. Farr (Eds.), *Aptitude learning and instruction* (pp. 152–188). London: Lawrence Erlbaum Associates.

Malone, T. W., & Lepper, M. (1987b). Making learning fun: a taxonomy of intrinsic motivation for learning. In R. Snow & M. Farr (Eds.), *Aptitude learning and instruction* (pp. 223–253). London: Lawrence Erlbaum Associates.

Peters, V., Vissers, G., & Heijne, G. (1998). The validity of games. *Simulation & Gaming*, *29*(1), 20–30.

Prensky, M. (2001). *Digital game-based learning*. New York: McGraw-Hill.

Rittel, H. W. J., & Webber, M. M. (1973). Dilemmas in a general theory of planning. *Policy Sciences*, *4*(2), 155–169.

Rollings, A., & Adams, E. (2003). *Andrew Rollings and Ernest Adams on game design*. Indianapolis: New Riders Publishing.

Rollings, A., & Morris, D. (2004). *Game architecture and design: a new edition*. Indianapolis: New Riders Publishing.

Schön, D. A. (1983). *The reflective practitioner: how professionals think in action*. New York: Basic Books.

Tate, R., Haratatos, J., & Cole, S. (2009). Hopelab's approach to Re-Mission. *International Journal of Learning and Media*, *1*(1), 29–35.

Winn, B. M., & Heeter, C. (2006). Resolving conflicts in educational game design through playtesting. *Innovate Journal of Online Education*, *3*(2). http://innovateonline.info/index.php?view=article&id=392. Accessed 4 November 2009.

Game Bibliography

Blizzard Entertainment (2004). *World of Warcraft* [PC]. Irvine: Blizzard Entertainment.

Deltares, & Delft University of Technology (2006). *Levee Patroller: The Levee Inspection Simulator* [PC]. Delft, The Netherlands: Delft GeoSystems.

Epic Games (2004). *Unreal Tournament 2004* [PC]. New York: Atari.

Filament Games, & Our Courts (2009). *Do I Have A Right?* [Web]. USA: Our Courts.

ImpactGames (2007). *PeaceMaker: A Video Game to Promote Peace* [PC]. Pittsburgh: ImpactGames.

Kojima, H., & Konami Computer Entertainment Japan (2004). *Metal Gear Solid 3: Snake Eater* [Playstation 2]. Tokyo, Japan: Konami.

Level-5 (2007). *Professor Layton and the Curious Village* [Nintendo DS]. Tokyo, Japan: Nintendo.

Maxis Software (2000). *The Sims* [PC]. Redwood City: Electronic Arts.

Rockstar North (2008). *Grand Theft Auto IV* [Playstation 3]. New York: Rockstar Games.

Simulearn (2003). *Virtual Leader* [PC]. Norwalk: Simulearn.

Level 7
Game Over?

Imagination is the beginning of creation. You imagine what you desire, you will what you imagine and at last you create what you will—George Bernard Shaw

And who says they cannot be? Make them beautiful. It depends on you. You have complete freedom to design them however you think best—Anciana gives advice to Odaer who complains that insects are not beautiful

My journey ended on October 10, 2006. That day the first ready-to-use version of *Levee Patroller* was presented.[1] Although this version certainly did not have all the functionalities we had in mind, I thought in line with Kolb (1984) that it was time to stop doing and reflect about the experience. That is exactly what I attempted with this book: a reflection on how *Levee Patroller* was designed and what this could possibly mean for designing games in general.

While reflecting on the design process somebody handed to me a children's book called "The Butterfly Workshop" (Belli and Erlbruch 2006). At first I thought to myself "Why should I read this?" However, after reading a bit, I was struck by how much it parallels the design of a game with a meaningful purpose. Sometimes the best notions come from simple stories.

The story is—not surprisingly—about "creation." All living things, animals, and plants are invented by the "Designers of All Things" who are divided into various workshops. Strict rules guide the Designers and prohibit them from mixing the animals of the Animal Realm with the flowers, fruits, and plants of the Vegetable Realm.

The protagonist of the story is Odaer, a young designer in the Insect Workshop. He feels the rules are too restrictive and becomes obsessed with how to make an insect beautiful. Specifically, he wants to *mix* the beauty of a flower with that of a bird, but this combination would be strictly forbidden under the current system. The

[1] At the moment of writing, the third version of *Levee Patroller* has been released.

DOI 10.1007/978-1-84996-157-8_7,

challenge is to pursue this dream within certain boundaries. After many attempts and failures—he creates amongst others the bat and the dragonfly—to achieve this, he does not give up and eventually designs the "butterfly."

The quest of Odaer has many deeper meanings and can result in different interpretations in what this story symbolizes (cf., González 2007). To me, it was a metaphor for designing games. When attempting to design, for example, an educational game, designers try to find a perfect mix of using entertainment game technology with a pedagogical strategy and the content of a certain subject. Each aspect belongs to different "Realms" as TGD proposes: the worlds of Play, Meaning, and Reality, respectively. Finding this mix is difficult: it will need many attempts and it will lead to many failures before a balanced game, a "butterfly," is designed.

Odaer's quest indicates that the key to success lies in the possibilities of the *imagination*. Achieving "artistic perfection" without contradicting the system or breaking the rules of creation, requires aside from persistence and a conviction to "think-out-of-the-box": to be creative and think "differently" about the possibilities. Odaer is eventually successful, because he approached his possibilities from a new perspective, synthesizing and merging apparent differences to produce a new and unique creation. This is the sort of thinking game designers also need to possess to ultimately become successful (i.e., "There is no spoon," see Level 1).

But "danger" is lurking around the corner. Anciana, the boss of the "Designers of All Things," warns Odaer at the beginning of his experiments:

> In your search for the perfect design, you can create monsters. Your urge to make life better and more beautiful, if you are not careful, can result in pain and fear for other creatures in nature. (p. 10)

She further asserts that although finding a mix of the beauty of a flower with that of an animal is an admirable goal, one must carefully monitor its means. This relates to game design as well. While games may not distort ecological systems on this planet and will not hurt anyone (except for maybe some people's pockets...), they can have severe negative side-effects, such as false memories, overconfidence, and inaccuracy.[2] Games can also have the "reverse effect" of what they attempt to achieve.

The latter is what more or less happened with *The Howard Dean for Iowa Game* (Fig. 7.1). Instead of promoting the presidential candidate Howard Dean, players left the game with an impression that he is not any different from the other candidates (Bogost 2007). In this game, players need to do sign-waving, canvassing, and pamphleteering, things volunteers also need to do for other candidates—so what makes Howard Dean different from the others? The impression of indifference certainly does not make one a president. He also did not make it, but, of course, it goes

[2] As far as I am aware, the mentioned negative effects of games are only "claims" and are thus not yet proven. It is nonetheless an important point to be made, because designers need to be aware that a game does not necessarily always lead to positive effects. False memories can occur when players come to confuse in-game experiences for real life experiences. Overconfidence happens if players become overconfident of personal skills or capabilities in dealing with real life complexities after playing a game. Finally, inaccuracy occurs when invalid or inaccurate representations are given of real life which could lead to errors in real life situations.

Fig. 7.1 Recruiting volunteers by sign-waving in *The Howard Dean for Iowa Game*. In this mini-game the goal is to attract the attention of as many people as possible by holding up the sign at the right moment. ©2003 Dean for America. Used with permission

way too far to blame the game for this. What we can learn from this is that careful monitoring to see whether the means are achieved is also necessary for games.

When reading the story I felt like I had been Odaer. I was similarly to him in search of something, in my case something meaningful rather than beautiful. The story helped me—amongst other influences—in articulating what I experienced while designing *Levee Patroller*. From this reflection the idea of Triadic Game Design (TGD) was eventually born. This idea has been extensively discussed in the previous levels of this book. This "level" now marks the ending. It is game over.

But is it really? Many issues related to TGD still need to be stressed, like how a balance is found (see "Finding Yin and Yang"), what the actual usefulness is of TGD for designers and researchers (see "So What and Who Cares?"), the "transfer" of the idea to others (see "Toward a Shared Understanding"), and what happens when the game is finished (see "Life After the Design"). This level delves into these issues and from it, it will become clear that although this book is "game over," it is everything but "over" for the design and research of games (see "Going to the Next Level").

Finding Yin and Yang

Yin and Yang is a Chinese conception. They are the two complementary opposite elements of the universe. They only exist in relation to each other: if there is a Yin, there is always a Yang. For example, darkness only exists when light exists. The symbol depicts further that Yin and Yang are two interdependent elements within a greater whole. If Yin changes, Yang changes, and the other way around. They are even able to flow into each other. Yin becomes Yang and the other way around. The most important message of this symbol is that the two elements need to be in *balance*. The two elements are equal to each other and this requires an equilibrium at all times.

This Chinese symbol is strikingly similar to TGD and its three worlds. The worlds are also complementary to each other. Play involves always some connection with Reality and has always Meaning. If any of the worlds are absent, the whole structure collapses. And when one world changes, the other two change as well, because they are interdependent on each other. If Reality is made more abstract, the message of the game may become more general, and the game more simple and straightforward. This close interdependency shows that designers have to think and take care of all three worlds at the same time.

The worlds can further "flow into each other." An engaging experience may, for example, make a player more curious about a subject and hence become more motivated to know about it. This idea is even famously—for Dutch people at least—described in the first lines of a poem by Hiëronymus van Alphen (1746–1803):

> Mijn spelen is leren, mijn leren is spelen,
> En waarom zou mij dan het leren vervelen?
>
> I translated this freely to:
>
> My playing is learning, my learning is playing,
> and why then should my learning bore me?

From this, we could retrieve that learning can become playing and playing can become learning. But similar to how with Yin and Yang we can infer that extreme good will turn to evil and extreme wealth to poverty, extreme playfulness may lead to not learning or unlearning.

This brings me to the final similarity with Yin and Yang which is to have a balance, an equilibrium. To prevent extreme playfulness, extreme realism, or an overload of information provision or extraction, harmony should be found between the three worlds. While the Yin and Yang philosophy is about finding a balance between the Yin and Yang element in everything, the philosophy of TGD is about finding a balance between the worlds of Reality, Meaning, and Play. To achieve this, designers need to consider the aspects and criteria of each of these worlds. Table 7.1 gives an overview of the different elements that can be derived from these worlds and that need to be considered.

How can we keep Yin and Yang in an equilibrium? This is difficult to answer. The conceptual meanings of Yin and Yang are hard to define. We need to avoid extremes, but how do we recognize them, and if so, what can we do about it? Much similarly, how can we create a balanced game? We have an idea of what aspects and criteria need to be taken into account according to the different worlds, but how do we put them together and create harmony?

Table 7.1 Overview of the elements of each world

	Reality	Meaning	Play
Aspects	Problem	Purpose	Goal
	Factors	Strategy	Gameplay
	Relationships	Operations	Gameworld
	Process	Context	Technology
Criteria	Flexibility	Motivation	Immersion
	Fidelity	Relevance	Engagement
	Validity	Transfer	Fun
Output	Model of reality	Value proposal	Game concept

Admittedly, it is hard to exactly say "how" the different aspects and criteria need to be considered in detail. Game design remains above-all an "art." It requires creativity, imagination, and thinking-out-of-the box to create a game—all of this makes it hard to pinpoint how game design exactly works. What happens in between the input—a problem for which a game needs to be developed—and output—the eventual game—seems for this reason sort of magical and this makes game design a kind of "black magic."

This is also exemplified by the "juggler model" (Fig. 2.3). Jugglers are artists who know a good trick: holding three balls in the air at once. Game designers know a similar sort of trick, but instead of balls they are able to consider three worlds at the same time. How designers do this is a bit of a mystery and this makes designing a game a magic trick. And it should stay magic to a large degree, because creativity and imagination are at the essence of creating innovative games and for being able to deal with the tensions resulting from the three worlds. This means that game design should not become some highly systematized and organized activity. Chaos and serendipity are inherently needed and part of this process.

Yet, jugglers are certainly not people who suddenly—out of the blue—are able to do a trick. They learned this. They know exactly what is needed to keep the three balls constantly in the air. Translating this to TGD, it means that this philosophy helps designers in developing a way of thinking of how to look and work in designing a game. TGD gives some insight into the "magical" process of what game design constitutes and this understanding may eventually lead to keeping the worlds of TGD "in the air"—to make the right decisions and creating a harmonic game in the end.

The insight TGD gives, does, however, not tackle the problem that it remains hard to specifically judge when "harmony," the ultimate criterion of TGD, is reached. To judge this, another criterion—a proxy for harmony—may bring revelation. This concerns the criterion of *satisficing*. The term "satisficing" has been coined by Simon (1957) to indicate that human beings lack the cognitive resources to find optimal solutions. We can rarely evaluate all possible outcomes with sufficient precision besides that our judgement may not be that reliable. That is why we stick to solutions that satisfy us.

Aside that an "optimal" solution is unlikely to exist when it comes to designing games with a serious purpose, it is just as unlikely that designers keep on optimizing the three worlds endlessly till near perfection is reached—especially when we take the constraints of designing a game, such as time and budget, in consideration. At some point, when designers think that some "balance" has been achieved, when they reached a sort of "optimum" they had in mind, they are satisfied with the situation and leave it at that. As regards to games, satisficing means that after many decisions on how to balance the game and many iterations to test and evaluate the results of the balancing process, the design reaches a point that is considered "good" by the designers and other stakeholders.

As for *Levee Patrollers*, although we were still struggling with some of the dilemmas and trilemmas and much of the design could still be improved, we reached such a point of satisfaction and released the first version on October 10, 2006. And our judgment has not less us down if we would define a "good" game as a game that is being used and receives positive responses from clients as well as players. Since its initial release the game has been used by the clients, the water boards, and until this very day the game is still upgraded—on demand of the clients—by including, for example, more failures and adding audio. The players have further indicated that they find it very realistic and learn much from it. Additionally, they enjoy playing it and are quite engaged. Often, patrollers tell me they want to continue playing at home, because they have to get a 100% score.

But to have a more accurate judgement, to see if we really created a game with "harmony", a proper evaluation is, of course, needed. The first steps for such an evaluation have been made and future research will provide the—hopefully—"definitive" answers on whether *Levee Patroller* can be considered a "good" or harmonic game.[3] However, such a rigorous evaluation can only be done if the game is delivered—when it is finished. Due to this, designers are dependent on the criterion of satisficing for judging the quality of their game in the first place.

To summarize, TGD gives us insight in the Yin and Yang of game design. Although the eventual harmony may be hard to observe, by striving to it and by being aware of the need we can reach a point that is satisficing for the designers and all other stakeholders. While this clarifies that TGD as a "design philosophy" can be useful for designers to perform their tricks, it does not precisely tell in what ways TGD contributes to the field of game design. Let me elaborate on this.

So What and Who Cares?

When I present my ideas, people always tell me "so what?" Ideas can be great, but "who cares?" What is—basically—in it for us? TGD sounds like a nice theoretical framework but how will it affect designers and researchers? Clearly, designing

[3] As part of my Ph.D. research I set up a training program with *Levee Patroller* of three weeks at three of the participating water boards. Around 150 patrollers participated in this training. The eventual analysis should provide a more rigorous answer to whether the game is being successful in achieving its purpose.

games has always been about making decisions and dealing with trade-offs. That is nothing new. What gives TGD something extra beyond what we already know? What becomes different for designers and researchers if they use TGD when compared to their existing practices?

The "easy" answer to this is that this framework goes beyond identifying the problems with designing games. It offers a new way of looking at the design process and offers information on which to base sound, pragmatic decision making when involved in designing a game and on which to base sound, rigid analytical inferences when involved in researching a game. But specifically, the usefulness of TGD for practitioners and researchers relates to three different yet related uses: the use of TGD as an "analytical lens," "application tool," or a "puzzle frame."

Analytical Lens

In designing a game with a meaningful purpose, a myriad of elements have to be taken into account. Even when one is able to grasp this wide variety of elements, it is difficult to understand how they relate to each other. To get an understanding of the complexity of a game, it helps to have an *analytical lens*, something that can point out to what is important, what needs to be considered, and how things work. Constituting a lens in understanding design is exactly one of the things that TGD can offer.

TGD explains what designing a game is about and what needs to be considered to do this. Knowing this upfront helps to have a constant overview: to see the "big picture." This helps designers to remain focused and pay attention to certain elements that would otherwise remain unnoticed and neglect those that are irrelevant. During the design TGD could further shed some light on specific issues. And afterward it can help to explain what has occurred during the design. It could explain why certain decisions were made or it could help to get an understanding of the effects of a game.

Let me elaborate on this with a game called *BioShock*. In this adventurous first-person shooter, players encounter the so-called "Little Sisters." These are genetically modified young girls with zombie eyes and a large syringe. The Little Sisters carry important resources that players can use to upgrade their powers. But to obtain these resources, players first have to defeat the "Big Daddies," large biomechanical monsters that protect the Little Sisters, and then kill the Little Sisters. With these game elements in place, players are confronted with a dilemma: will they kill the Little Sisters and harvest their resources, or will they let them live, and survive with fewer resources but with a cleaner conscience?

Sicart (2009) points out that the implementation of this dilemma is problematic, because there is barely any difference between letting the Little Sisters live or die. If they are left alive, players will receive the wanted resources in a quantity similar to what they would get after killing them. It only has an impact on the ending of the game and not on its progression. This way, according to Sicart the choice is deprived of all meaning.

It is deprived from all meaning, because from an ethical perspective, this seemingly interesting ethical choice is actually turned into a resource management process that does not require any type of moral reasoning for the player to succeed. Moral actions ought to be supported by the gameplay by providing a sufficiently distinct outcome so players feel that their actions are of moral nature. *BioShock* does not provide such distinction.

Sicart (2009) gives two specific reasons for why the designers may have implemented the Little Sister game mechanic in this way. The first concerns a "dominance of the narrative." This refers to the fact that the ethical choice does affect the unfolding of the storyline but not the progression throughout the game. If the moral actions would affect the progression, it would increase the interactivity and thus the player's agency, but it would also be required to reconcile the story with the player's actions. The gameworld would need to constantly respond and change in accordance to the player's actions. This is much tougher to implement than only letting the actions be dependent on the eventual ending of the game. In the end, the designers have chosen to deal with this Play dilemma by choosing linearity over interactivity.

The second reason is an "obsession with gameplay balance." About this reason, Sicart (2009) says the following:

> In classic conceptions of game balance, this is probably a positive thing; the game is balanced to different play styles. But when it comes to developing ethically relevant games, this balance is ineffective, since it is disconnected from player agency. There is, then, the possibility of thinking about some kind of ethical balance, a design choice that needs to be made when creating the game system, and that is related to how the game reacts to actions in which the player's ethical agency is at stake. In this sense, game imbalance can yield interesting ethical balance—and of course the task of the game designer is to allow for the game to be playable, despite these imbalances. (p. 162)

From a TGD perspective the above can be interpreted as a Meaning-Play dilemma. To get an ethically relevant game, an imbalance is wanted, while a balance is wanted from the classic conceptions of game balance to assist different play styles. The designers of *BioShock* eventually chose the world of Play over Meaning. They may have made this design choice consciously. From early playtests they may have observed that many players did not want to kill the Little Sisters and became very frustrated by the subsequent increased difficulty to finish the game. The players may have thought that it was awkward that they were being punished by the game system for being "good."

It could also be that the designers were indeed so "obsessed" with gameplay balance that they forgot to see the big picture and lost sight of their actual aim to incorporate ethical choices. Or it could be that the designers do not have any lenses to consider the implementation of ethically relevant game choices yet do have a lens, the classic conceptions of game balance, onto which they can rely on. As they can rely on the latter and on most likely many other lenses from the world of Play (cf., Schell 2008), a dominance by the world of Play as a result is not so strange.

From this example of *BioShock*, we can see that TGD helps to make sense of the design of a game. TGD provides concepts and terminologies to describe phenomena accurately and it gives insight into the complex nature and relationships of the elements that relate to the game design process.

And if the designers of *BioShock* would have known of TGD, it may have helped them in dealing with the tensions that resulted from the Little Sister game mechanic. This brings me to the second implication: to use TGD as a "application tool."

Application Tool

When using TGD as an analytical lens, it can be seen as a "descriptive framework" in understanding (parts of) the design. From such understanding better games may be the result if it is applied during the design. If it is applied in retrospect, the reflections may help designers and others to learn from it for future projects.

In contrary, when TGD is used as an *application tool*, it should be seen as a "prescriptive framework" that is actively and dominantly used in designing a game. It urges designers to take multiple worlds at the same time into account, gives a set of aspects and criteria that need to considered, and stresses that in the end a balance needs to be perceived between the three worlds.

The most important distinctions between the use of TGD as analytical lens and as application tool is that within a project TGD as a lens could be applied at will and is only one of possibly many lenses that are used. However, for TGD as a tool the designers really have to live by what the design philosophy outlines. Other tools may be used but they have to fit into the idea of TGD.

To illustrate this use, let us assume that we are asked, much similar to the game *PeaceMaker*, to create a game about the Israeli-Palestinian conflict. After an initial investigation, we decide that the problem can be decomposed into two subproblems. First of all, many people in the world have only a slight understanding what this conflict is about. Secondly, what people hear is all about politics—they have hardly any idea of how the people in that area, from the average citizen to the soldier, think about the conflict.

In fact, we have hardly any idea ourselves! To change this we need to delve into the subject ourselves, see what factors are involved and how they relate to each other. We may need to consider some processes as well, but this actually depends on how we want to achieve the actual purpose of the game, to bring forth an awareness and a conceptual understanding of the Israeli-Palestinian conflict on a local level.

After thinking deeply of the possibilities we realize that we learned a lot about the Israeli-Palestinian conflict ourselves. This realization gave us a Eureka! moment in coming up with a strategy to achieve the purpose of the game: why not let the players investigate as well? By letting them investigate themselves, they actively construct and self-initiate an understanding and such an understanding will definitely be "grokked" a lot better than if they are being told what it is all about.

This sounds good, but this investigation needs to have a goal. It also needs to be interesting. Moreover, immersion is incredibly important as players need to get a clear idea of the different perspectives of the people who are dealing with the conflict on a daily basis. After some consideration, the worlds of Play and Meaning seem to perfectly fit together by making the players journalists who have to write

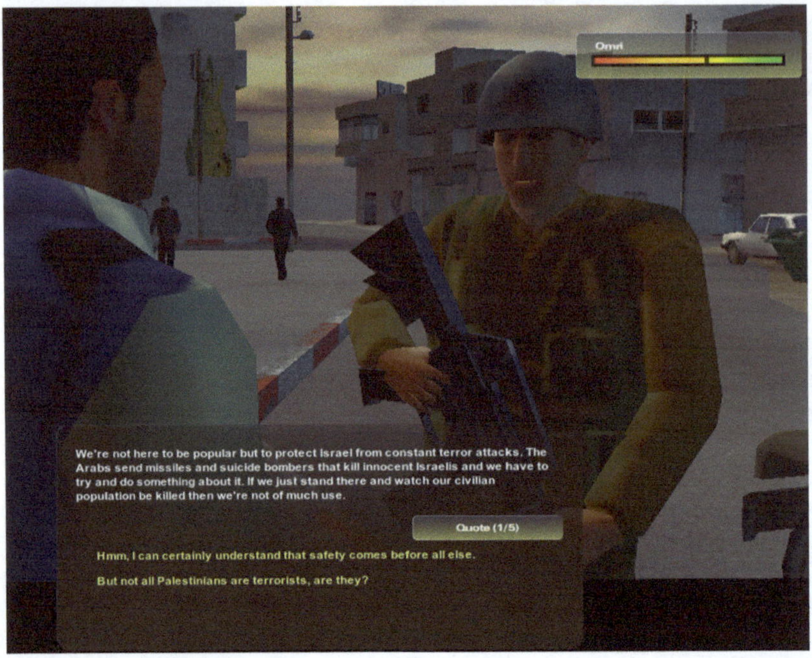

Fig. 7.2 Reporting events as a journalist in *Global Conflicts: Palestine*. Here I talked with an Israeli soldier who explained that he is needed to protect the Israelis from Arab terrorists. ©2007 Serious Games Interactive. Used with permission

articles based on their talks with local people. The challenge is to write articles that are well-received by the audience and are newsworthy.

This thought experiment shows that the design process until so far is completely led by TGD. It is not just used to look at a particular issue, such as with the Little Sister game mechanism, but it is pervasively involved in every part of the design. When this game will be further developed, TGD will also be used as a tool in dealing with the tensions and evaluating whether the ultimate criterion, harmony, is reached.

And, as a matter of fact, the game I just described actually exists. It is the much lauded *Global Conflicts: Palestine* (Fig. 7.2). Although the actual design process of this game might have been far from different than what I described here, with TGD it is not unimaginable that the design process could have proceeded as this.

Therefore, from the example of *Global Conflicts: Palestine* we can retrieve how TGD could have aided in designing this game. When TGD is used as a tool, it gives an outlook on how to create a harmonic game and it enables to infer whether such a balance has been found. But the use of TGD is not solely restricted to individual projects. It can also be applied as an overarching theoretical framework. This is what the last usage is about.

Puzzle Frame

In designing and researching games a number of "larger" questions exists that extend beyond the development of an individual game, like "How do we apply games in classroom settings?" and "What role does gender play for applying games for education?" In being able to answer such questions a theoretical grounding is necessary, as Selfe (1990) notes for the educational use of computer technology:

> [An] atheoretical perspective...not only constrains our current educational uses of computers, but also seriously limits our vision of what might be accomplished with computer technology in a broader social, cultural, or educational context. Until we examine the impact of computer technology...from a theoretical perspective, we will continue, myopically and unsystematically, to define the isolated pieces of the puzzle in our separate classrooms and discrete research studies. Until we share some theoretical vision of this topic, we will never glimpse the larger picture that could give our everyday classroom efforts direction and meaning. (p. 119, as cited in Mishra and Koehler 2006)

If we rephrase this quotation in light of games and the usefulness of TGD, it would become something like this:

> [An] atheoretical perspective...not only constrains our current *purposeful* uses of *games*, but also seriously limits our vision of what might be accomplished with *games* in a broader social, cultural, or *meaningful* context. Until we examine the impact of *games*...from a theoretical perspective, we will continue, myopically and unsystematically, to define the isolated pieces of the puzzle in our separate *practices* and discrete research studies. Until we share some theoretical vision of this topic, we will never glimpse the larger picture that could give our efforts *of designing and applying games* direction and meaning. (words in italic are changes to the original text)

At the moment, most game design research consists of case studies and examples of best practices. Of course, such efforts are certainly valuable for building an understanding. But these "isolated pieces of the puzzle" do not allow us to compare across diverse cases and examples of practice. The rephrased quotation explains that to be able to move the field forward, to "solve the puzzle" and get a glimpse at the larger picture, some theoretical perspective or vision is needed that ties the separate practices and research together and gives meaning and direction to the efforts that have been done.

TGD might offer such a perspective. If used in such a way, TGD can be seen as a *puzzle frame* in which different puzzle pieces can be put together to eventually solve the puzzle. It concerns an *integrative framework* in this case. However, to be able to serve as a puzzle frame, the integrative theoretical framework should be able to be used for a wide variety of games. To show that TGD can actually be applied to such a wide variety, I will explain how it can be related to an interesting yet quite different game called *Braid*.

At first glance, *Braid* looks and feels like a platformer, as it involves running and jumping through linear levels, but at its heart it is a puzzle game. The puzzles are built around the ability to manipulate time. In some levels, players can rewind the time, in others they can slow down game elements with a ring or create a shadow doppelgänger to repeat actions previously performed (Fig. 7.3).

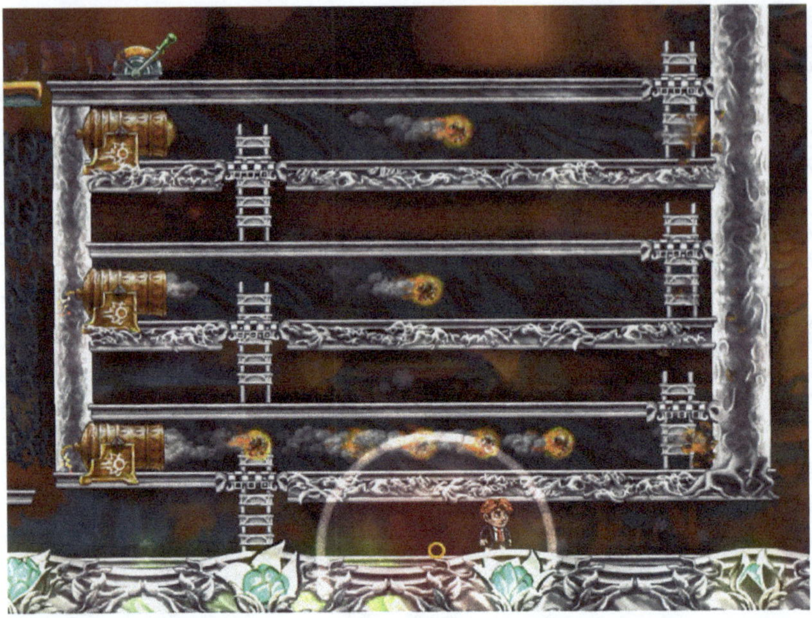

(a) Slowing down other game elements — the cannonballs in this picture — with a ring

(b) Using a shadow doppelgänger to solve puzzles

Fig. 7.3 Two different gameplay abilities for manipulating time in *Braid*. ©2009 Number None. Used with permission

As for the story, the game involves the protagonist Tim who is a man searching for a princess who "has been snatched by a horrible and evil monster." The relationship between the two is vague. The only clear part is that Tim has made some mistake which he hopes to make up for or undo. Throughout the game, the plot is further explained by ambiguous textual fragments, such as "She could not understand why he chose to flirt so closely with the death of the world" and by its game mechanics. At the end of the game, which is actually the start of the plot, Tim is revealed to be the "horrible and evil monster" the princess is escaping from.

The purpose of the designer was to make a statement against the status quo of the industry. The game has deconstructed traditional gameplay concepts, such as jumping on enemies and saving princesses, and re-used these elements in this game in an unfamiliar way to players, forcing them to think about what all of this means. In other words, the game uses contradictions to spark the interest of the player. Things are not what they seem.

For example, while *Braid* is a platforming game and the player largely scrolls linearly from left to right, a gaming convention we expect from these types of games, the sequence of the levels is not played linearly. Moreover, we expect to save the princess from the evil monsters in most games, but in this game it turns out that the player-character is the actual monster.

By using TGD we can elaborate on the design of this game. Looking at the game from the world of Play, it uses and harnesses game elements familiar to platform and puzzle games. If players neglect the whole storyline, they just play a game consisting of a number of aesthetically pleasing levels in which puzzles need to be solved with innovative gameplay elements that involve manipulating the time.

The world of Reality only pertains to the classic gaming conventions, because the problem concerns the status quo of the game industry. The model of reality more or less consist of all factors that make up these conventions, such as jumping on top of enemies. By having this model, the designer has an overview of all the classic gaming interventions that he wants players to be confronted with and is able to translate them into a gameworld.

For this to happen meaningfully, a strategy needed to be conceived from the world of Meaning. This strategy concerned to break down the conventions and use them in for players unfamiliar ways. The operations to reach this concern reversing plot and gameplay, making parts non-linear, and using surprise by making sure that the expected never happens.

The reason why *Braid* works so well is that despite that the story can be neglected, it will be hard not to, because the player's curiosity is raised enormously by the contradictions experienced and the ambiguous references to what it could all possibly mean. And when thinking about this, it may not become clear what the story means, but it does become clear that while the game looks familiar with classic gaming conventions, it actually breaks with many of them. Things are simply not what they seem. This shows that the game has neatly intertwined the three different worlds in achieving its purpose.

From the example of *Braid*, we can see that TGD can even be extended to beyond what we "traditionally" conceive as games with a serious purpose (see Level 2).

Although this example certainly does not guarantee this, it does indicate that TGD can be used as a "puzzle frame" to compare all sorts of games with each other. Therefore, TGD may be a way to put all the "isolated pieces of the puzzle" together.

Nevertheless, TGD is first and foremost developed to have an impact on the actual practice of designing games with a meaningful purpose—by being used as an analytical lens or application tool. To be successful in this regard, it would be better if more than one person has an understanding of TGD when designing a game (see "Toward a Shared Understanding"). It is further critically important to consider what happens when the game is eventually finished (see "Life After the Design").

Toward a Shared Understanding

A game is mostly not designed by a single individual. Rather, it is designed by a team which can consist of as small as three to five people and as big as up to over 100 people. The larger the number of members on the team, the more difficult it becomes to make sure that the efforts of the team are coherently integrated into a single whole. Aside from the design team itself, frequently stakeholders beyond the team are involved during the process, from clients to the marketing department. Designing a game is, therefore, an enormous collaborative effort.

To make sure the process runs smoothly, different variables can play a role. The management of a project in general can, for example, make an important difference in having a successful project. But as designing games is inherently interdisciplinary if not trans-disciplinary, by involving a variety of people and disciplines and integrating their efforts together, it would certainly be beneficial if all of those involved have some "shared understanding" of what designing a game is about and to have a common vocabulary to talk about it.

How can a *shared understanding* be achieved? It is possible to have a couple of meetings to exchange thoughts or do some team building activity like creating a sand castle or playing an entertainment game together. While the first is a traditional yet somewhat cumbersome, inefficient, and ineffective way of getting to understand each other, the second only socially bonds members together. Such bonding is certainly beneficial for collaboration, but it is not meaningfully related to the work that needs to be done to design a game. To achieve a meaningful understanding an alternative would be to let everybody read the same articles and books and discuss these. However, aside that this is very time consuming, this simply cannot be expected from everybody—especially not from the clients.

For TGD to have an effect on the actual practice of designing games, I realized that writing this book may not be sufficient. Of course, it is most crucial that the game designers on the team are aware of TGD and are able to use the insights of this design philosophy to develop a concept and implement this, but it would be more fruitful if other members, and even stakeholders beyond the team, have some understanding as well. To make this possible, I developed parallel to this book "The

Triadic Game Design Workshop" (see "Workshop").[4] Before I explain what this workshop is all about, I will first elaborate on the importance of "collaboration."

Collaboration

In designing games project teams consist of people with different backgrounds, knowledge, skills, and interests. Any team has, for example, artists, game designers, modelers, and programmers. If a non-entertainment game is created it would be beneficial to include an expert affiliated with the world of Meaning, such as an instructional designer, and a subject-matter expert which is affiliated with the world of Reality. The different roles are outlined below.

- **Artist**: the artist can be a writer, a musician, or a graphics artist. The artist basically does most of the creative work, inspired by the game designer. The artist delivers content directly to the programmer or level designer or in case of the graphics artist, lets a modeler convert the sketches to bits and bytes.
- **Game designer**: this person takes the game as a system into account. The rules of the game, the look and feel, et cetera. This and more is described in a conceptual design document by the game designer.
- **Level designer**: the level designer is someone who uses the framework of the programmer and the objects of the modelers to create compelling environments. To do this, the level designer, depending on what type of equipment is used for the development, works in a level editor.
- **Modeler**: this person is involved with creating the objects in the game world. The modeler uses computer graphics tools as Adobe Illustrator, Photoshop, 3D Studio Max, and/or Maya to create the objects.
- **Programmer**: the programmer brings the concept of the game designer to life. This is done by coding the ideas with some programming language such as C, C++, Java, or Python, and with or without tools, such as a game engine.
- **Instructional designer**: this person is involved with the educational philosophy behind a game. This means that this person looks at what the player needs to learn and how this is achieved by playing the game. If the game does not have an educational purpose another type of expert has to be involved. For example, when a game for data collection is developed a data mining expert needs to be involved and when it is about attitude change an expert in rhetoric could be helpful.
- **Subject-matter expert**: this person knows a lot about the subject. The expert's knowledge needs to be converted in some way to the game.

A strong collaboration between these diverse roles is needed to synchronize all the efforts. And this may be hard, because as Rollings and Morris (2004) argued

[4] I did not develop The Triadic Game Design Workshop completely by myself. Rens van den Bergh, game developer at Deltares and a previous project member of the *Levee Patroller* team, developed it together with me. Another Rens, Rens Kortmann, made some valuable contributions in improving it.

"You may have heard the saying that programmers cannot see the wood for the trees, while designers cannot see the trees for the wood. It is true, except that programmers sometimes cannot even see the trees for the leaves on the trees" (p. 95). Besides a different way of working and inability for some to see the larger picture or the inverse, to see the details, language plays a role as well. I remember vividly how one of the programmers always ordered a "C++" each time a coffee round was proposed. This caused many other programmers to smile but it raised the eyebrows of all the other project members (including me). C++ is a programming language, but in this case the programmer meant to say he wanted a "cappuccino extra strong with extra sugar." Although it was just a joke, to me this request does indicate how members have diverse backgrounds to which a different language can be affiliated with (and even a different type of humor...).

To ensure that the game becomes a complete whole, it is important that project members do not work in isolation from each other. They should work together by—at the very least—exchanging information with each other. Otherwise it could happen that some project members go into the opposite direction of others and this may "disjoin" the whole. To prevent this from happening, it is fundamental that team members are aware of their role and the need to integrate their part with others to create a synthesis. They should be aware that trade-offs are going to be made during the process and that their choices have effect on the work of others.

From the side of the clients and other stakeholders, it is also important to understand what the game design process is about. They will definitely understand the need to make decisions based on time and budget, but in addition they will need to get an understanding of the balancing process of the worlds of Reality, Play, and Meaning to see why certain choices are made and to think constructively with the design team how a synthesis can be achieved. For all people involved, awareness about the process leads to a higher acceptance of the decisions made and a tendency to look for solutions when tensions are encountered instead of being frustrated or unsatisfied.

Having a person on the team who sees the larger picture and manages the project is of great value. However, it would of course be much better if the team and stakeholders see the larger picture as well. If not, everybody operates from their own ivory tower and the overseeing manager needs to jump in and out, correcting and adjusting the process almost like a police officer. To avoid this, a "shared understanding" of the design process would be very valuable.

Creating a shared understanding is easier said than done. In fact, according to Weick (1995) it is impossible to achieve a shared understanding. People are simply too different in terms of background, previous experiences, personality, and so on, to expect that they think alike. Instead of trying to achieve a shared understanding, he proposes that we should create "shared experiences" to make a common understanding possible. Although people may still think differently about the experience, the experience becomes a common reference which is the same for everybody. This enables to talk and refer to events like "Do you remember when X happened?"

Workshop

To create a "shared experience" was the main reason to develop a participatory workshop (for details, see Appendix B). A workshop is much more "experiential" than having a meeting, reading a book, or attending a lecture, and much more "educational" than doing a team building activity. The workshop attempts first and foremost to educate participants about TGD. It does this by letting participants work together in teams on developing a game conceptually. This means that a game is only developed on paper. At the end of the workshop ideas are presented and not playable prototypes. As these ideas can still be used as an input for further development, another use of the workshop is as a "brainstorming tool."

Before the final concept is presented, three steps need to be taken during the workshop. First, teams will blindly draw a theme. This theme relates to the domains that can be derived from the world of Reality. They could, for instance, relate to business & management or health (see Level 2). Based on the theme, teams need to develop a "model of reality." Worksheets are handed out that help teams to think about what aspects and criteria they need to consider in creating such a model (see Appendix C). In this step, it is also possible to not hand out themes but let everybody work on the same topic.

The second and third step are similar to the first, except they involve the worlds of Meaning and Play, respectively. With the second step, teams blindly draw a "value," such as attitude or knowledge. This time participants are required to (re)consider what the game needs to achieve beyond the game itself by taking their value and the earlier developed model of reality into account. To guide teams in creating a "value proposal," they also receive a worksheet in this step.

With the third step, the teams have to think of a "game concept" based on the outcomes—a model of reality and a value proposal—of the previous two steps and with the help of another worksheet. This concept further needs to be based on some of the characteristics of a "genre" that the participants blindly picked. This means teams are forced to think about what characteristics they use from, for example, the action or adventure genre in their eventual concept.

By using these steps participants learn in an incremental, social, and experiential way about TGD. Participants are not overwhelmed but get the time to learn to appreciate each world, while the challenge is steadily increased, as in each step the results of the previous step(s) have to be taken into account as well. The sequential order serves another educational purpose as well. After every step teams will have to revise or rethink their ideas and will realize that the different worlds are heavily interdependent on each other. This way, participants will understand that the worlds need to be considered concurrently.

To make the experience more fun and engaging but also increase its educational effectiveness, the previously described procedure has been embedded in an actual game. The goal of the workshop—not the purpose—is to actually score the most points as a team. Points can be received in-between steps and at the end. At these occasions teams have to present their work to the other teams. After the presentations, teams need to award each other (themselves not included) with points. The facilitators collect the awarded points and make the scores either known right away or only at the end. The resulting competition between teams makes the workshop fun and engaging to participate in.

The game elements have, however, an educational function as well. The rules of the game force teams to listen to each other and judge their ideas. Why would a team bother listening to the creations of others if it does not further affect them? From experience I know that teams are so preoccupied and enthusiastic about their own concept that it is hard to get their attention at any point during a workshop. Whether teams award points strategically or not, by introducing this competition between teams, teams are required to discuss the ideas of others and think about what makes something a good or bad design.

It is important to emphasize that although the workshop (and also this book) give a seemingly structured way of approaching the design of a game, the aim is above-all to give participants a feeling of what it is like to design a game and what needs to be considered. This feeling coupled to having already designed a game together makes up for a "shared experience" that will help the design team and the stakeholders to be prepared for doing the same thing for real. This way, the workshop gives a "common understanding" and "common vocabulary" that is needed for a solid collaboration.

But aside from considering in what ways a project runs smoothly during the design, it might also be wise to already start thinking about what happens when a game is finished. This I will discuss now.

Life After the Design

Suppose the project is managed to the extent that the game is actually finished and released. What happens next? The obvious first answer to this is to make sure it is actually used. However, the *deployment* of a game, a sub-aspect of the world of Meaning (see Level 4), is not something that should be taken lightly. In fact, it is often one of the most critical parts for having a successful game.

The extent to which it is critical depends, of course, on the game—for a persuasive game as *September 12th* this is of less importance than say a data collection game as *Foldit*. The latter requires much maintenance and its success is completely dependent on usage, while the first, *September 12th*, more or less only had to be put online by its designers. If a game is even used for education or training, many more things have to be thought of, such as how the game integrates into the overall curriculum and to make sure the facilities are up and running to play the game.

This sort of "life after the design" should not be taken lightly, because aside that the creation of meaning actually finds place during the deployment, it is not unlikely that a game ends up not being used. For example, if a game is specifically designed for clients, such as with *Levee Patroller*, the danger is that clients receive the game and that quickly the game ends up somewhere on a shelf deeply hidden away from anybody to find, let alone use it.

This seems like a "doom scenario" but it is more likely to happen than not. Organizations are dynamic: people change from position and interests change frequently as well. If people change from position, especially if they are the initiators and the proponents of the game, it could possibly happen that their replacers are not as enthusiastic, have other priorities, or even do not know about the existence of it.

The latter may seem awkward, but again, it is more likely to happen than not. In fact, it happened with *Levee Patroller*. Once we were called for information about the game, because one of the water boards was interested in getting a license. However, this water board already had a license! As for changing interests, one year an organization may want to train procedures, another year they would like to focus on communication. I mentioned "flexibility" as one of the criteria and I will soon talk about the versatility of games, but it remains to be seen whether an already constructed game can keep up with the changing demands of an organization.

Another example of a "showstopper" concerns the "knowledge transfer" to use the game. Most games come with a manual that explains the functionalities, such as what the controls are and what options are available. To make sure a game is used well, it could require more than such manual instructions, certainly if clients want to use the game themselves. For example, an explanation is needed of what the game is about and how it could be used most effectively. This can be explained in a more elaborate manual or it could be done in a "teach-the-teacher course." With the latter, the potential facilitators guiding the game sessions will be instructed by somebody, for instance the designer, who has the knowledge about how to use the game. But if all of this does not happen, nobody knows how to use it and the game will end up not being used.

Of course, all of this may not matter so much if a rather "simple" (online) low budget game is developed which speaks pretty much for itself, such as the *The McDonald's Video Game* or, again, *September 12th*. But even in these instances, the life after the design matters to some degree. Putting a game online is easily done. It requires some effort in terms of marketing to actually make sure that it is going to be noticed and hence played. These types of games currently get a lot of media and academic attention which make it a bit easy to get noticed. However, when this is over, when such games are considered "normal," and thousands of others are jumping around for attention as well, developers need to look for ways to be seen.

The life after the design goes, however, also beyond the deployment. The second and less obvious answer to "What happens next?" is to re-use the design. It takes a lot of time, people, and budget to develop a game at first. When a certain game turns out to be successful, developers will try to get as much out of it as possible. We do not only see this in the entertainment industry, where sequel upon sequel is released, but also in the field of games with a meaningful purpose, and in particularly two ways.

The first concerns *recycling* successful concepts. In the wake of *Global Conflicts: Palestine* (Fig. 7.2) two successors, *Global Conflicts: Latin America* and *Global Conflicts: Sweatshops*, appeared. In all three games, the player plays a journalist who has to delve into the problems of an existing region in the world. While in the Palestine edition players have to write stories and observe events from the Israeli and Palestine perspective, in the Latin America edition, players have to note stories and observe events as well, only this time debt slavery, corruption, and trafficking

Fig. 7.4 Looking for a place to make a cone penetration test in *CPT-Operator*. Notice the similarity between this gameworld and the one of *Levee Patroller*

of humans are at the matter. With the Sweatshop edition, players have to immerse themselves into the issue of child labor in Bangladesh.

Using the same concept for a completely other game can also be seen with the *ESP Game* and *September 12th*. After the *ESP Game*, similar "data collection" type of games have been developed, such as *Verbosity*. With this game, players alternate between "describer" and "guesser" of a word. The describer enters a maximum of words on predefined descriptions such as "It has..." and "It looks like...." And a bit similar to the *ESP Game*, the faster the guesser guesses the describer's word, the more points both earn. This way, the game collects commonsense facts to train reasoning algorithms.

September 12th, on the other hand, is a game that is closely affiliated with a predecessor called *Kabul Kaboom!* and a successor called *Madrid*. All these games relate to political events, to the War on Terror, the invasions of Afghanistan, and the Madrid train bombing, respectively, and use a similar sort of rhetoric to persuade the player—one of failure.[5]

With *Levee Patroller* something comparable happened as well. With much of the game's material another game has been developed called *CPT-Operator* (Fig. 7.4). CPT stands for "Cone Penetration Testing." In this game, the player has to get his equipment in his office, drive to the desired location to initiate a cone penetration

[5]For a detailed explanation of *Kabul Kaboom* or *Madrid*, see the explanations by Bogost (2007, pp. 84–89).

test, which involves taking a soil sample, and do the test. Throughout the game, the player learns about the procedures of taking a soil sample and learns how to analyze these.

Another tendency which I at least observed with *Levee Patroller* but which can occur with any other game, is its usage for completely other purposes. Over time, a part of the game has been used to measure to what extent people are willing to invest in safety measures against flooding, as an educational tool at technical schools, and as a component of a multiplayer game that involves multiple organizations that try to prevent a flood from occurring.

A mini version has also been created which adopts an "arcade" style of gameplay. This version, called *Levee Arcader*, requires players to find and name all problems within two minutes. This version has been exhibited at the Nemo Science Museum in Amsterdam. This museum is foremost aimed at letting children "play" with science. In this case, the idea of installing the game was to let children become more aware about the Dutch landscape. It was great to see that one of the children corrected his parent in playing the game: "No dad, this is not micro-instability. It is macro-instability."

This shows that games can be quite *versatile*. Similar to how *SimCity* and *Civilization* have been repurposed to be used for serious purposes, games with a serious purpose themselves can be repurposed themselves as well.

To conclude, life after the design of a game definitely exists. This life involves making sure that the game is actually used and/or it could involve re-using the design concept or repurposing the game itself. This life is even quite important. The usage of a game is the "oxygen" that makes a game "breathe"—without any players there is no game. Moreover, the ability to re-use or repurpose a game makes for a strong "business model" that allows developers to get some return-on-investment. It is the "oxygen" for a sustainable industry. This shows that except for the actual design itself many other considerations have to be made to be successful.

But generally speaking, for ensuring that the field of games with a serious purpose remains "sustainable," that games continue to make an impact on society, and that games are taking serious as a potential tool for serious purposes, we above-all need to bring the field to "the next level."

Going to the Next Level

Some games are never-ending. Playing *SimCity*, for example, does not stop until players have gone bankrupt or decide that they have enough of it. Most games, however, do end. After the princess is saved, the evil monster is defeated, or the mystery is solved, the game comes to an end. Of course, players can always play it again to see if they can beat the game on a higher difficulty, in a shorter amount of time, or discover some more "goodies" that they have not found on their first travel.

This book is like any other more like these latter games. It has come to an end. There are no more "levels" to be read. It can be re-read but unlike games it does not offer a new challenge unless one is thought up, like "trying to finish it in a single day" or "looking up how many times TGD is mentioned throughout the book."

But is it really game over? This is something many players wonder when they finish a game. Sometimes the game offers, like movies, clear—I will be back to defeat you Sonic!—or unclear—the world is safe for now...—references toward another challenge that is awaiting the player. I will give a "clear reference" about the ending of this book. This book, based on the development of a game called *Levee Patroller* and about balancing three different worlds, does not end with an "and they lived happily ever after." It is more like a "and they started to live" ending and for two major reasons.

First, although the use of games for serious purposes is not new, it is not until recently that it is widely considered and used in a variety of domains. In addition, the general field of gaming has been quite dynamic with many new developments over a relatively short amount of time, ranging from the introduction of the computer to support gaming, to fully-fledged digital games, to virtual worlds, to whatever is bringing us in the nearby future. These technological advances have pushed our possibilities to use games and at the same time have changed our notions of what "gaming" is and what its impacts are. This means that when it comes to digital games, many "unknowns" still exist and this book only adds a little bit to the vast amount of research that needs to be pursued.

When it comes to exploring the many unknowns, the documentation and reflection on the design of games, such as presented in this book, should not be neglected. Unfortunately, compared to the increasing amount of research into games in general, research into game design for games with a serious purpose is currently structurally lacking. Little insight is provided into *how* such games have been developed and *how* this needs to be done. These insights are also important, because they push the field forward as well.

As I stressed before, if we gain more knowledge about the design, it can be expected that better empirical results are achieved. Of course, conversely those empirical results help to improve and better understand the design. That is why we need different types of research to bring this field to "the next level": away from those standard "look at all these developments" reports, promises what it may possibly bring, and "look, we also made a cool game about sustainability that everybody loves"—comments, toward structural (design, analytical, or evaluation) approaches that really try to get to the bottom of it.

This brings me to the second reason for why this story ends like an "and they started to live" ending. Besides the relatively newness of this field for why everything is actually starting, this book actually described a structural design approach to bring the field to the next level. In a nutshell, this approach puts forward:

1. that the design of a game poses a multi-objective problem in a design space involving three equally important worlds: the worlds of Reality, Meaning, and Play;
   a. A game needs to be related to the domain and subject for which the game is developed (Reality);
   b. A game needs to attain a value beyond the game itself (Meaning);

   c. A game needs to have elements that characterize play and make it a powerful tool to use (Play);
2. that each world has its own people, disciplines, aspects, and criteria on how to design a game;
3. that various tensions can arise within and between the three worlds, forcing designers to make trade-offs;
4. that it is fundamental to keep these three worlds in balance to create a "good" game—a game that accomplishes its meaningful purpose;
5. that a balance can be achieved by designing the core of the game concurrently—by taking different design problems and various perspectives at the same time into account; and
6. that an eventual "optimum" is found when the design is satisficing in accordance with the criteria of the worlds of Reality, Meaning, and Play.

With this approach written down, it becomes possible to use, criticize, and build forth onto what has been presented in this book. It is not game over—it is time to live. It is time to stop making "animals" or "insects" and to start making "butterflies."

Actually, come to think about it, the ending of this book is more like a "and they started to *dance*." And they danced the tango to be precise. Because it takes two to tango, but it takes three to design a game with a meaningful purpose.

Bibliography

Literature Bibliography

Belli, G., & Erlbruch, W. (2006). *The butterfly workshop*. New York: Europa Editions.

Bogost, I. (2007). *Persuasive games: the expressive power of videogames*. Cambridge: The MIT Press.

González, A. (2007). *Transgressing limits: Belli's el taller de las maripo-sas*. http://www.lehman.edu/ciberletras/v17/gonzalez.htm. Accessed 3 November 2009.

Kolb, D. A. (1984). *Experiential learning: experience as the source of learning and development*. Upper Saddle River: Prentice Hall.

Mishra, P., & Koehler, M. J. (2006). Technological pedagogical content knowledge: a framework for teacher knowledge. *Teachers College Record*, *108*(6), 1017–1054.

Rollings, A., & Morris, D. (2004). *Game architecture and design: a new edition*. Indianapolis: New Riders.

Schell, J. (2008). *The art of game design: a book of lenses*. Burlington: Morgan Kaufmann.

Selfe, C. (1990). Technology in the English classroom: computers through the lens of feminist pedagogy. In C. Handa (Ed.), *Computers and community: teaching composition in the twenty-first century* (pp. 118–139). Portsmouth: Boynton/Cook.

Sicart, M. (2009). *The ethics of computer games*. Cambridge: The MIT Press.

Simon, H. A. (1957). *Models of man: social and rational*. New York: Wiley.

Weick, K. E. (1995). *Sensemaking in organizations*. Thousand Oaks: Sage.

Game Bibliography

Blow, J. (2009). *Braid* [PC]. San Francisco: Number None.

Deltares (2008). *CPT-Operator* [PC]. Delft, the Netherlands: Deltares.

Deltares, & Delft University of Technology (2006). *Levee Patroller: The Levee Inspection Simulator* [PC]. Delft, the Netherlands: Delft GeoSystems.

Deltares, & Delft University of Technology (2007). *Levee Arcader* [PC]. Delft, the Netherlands: Deltares.

Firaxis Games (2005). *Sid Meier's Civilization IV* [PC]. Hunt Valley: 2K Games.

Frasca, G. (2001). *Kabul Kaboom* [Web]. Published independently.

ImpactGames (2007). *PeaceMaker: A Video Game to Promote Peace* [PC]. Pittsburgh: ImpactGames.

Irrational Games (2007). *BioShock* [PC]. Novato: 2K Games.

Maxis Software (2003). *SimCity 4* [PC]. Redwood City: Electronic Arts.

Molleindustria (2006). *The McDonald's Video Game* [PC]. Italy: Molleindustria.

Persuasive Games (2003). *The Howard Dean for Iowa Game* [PC]. Burlington: Dean for America.

Powerful Robot Games (2003). *September 12th* [Web]. Montevideo, Uruguay: Newsgaming.com.

Powerful Robot Games (2004). *Madrid* [Web]. Montevideo, Uruguay: Newsgaming.com.

Serious Games Interactive (2007). *Global Conflicts: Palestine* [PC]. Copenhagen, Denmark: Serious Games Interactive.

Serious Games Interactive (2008). *Global Conflicts: Latin America* [PC]. Copenhagen, Denmark: Serious Games Interactive.

Serious Games Interactive (2009). *Global Conflicts: Sweatshops* [PC]. Copenhagen, Denmark: Serious Games Interactive.

Von Ahn, L., & Dabbish, L. (2004). *ESP Game* [Web]. Pittsburgh: Carnegie Mellon University.

Von Ahn, L., Kedia, M., & Blum, M. (2005). *Verbosity* [Web]. Pittsburgh: Carnegie Mellon University.

Appendix A
Solutions

Throughout the book I have mentioned a number puzzles—three to be precise—that needed to be solved: the spoon tutorial, the silhouette illusion, and the weights puzzle. The "solutions" to these can be found here.

The Spoon Tutorial

Figure A.1 presents the solution to the puzzle in Level 1. The puzzle can be solved by making sure that each spoon supports and is supported by another spoon. This way, a strong construction is made that is able to support quite heavy objects. This puzzle, as explained in Level 1, is a metaphor of TGD. Each spoon represents one of the worlds: Reality, Meaning, or Play. Like the spoons, these worlds also need to support and be supported by one another.

The Silhouette Illusion

This ambiguous picture can be interpreted in two specific ways. We can picture the girl kicking the ball with her right or left foot. See Fig. A.2 for an explanation.

The Weights Puzzle

The initial thought people have in solving this puzzle is to divide the 12 weights by two. The problem with this, however, is that it does not give any new information. We do not know whether the unequal weight is lighter or heavier. This means that we do not know whether the unequal weight belongs to the lighter or heavier group of six weights. The only way to solve this puzzle is to make three piles of four. For the first measurement, two random piles of these three have to be picked. From this, two outcomes can be observed. Either one side is heavier or they are even.

C. Harteveld, *Triadic Game Design*,
DOI 10.1007/978-1-84996-157-8, © Springer-Verlag London Limited 2011

Fig. A.1 The solution to the spoon tutorial. Picture by Almar Joling

Fig. A.2 Explanation of the silhouette illusion by Akiyoshi Kitaoka. Used with permission

One Side Is Heavier

If this happens, we know that the unequal weight is amongst the eight weights used. We only do not know in which group of the weighed units it sits. Now comes the tricky part. To find out, we need to remove randomly three weights from the heavy side, move three weights from the light side to the heavy side, and place three weights not weighed the first time on the lighter side. After this, we get the following possibilities:

- **The previous heavier side is still heavier**: either the remaining weight on the heavy side is heavier than the others or the remaining weight on the light side is lighter than the others. By measuring one of the two against any other weight, the solution will become known.
- **The previous heavier side is lighter**: one of the three weights that were moved from the light to the heavy side is lighter than the others. For the third attempt, any two of these need to be weighed against each other. If they are even, the third and unweighed weight is the exception. Otherwise the lightest one of the two concerns the odd one.

- **Both sides are even**: one of the three removed weights is the odd one. Weigh two of these against other. If they are even again, the third weight is heavier than the others. Otherwise the heavier weight concerns the exception.

Both Sides Are Even

If this happens, it means that during the first attempt all used weights are equal. Place from the four remaining candidates randomly three on one side of the balance and take three out of the eight identified equal weights and place these on the other side. Now three possible outcomes can be observed:

- **The three remaining weights are lighter**: one of the three remaining weights is the odd one and is lighter than the rest. Take two of the weights and weigh them against each other. If they are even, the unweighed weight is the odd one. Otherwise the lighter weight can be considered the odd one.
- **The three remaining weights are heavier**: one of the three remaining weights is the odd one and is heavier than the rest. Take two of the weights and weigh them against each other. If they are even, the unweighed weight is the odd one. Otherwise the heavier weight can be considered the odd one.
- **Both sides are even again**: the unweighed weight is the odd one. By weighing this weight against any of the other 11, it will become known whether it is lighter or heavier.

Appendix B
Workshop

The Triadic Game Design Workshop is a game-based workshop that was developed parallel to this book to educate participants about TGD. It is flexible. It can be adjusted to the needs and wants of the context and those that attempt to use it. It can be deployed in educational settings to teach students about game design or it can be used—as suggested in Level 7—to get a common understanding between project members and stakeholders about the game design process. Everybody is free to use and change it. In this appendix, I give a further detailed description of this workshop in terms of its purpose, setup, procedure, scoring system, and debriefing.

Material of this workshop, such as the presentation and the worksheets, can be retrieved from http://triadicgamedesign.com.

Purpose

The purpose *of* the workshop is to educate participants about TGD. Other purposes could relate to exchanging knowledge about designing games or using it as a "brainstorming tool" to distill a number of concepts that can be used as an input to an actual design process. The goal of the game, is, however, to score the most points as a team. Points can be gained by performing well on the four assignments of the workshop.

Setup

To setup the workshop, the following aspects need to be kept in mind.

- **Location**: the workshop can be performed in any room that could facilitate about 20 people and which has a projector, a chalk board, or anything else to present with. Preferably, the furniture of this room, such as tables and chairs, can be moved. This makes it easy for teams to sit together.

C. Harteveld, *Triadic Game Design*,
DOI 10.1007/978-1-84996-157-8, © Springer-Verlag London Limited 2011

- **Participants**: teams need to be formed of three to five people. A group with less than three people will not facilitate any discussion. Two people agree quite quickly amongst each other. If a group of more than five people is formed, it is likely that we have "free riders": people who do not contribute anything and just listen. To ensure teams become competitive, the workshop needs at least nine participants. This makes it possible to create three teams of three people. More than 25 participants is not advisable. It will take too long to listen to all the presentations and it will be difficult for facilitators to pay attention to all the teams.
- **Time**: it is best to take half a day (about 3–4 hours) and have no "real" breaks. If it is shorter, not much time is available for discussion and reflection. If it is longer, people may become disengaged due to a lunch break or other reasons. The pressure-cooker effect is lost then. Make sure drinks (and maybe some snacks) are available in the room so people can grab these to meet their primary needs when these arise.

Besides the above-mentioned aspects, it is beneficial to bring some writing equipment and material just in case participants did not bring any, have some cups and spoons, and—not to forget—have one or two facilitators to run the workshop.

Procedure

The workshop consists of four assignments that are described below in the order they should be given during the workshop.

1. **Ice-breaker**: after forming the teams, the workshop can immediately start with an "ice-breaker." The ice-breaker I use is—of course—the "spoon tutorial" from Level 1. The first to solve the puzzle receives three points, the second two, and the third one point. If, after five minutes, nobody is able to solve the puzzle, nobody gets any points. Mostly I provide hints at some point to prevent this from happening. This puzzle will put everybody in a good mood and makes for a nice transition toward the rest of the workshop.
2. **The world of Reality**: the first world to be discussed concerns Reality. After some background information, teams are asked to blindly draw a *theme*. Themes can relate to any topic or domain, from globalization to the financial crisis. The goal of this assignment is to develop a "model of reality" based on the theme they picked. While working on this, teams should be explicitly asked to take the role of the "subject-matter expert."
3. **The world of Meaning**: the third assignment is centered on the world of Meaning. This time, teams have to blindly pick a *value*. This can range from certain skills to data collection. The idea is that teams develop a "value proposal" based on the value they retrieved and the earlier developed model of reality. Participants need to take the role of a professional who is knowledgeable about achieving a certain value. For example, when it comes to educational values, they should consider themselves as a "teacher" or "instructional designer."

4. **The world of Play**: the final assignment is related to the world of Play. Participants should act like "game designers." The goal is to create a "game concept" based on the previous two assignments and a *genre* that they blindly pick from a set of genres ranging from role-play to simulation.

During the drawing of themes, values, and genres, teams get a chance to change the theme, value, and genre once, but only once when they do not like it. For each of the last three assignments, teams should also receive a worksheet that they can use as a guideline. It is not necessary to strictly follow the items or fill out the complete worksheet, the items are just there to prevent teams from not knowing what to consider. The questions of the worksheets for each assignment can be found in Appendix C.

At the end of the last three assignments, teams should give a short "pitch" of about one minute (make sure to time this with a stopwatch or otherwise people will never stop talking) after which teams get time to deliberate to what teams they will award their points. The awarding of points happens secretly, so teams do not know from each other who awarded whom. Each team hands in their points and hand these over to the facilitator. Facilitators can start a discussion after the points are awarded.

Scoring System

The scoring system needs some explanation. First of all, by enabling teams to award points to each other, it is very likely that they will strategically award points. A team who is winning, will probably receive less support than another. If everybody does this, it is not a problem, because eventually everything will be balanced out. A simple way to solve the "problem" of strategic behavior—a Play dilemma—would be to only give feedback about the awarded points at the end of the workshop.

Although a viable option, I tend to give immediate feedback. I noticed that it increases the engagement of the participants. In addition, teams really pay attention to the scores and try hard to stay on top or get to the top. If nothing is known, teams may not make this extra effort. The scores give a reason to do better next time.

To foster the feeling that everybody is able to win and to prevent one or two teams from having much more points than others, a scoring system is developed in which each round the scores are increased. During assignment two, teams need to award the best team three points, the second best two points, and the third best one point. With the third assignment the best team gets six points, the second best four points, and the third best two points. Finally, with the fourth and final assignment, the best team gets nine points, the second best six points, and the third best three points. This scoring system should be unknown upfront. With this system, every team has a possibility to win until the end.

Debriefing

At the end of the workshop a number of important reflections need to be made. The first is that although participants have been involved in a game and have been trying to score as many points as possible, the purpose *of* the game is to actually teach them about game design according to the ideas of TGD. At this point, an explanation can be given of what TGD involves.

Following this, it should be stressed that the workshop forced teams to work sequentially to experience that the design process is actually one in which the worlds have to be considered concurrently. It is difficult to disentangle the three worlds and similar to the spoons each and every one of them is needed to create a single whole.

The final point that needs to be stressed is that while this workshop is heavily structured, it does not mean this should be followed in an actual design process as well. During the workshop participants should have acquired a way of thinking about designing games. This is the essence of the workshop, not the worksheets that structure it or the order in which the worlds have been discussed.

Appendix C
Worksheets

Based on Levels 3, 4, and 5, I developed three worksheets, one for each world, that I use for the workshop described in Appendix B. The worksheets can, however, also perfectly be applied for other occasions. The worksheets consist of a description and questions related to the aspects and criteria of the worlds of Reality, Meaning, and Play.

Answering the questions related to the aspects results in an initial "model of reality," "value proposal," and "game concept," for respectively the worlds of Reality, Meaning, and Play. These outputs can be judged against the criteria of the world they belong to. It is important to note that although it is difficult if not impossible to really answer the questions related to the criteria upfront, it is absolutely necessary to consider them in an early stage of the design, to simply know what is expected in the end. Furthermore, it is also worthwhile to determine how well the design may fulfill the criteria and to clarify what criteria are important and what are not.

The questions are by no means conclusive. They are a first good start to think about when designing a game. Do not feel the urge to first answer one question and then the other. Look at the questions, think about them, "play around" with them, and then start to fill them out like a juggler would do. Design concurrently.

Reality Worksheet

The world of Reality represents the people, such as experts and consultants, and disciplines related to the domain and subject of the game. It also represents a number of aspects and criteria and these are mentioned below.

Aspects

- **Problem**: the situation is in some state and we would like to move it into a desired state. An improvement is needed. Try to define the problem as precise as possible.

C. Harteveld, *Triadic Game Design*,
DOI 10.1007/978-1-84996-157-8, © Springer-Verlag London Limited 2011

- What is the problem to be dealt with?
- To what domain(s) does this problem relate to?
- Why would a game be suitable for this problem?

- **Factors**: these are "objects," people, organizations, artifacts, or phenomena, that play a role in the problem. A distinction should be made between critical factors and environmental factors. The critical factors are the most important factors, at least for the problem at hand and how it is defined. Environmental factors are those other factors, the ones that do influence the problem, but who are certainly not the focal point.
  - Who or what is involved?
  - What are the critical and what are the environmental factors?
- **Relationships**: factors are not isolated objects. They relate in certain ways to each other. In what way is what needs to be considered when "drawing relationships." Some factors are simply an input of the model that influence the factors inside the "imaginary box"—a box drawn around the critical and other relevant factors—and others concern an output. The latter is what the model produces. Try to draw a diagram to make the relationships clear.
  - How do the factors relate to each other?
  - What concerns an input, what is included in the "imaginary box," and what are the outputs?
- **Process**: a model, especially when implemented in a game environment, is not static. Relationships, and thus their factors, change over time. The way something changes from one state to another relates to the process. In considering this, it also helps to draw this in a diagram.
  - How do the factors and their relationships change over time?
  - What happens?
  - When, how, and why does something happen?

Criteria

- **Flexibility**: the real world is diverse, chaotic, dynamic, and rich. This means it is difficult to create a single generalizable game that suits everybody, adaptations are needed over time, and it is impossible to take everything into account at once. Due to this, flexibility in use and design is often required.
  - To what extent is the real world related to the problem at hand diverse, chaotic, dynamic, and rich?
  - To what extent can the game be changed on the fly, for future developments, and for extra features?
- **Fidelity**: concerns the "level of realism" presented to the player. It measures the degree to what the game is similar to the real world.
  - Does the game look & feel realistic? (physical dimension)
  - To what extent is the interaction between player and game environment, in terms of information, stimuli, and response options, similar to the real situation? (functional dimension)

- **Validity**: whereas fidelity is about "similarity" in the appearance of a game, validity is about the correspondence of what in the game happens and what it does in the real world. The degree of correspondence between the game and the real world or to what extent it is isomorphic is what this criterion measures. To determine this, we have to look into the extend that investigation of the game provides the same outcomes as would investigation in the real world.
  - Do the factors and their relationships correspond to the real world? (structural validity)
  - Do the processes correspond to the real world? (process validity)

Meaning Worksheet

The world of Meaning is concerned with the creation of value beyond the game itself. In considering this creation, people, such as storytellers and teachers, and disciplines, like psychology and education, can be involved who can provide tips, suggestions, and ideas of how the value can be achieved. Similar to the world of Reality, this world also has a number of aspects and criteria.

Aspects

- **Purpose**: the intention for designing a game. It needs to have some sort of function aside from entertaining players and this relates to the type of values that need to be derived from the experience. It helps to specify the (general) purpose into concrete, measurable objectives.
  - What value(s) does it need to bring forth beyond the context of the game itself?
  - What is the purpose OF the game?
  - What concrete, measurable objectives can be specified based on the purpose?
- **Strategy**: for reaching the purpose, a plan of action needs to be thought of to achieve some value in the real world in the best way possible. Strategies can relate to existing games or other artifacts which embody some philosophy to create value ("we are going to do it like them") and/or to theories from one of the disciplines that are affiliated with Meaning.
  - How can the purpose in the best way possible be achieved?
  - What frameworks, theories, or other notions help in developing an approach to reach the purpose?
- **Operations**: a strategy roughly outlines what needs to be done and how this is going to be done. For implementing the strategy, the plan needs to be translated to concrete mechanisms that achieve the value. These mechanisms are called "operations." An operation can emerge on the basis of the interaction of game elements or it is a fixed element that helps establish the value, such as making sure that a scenario is never completely the same. This increases the possibility to replay scenarios and this is beneficial for players to keep on practicing.

  - How can the higher-level plan of action be translated to concrete operations? (top-down approach)
  - What specific mechanisms can possibly establish the value(s) and in what way will this happen? (bottom-up approach)
- **Context**: the use of a game takes place in a certain setting and this setting is influential for achieving the purpose. Additionally, the context can also be harnessed to derive even more value from playing the game. Therefore, in considering the context, we have to look into—amongst possibly other influential issues—the target group that is going to play the game as well as the deployment of the game.
  - For whom is the game intended?
  - Where, when, and how will the target group play the game?
  - What other elements surrounding the game can be used to reach the purpose (e.g., website, books, or a field trip)?

Criteria

- **Motivation**: the willingness and persistence to invest time and energy into an activity. A game environment may be a great initial motivator to be involved in the first place but for continuous and further involvement to take place, the player needs to be motivated by the subject in accordance to the play elements, not just by the play elements alone.
  - Does the target group want to learn the subject of the game or are they willing to contribute to something valuable?
  - Is the target group willing to invest time and energy to achieve the purpose of the game?
  - To what extent are players intrinsically and to what extent extrinsically motivated?
- **Relevance**: something is "relevant" if it serves a means to a given purpose. Therefore, a game fulfills the criterion of relevance if it accomplishes its purpose. To look into the relevance of a game, it is necessary to see how pertinent, connected, or applicable a game is to its original purpose. This can be done in two ways: the connection with the purpose and what happens in the game (internal relevance) and the connection with the purpose and the value retrieved from the game (external relevance).
  - To what extent is the player really involved with the purpose of the game when playing? (internal relevance)
  - Does the game accomplish its purpose? (external relevance)
- **Transfer**: a value, be it attitude change, data collection, or exploration, can be highly relevant but still not achieve a real world impact. For this to happen, a transfer needs to occur from the game environment to another environment.
  - What variables make it difficult for a transfer to occur?
  - To what extent and in what sort of situations does a transfer occur?

Play Worksheet

Games are first and foremost a specific tool (or medium). In creating such a tool people and disciplines are involved that know how to do this. Such people, like programmers and artists, and disciplines, like media studies and computer science, are affiliated with the world of Play. Some aspects and criteria are affiliated with this world as well. These are discussed below.

Aspects

- **Goal**: a goal is an explicit or implicit statement at the beginning of the game that explains what the player needs to do. It defines the sort of in-game objectives, like saving the princess or planet earth, that players need to achieve to reach the desired end-state. In thinking about this, it is also useful to consider the type of genre(s) to which the game belongs, as they largely determine what sort of goal(s) the game has.
  - To what genre(s) does the game belong?
  - What is or are the goals IN the game?
  - How does the player know when this goal or these goals are achieved?
- **Gameplay**: consists of a combination of the challenges players face, the actions that are available to them, the way they execute these actions, and the rules that connect all of these previous elements. The rules, for example, tell what the consequences are of executing an action.
  - What challenges does the game offer?
  - What actions can players perform to overcome these?
  - What are the rules of the game?
- **Gameworld**: playing a game takes places in fictional play space called the gameworld. Such a gameworld can be looked at from a physical, temporal, environmental, emotional, and ethical dimension. In thinking about these dimensions, elements, like graphics, audio, and text, have to be considered. It is further incredibly important to look into the coherence of the gameworld: every part has to be made explicit and connected to other parts. To see the linkages, it helps to draw a diagram.
  - Where and when does the game take place?
  - What is the look & feel of the game?
  - What is the story?
  - What happens in the game and how does it possibly end?
  - What other types of aesthetics play a role?
  - How does everything fit together?
- **Technology**: in designing and facilitating a game, technologies (e.g., game engines, hardware, Internet) are used. These technologies make a lot possible but also have their restrictions in what can be accomplished. For designing a game, it is for this reason necessary to carefully consider what to employ.
  - What technologies are used for the game and how are they used?
  - What are the affordances and limitations of these technologies?

Criteria

- **Engagement**: refers to the connection between a player and a game. This connection can be real-time when players are that much intrigued by the game that they keep on playing and playing. The other connection is "offline." Players may not actually play the game, but they are thinking about it while "engaged" with something else and/or are willing to play the game anytime soon again.
  - To what extent are players willing and committed to play the game?
  - What factors can explain for their engagement (e.g., fantasy, curiosity, or control)?
- **Immersion**: the feeling of being somewhere else even when one is physically situated in another—in the game environment. In getting immersed, players suspend their disbelief about not being situated in the real world but also actively create belief by filling in the gaps that the virtual environment has.
  - Do players have the feeling of being somewhere else?
  - In what ways do players suspend their disbelief and in what ways do they create belief?
- **Fun**: is an emotion that is triggered at certain occasions when playing a game. It may happen out of mastery (hard fun), when interacting with a fictional world (easy fun), when creating something of value outside the game itself (serious fun), or by simply interacting with people (people fun).
  - Do players enjoy the game?
  - What factors can explain for their enjoyment?
  - If the game is not about fun, what other emotions does the game evoke?

Index

C. Harteveld, *Triadic Game Design*,
DOI 10.1007/978-1-84996-157-8, © Springer-Verlag London Limited 2011

FSC
www.fsc.org
MIX
Papier | Fördert
gute Waldnutzung
FSC® C083411

Kolibri 360 GmbH
Ferdinand-Jühlke-Straße 7
99095 Erfurt, Deutschland
produktsicherheit@kolibri360.de